MW01628663

Kansas City
MISSOURI

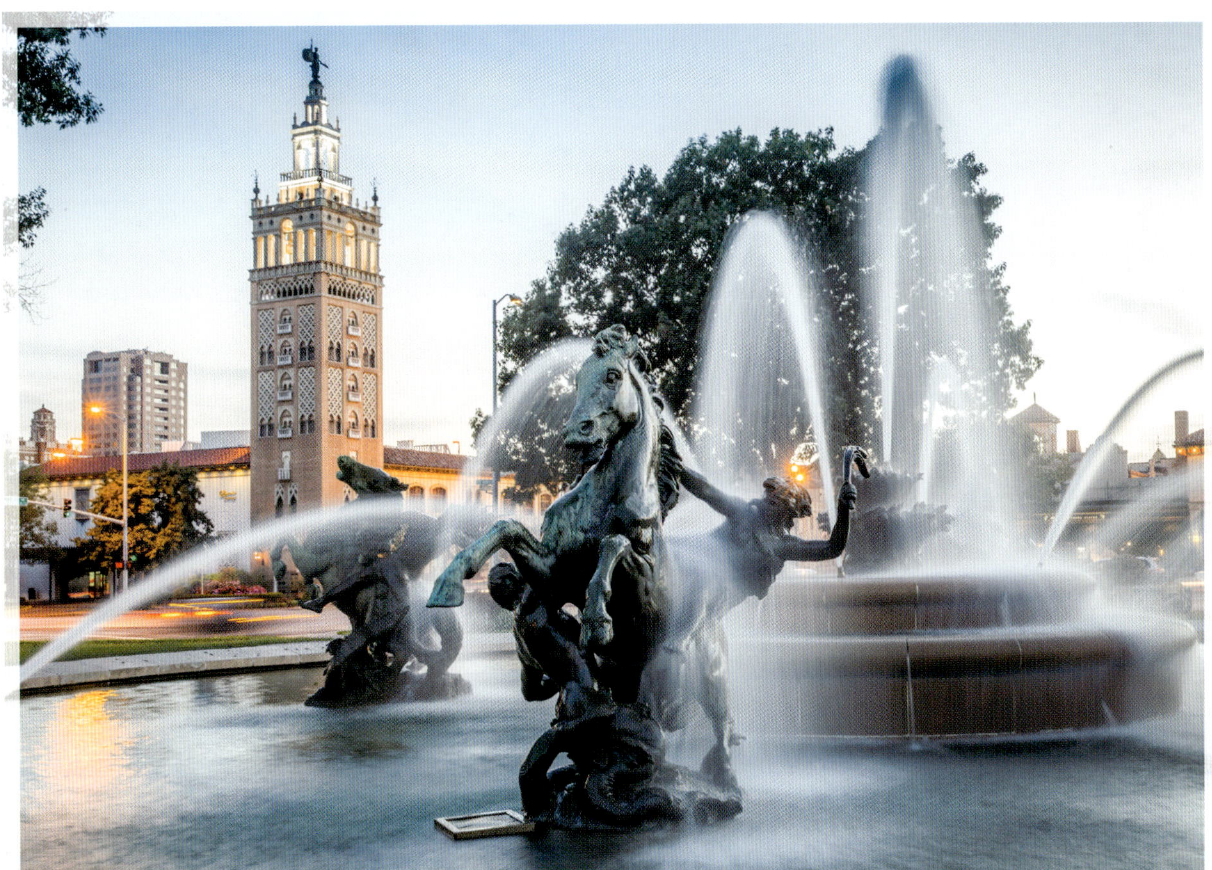

A PHOTOGRAPHIC PORTRAIT

PHOTOGRAPHY BY
Roger Ridpath

NARRATIVE BY
David Banks

TWIN LIGHTS PUBLISHERS | ROCKPORT, MASSACHUSETTS

First published in the United States of America by:

Twin Lights Publishers, Inc.
Rockport, Massachusetts 01966
Telephone: (978) 546-7398
www.twinlightspub.com

ISBN: 978-1-934907-37-5

10 9 8 7 6 5 4 3 2 1

(opposite)
The Scout overlooking Kansas City

(*frontispiece*)
J.C. Nichols Fountain

(*jacket front*)
The Scout overlooking Kansas City

(*jacket back*)
Union Station, Kauffman Memorial Garden

Book design by:
SYP Design & Production, Inc.
www.sypdesign.com

Printed in China

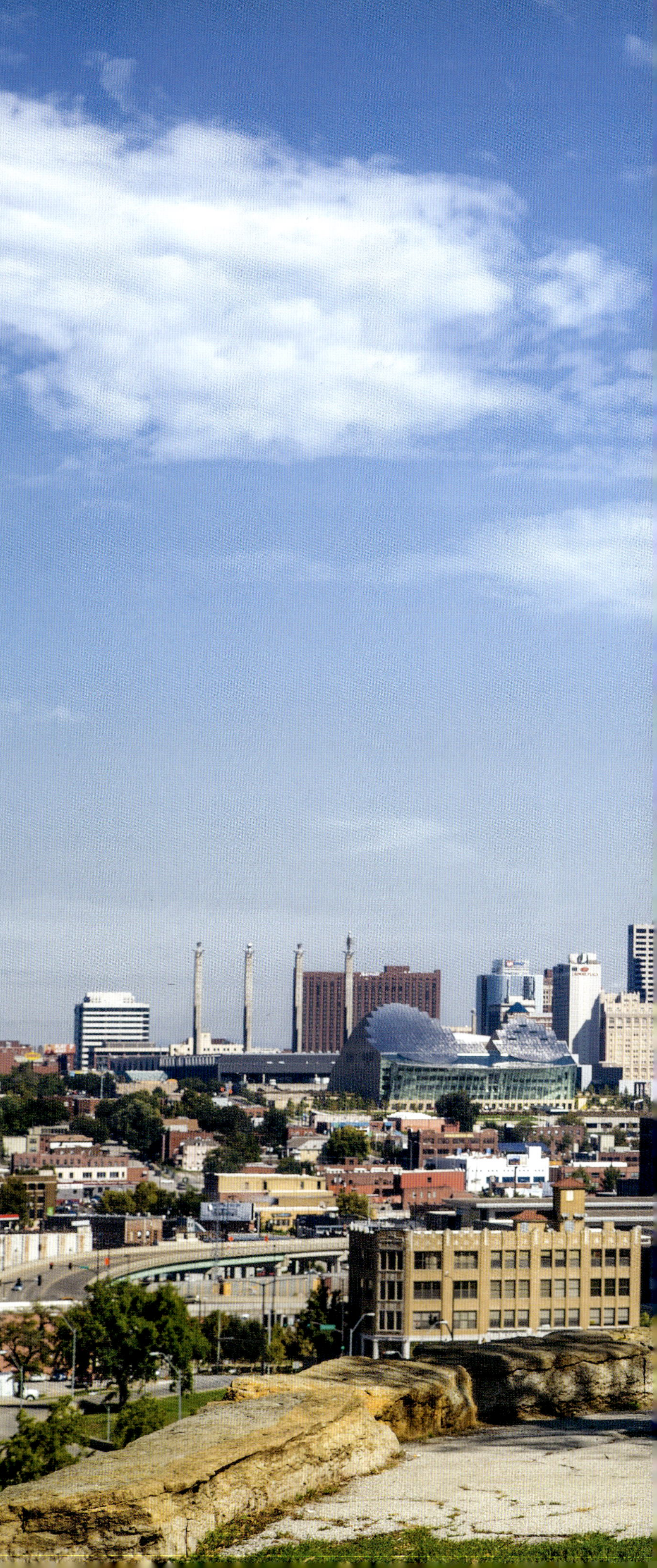

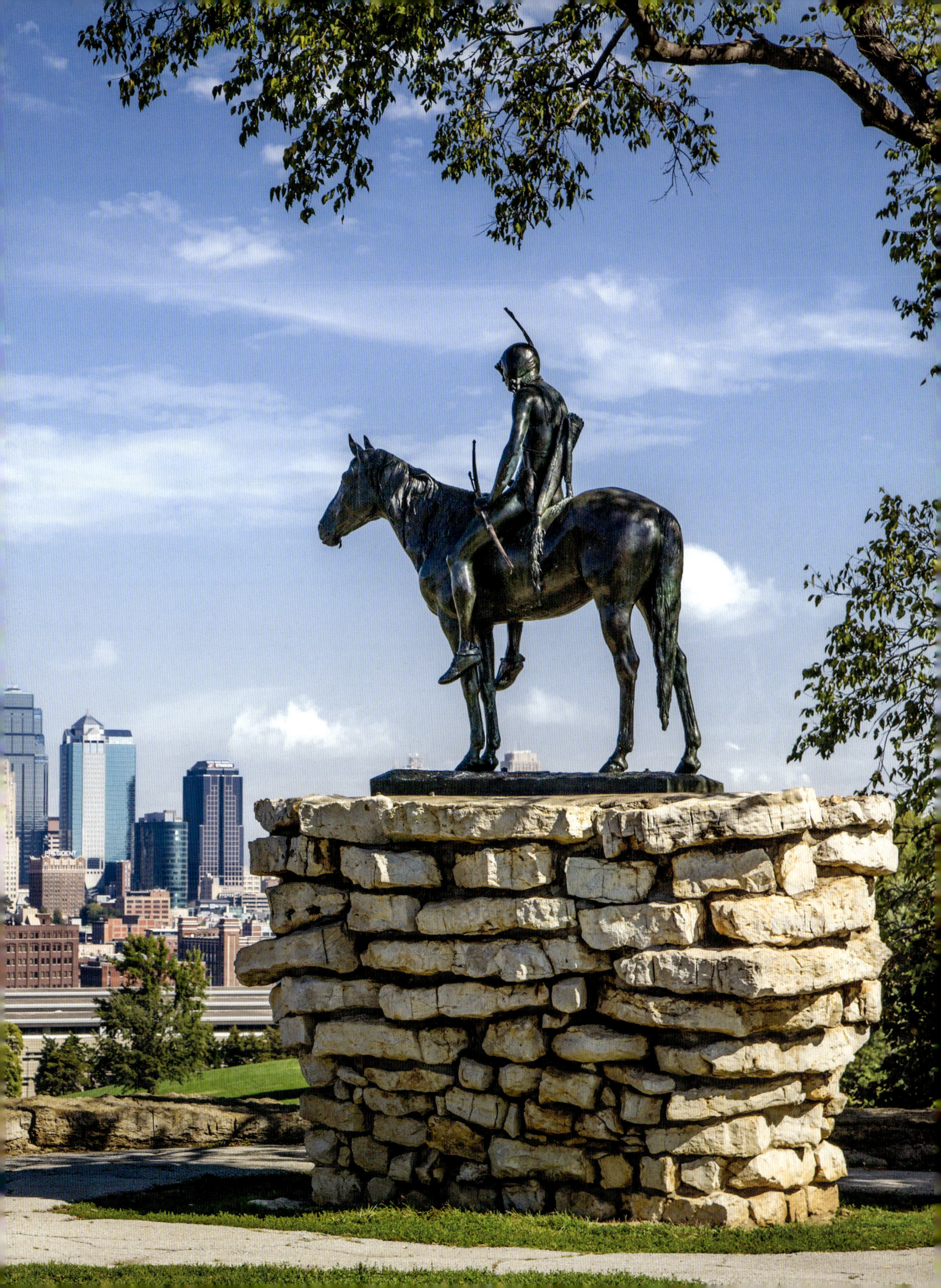
PRESIDENT

There are many reasons to fall in love with Kansas City. It's a town with a rich history, from Lewis & Clark's exploration of the city's rolling hills and towering bluffs to bloody Civil War battles and a fierce border war.

Later, the city was known as the "Crossroads of the Country" as pioneers bought supplies before setting off for the territories and those traveling back east became reacquainted with civilization. As the railroad striped the country, the city reinvented itself again and was known as "Cow Town" for its expansive stockyards and unmatched steaks.

From the famous Kansas City strip steak, local restaurants experimented and learned to perfect barbecue. Some of the best barbecue restaurants in the world have always been found in KC. Walking around town, the savory smoke from a hickory-fired oven can draw you in like a magnet. As the city grew, it became one of the hotbeds for jazz, with many of the biggest names calling Kansas City home.

Today, no longer a cowtown, Kansas City boasts more tree-lined, picturesque boulevards than anywhere in the world except Paris and more elegant and artistically flowing fountains than anywhere but Rome. Its museums and public spaces have been molded by world-class architects. Everywhere, neighborhoods have been revitalized and the city is constantly reinvesting in itself.

But more than its storied history, natural beauty, diverse culture, or breath-taking architecture, Kansas City is known for its people. Warm and hospitable to a fault, Kansas Citians are neighborly and incredibly proud of their fine city. Ask for directions and you're as likely to have someone lead you to your destination as just being pointed the way. It's that kind of place. Turn these pages and you just might fall in love with Kansas City.

Kauffman Memorial Garden *(opposite)*

Beloved Kansas Citians Ewing and Muriel Kauffman made a tremendous impact on the city's business, sports, and philanthropic landscapes. This lush, urban garden pays tribute to their legacy. The tranquil oasis, open year-round, features playful fountains, fragrant flowers, seasonal plantings, and many places for all to visit and relax.

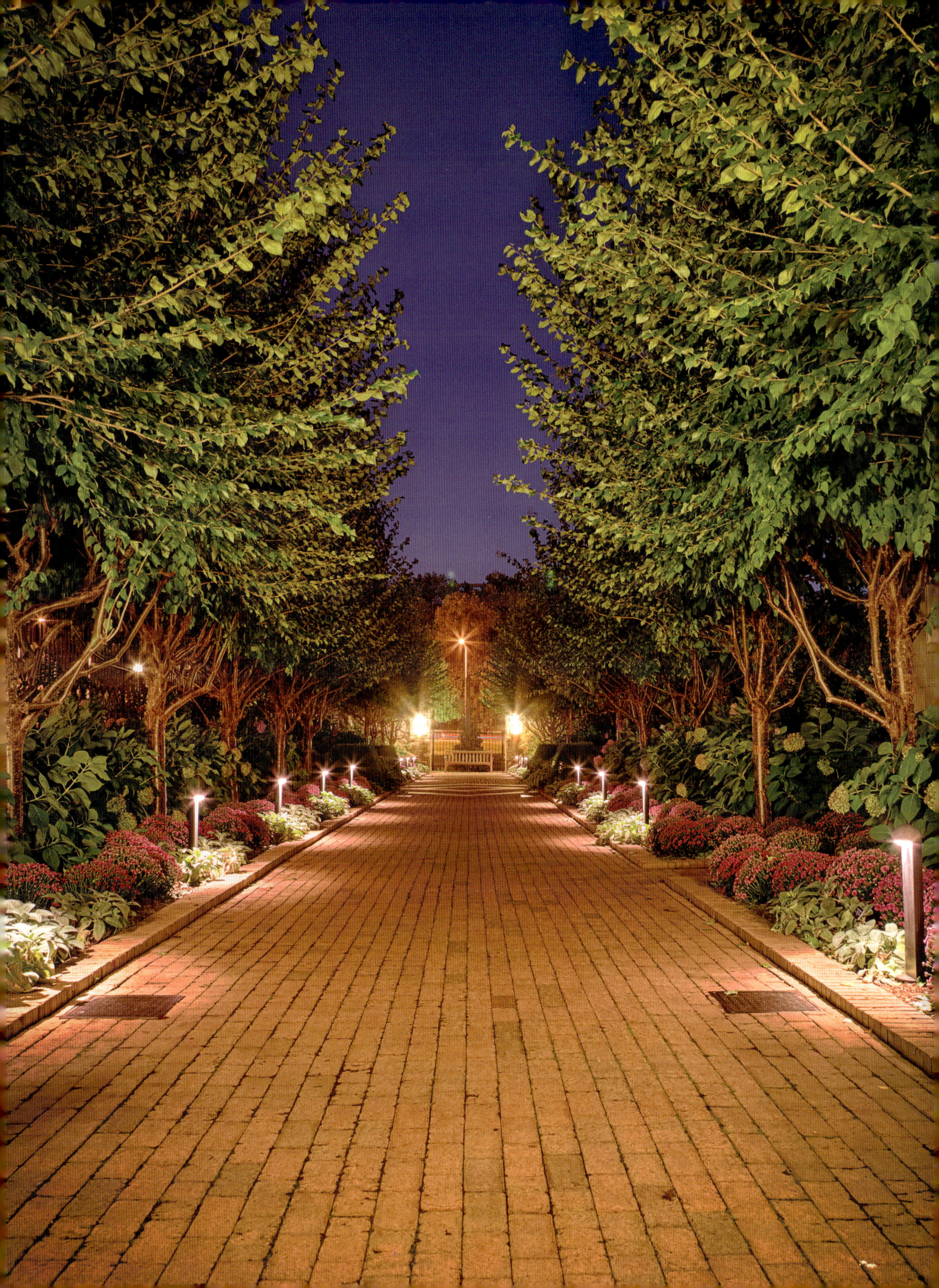

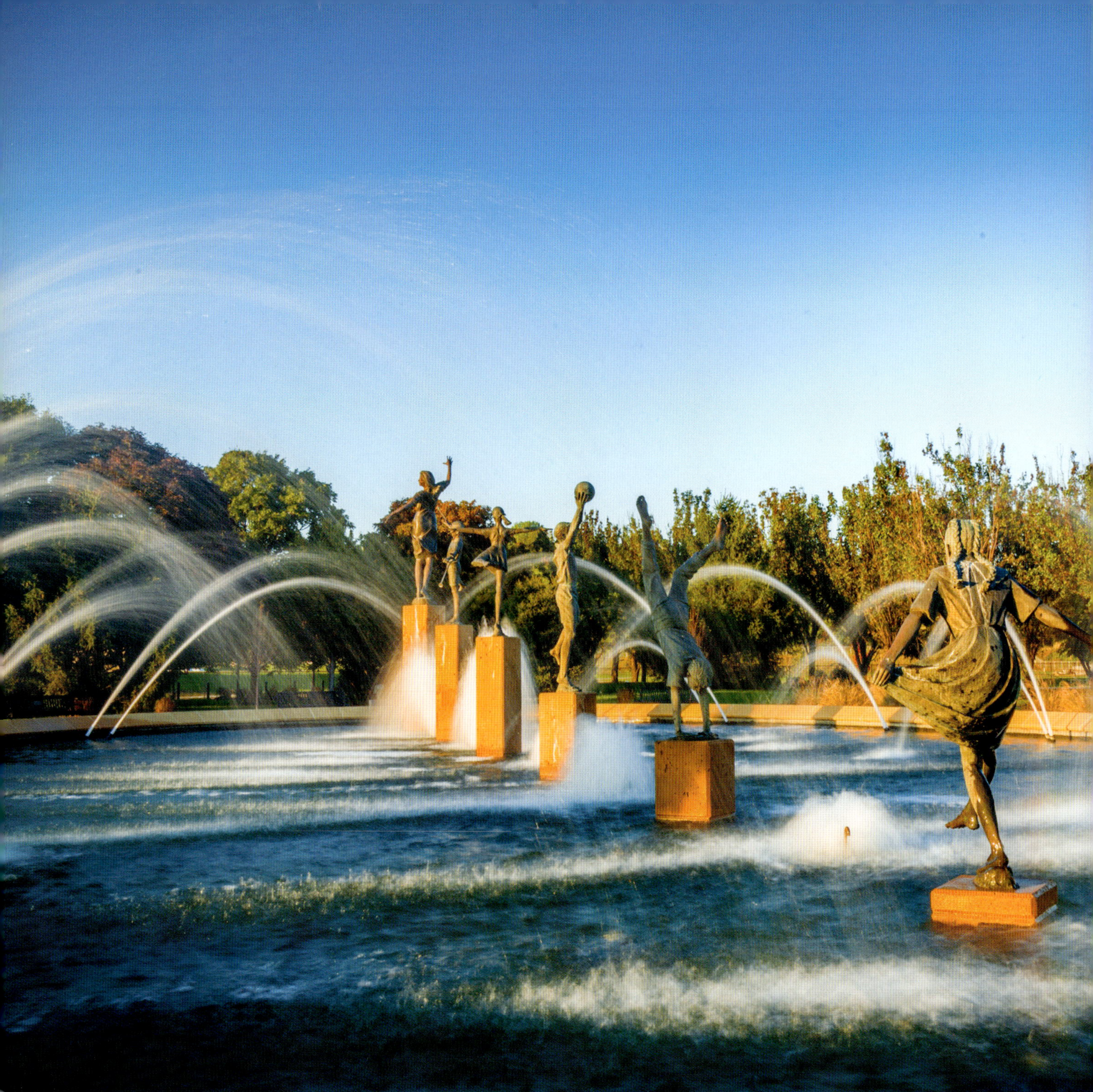

Children's Fountain

In the Waterworks Park, considered an entrance to Kansas City's Northland, you'll find this fountain dedicated to the city's children. Kansas City kids were used as models for the statues and a variety—from soccer players to a boy on crutches to a ballerina—are featured.

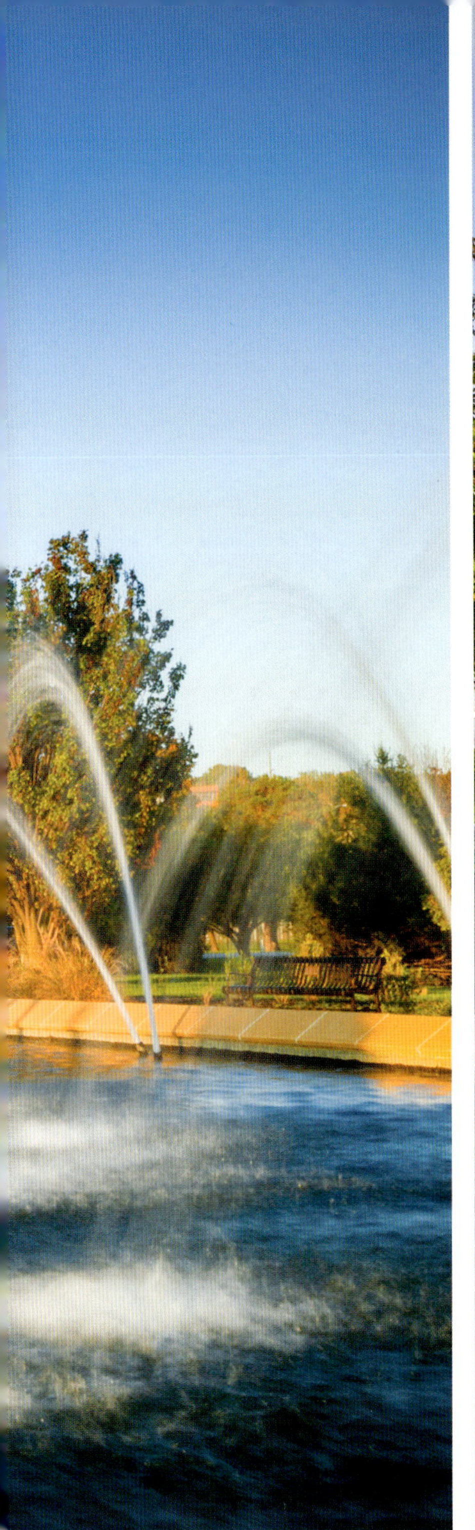

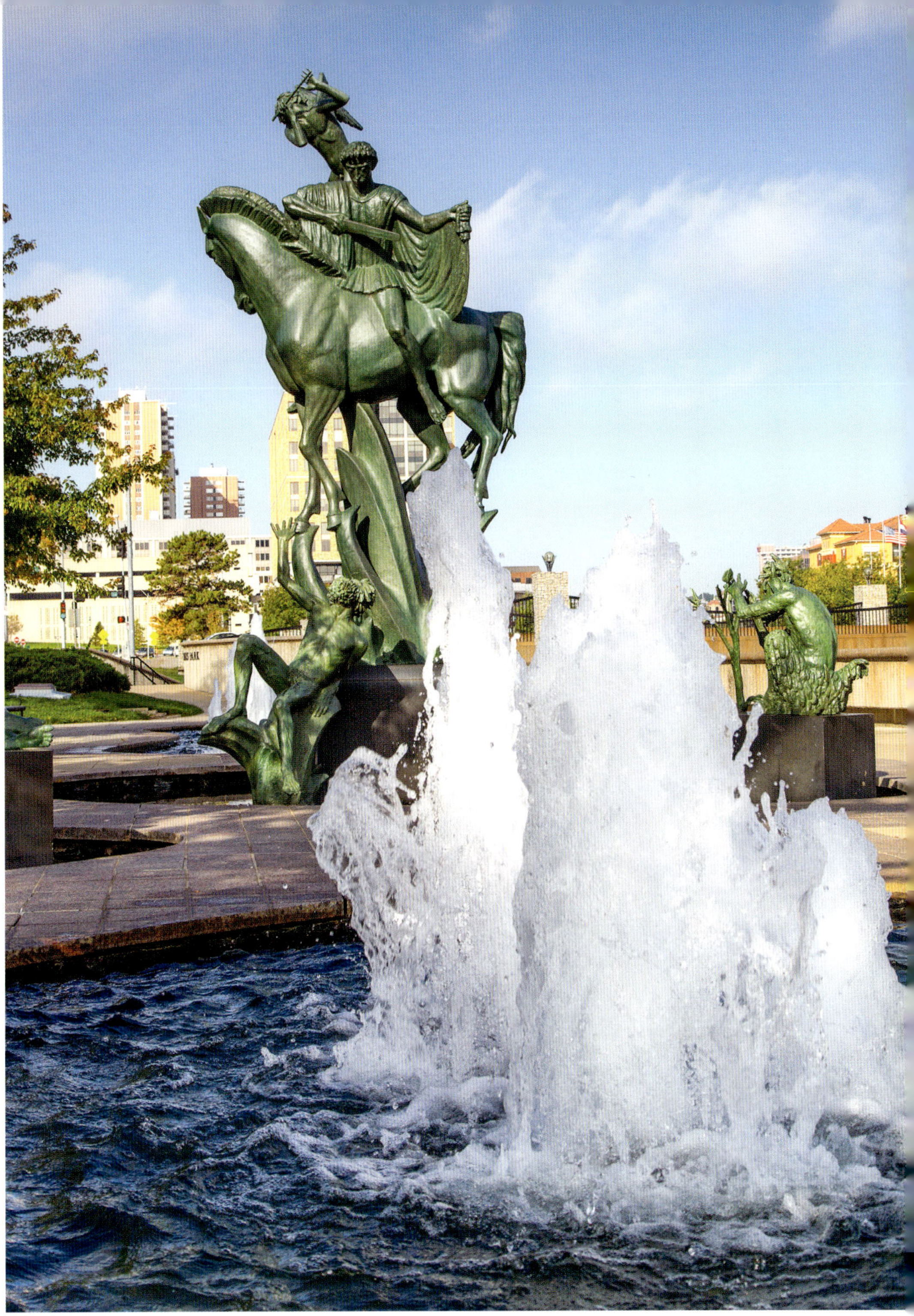

William Volker Memorial Fountain

Just outside the campus of the University of Missouri-Kansas City sits this fountain, dedicated to William Volker, an entrepreneur and philanthropist. Volker built an empire based on picture frames and window shades during the late 1800s, before anonymously giving most of it away to benefit the city he loved.

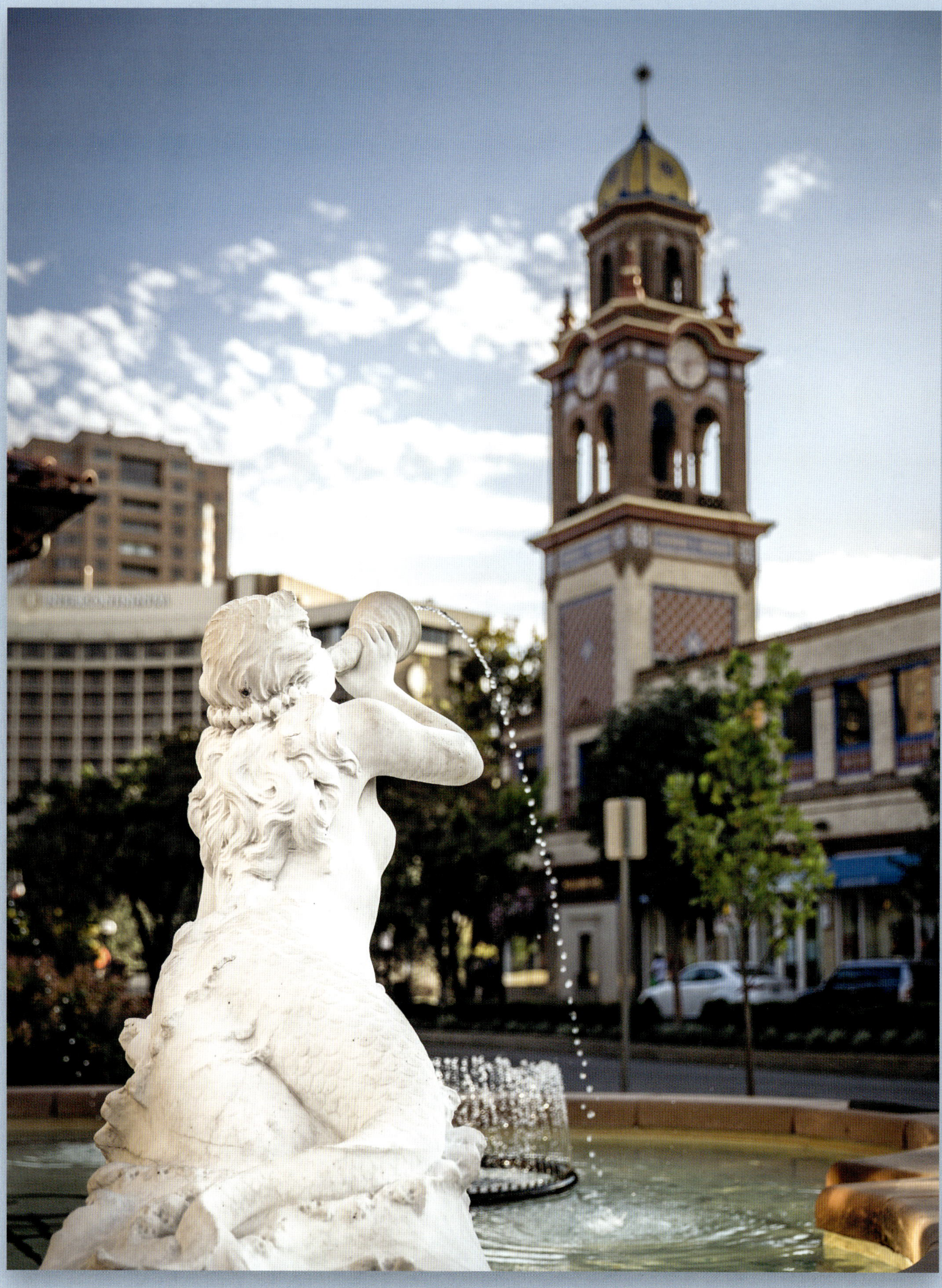

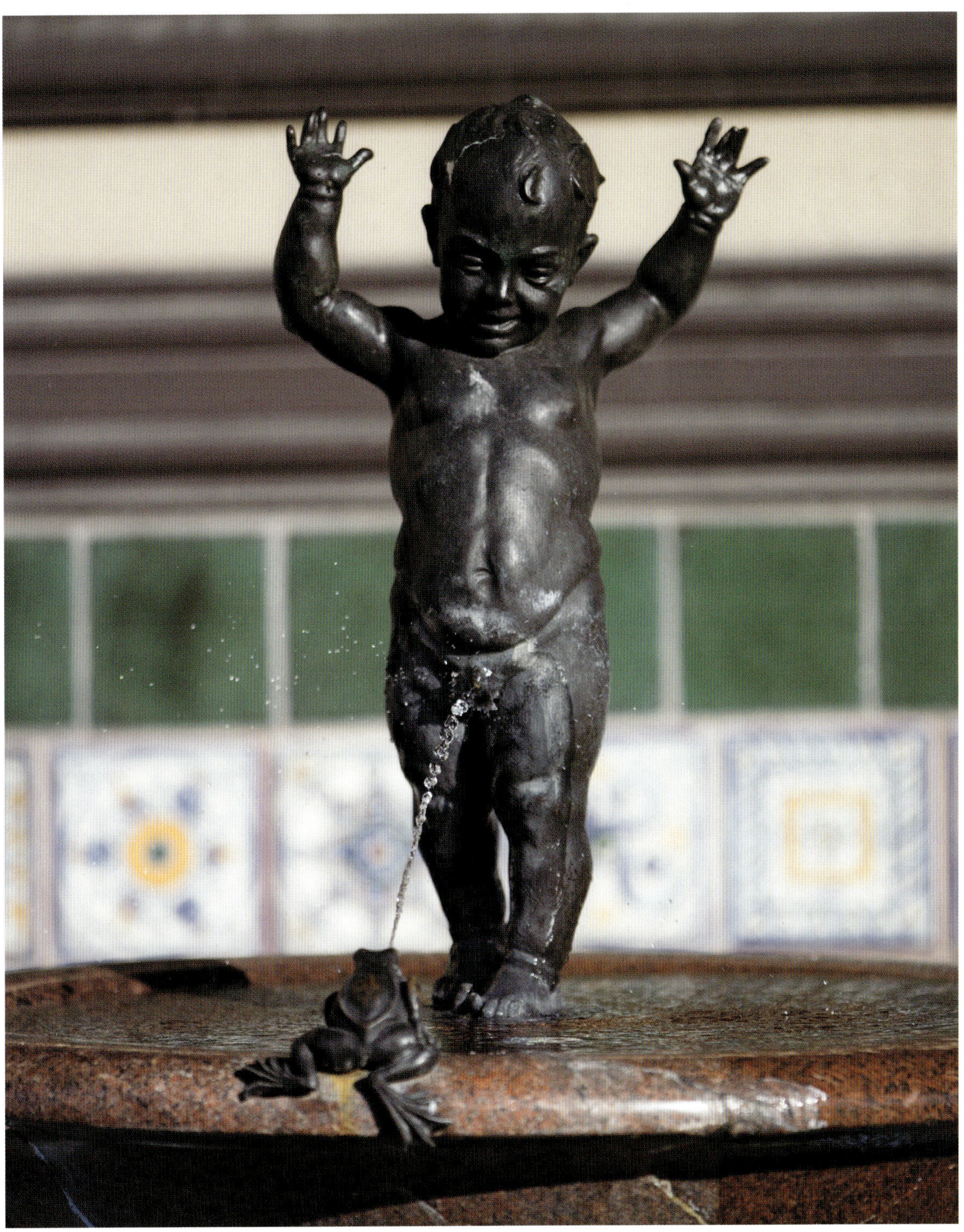

Mermaid Fountain *(opposite)*

Located in the heart of the Country Club Plaza, the Mermaid Fountain is a familiar meeting spot for locals and visitors, alike. A small bronze of a praying child sits in the center and it is customary to toss coins in this fountain with all proceeds donated to Children's Mercy Hospital.

Boy and Frog Fountain *(above)*

Atop a bowl of rose-colored Verona marble, this bronze statue depicts a boy shouting in delight at the surprise shower he is receiving from a frog. This playful fountain was imported from Florence, Italy in the 1920s and is a favorite of many photographers on the Country Club Plaza.

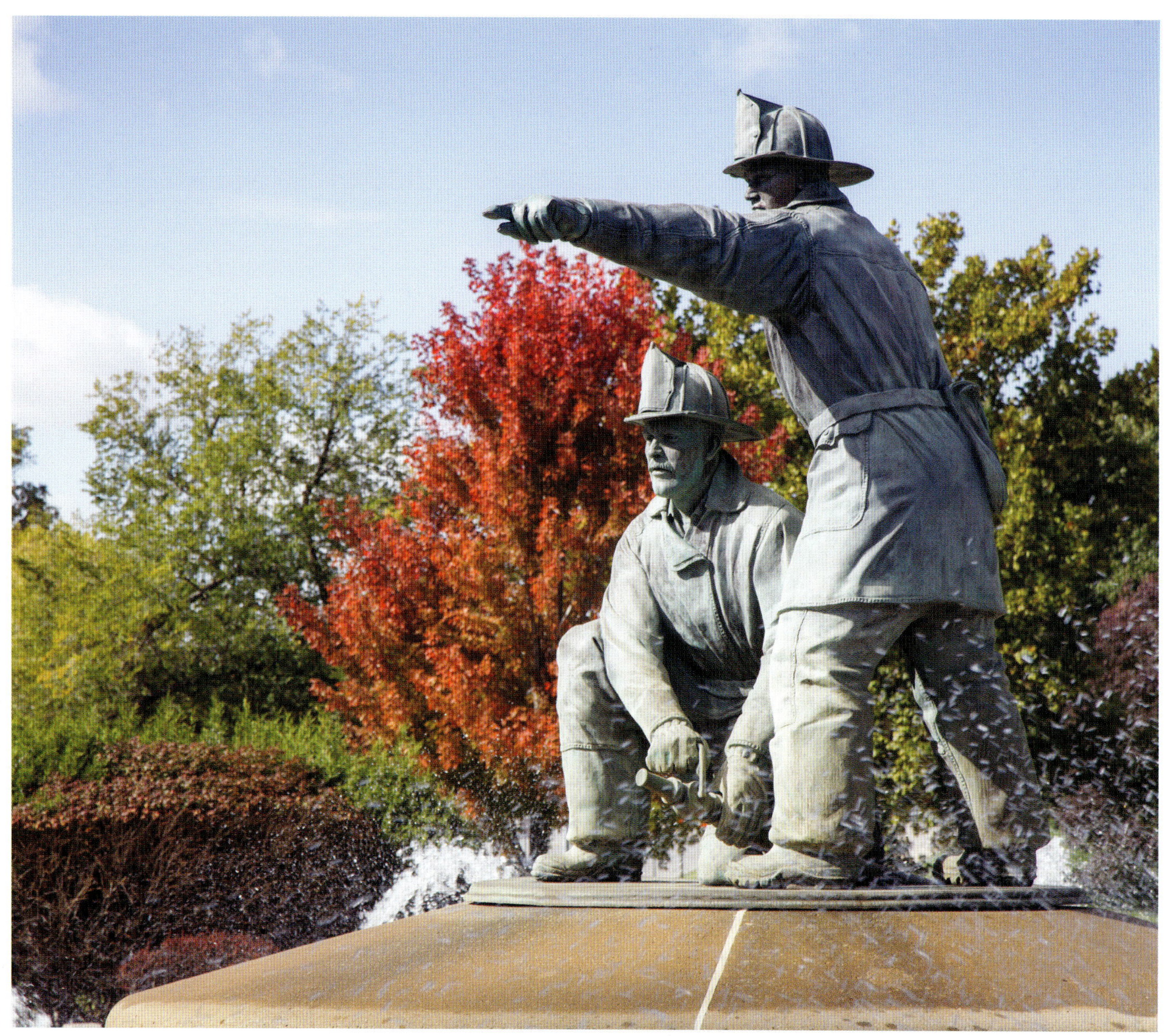

Firefighters Fountain *(above)*

One of the largest fountains in the city, the Firefighters Fountain is dedicated to those men and women of the city's fire department whose lives have been lost in the line of duty. Two bronze firemen are at the center of this fountain that is more than 80 feet wide.

Firefighters Fountain *(opposite)*

Also known as "Lest We Forget," the Firefighters Fountain is backed by a curved wall, which is backlit at night and includes the names of the city's fallen firefighters. To the north of the fountain is a larger-than-life bronze sculpture of a fireman with his head bowed.

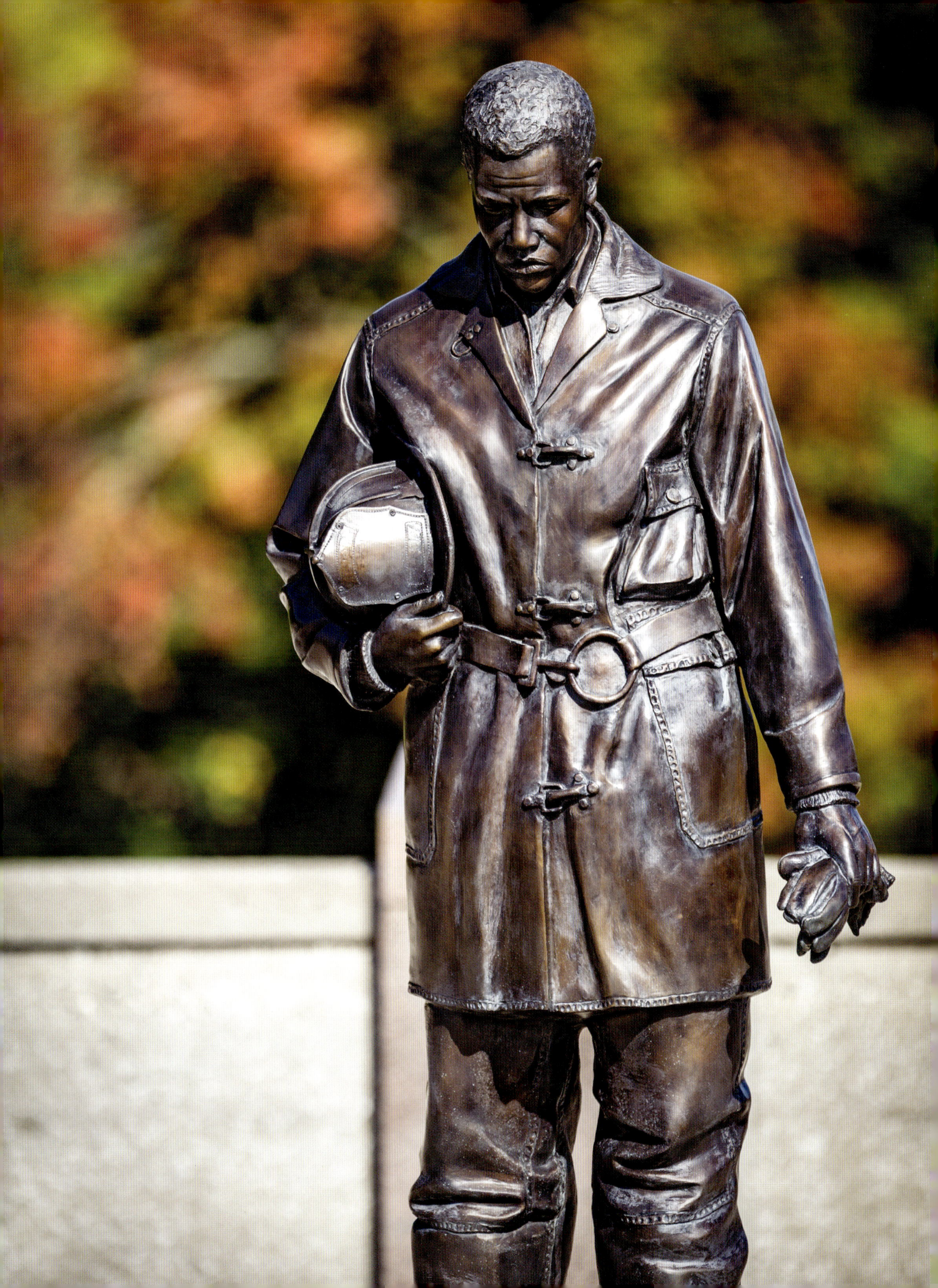

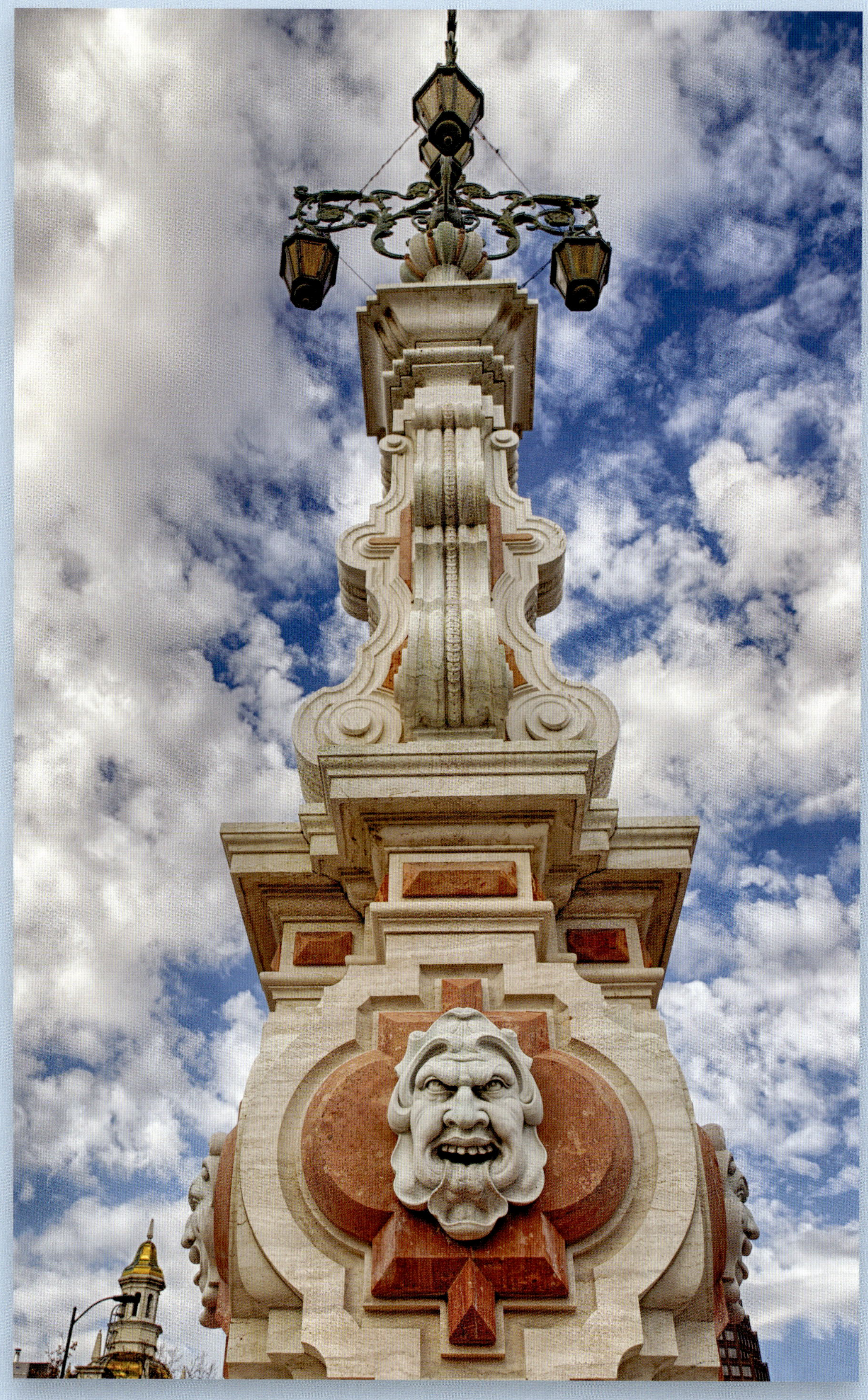

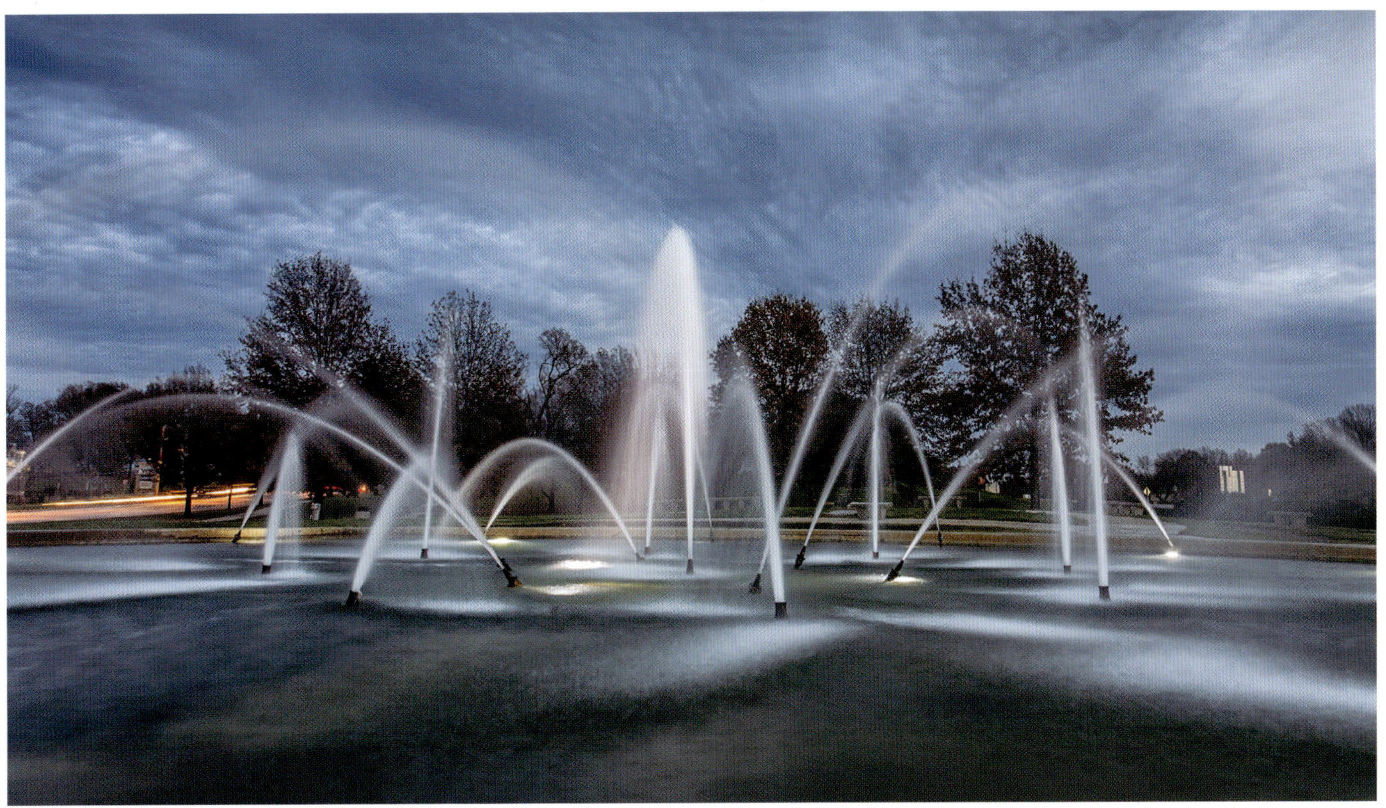

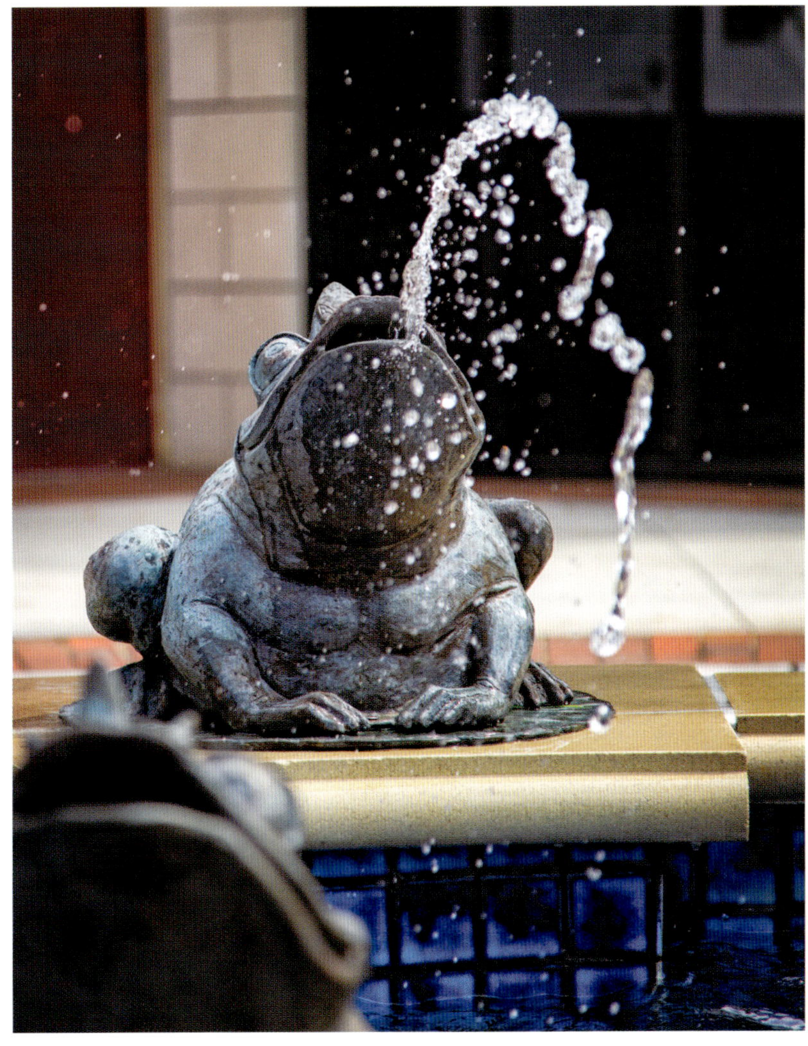

Northland Fountain *(above)*

The Northland Fountain is a large fountain representing the cooperation between public and private enterprises. It's unique because it's one of the few fountains that operates year-round. During the coldest days of winter, the fountain becomes a beautiful ice sculpture, changing its shape daily.

Frog Fountain at Zona Rosa *(right)*

The Frog Fountain is really two fountains located in the Zona Rosa shopping district. Brave visitors can walk between the fountains as these fun frogs spit water at each other, over the visitors' heads. The Frog Fountain is a favorite of young and old, alike.

Seville Light Fountain *(opposite)*

Many of Kansas City's buildings are heavily influenced by Spanish architecture, especially on the Country Club Plaza. This tall fountain is an exact replica of the Plaza de Los Reyes fountain found in Seville, Spain. Water pours out from all four sides and its lamps welcome visitors to the shopping district.

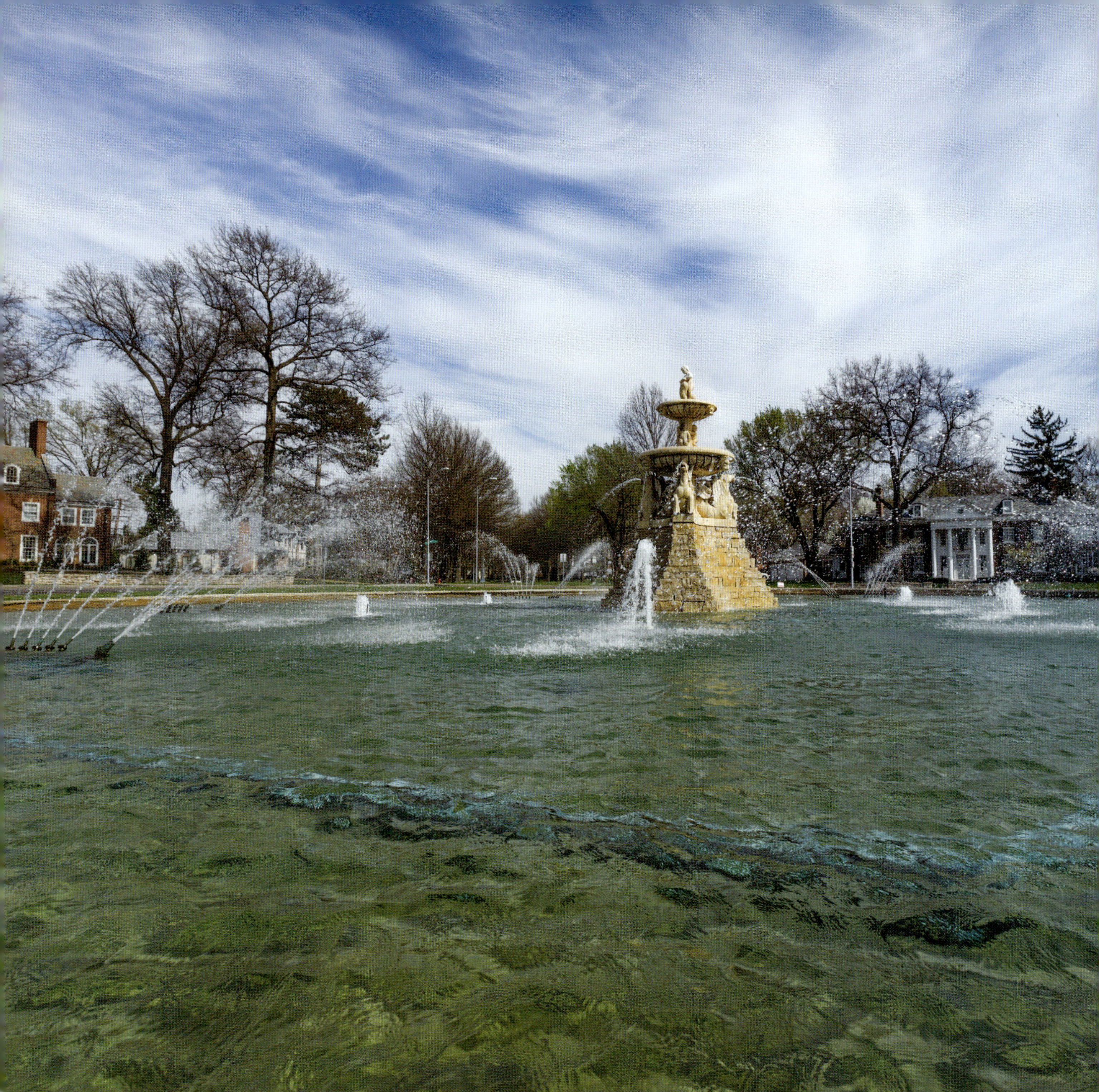

Meyer Circle Sea Horse Fountain

(above and opposite)

Kansas City is a city of boulevards with none more celebrated than Ward Parkway. The Meyer Circle Sea Horse Fountain sits in the center of the boulevard and is surrounded by luxurious mansions. The fountain dates to the 1700s and was brought from Venice to Kansas City in the 1920s.

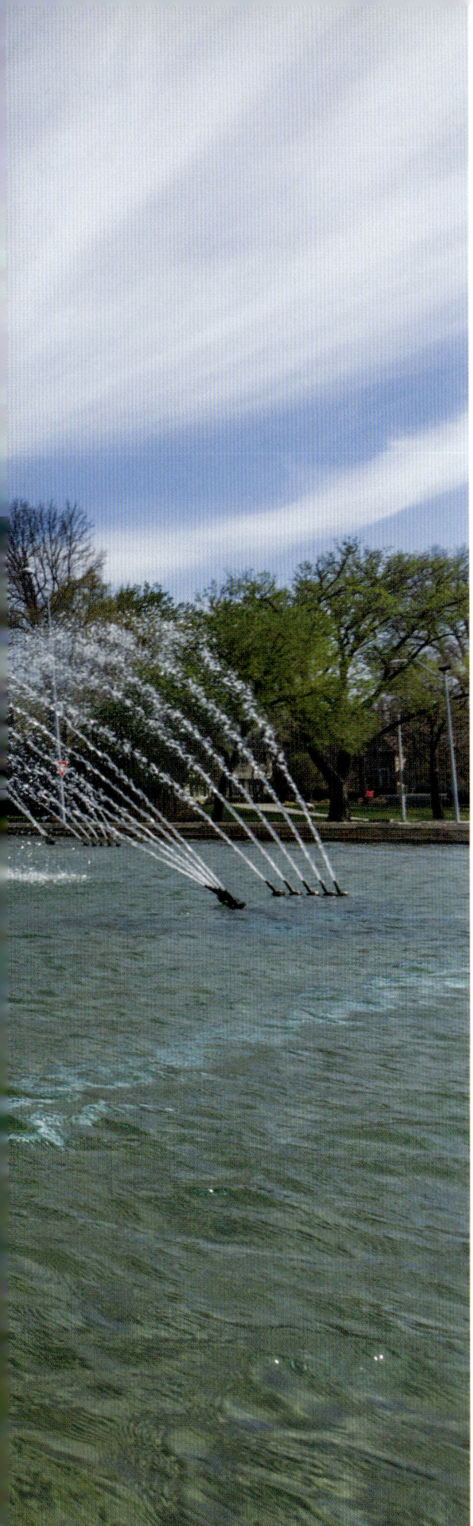

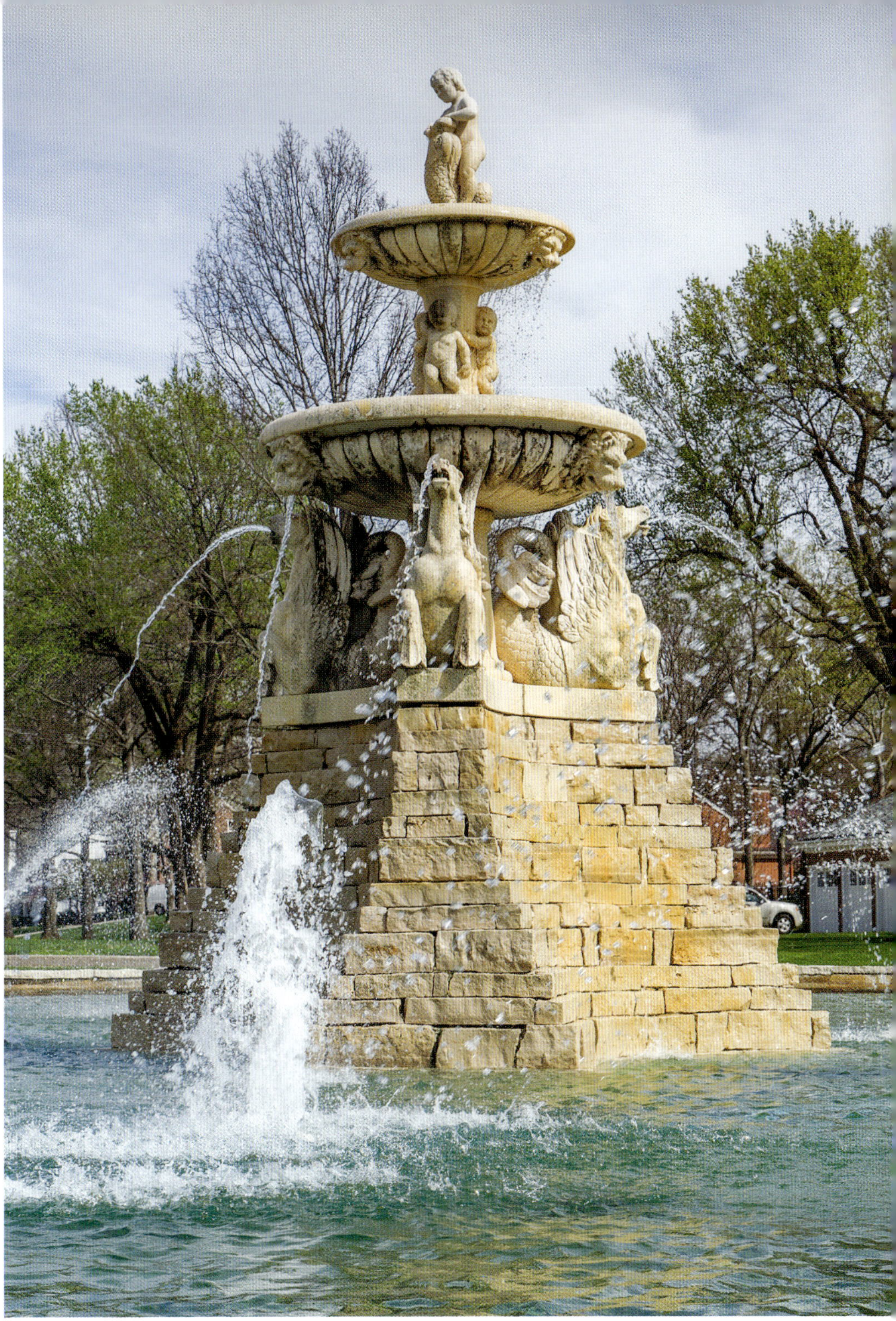

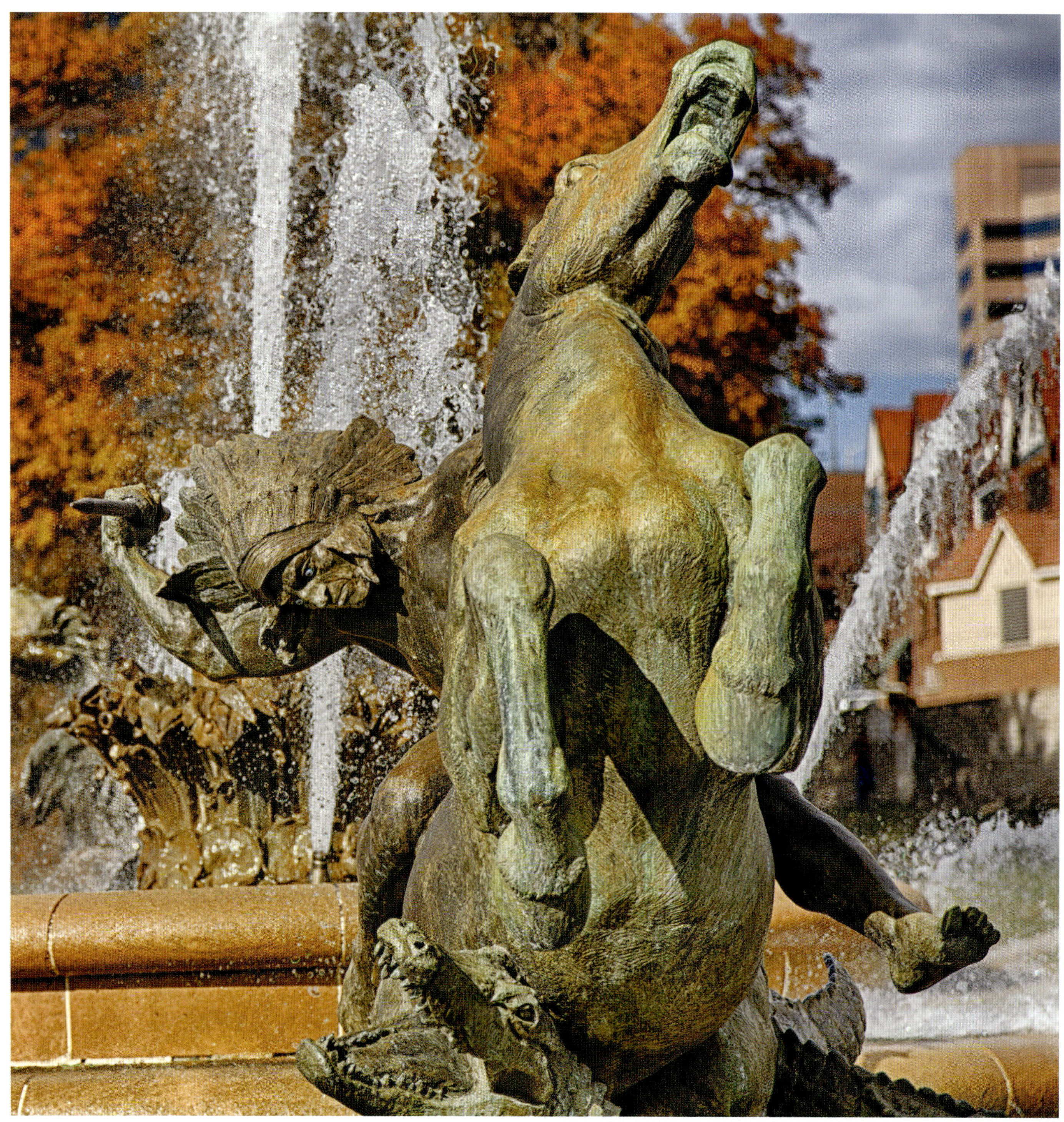

J.C. Nichols Memorial Fountain

(above and opposite)

Kansas City is known as the "City of Fountains" and none is more popular, or photographed, than the J.C. Nichols Memorial Fountain. The majestic fountain sits on the edge of the upscale Country Club Plaza shopping district, one of Nichols' greatest achievements as a real estate developer.

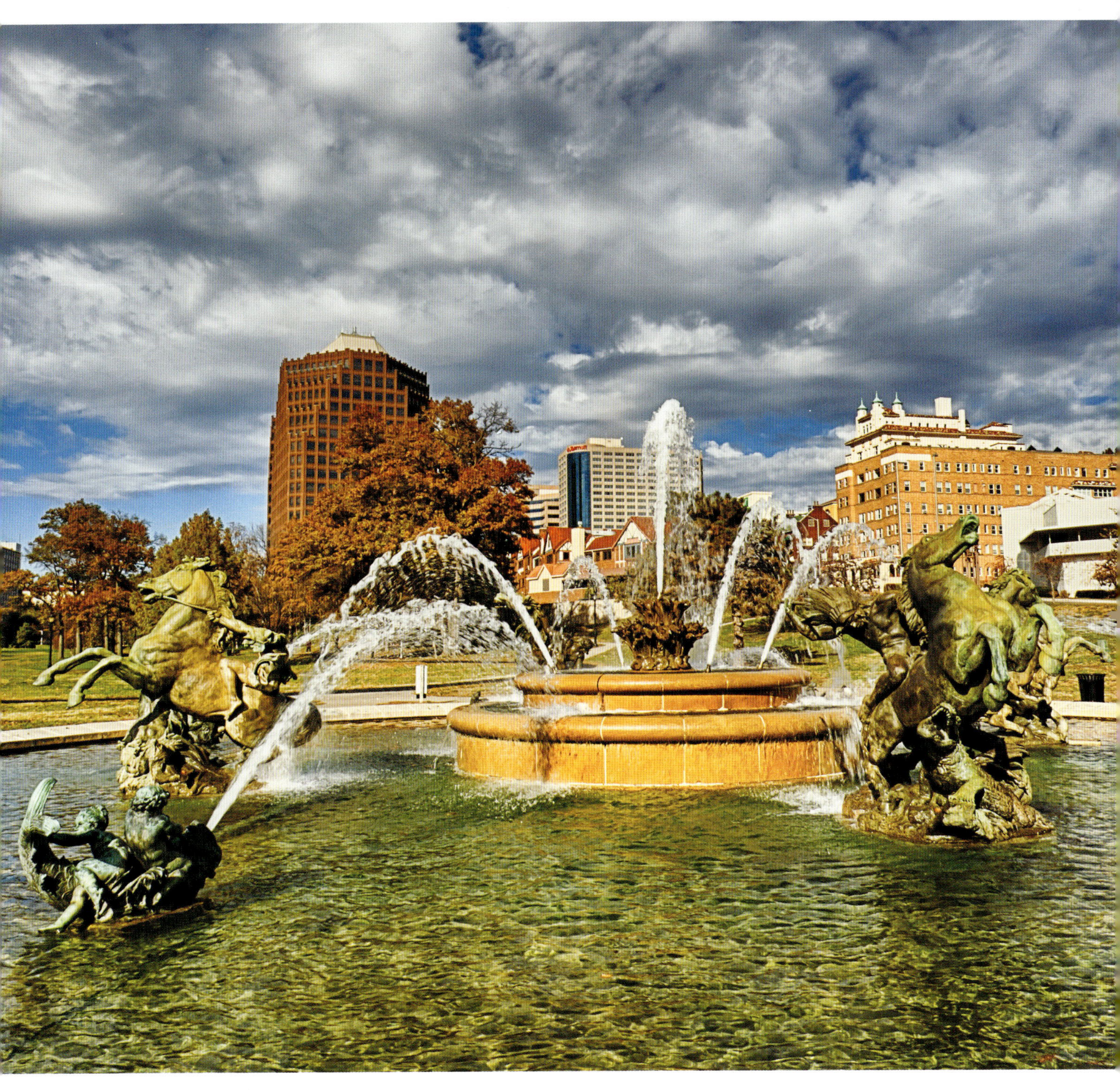

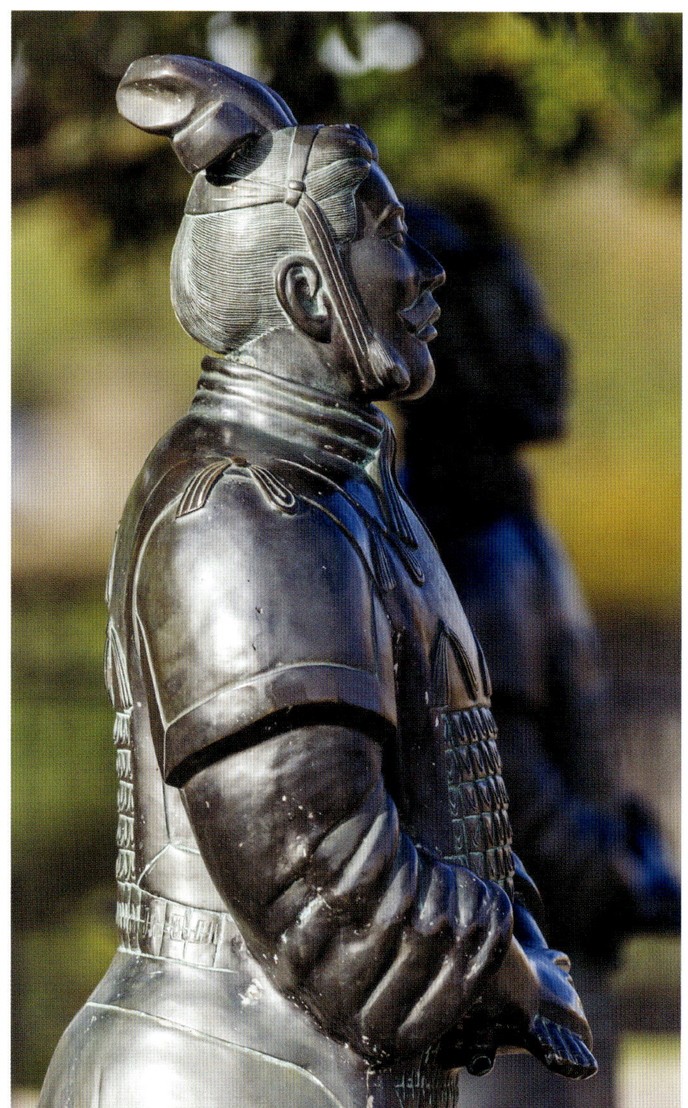

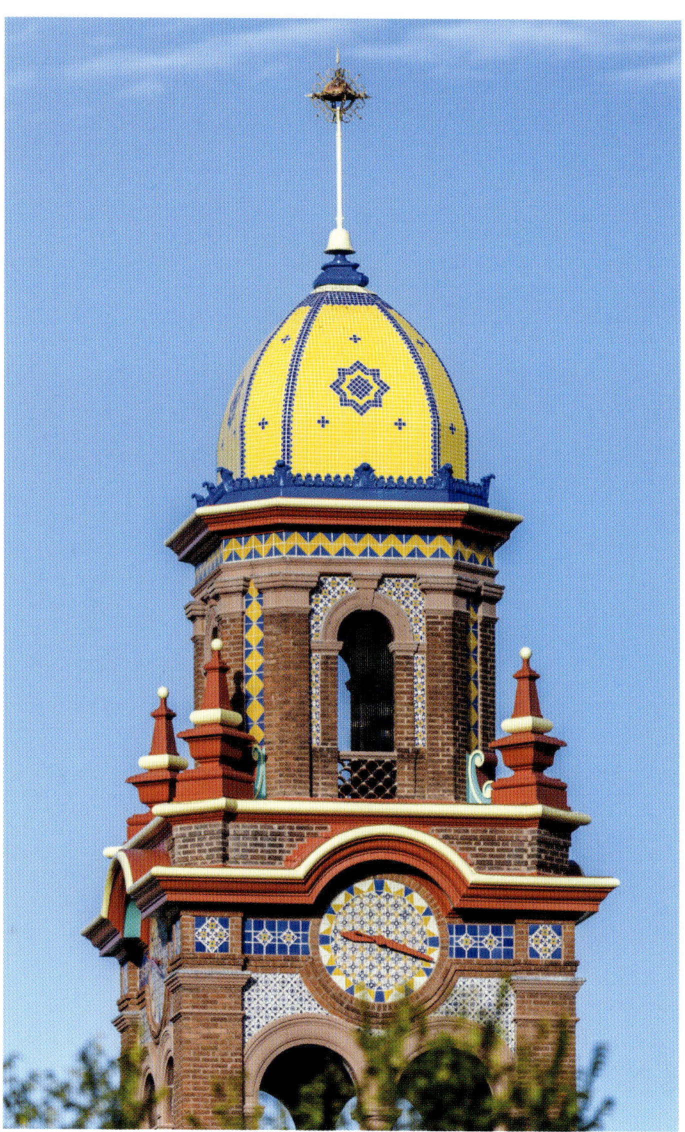

Chinese Warrior Statues *(left)*

Kansas City is a sister city to X'ian, China and guarding the entrance to the Sister Cities International Bridge over Brush Creek are bronze statues of two Chinese warriors. The bronzes are replicas of concrete figures that X'ian sent to Kansas City as a symbol of friendship between the cities.

Time Tower Building *(right)*

Echoing the architecture of Seville, Spain, numerous towers punctuate the skyline of the Country Club Plaza. Chief among those is the striking Time Tower Building, with its iconic yellow tiled dome. On all sides of the tower, clocks look out over the shopping district, letting passers-by know the time.

Pomona Fountain *(opposite)*

This fountain is nestled comfortably in a courtyard on the Plaza. Standing proudly above the fountain is a life-sized statue of Pomona, the Roman goddess of fruitful abundance. She stands atop a bowl of polished marble, from which a continuously cascading curtain of water falls into a pool below.

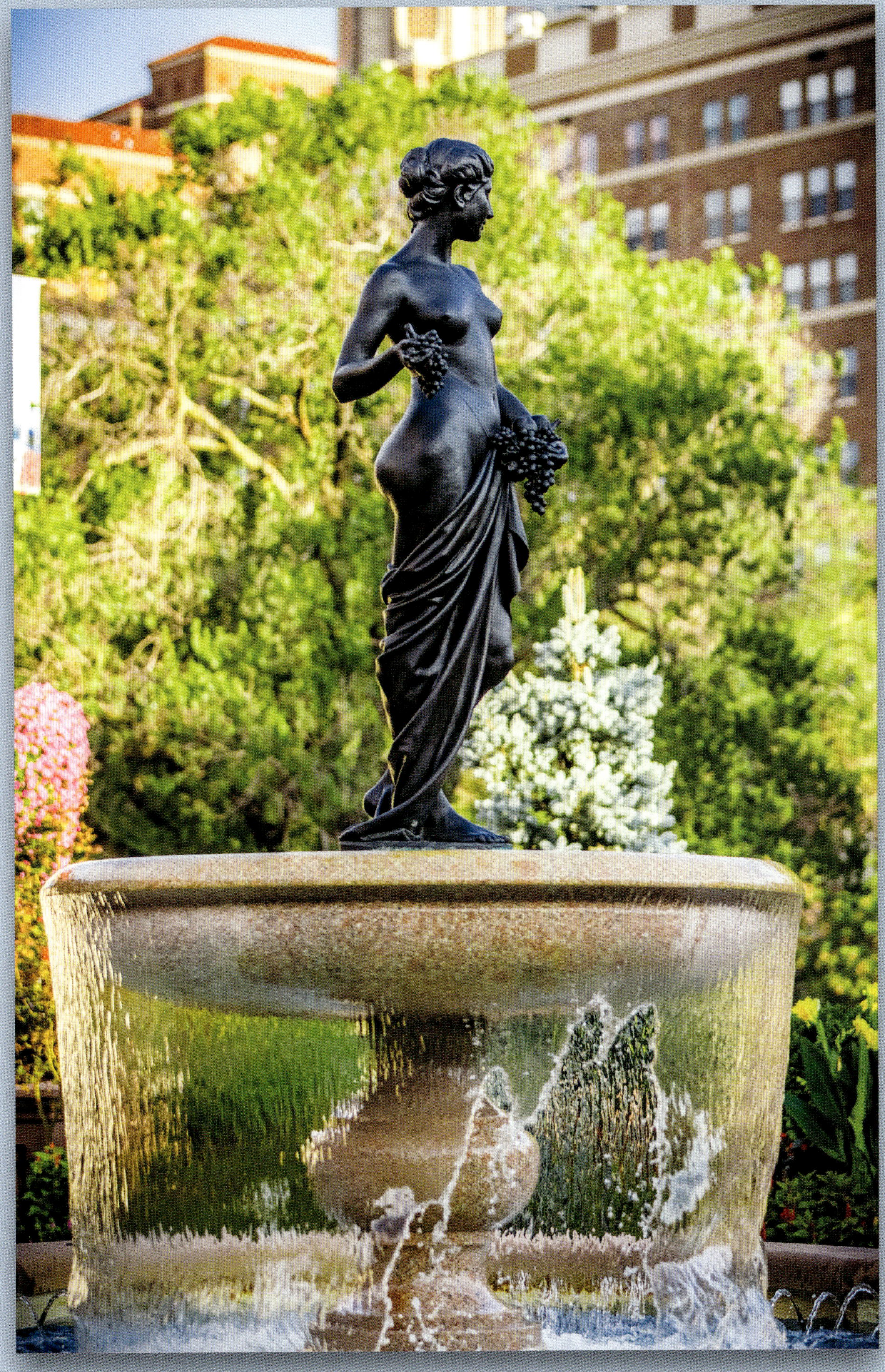

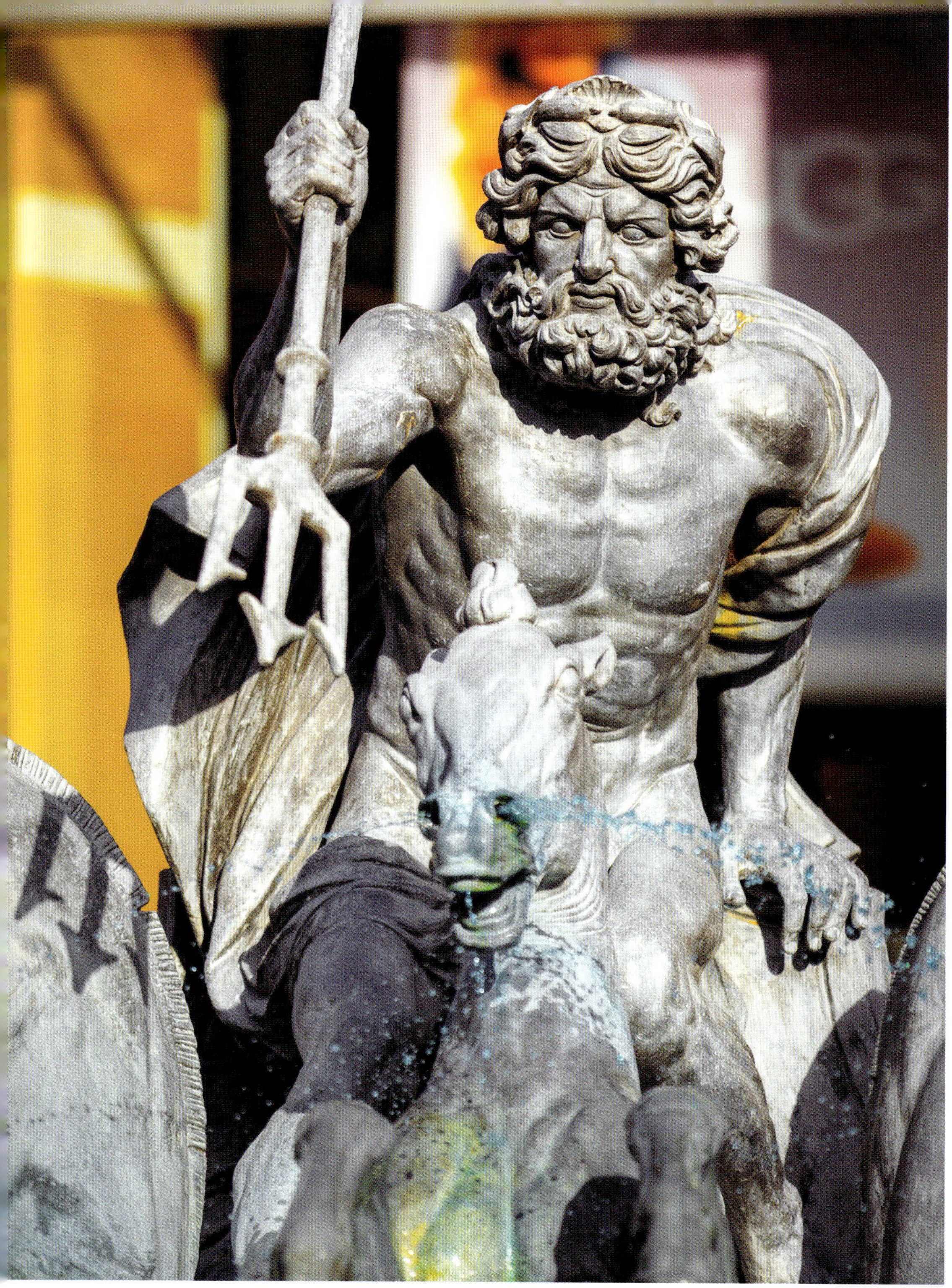

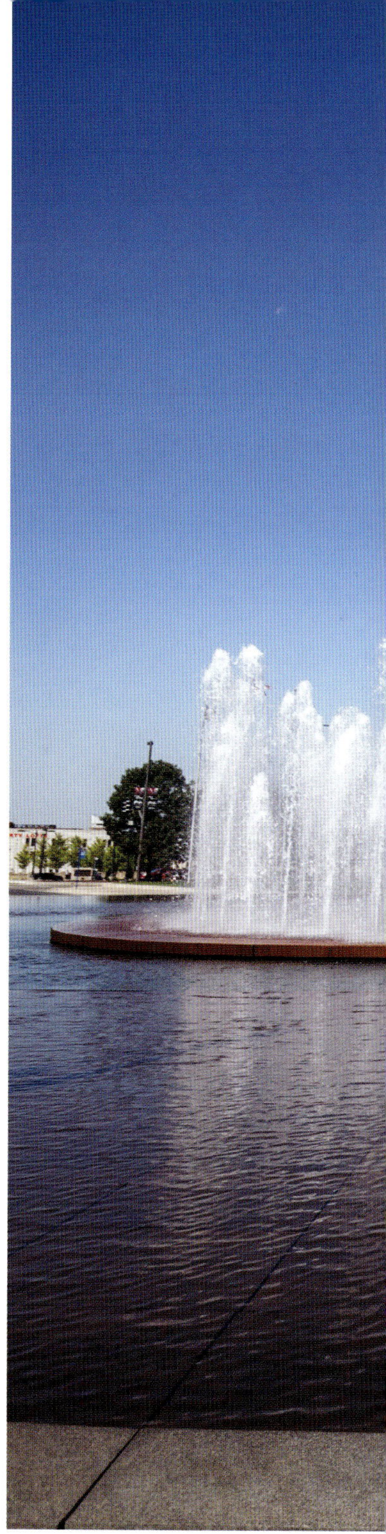

Neptune's Fountain

A common theme found in fountains is a tribute to Neptune, Roman god of the sea. Kansas City's Neptune Fountain depicts the god in his chariot, being pulled by dolphins and sea horses as he thrusts his trident. The fountain weighs more than 8,000 pounds and is cast in lead.

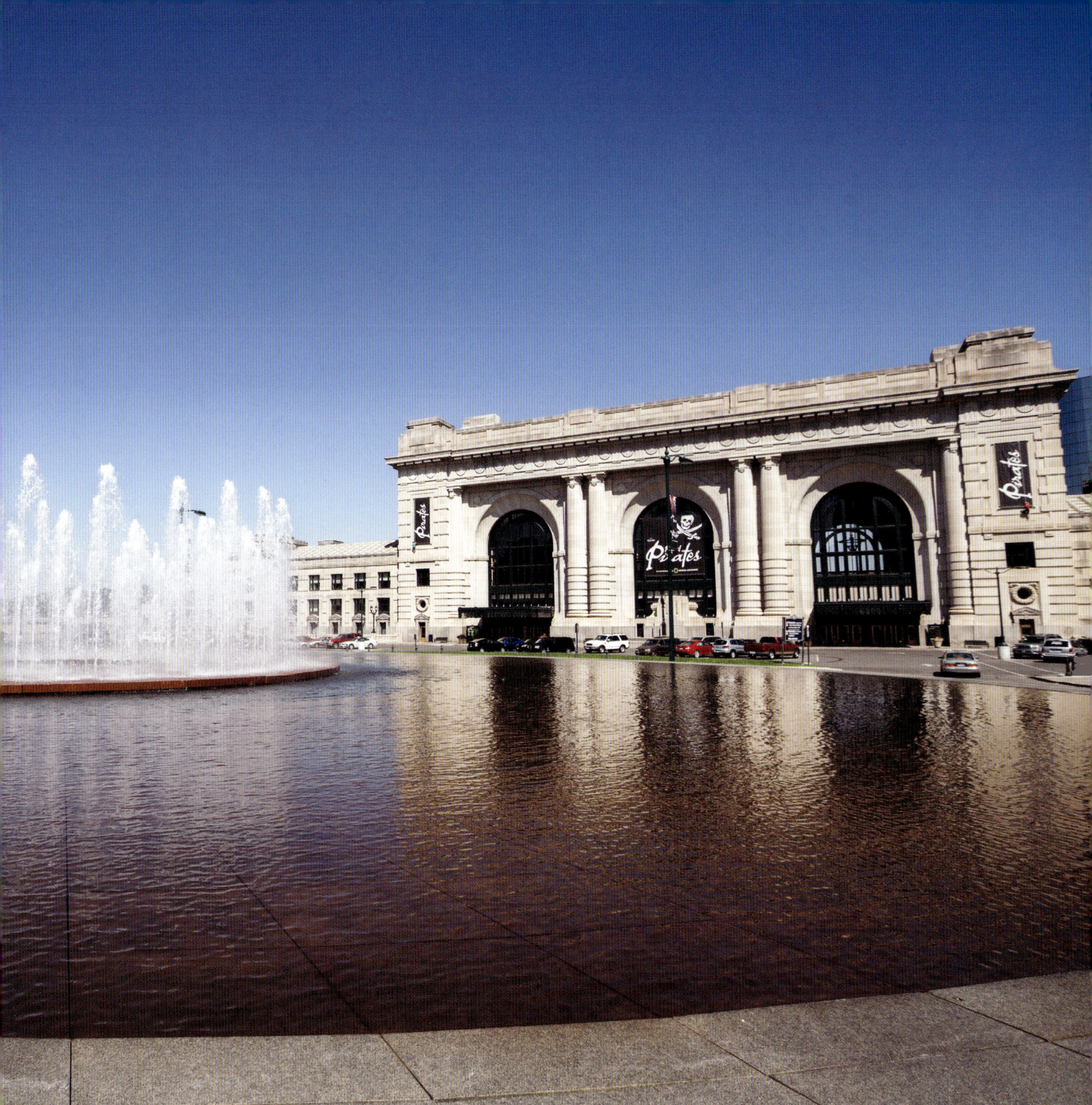

Henry Wollman Bloch Fountain

Outside historic Union Station is the expansive Henry Wollman Bloch Fountain, a gift to the city from the founder of H&R Block. Its large pool reflects the facade of the train station and its 232 computer-controlled jets put on a spectacular water show every 90 minutes.

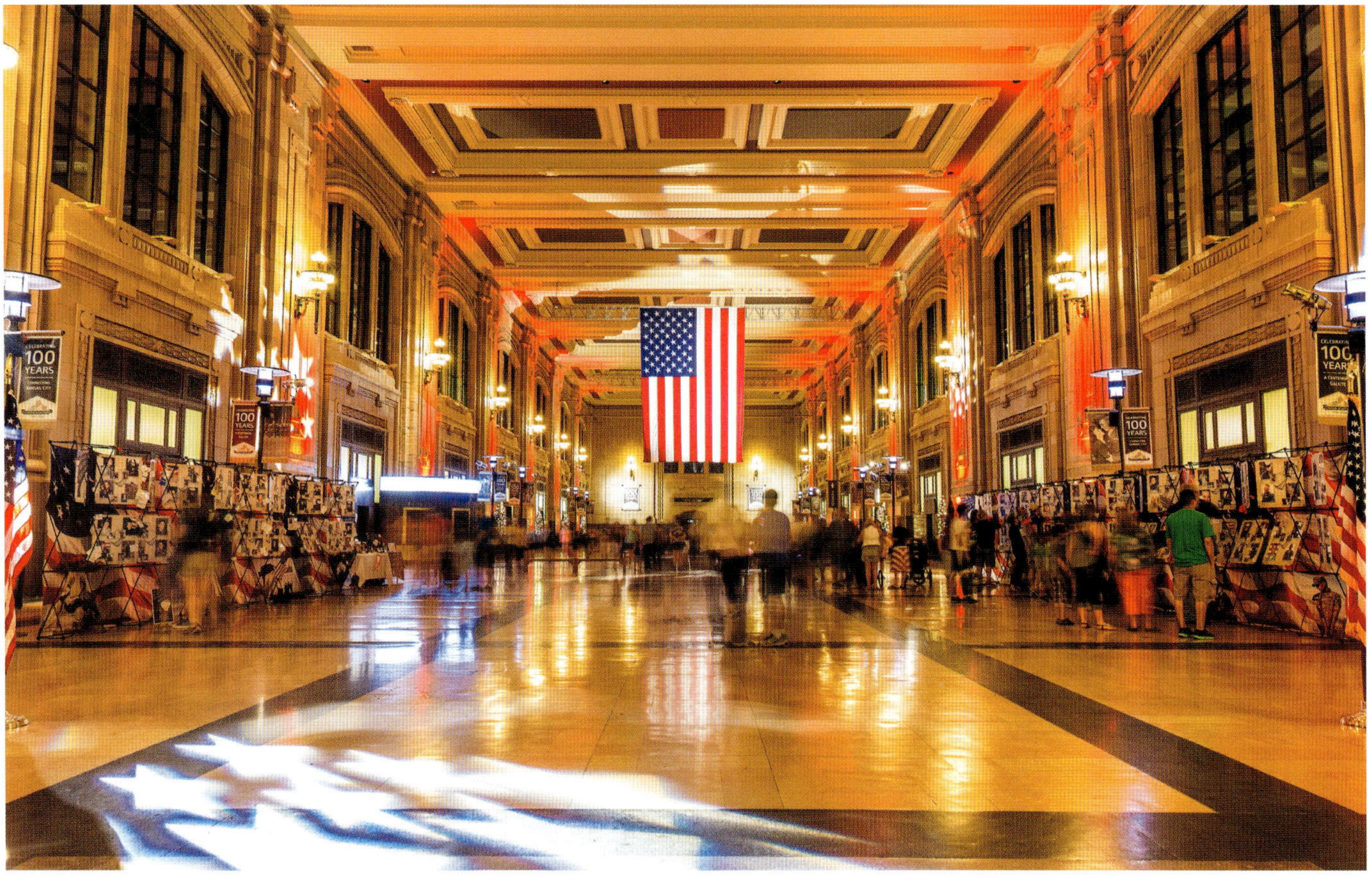

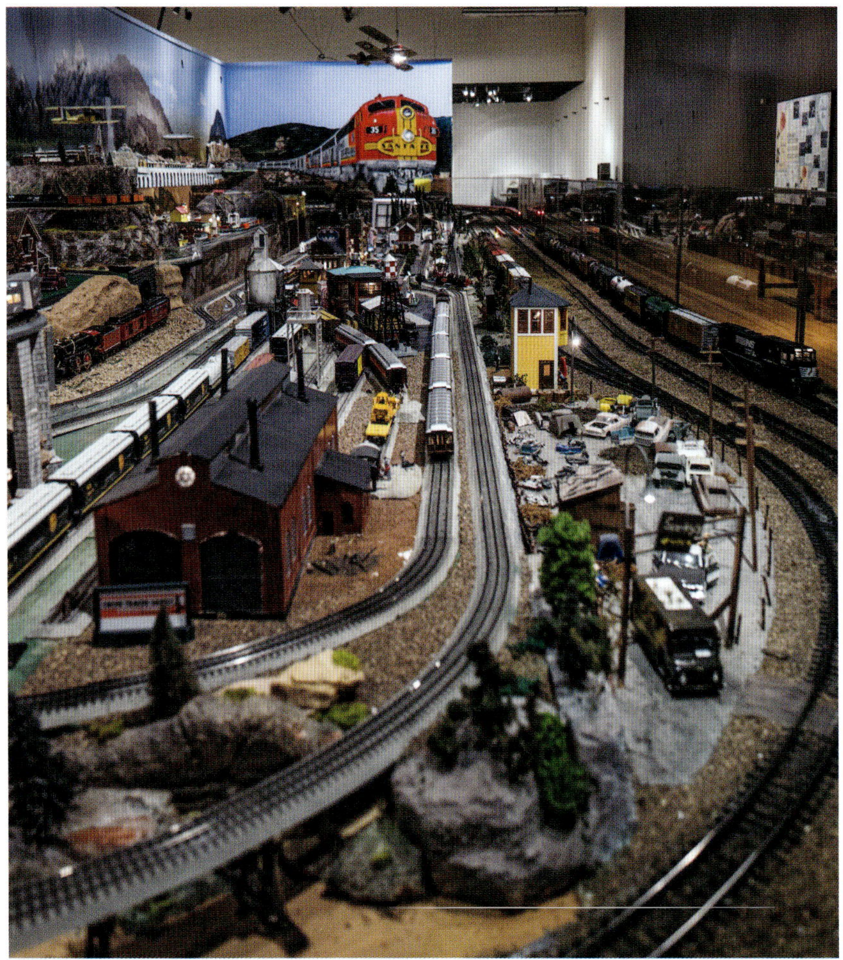

North Waiting Room, Union Station *(above)*

This cavernous room once held up to 10,000 people as they shopped, dined, and waited for trains to take them to new adventures. During World War II, a million travelers walked this hall, many on their way to Europe or the Pacific. Now, it is home to festivals and parties.

Model Railroad Experience *(left)*

A miniature countryside sits before you, complete with general stores, power plants, and lots and lots of trains. There are lights, noises, and movement everywhere you turn. The Model Railroad Experience has more than 8,000 square feet of tracks and models, and best of all, admission is free.

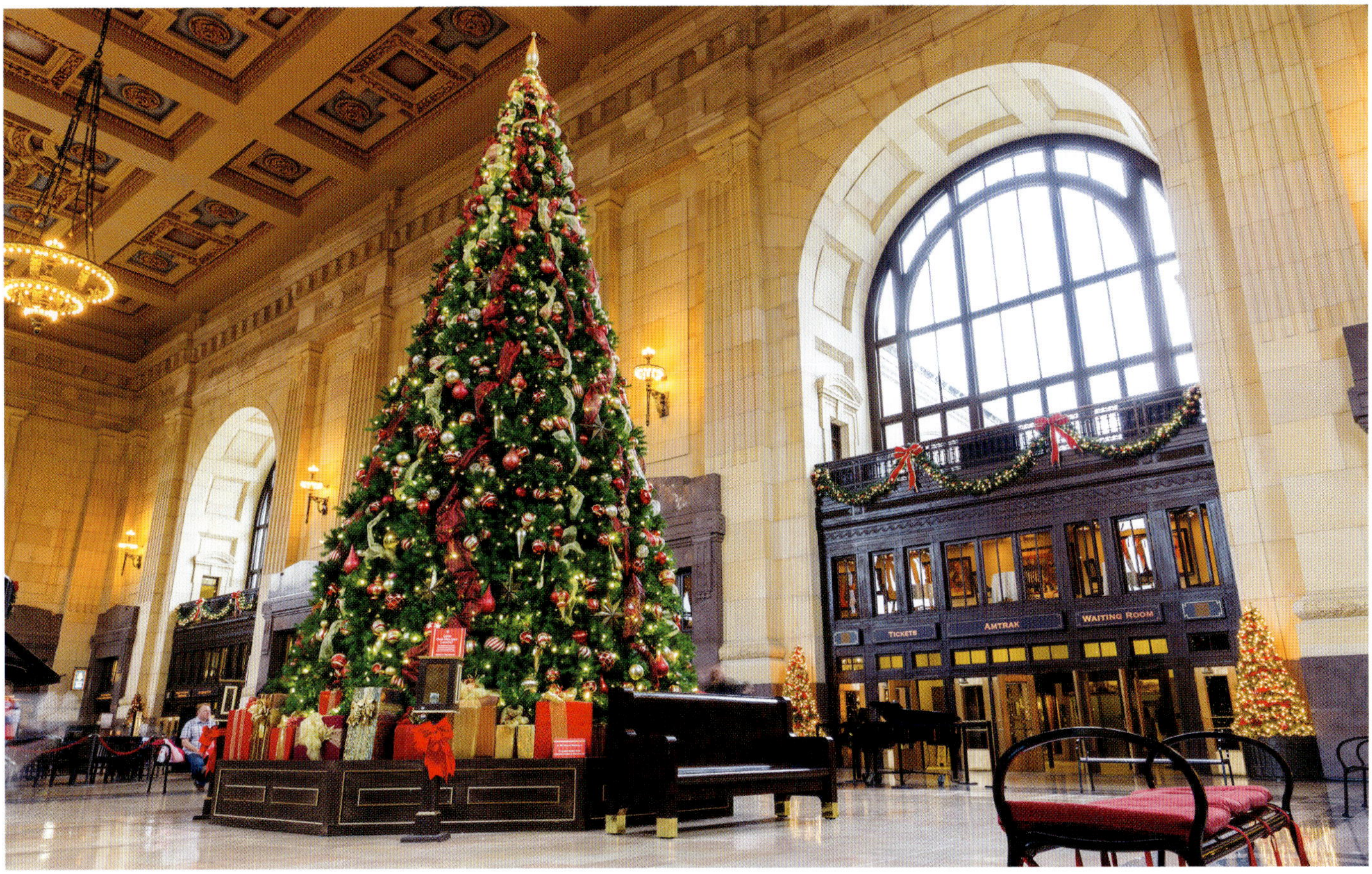

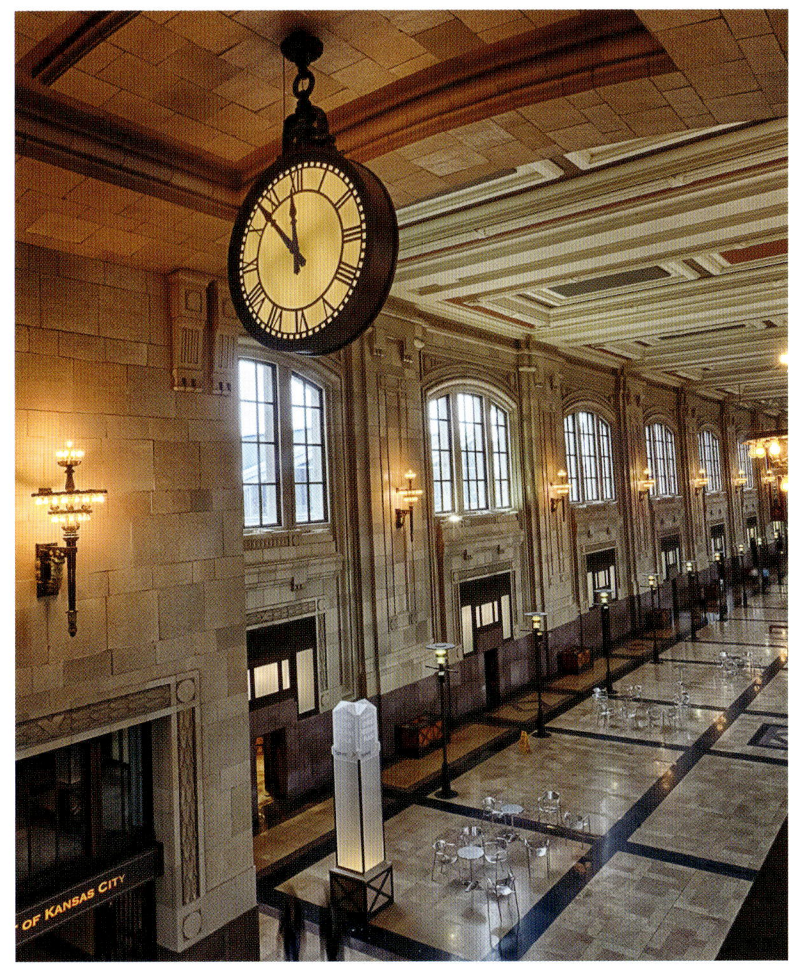

Union Station Grand Hall and North Waiting Room *(above and right)*

Union Station sat abandoned not long ago. Now refurbished, it is a near constant bustle of activity. From weekly fairs, which attract thousands, to months-long exhibitions, the functioning train station has a rich history as a gathering spot, of transport, and even a gangland massacre.

Night Settles on Kansas City
(pages 24 - 25)

Modern Kansas City meets its past in this view north from Liberty Memorial. To the left sit the tall pylons of Bartle Hall and the scalloped roof of the Kauffman Center for Performing Arts. To the right, the UFO-shaped Sprint Center, and in the foreground is historic Union Station.

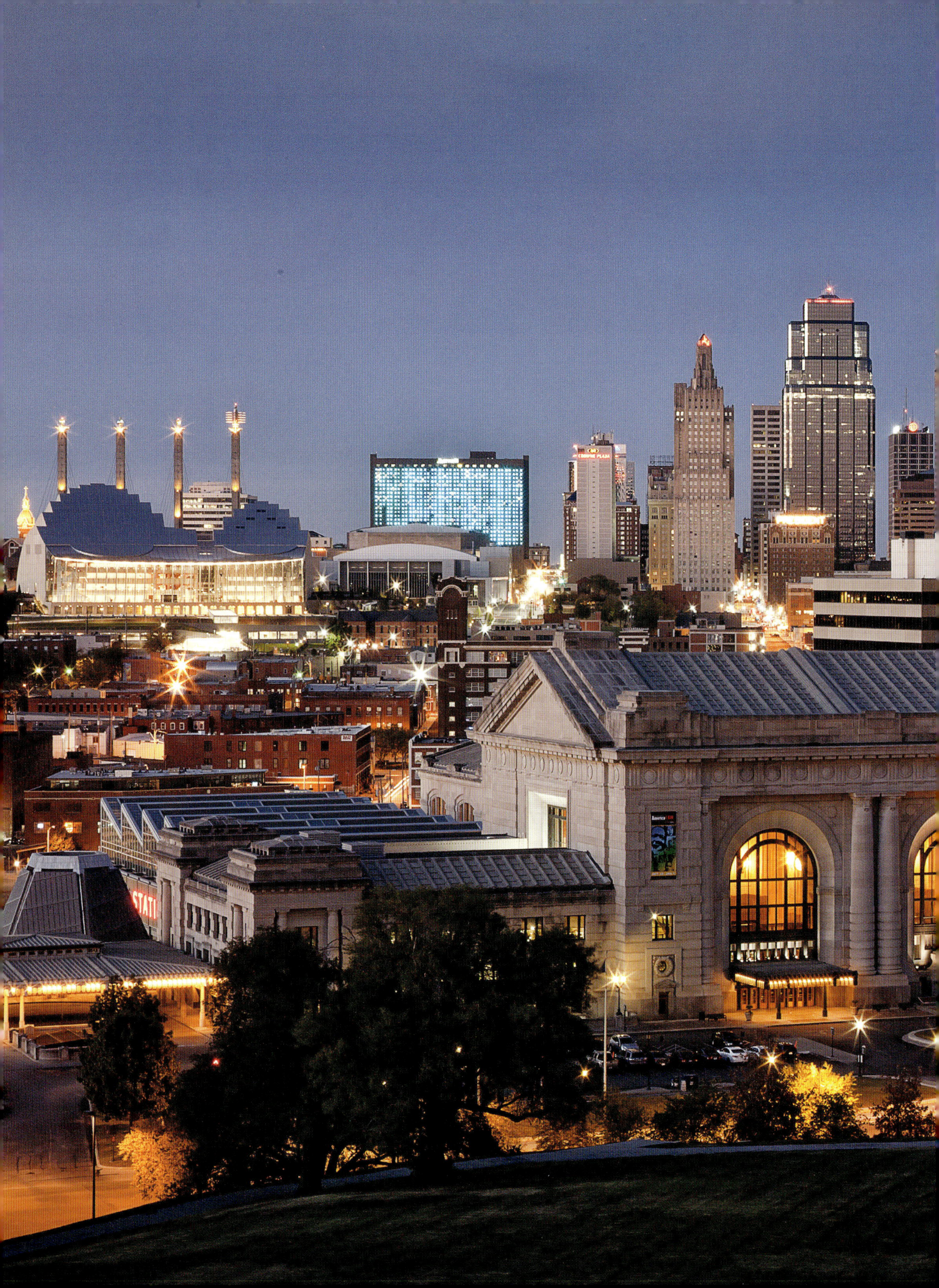

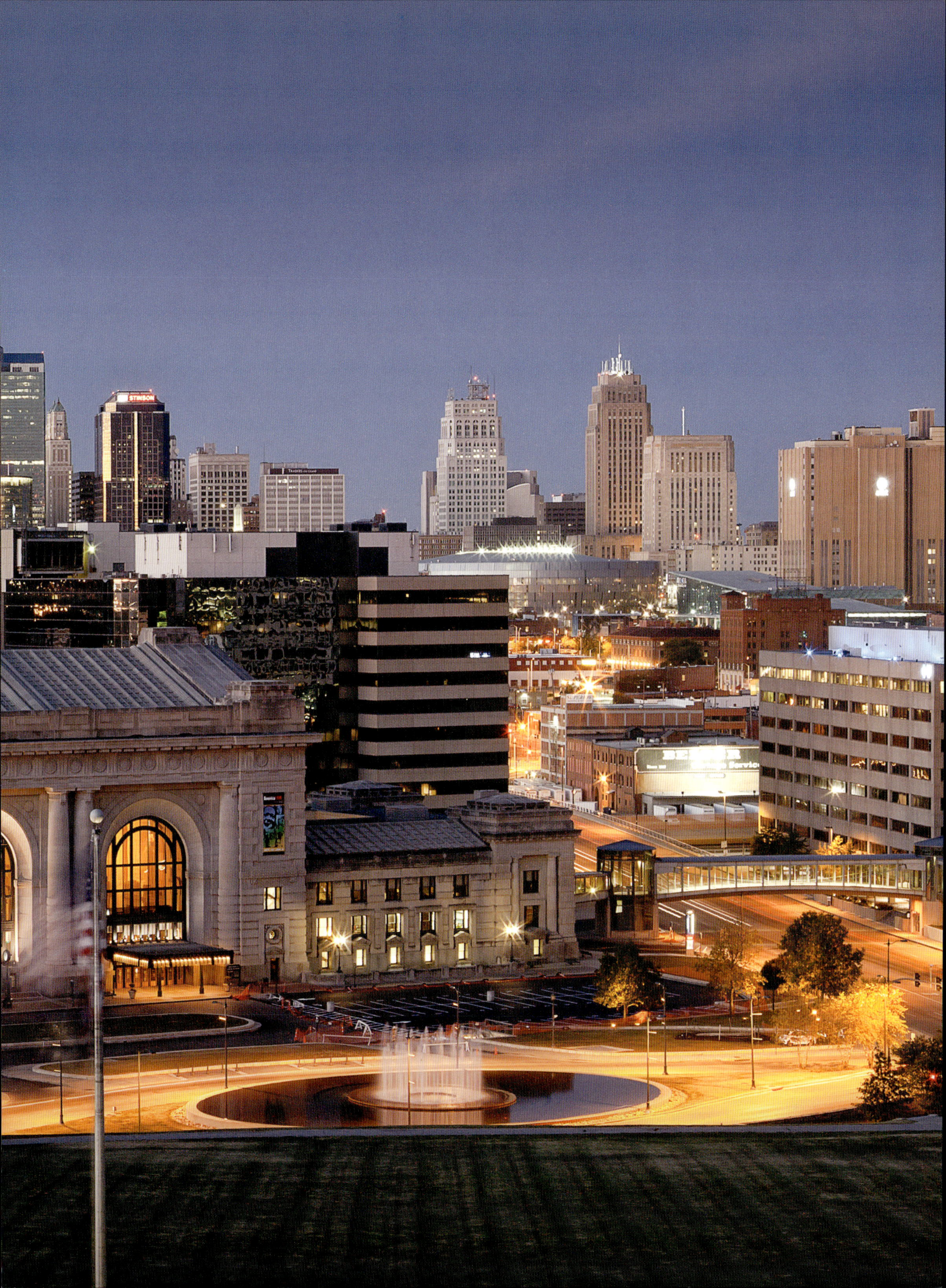
STINSON

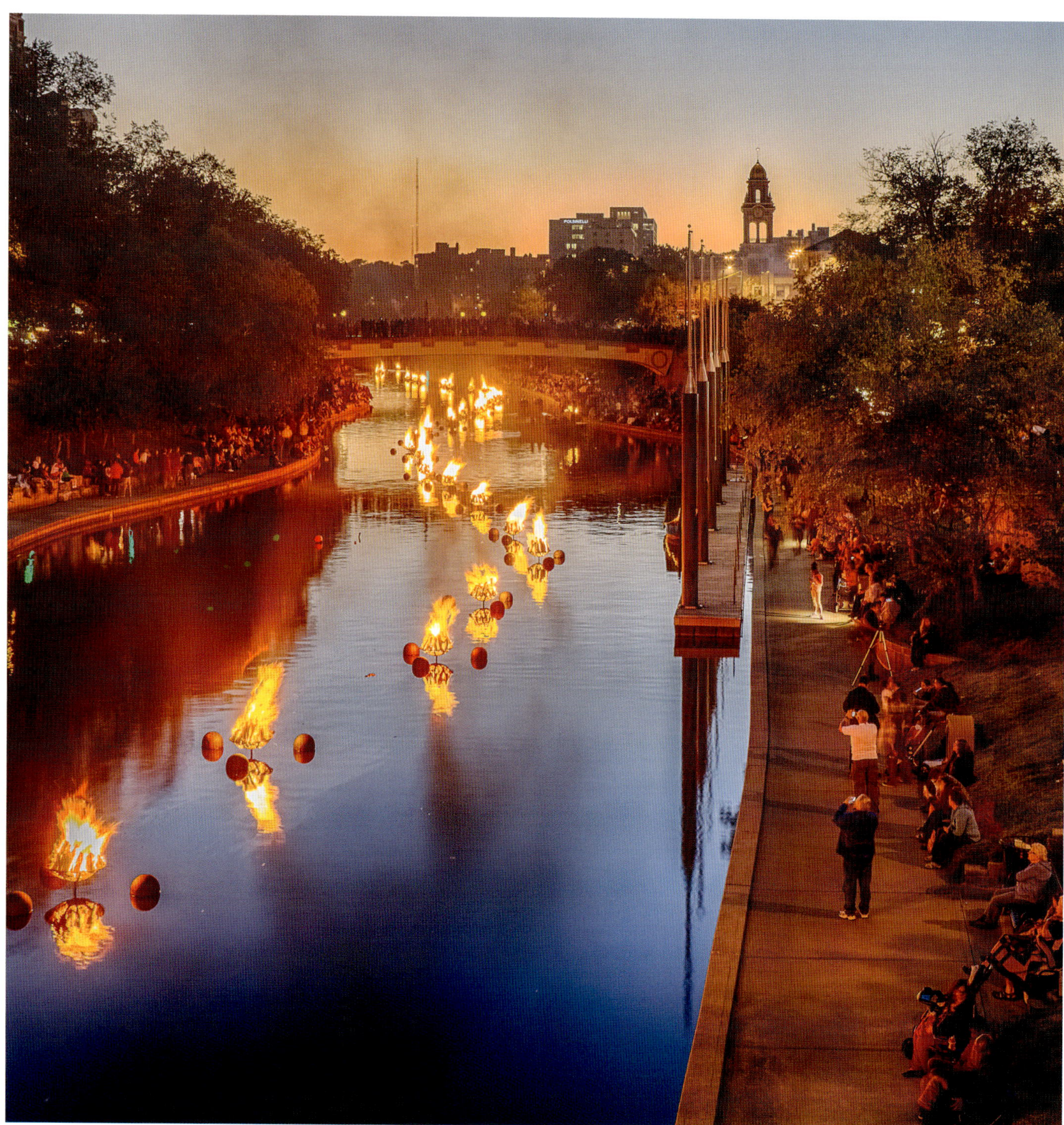

WaterFire *(above)*

Every fall, Kansas Citians gather along the banks of Brush Creek to watch the iconic WaterFire performing arts festival. Lit braziers float in the waterway, setting the stage for dance, drama, music, and more as rich and complex stories are told against the contrasting backdrop of flame and water.

Brush Creek Waterway *(opposite)*

The Battle of Westport, the largest Civil War engagement west of the Mississippi, was waged across the banks of Brush Creek. Today, the peaceful waterway flows through the middle of Kansas City, connecting neighborhoods and suburbs. Along its ten-mile length, fountains have been placed to accentuate its beauty.

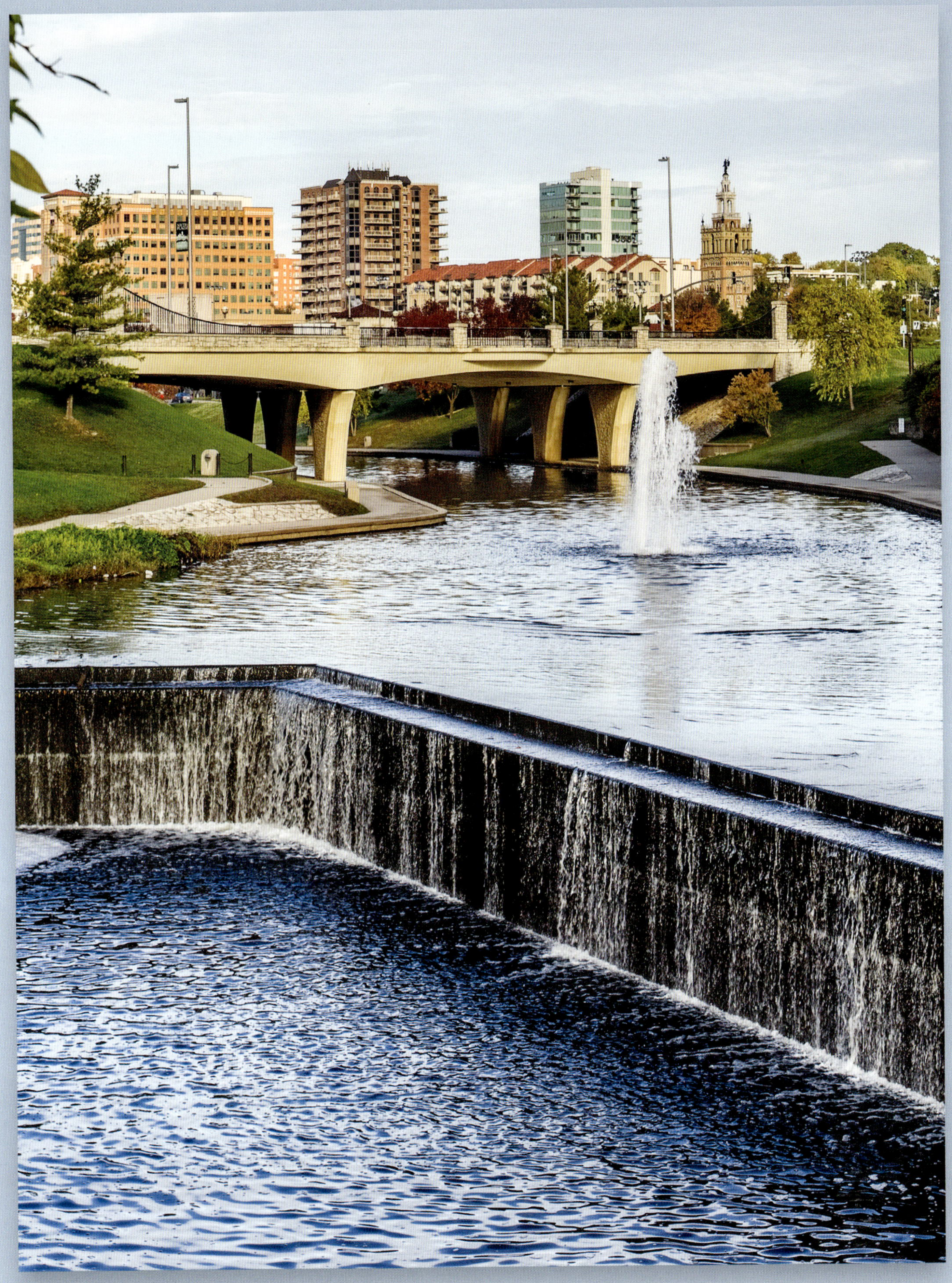

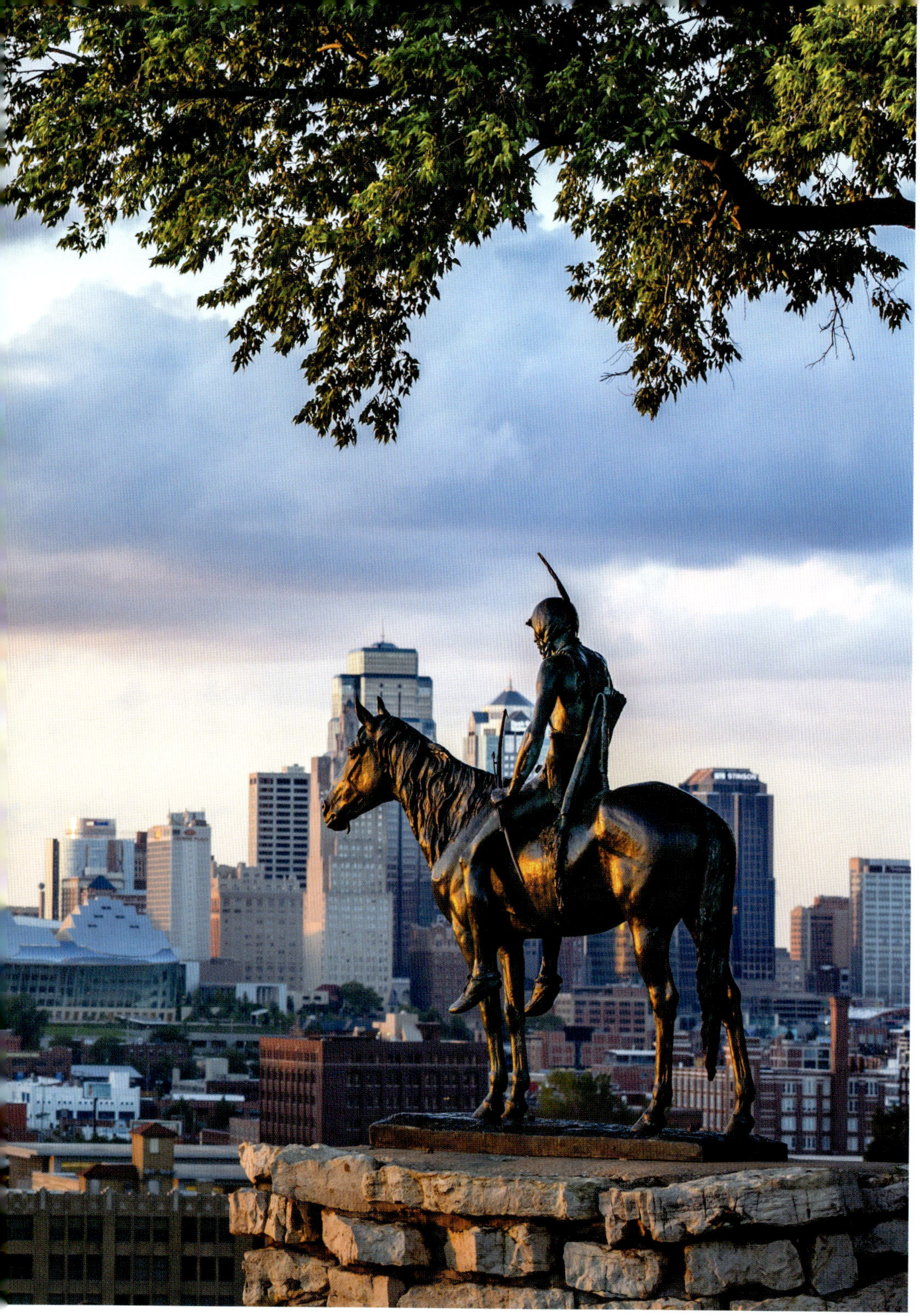

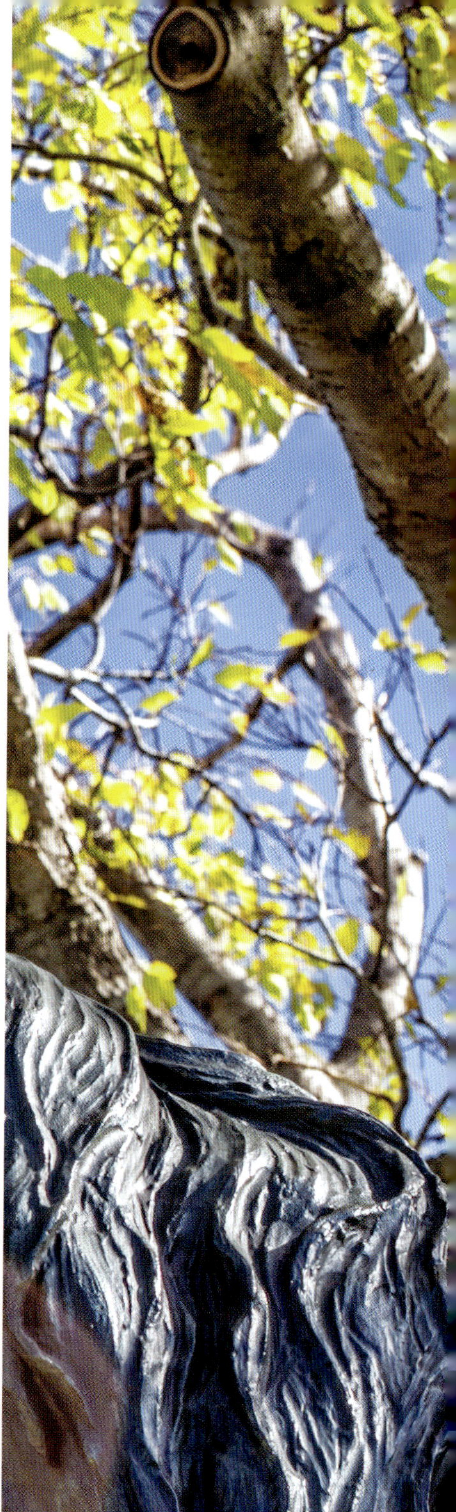

The Scout *(above and opposite)*

On a bluff overlooking the downtown skyline, sits an oversized bronze statue of a Sioux scout. Kansas City has a rich historical connection with Native Americans tribes, thanks to its role as the last stop before the western frontier, and the Scout statue is a proud reminder of that past.

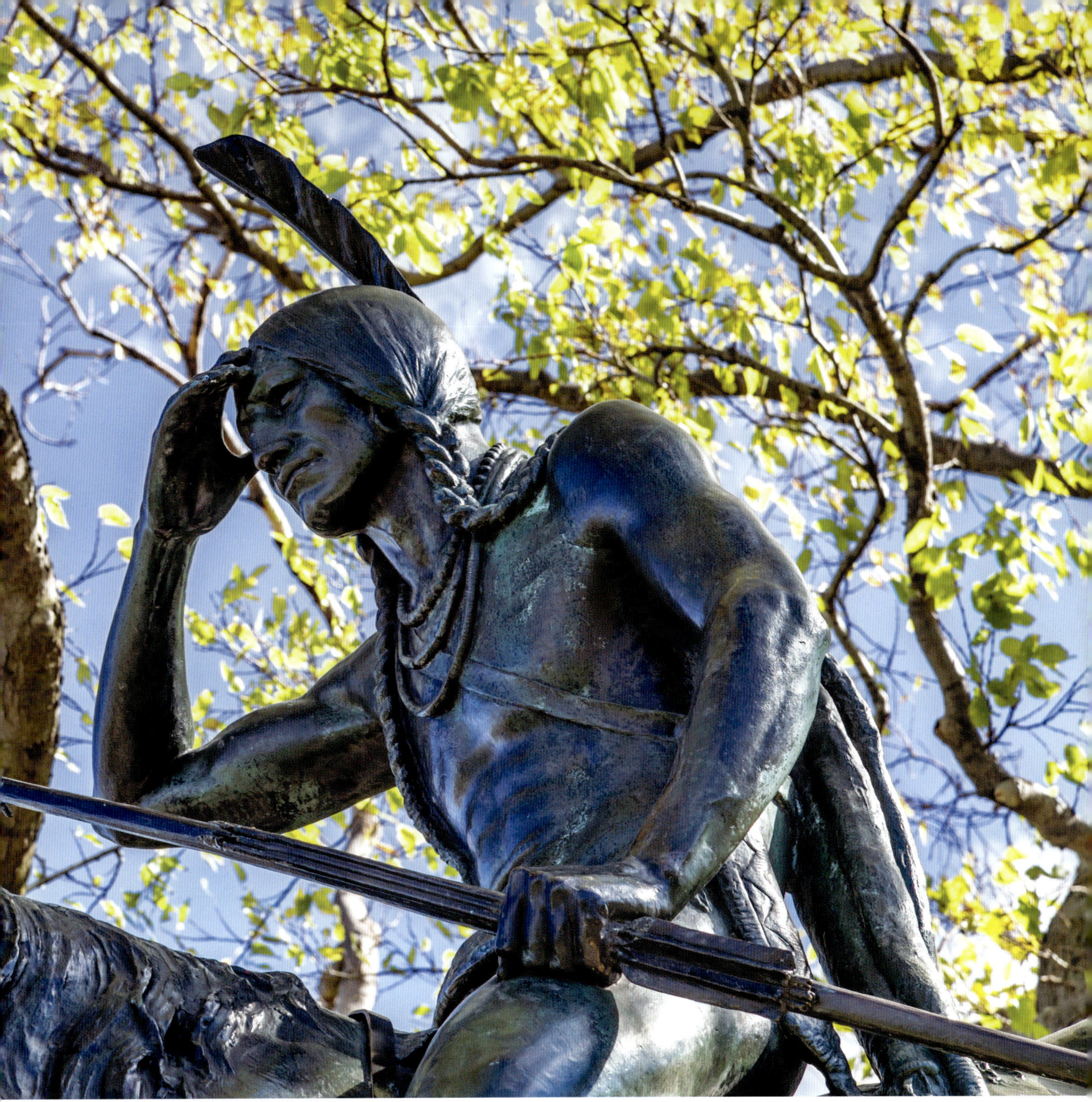

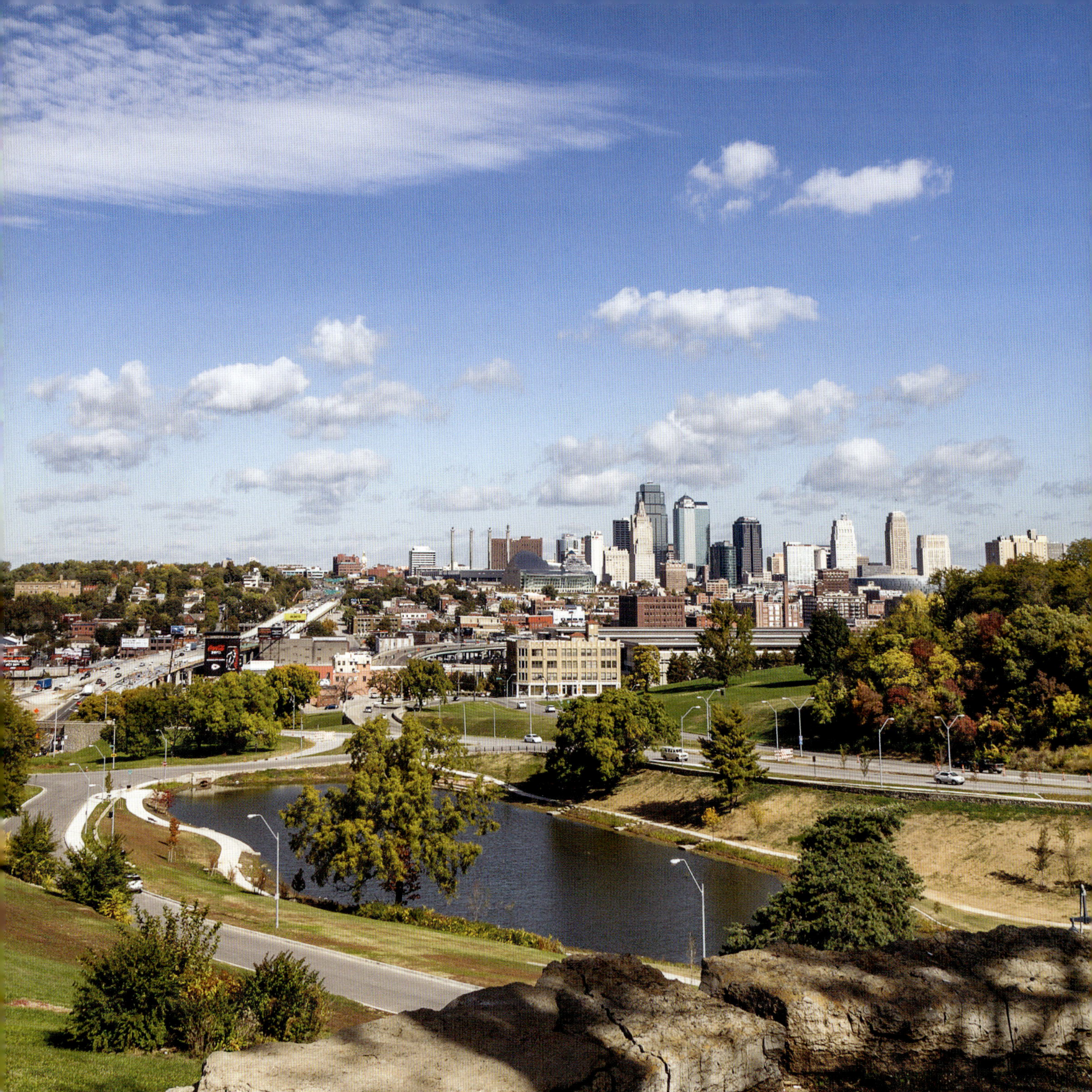

Kansas City Skyline

The city is set among bluffs and valleys, making for some beautiful and breathtaking viewpoints, like this one, which looks north at downtown. From the left, the art-minded Westside, with its restaurants and galleries, meets the headquarters and businesses of downtown in a seamless integration of neighborhoods.

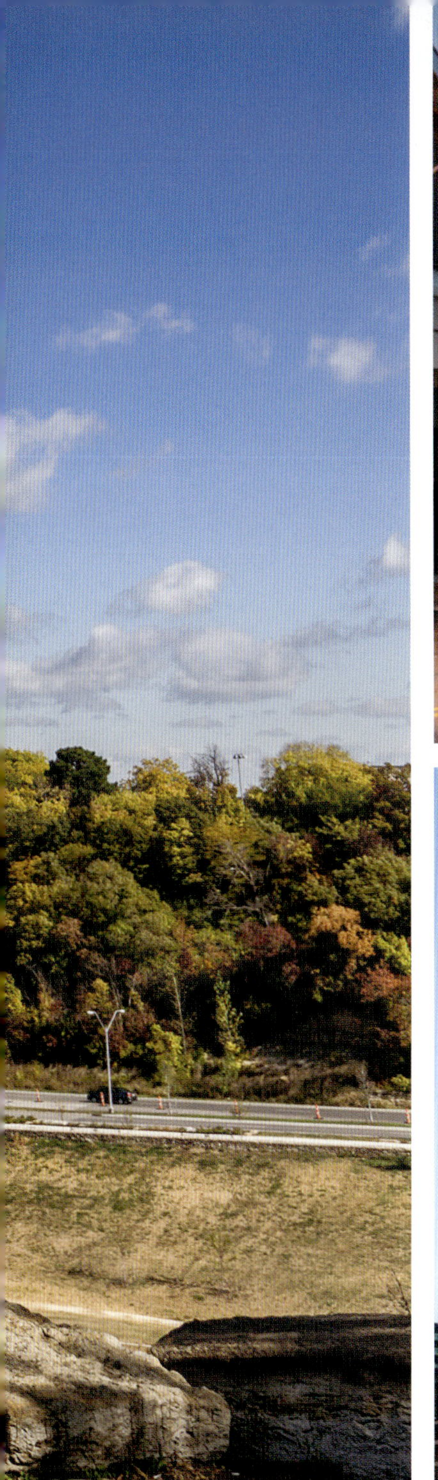

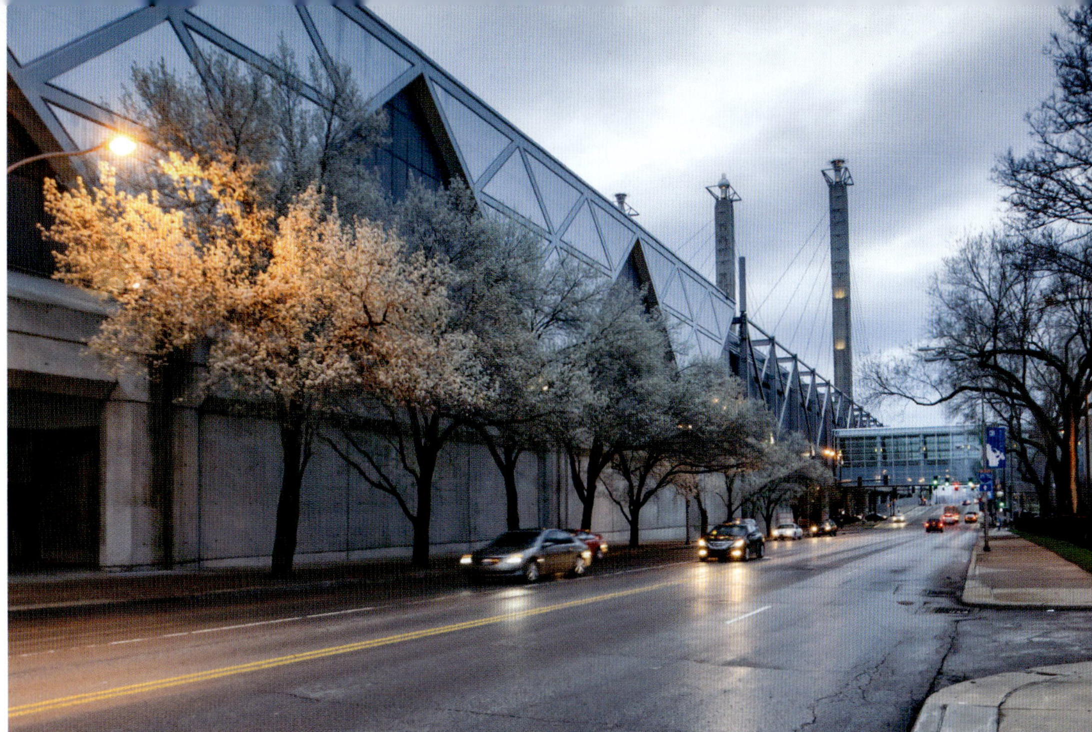

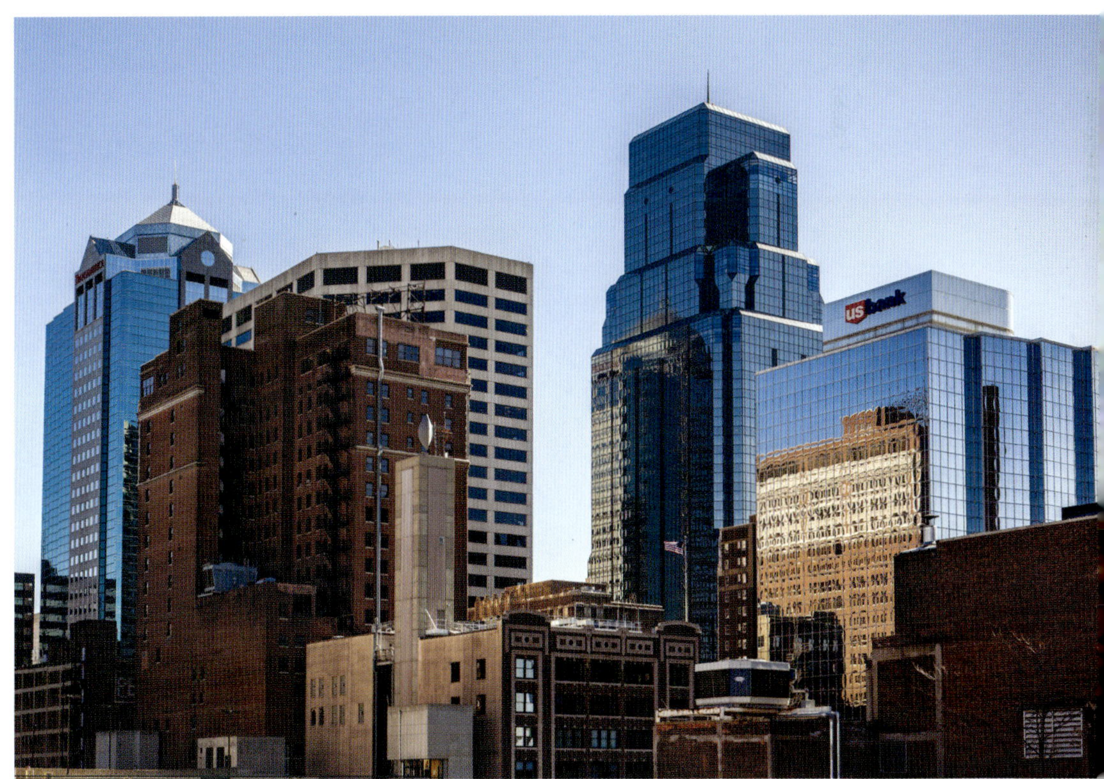

Bartle Hall and Broadway *(top)*

Kansas City's convention space is located in the heart of downtown and is immediately recognizable by its four art deco inspired pylons. The convention center occupies eight city blocks and has hosted national conventions for both political parties. The largest hall in the complex, Bartle Hall, sits prominently on Broadway.

Downtown *(bottom)*

Kansas City has long been known as a crossroads where travelers heading west met with those returning east. Those contrasts are still evident as historic brick buildings sit among modern glass and steel headquarters in downtown. A revitalization effort has repurposed many old buildings, permanently tying Kansas City to its past.

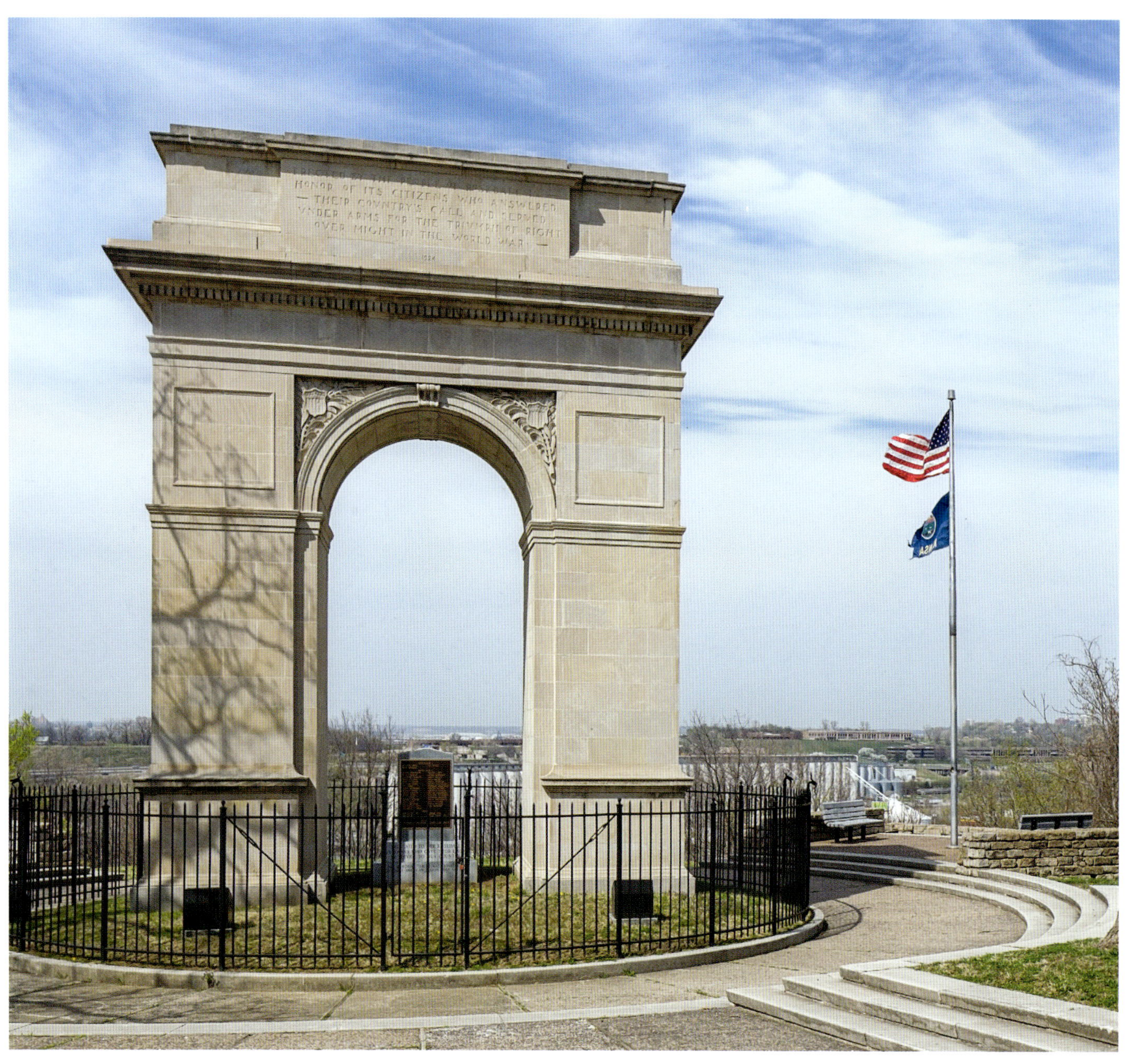

Rosedale Memorial Arch *(above)*

This arch, a tribute to men from the Rosedale neighborhood who died during World War I, was inspired by the Arc de Triomphe in Paris. The memorial sits high on a bluff with a panorama of downtown to the east and the Kansas River and west bottoms to the north.

City Hall *(opposite)*

Kansas City's seat of government has the distinction of being the fourth-tallest city hall in the world. The public can access an observation deck atop its 29 stories for a stunning view of downtown and the surrounding areas. Inside, the building is rich with art deco ornamentation and details.

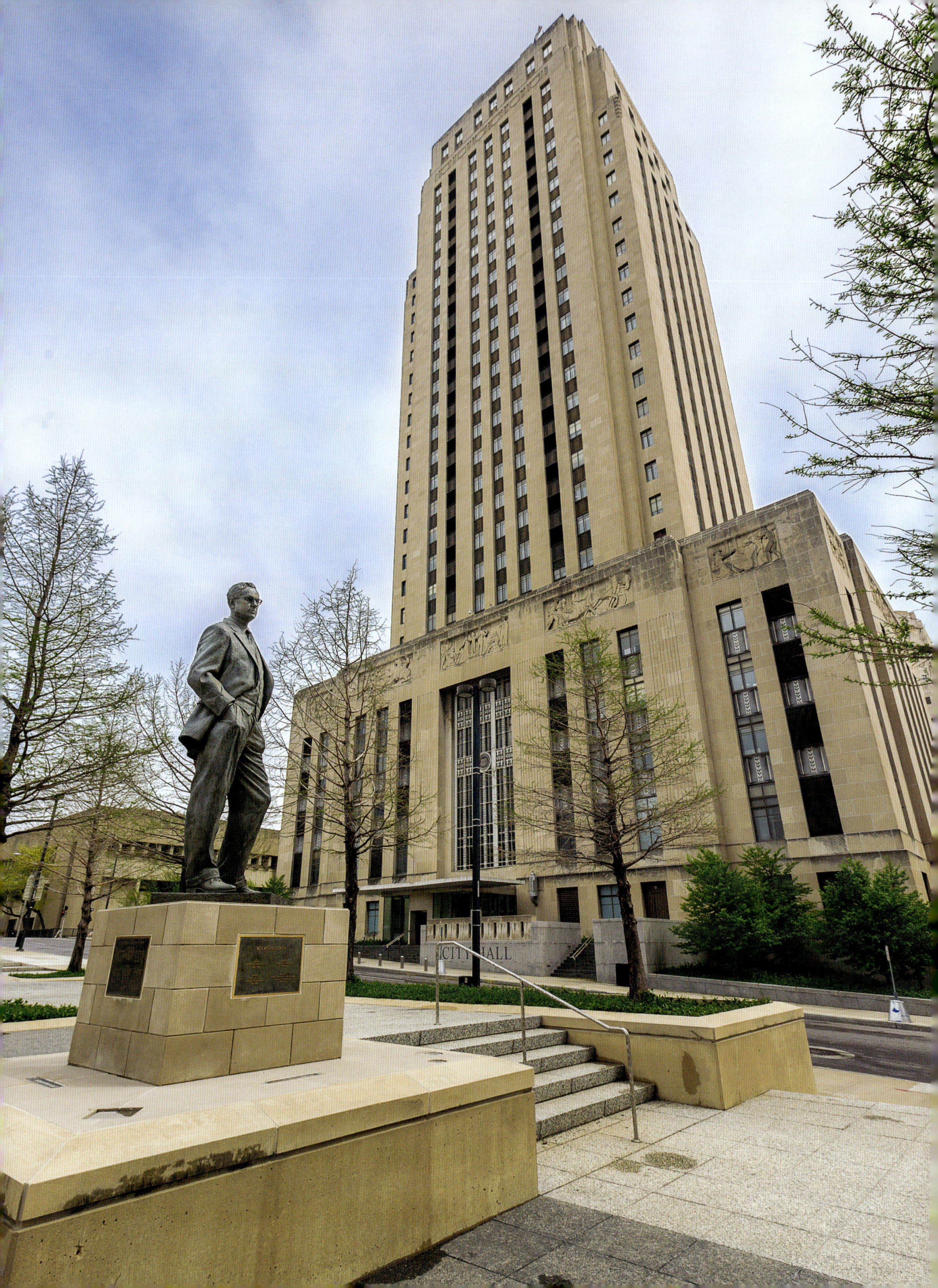
CITY HALL

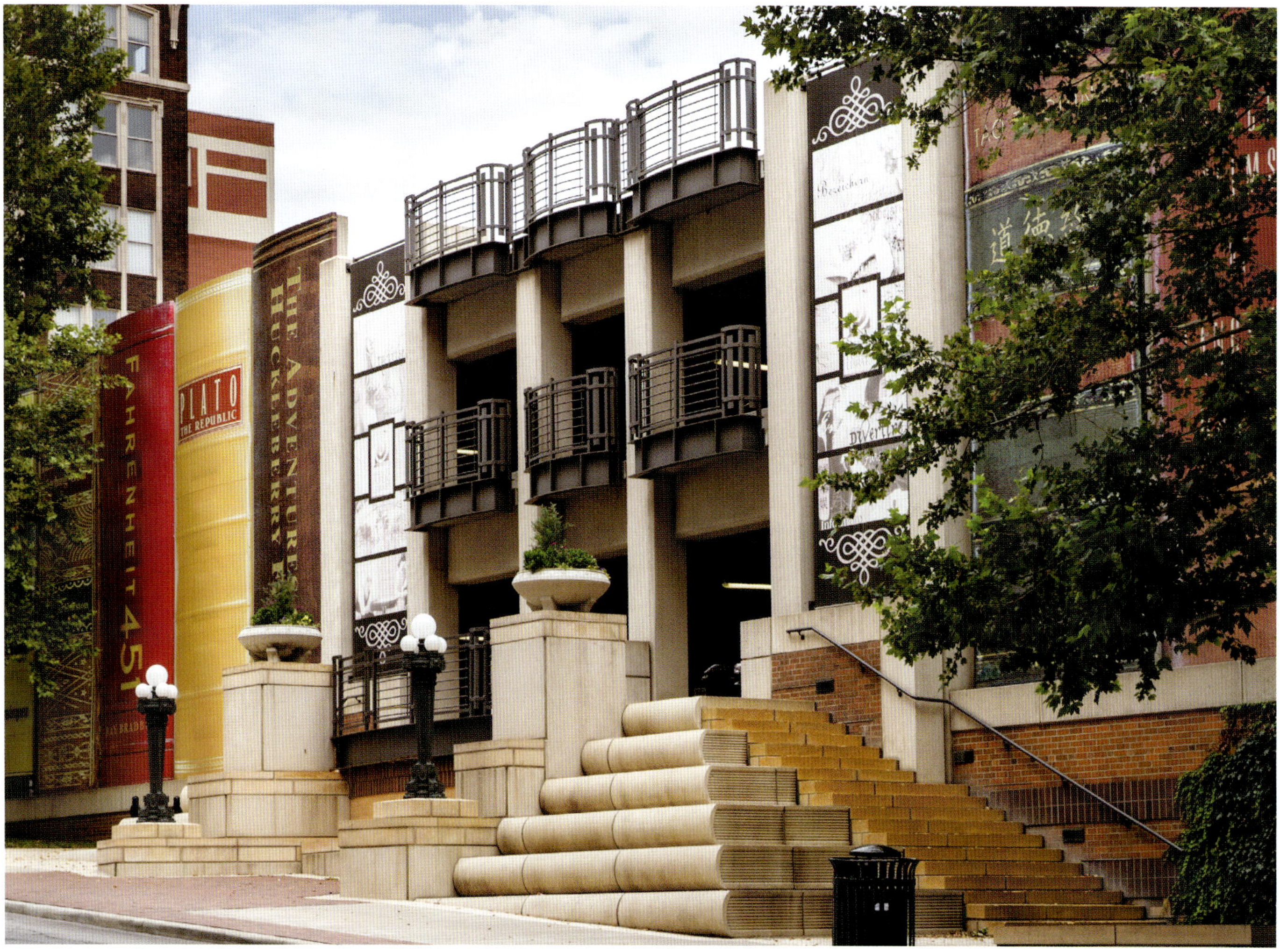

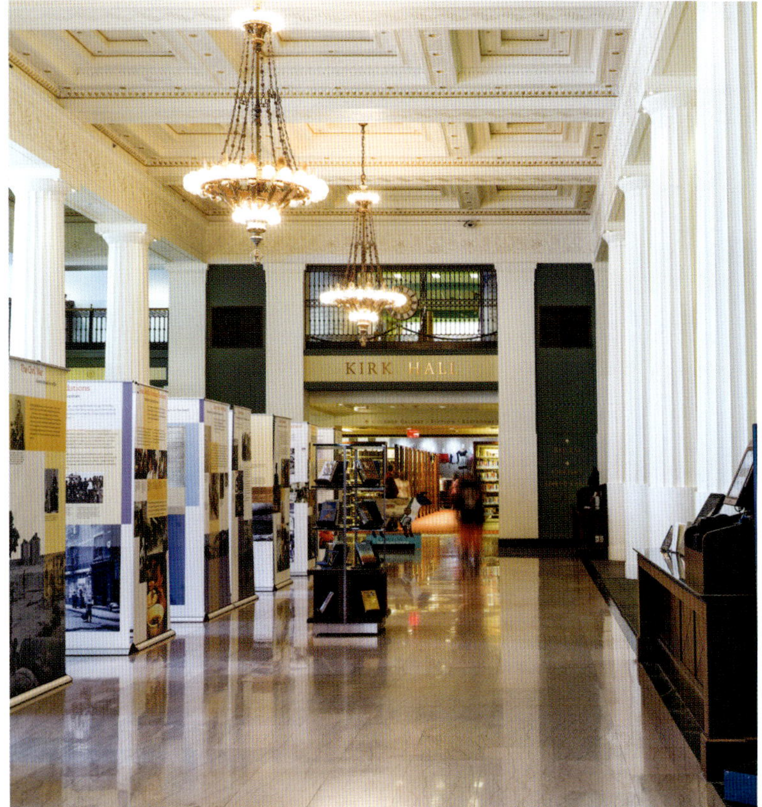

Kansas City Public Library

(above and left)

This library has been in operation since 1873 and its collection specializes in local history and African-American culture. The connected garage is adorned with huge replicas of books, making it look like an oversized bookshelf and earning a place as one of the world's most unique buildings.

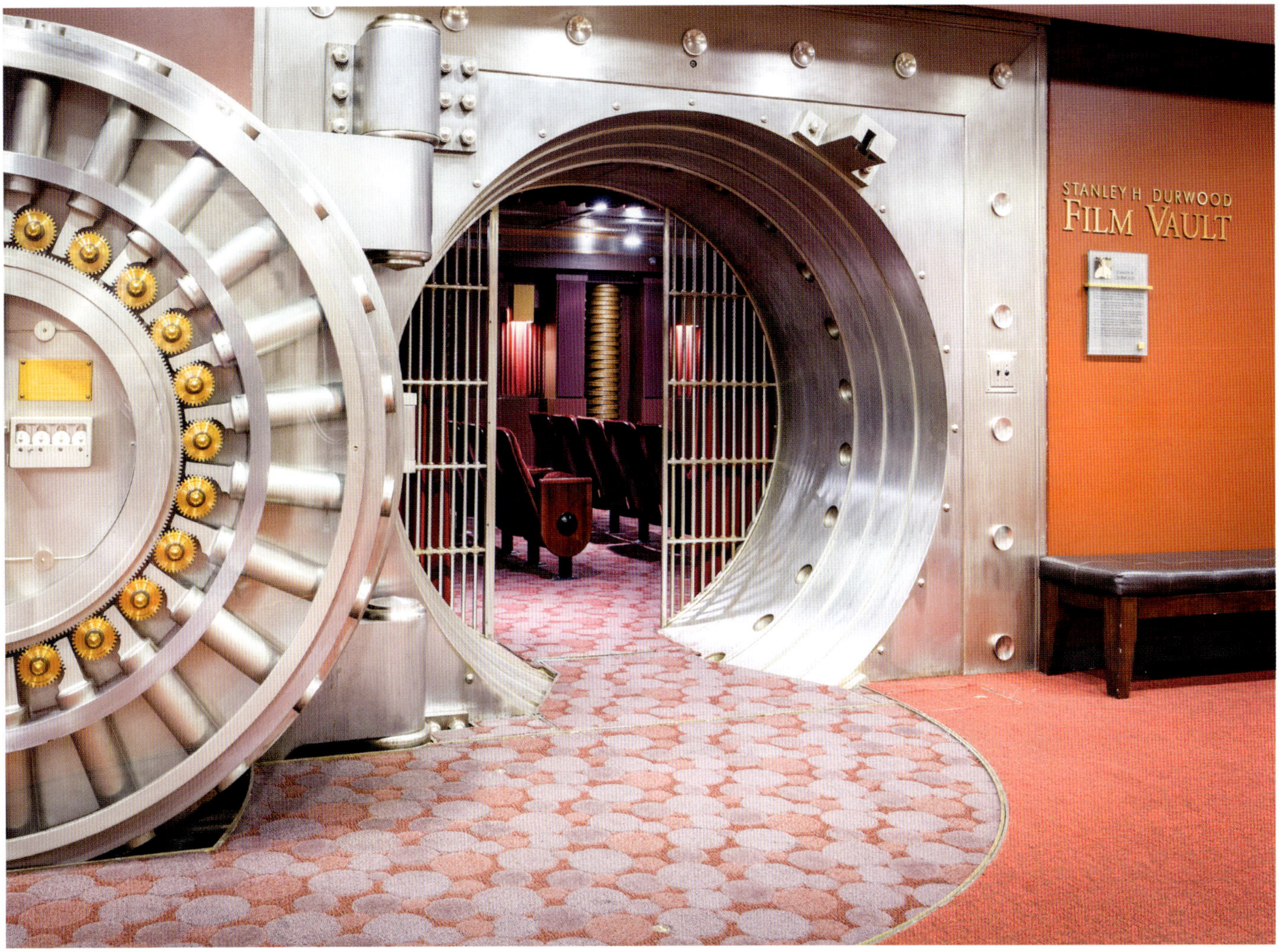

Durwood Film Vault *(above)*

When the library annexed an old bank, they repurposed the vault into a small movie theater. The vault, seating just 28, is used for film viewings or as a meeting space and is unique for its 35-ton steel vault door, which serves as a remembrance of the building's past.

Kansas City Public Library Rooftop Terrace *(right)*

Popular for its urban views and contemporary setting, Rooftop Terrace has hosted wedding receptions, birthday parties, and corporate events. On a sunny weekend afternoon or a warm summer night, it's also the ideal place to challenge a friend to a game of life-sized chess.

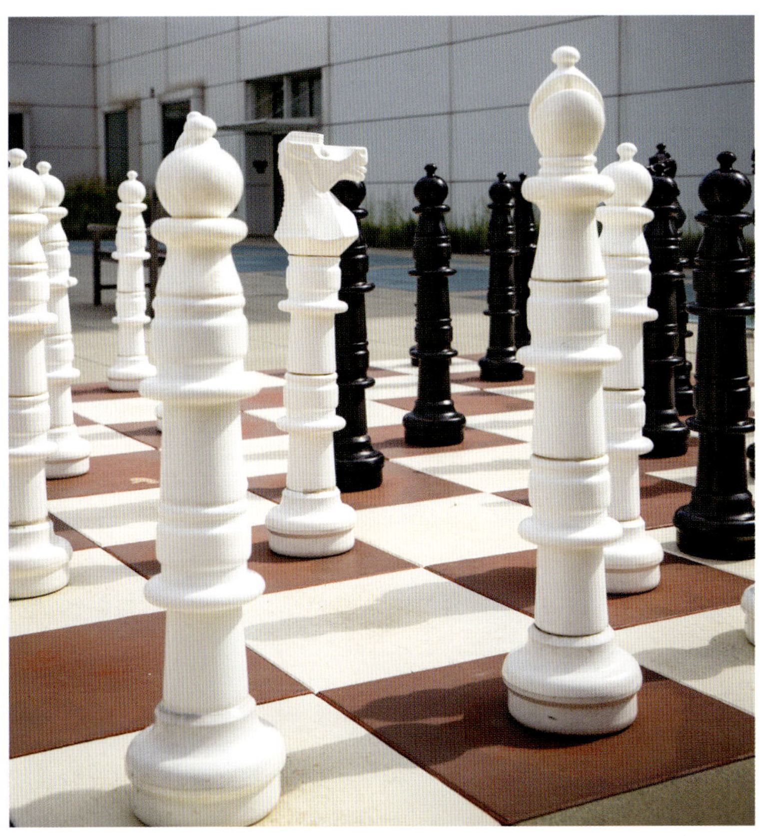

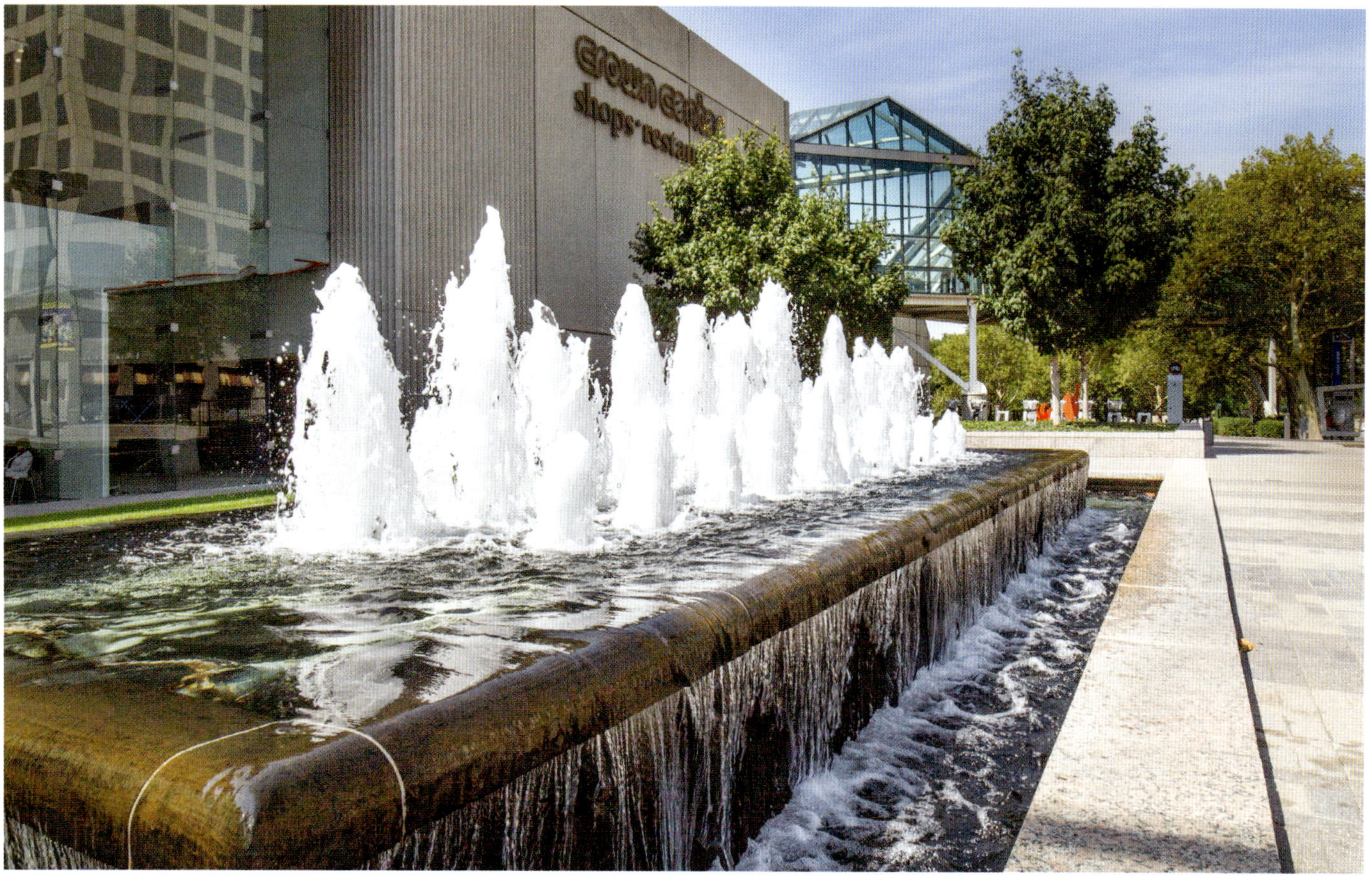

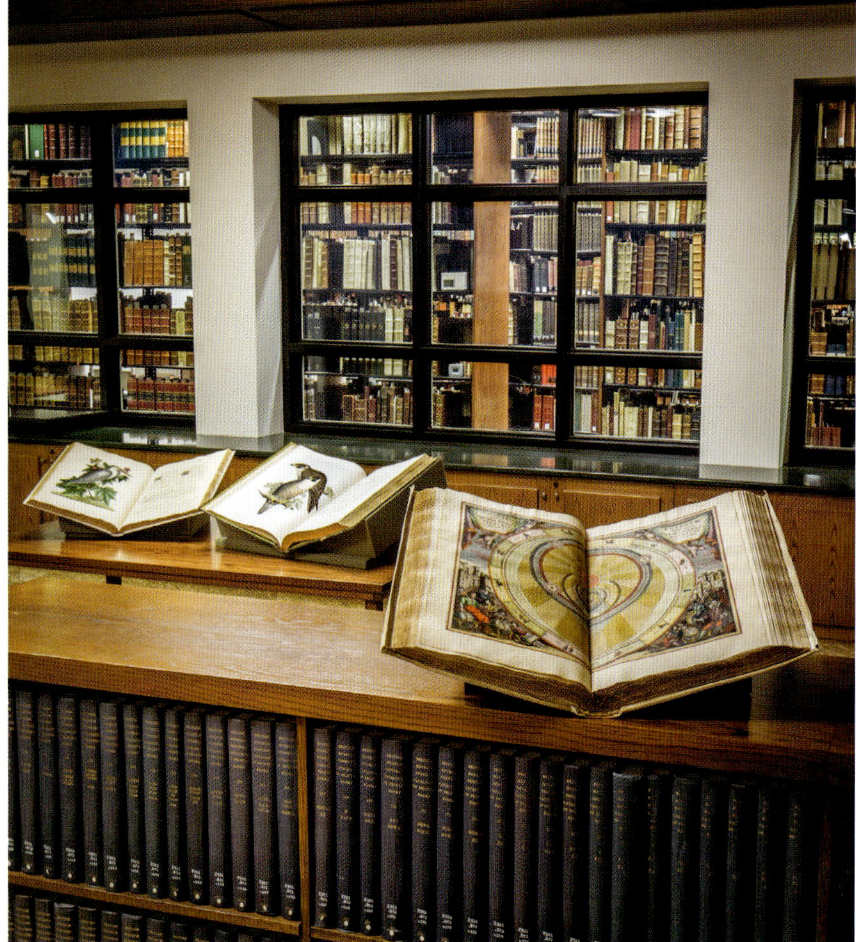

Crown Center *(above)*

This shopping center acts as a gateway that connects busy downtown to the lazier suburbs to the south. The complex boasts a variety of shops, hotels, theaters, and Missouri's only four-star restaurant, The American. Its plaza is home to numerous festivals and the mayor's Christmas Tree during the holidays.

Linda Hall Library *(left)*

Nestled among 14 acres of gardens and tree-lined footpaths, the Linda Hall Library is one of the largest science libraries in the world. The private collection contains more than two million items on science, technology, and engineering, making it a favorite destination for researchers, students, and curious visitors.

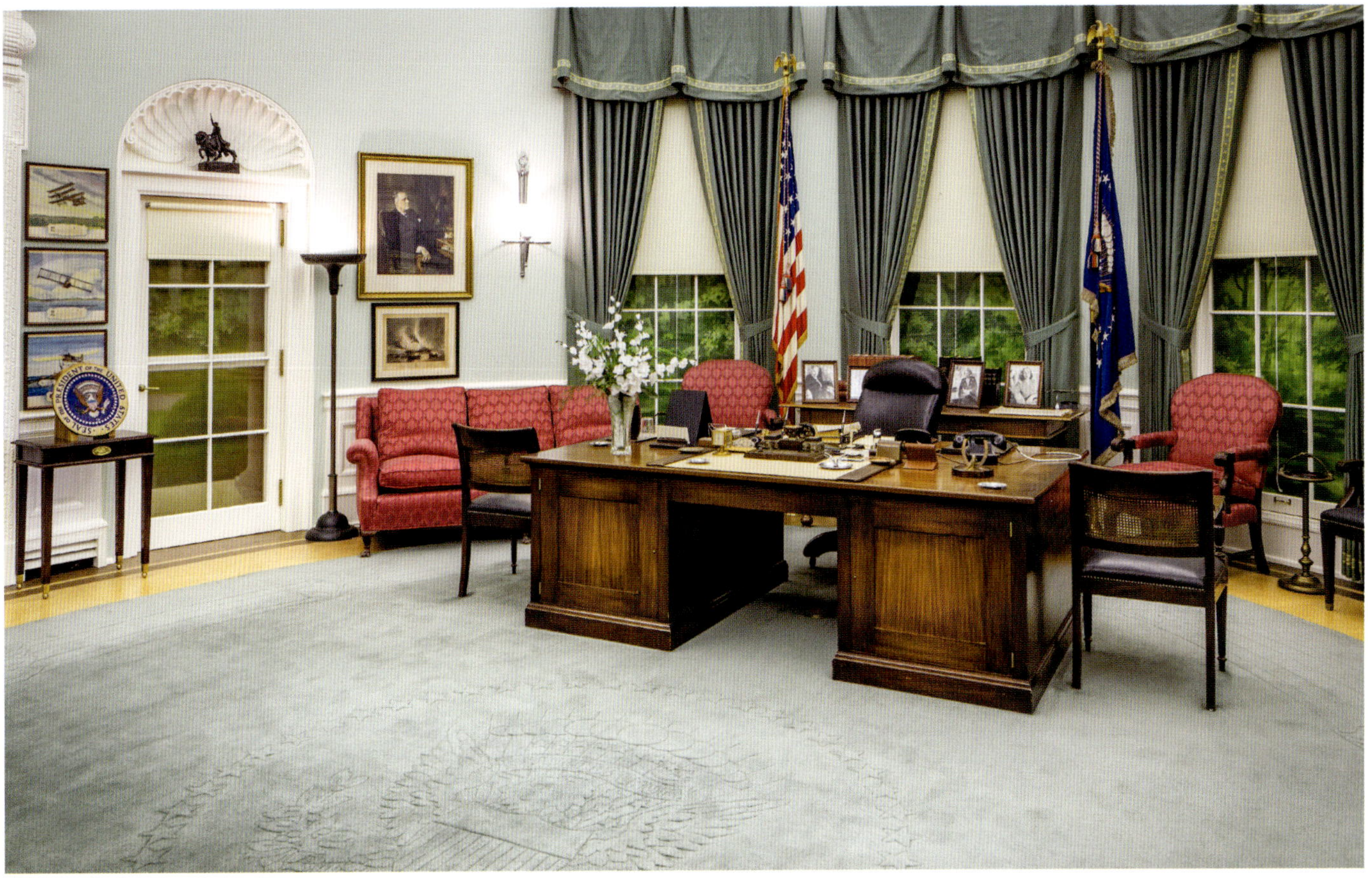

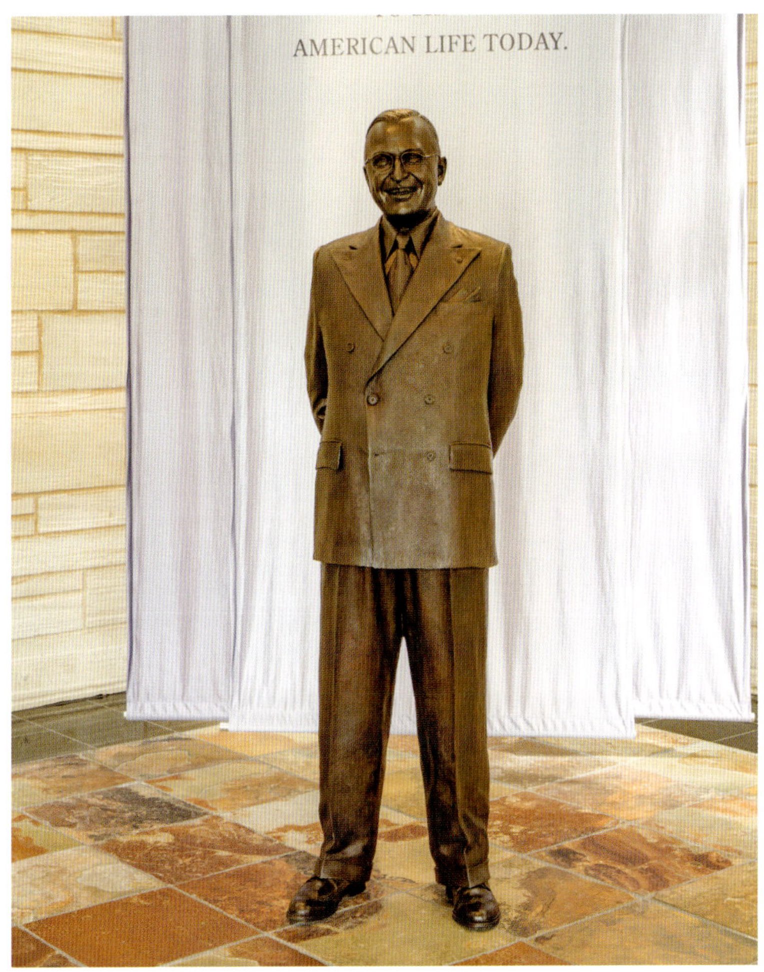

Harry Truman Presidential Library and Museum *(above and right)*

America's 33rd President, Harry S. Truman, left his effects to the first Presidential Library managed by the National Archives. The facility includes many important artifacts and documents of Truman's presidency, which saw the bombing of Japan and conclusion of WWII. Truman and his wife are buried in the library's gardens.

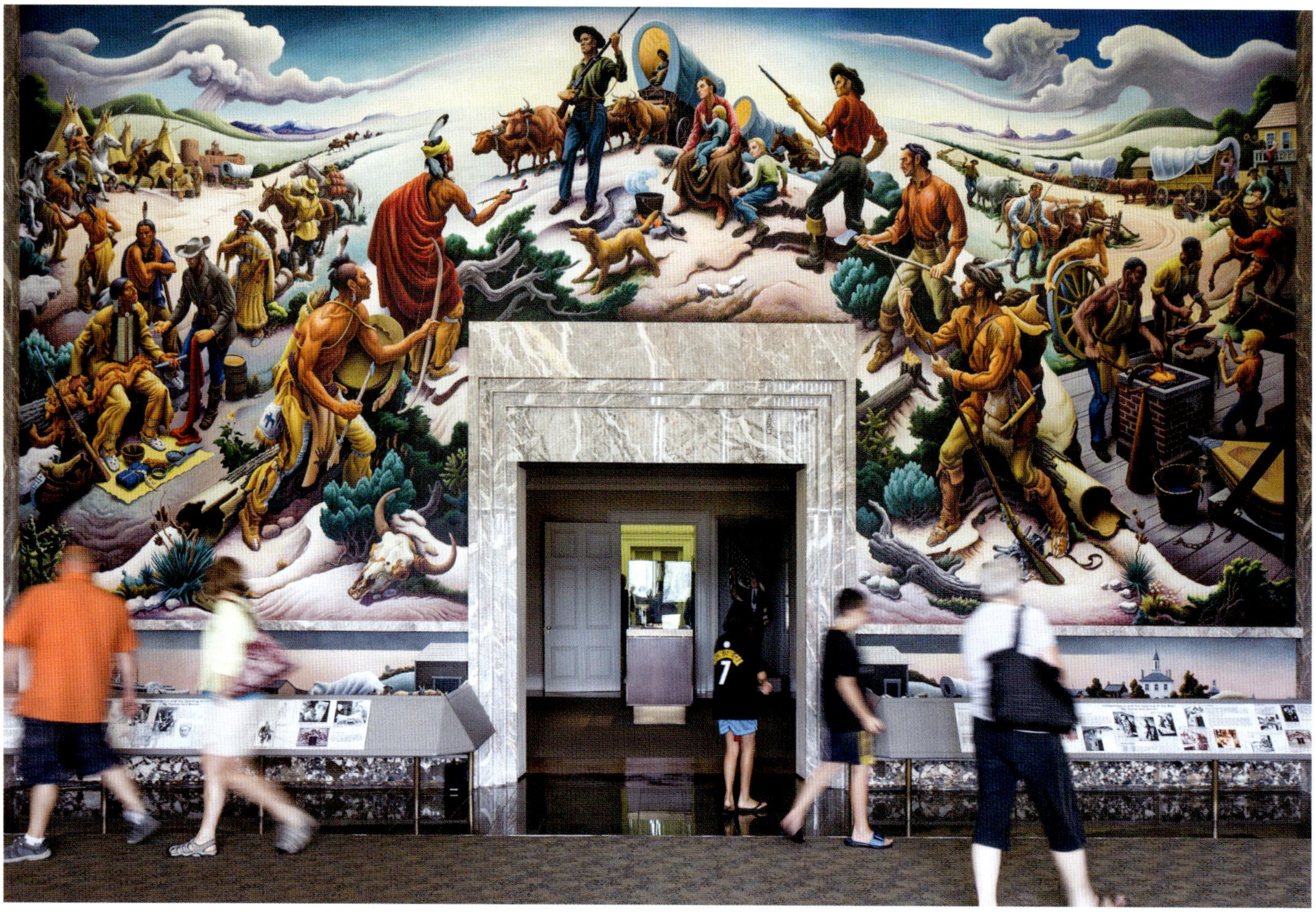

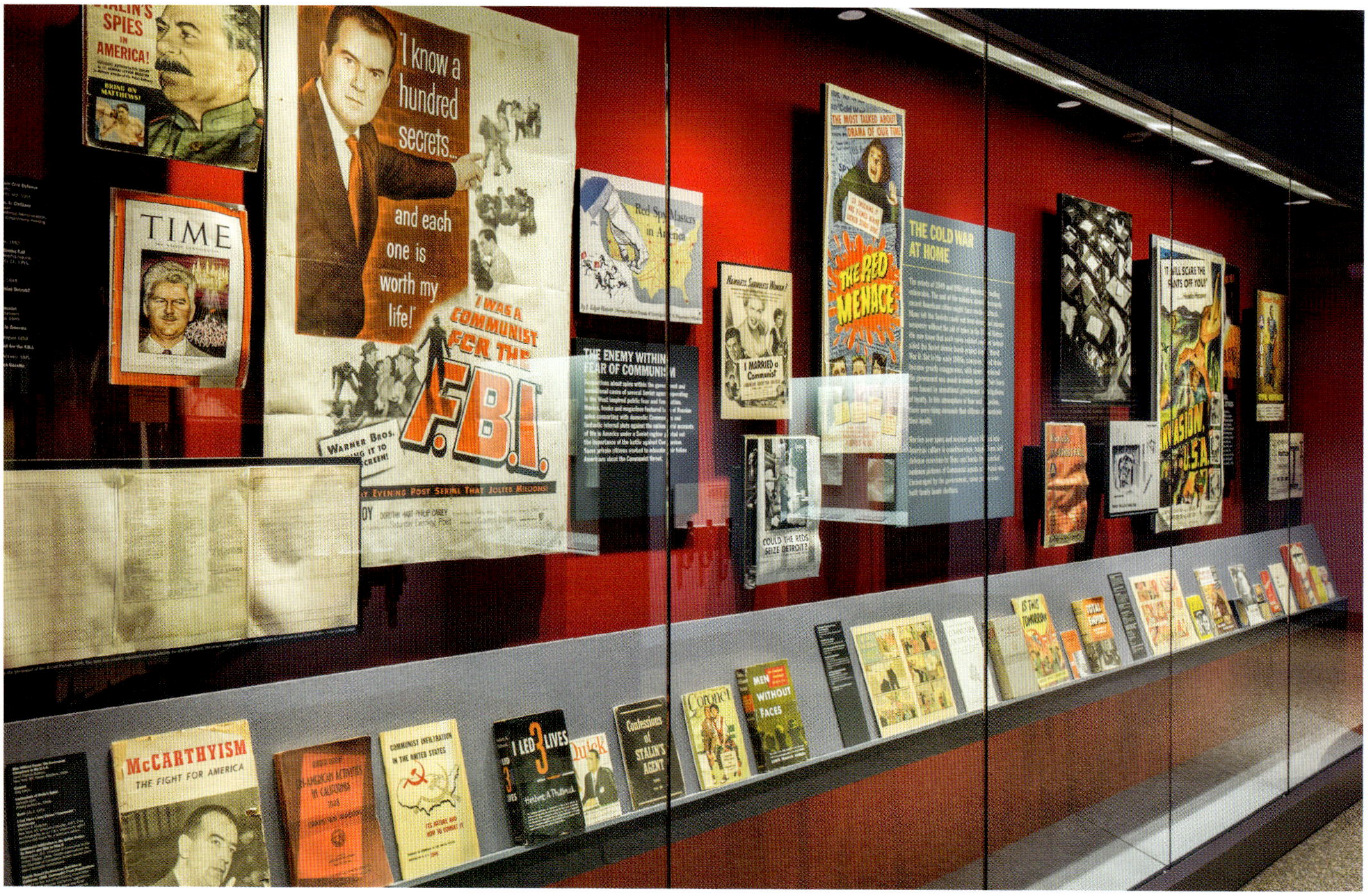
STALIN'S SPIES IN AMERICA!
TIME
"I know a hundred secrets...
and each one is worth my life!"
I WAS A COMMUNIST FOR THE F.B.I.
WARNER BROS.
THE ENEMY WITHIN
THE MOST TALKED ABOUT DRAMA OF OUR TIME
THE RED MENACE
THE COLD WAR AT HOME
I MARRIED A Communist
COULD THE REDS SEIZE DETROIT?
INVASION U.S.A.
McCARTHYISM THE FIGHT FOR AMERICA
I LED 3 LIVES
Confessions of STALIN'S AGENT
Coronet
MEN WITHOUT FACES

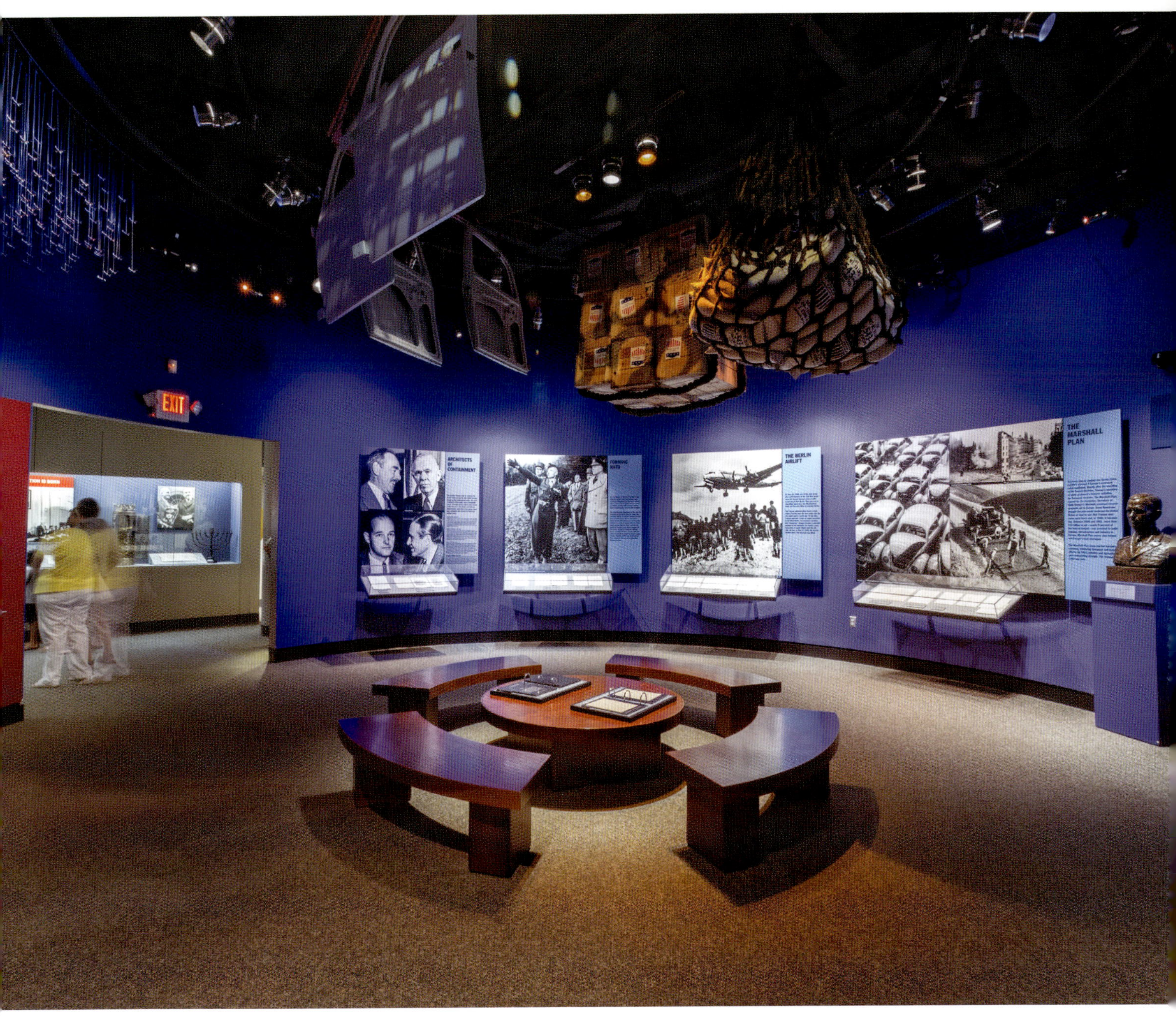

Harry Truman Presidential Library
(opposite, top and bottom)

At the library entrance is a mural by Thomas Hart Benton. The painting represents the nation's westward expansion, which had a departure point near the library's location. Beyond the mural, displays capture the atmosphere of American culture during and after Truman's presidency.

Harry Truman Presidential Library
(above)

Truman became president with President Franklin D. Roosevelt's passing and inherited a war as well as other challenges. The museum exhibits life during Truman's presidency, the obstacles he faced, and how he tackled them. After his presidency, he maintained an office on the library grounds.

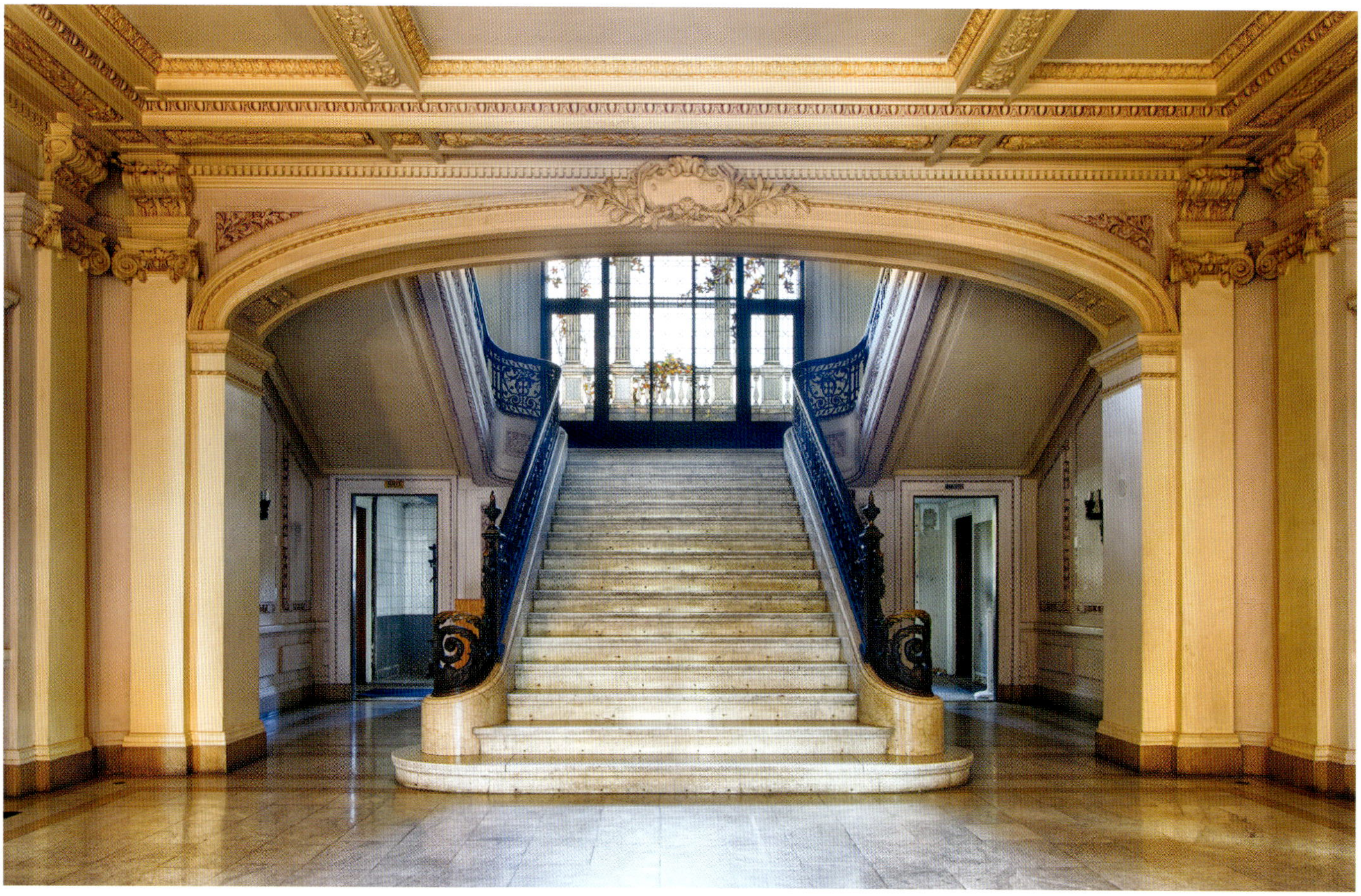

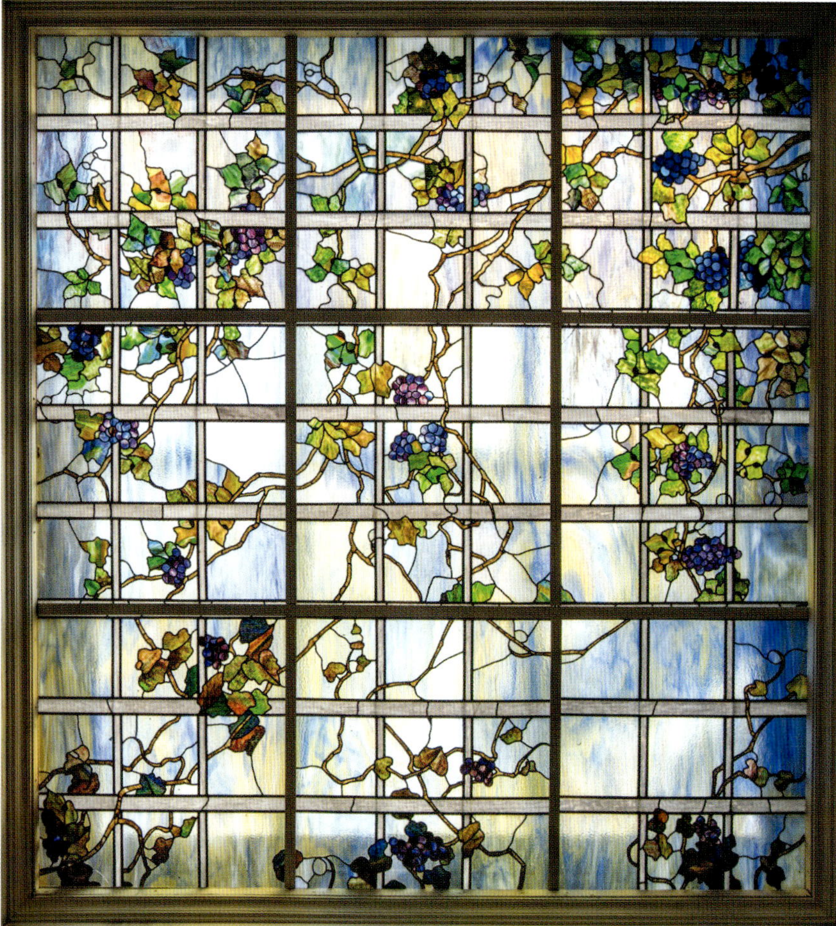

Corinthian Hall at Kansas City

(above)

The main building for the Kansas City Museum is known as Corinthian Hall, reflecting the many Corinthian columns outside its entrance. The magnificent French Renaissance mansion is the former home of lumber magnate Robert A. Long and was Kansas City's first million dollar home when it was built in 1911.

Stained Glass Collection at Kansas City Museum *(left)*

The stained glass collection at the Kansas City Museum includes many pieces that belonged to the Long family, plus other pieces, added later. Many pieces of the beautifully assembled colored and textured glass evoke nature scenes and acknowledge the museum's long history as an institution of natural science.

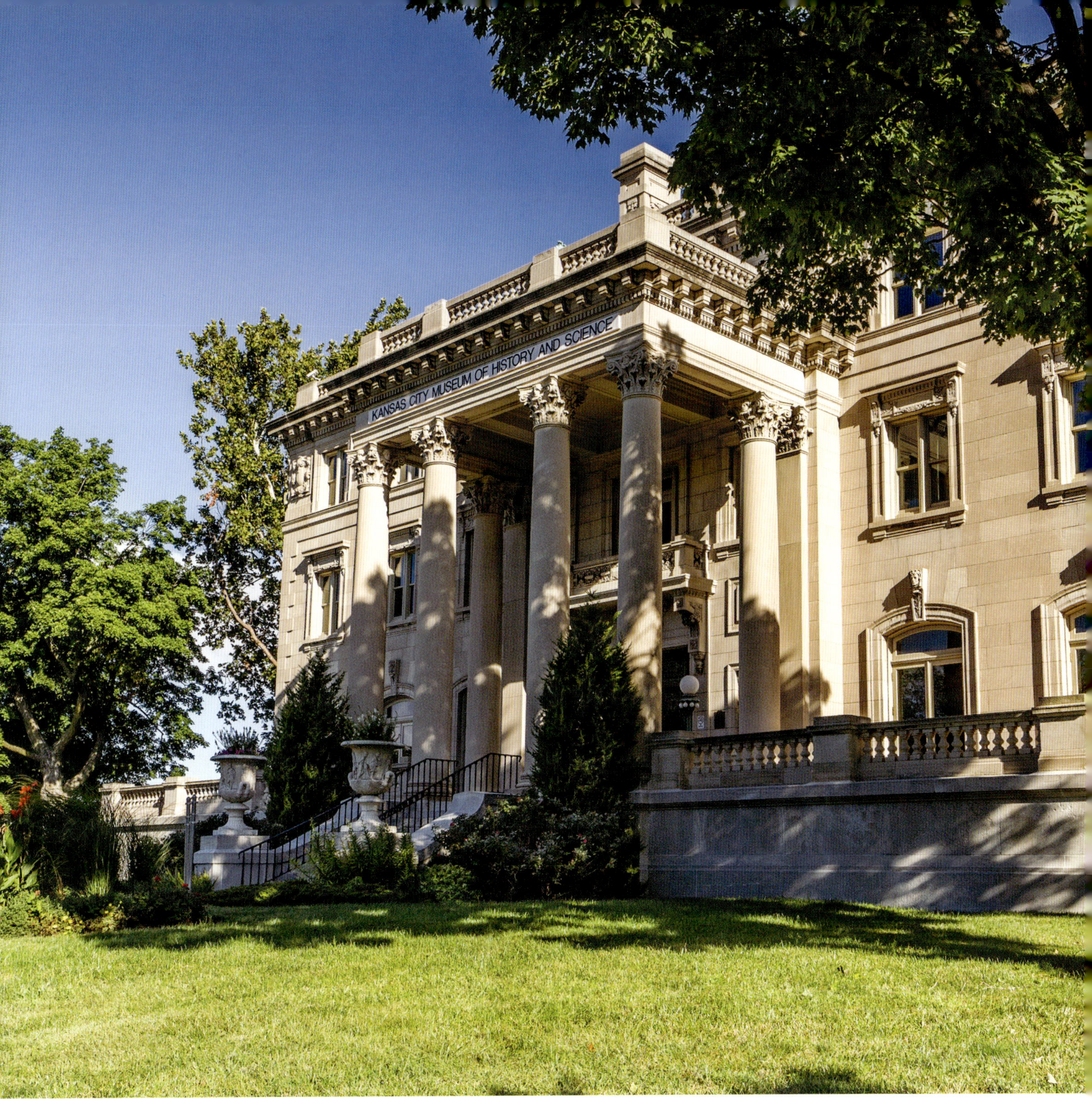

Kansas City Museum

Kansas City's first museum features local and regional history, with a focus on natural sciences. The museum also has a small planetarium, a soda fountain, and lush gardens on its three-acre property. Exhibits at the museum are regularly rotated, so there's always something new to see.

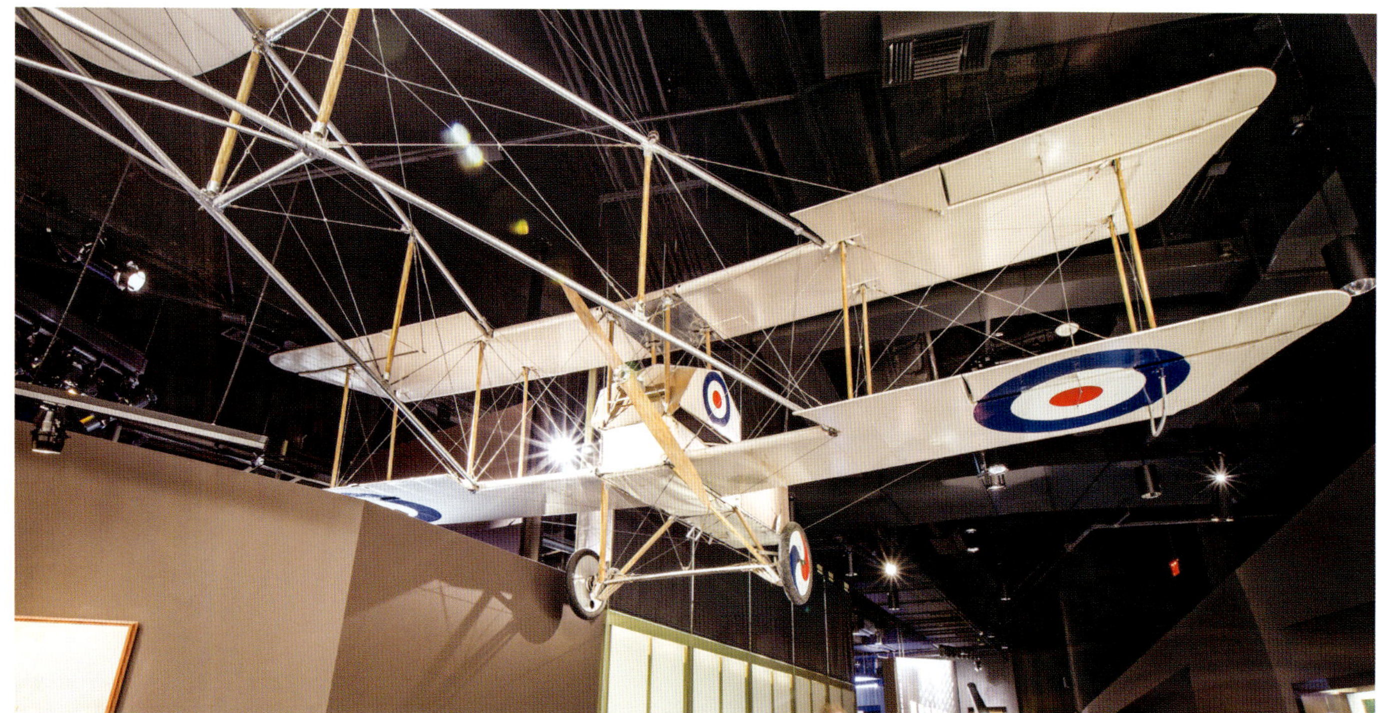

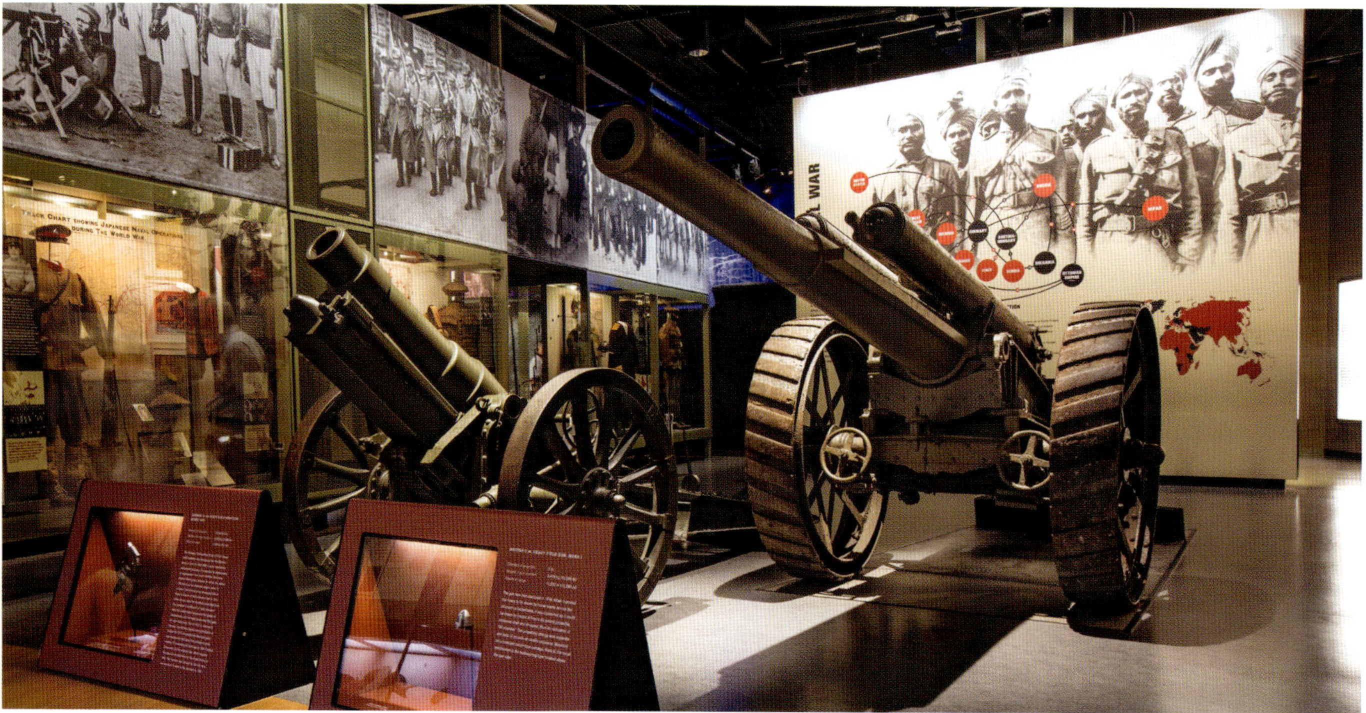

National WWI Museum *(top)*

World War I marked the first time planes were widely used in warfare, and they developed quickly and dramatically over the duration of the conflict. The museum has examples of several planes used in the skies over Europe, including this very early open-framed biplane from the UK's Royal Air Force.

Artillery Guns, National WWI Museum *(bottom)*

One of the unique things about the museum is that it doesn't discriminate between the war's participants. Stories are told neutrally and German propaganda hangs alongside that from the British. The same is true of its three-dimensional artifacts; uniforms, weapons, and gear.

National World War I Museum and Liberty Memorial *(opposite)*

One of the finest museums in the country and one of the best Great War collections in the world, the National World War I Museum is a stunning and sobering look at the first time modern nations clashed. The museum is situated beneath the Liberty Memorial, a National Historic Landmark.

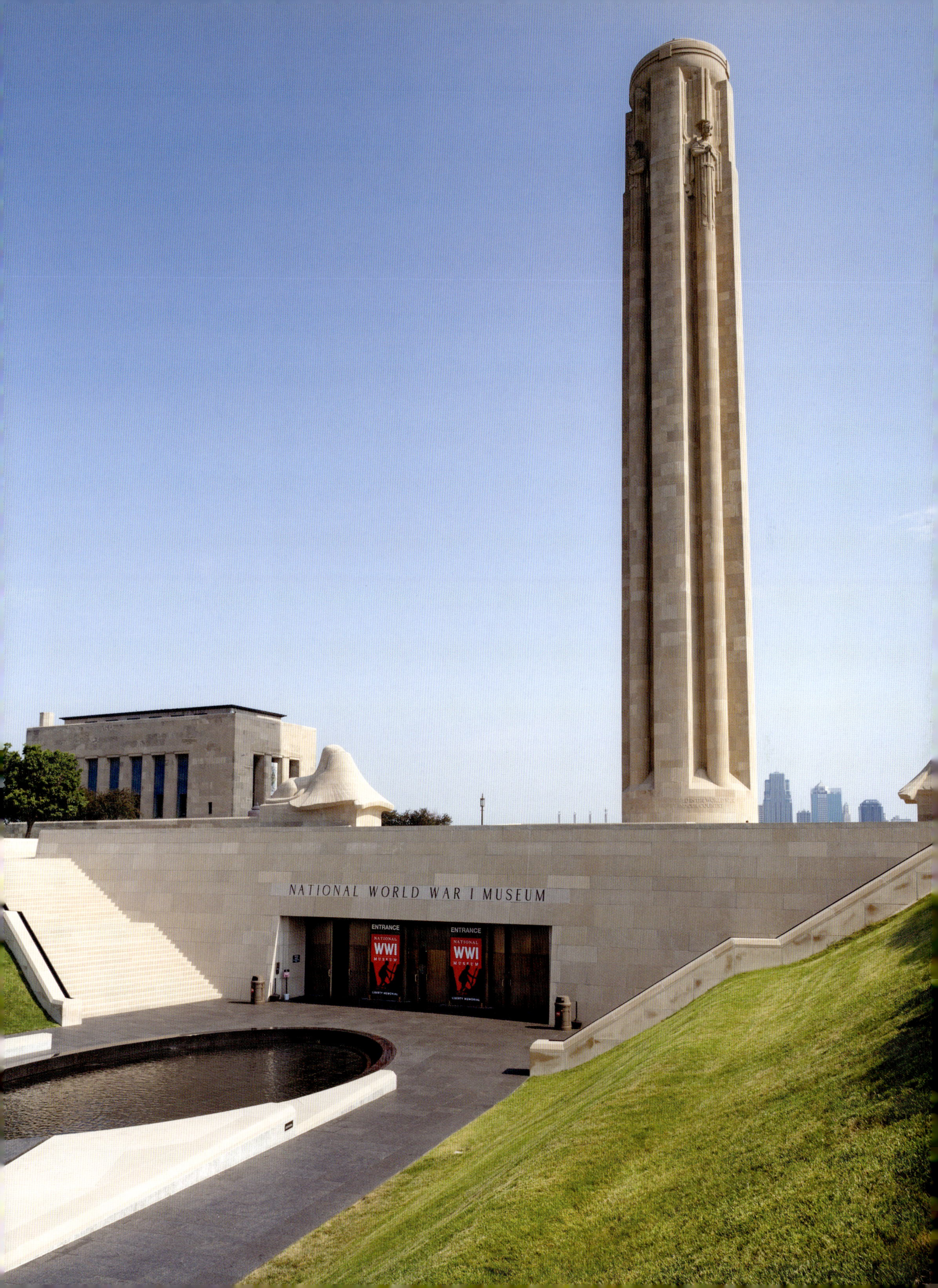
NATIONAL WORLD WAR I MUSEUM
ENTRANCE
NATIONAL WWI MUSEUM
LIBERTY MEMORIAL
ENTRANCE
NATIONAL WWI MUSEUM
LIBERTY MEMORIAL

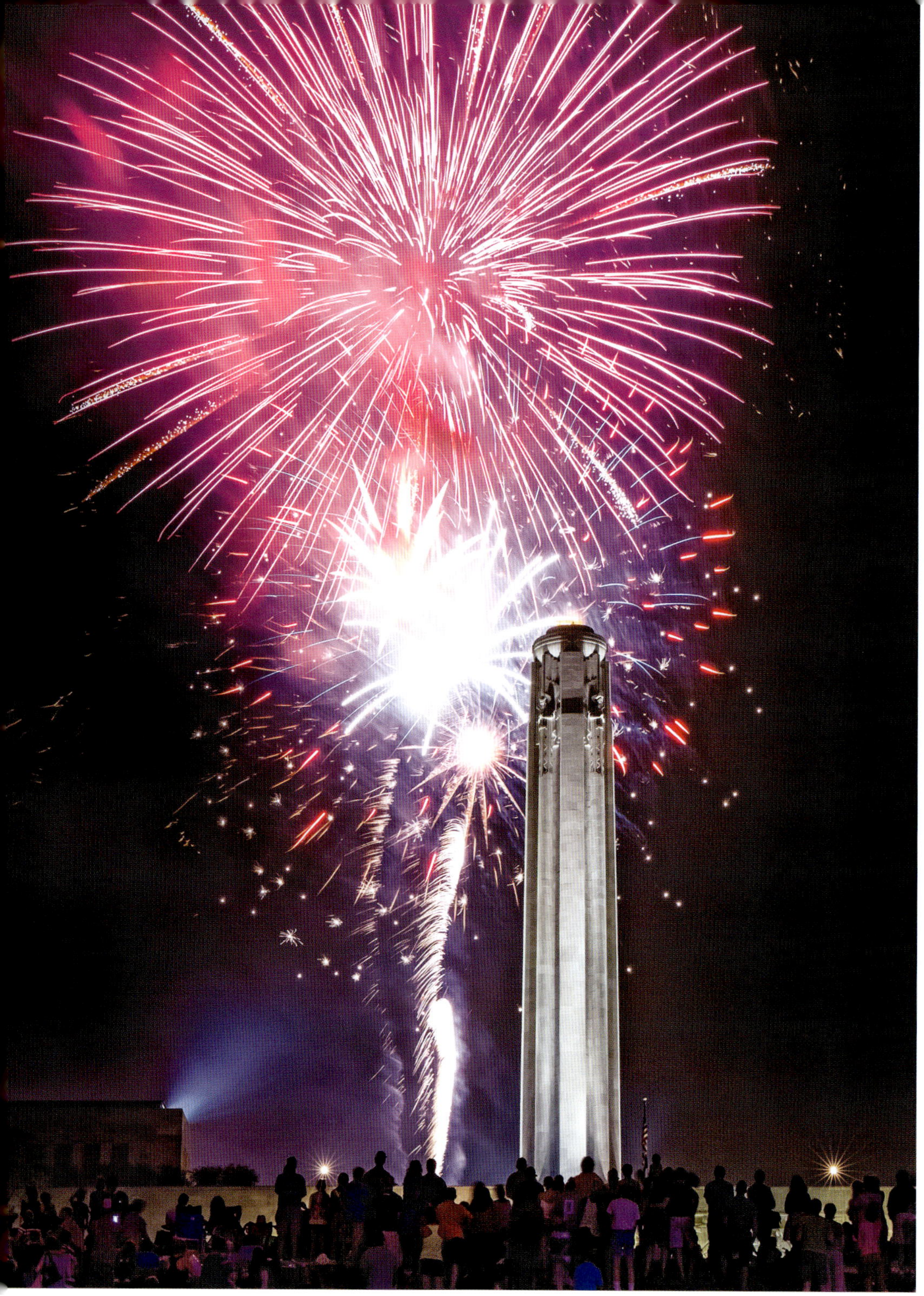

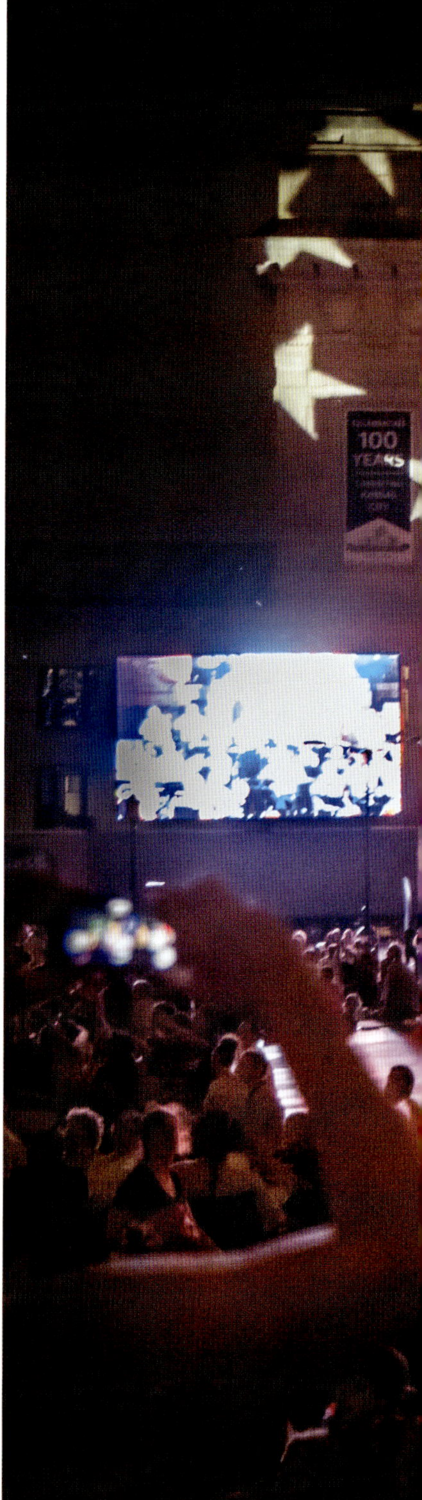

Memorial Day Celebration

Each year on Memorial Day weekend, thousands of Kansas Citians bring their blankets and sit on the north lawn of the Liberty Memorial to watch the largest fireworks display of the year. The free event is preceded by picnics and activities for the young and young at heart.

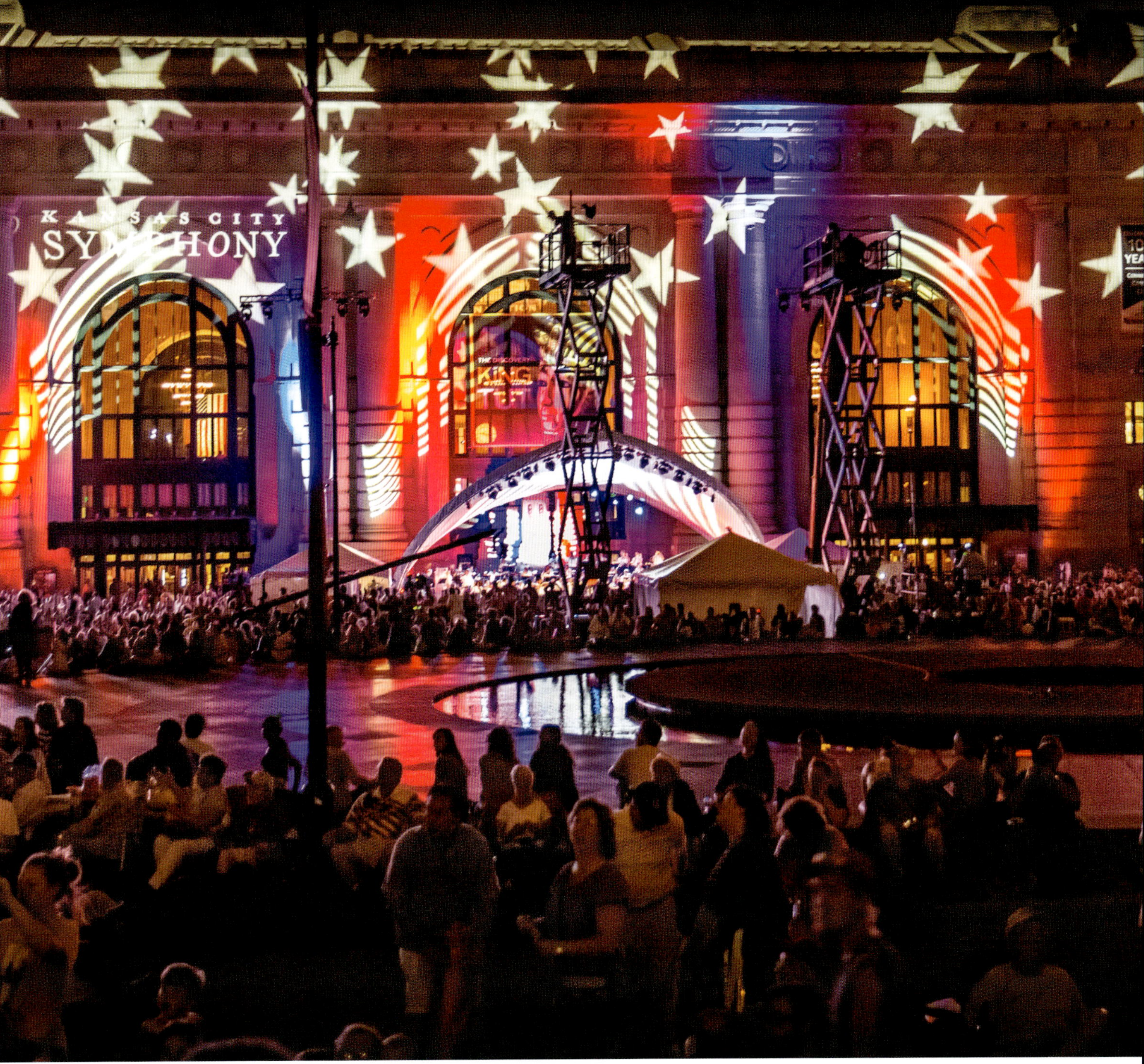

Celebration at the Station

Prior to the Memorial Day fireworks, the Kansas City Symphony puts on a rousing and patriotic concert performance. The music is accompanied by a spectacular light show, which is cast against the facade of Union Station. The event is the largest Memorial Day celebration in the Midwest.

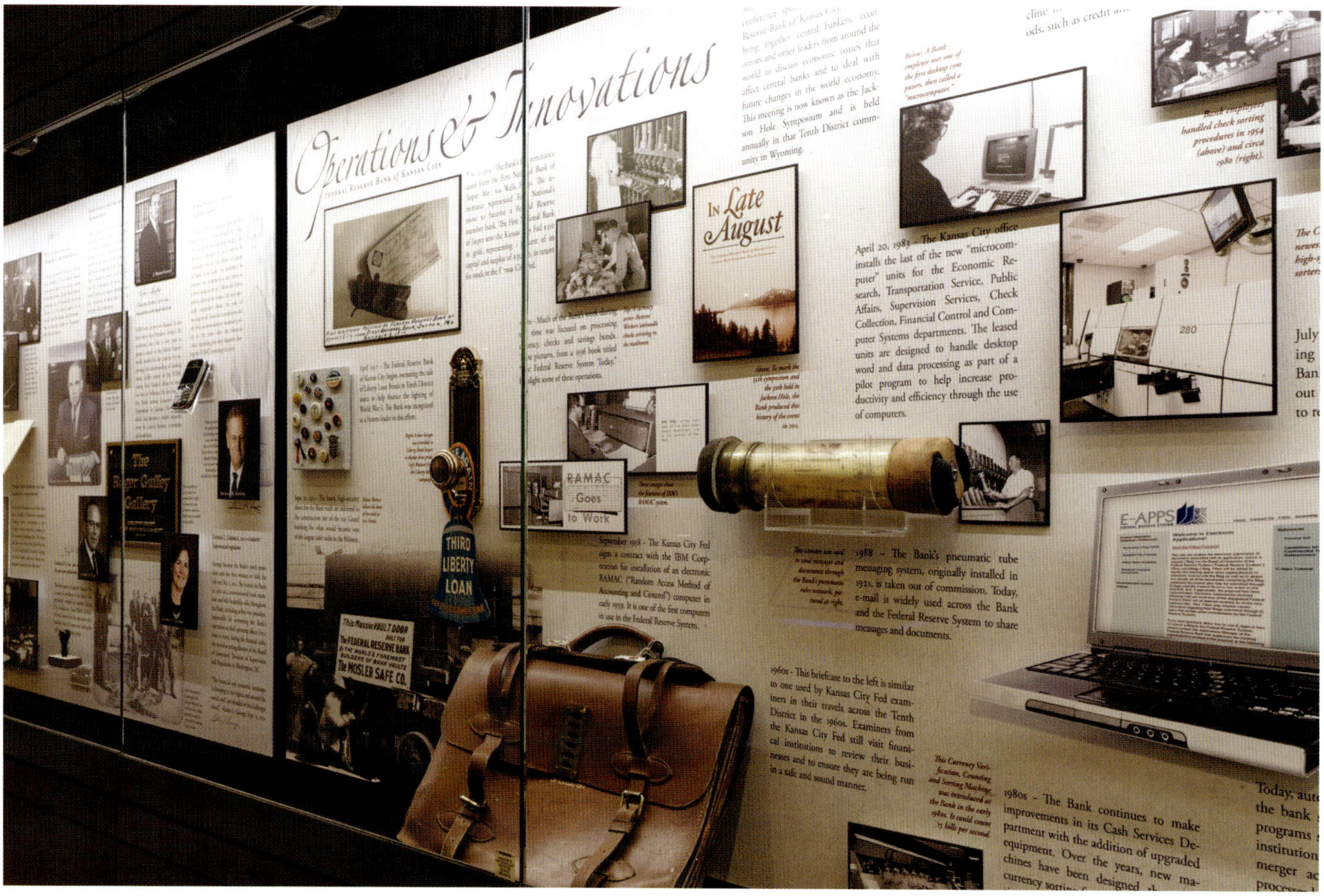

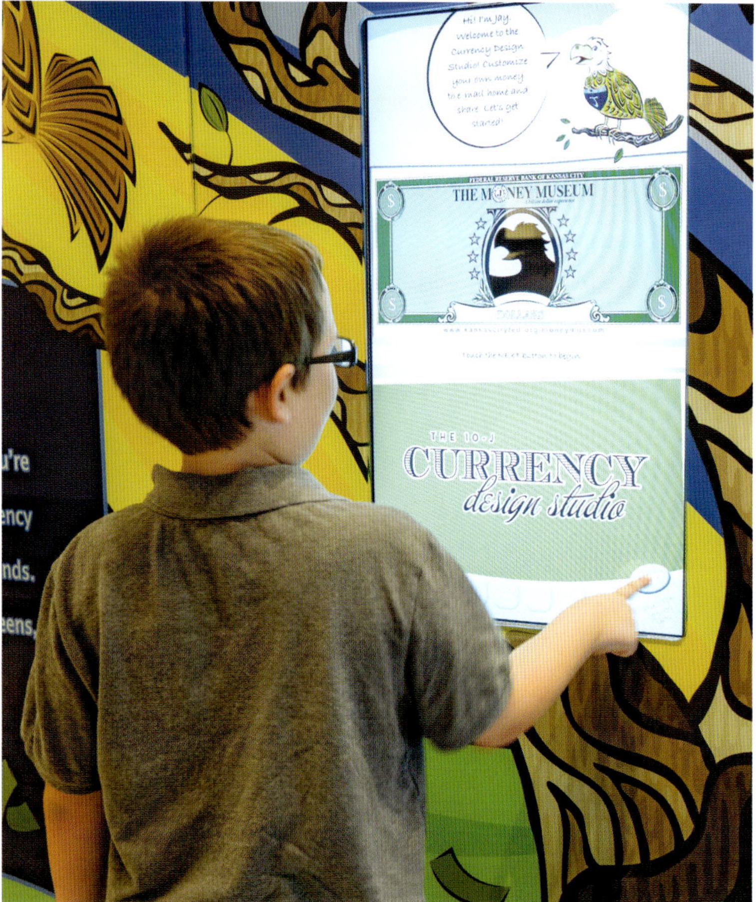

A Billion Dollar Experience *(above)*

Located within the Federal Reserve Bank of Kansas City is The Money Museum. There are lots of interesting things to see and do. Can you lift a 400 ounce gold bar? What does a million dollars look like? You'll see it all as robots move hundreds of thousands of dollars before your eyes.

The Money Museum *(left)*

See how money is counted and sorted while learning more about how our currency system works. There are interactive exhibits and kids can design their own currency. At the conclusion of this short tour, you'll receive a free bag of money. Unfortunately, the cash has been shredded.

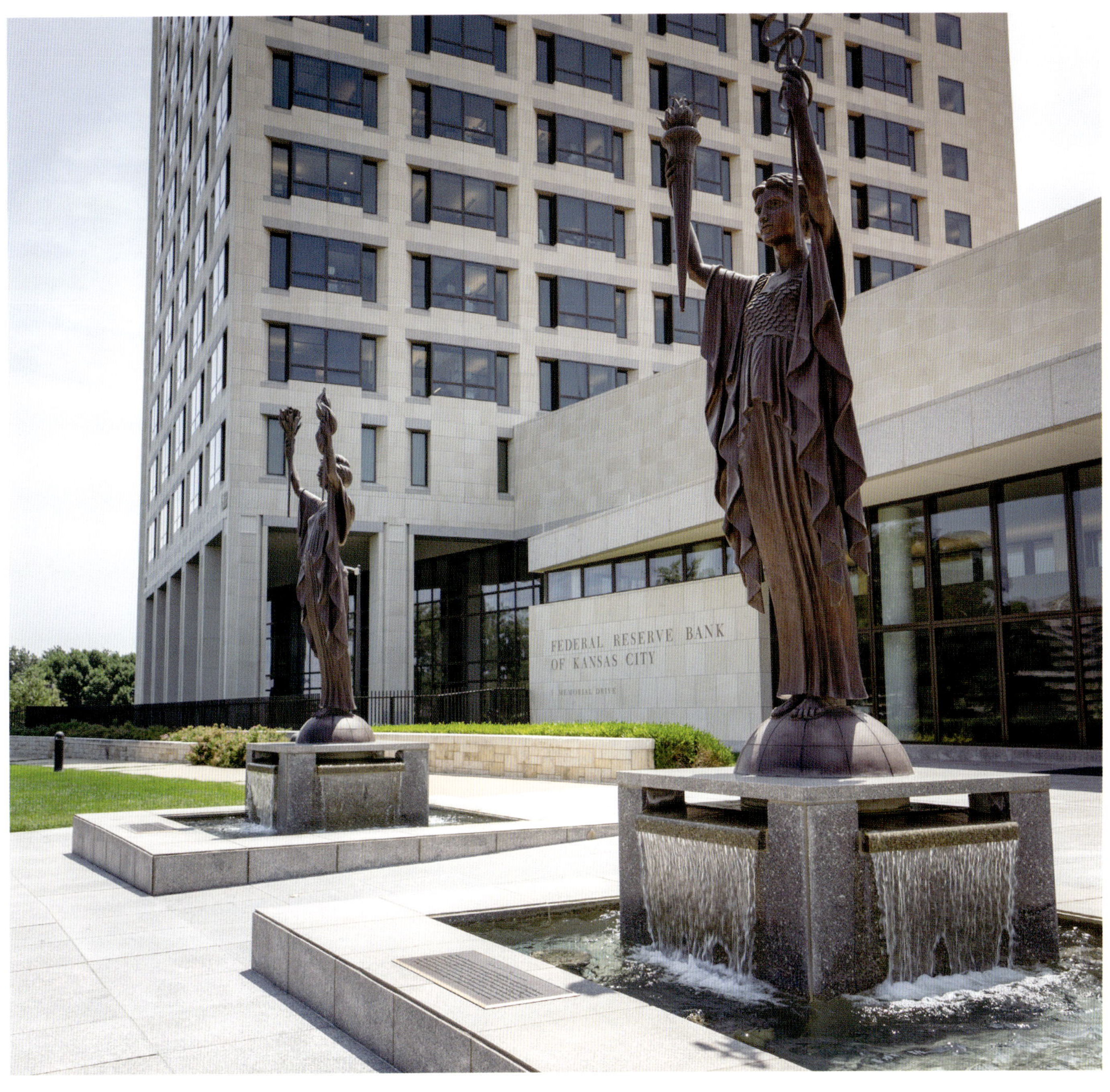

Federal Reserve Bank

The 10th District of the Federal Reserve covers a massive geography, serving all or part of seven western states, and is headquartered in Kansas City. The bank, like other Federal Reserve Districts, is responsible for regulation and oversight of public and private banks and the implementation of monetary policy.

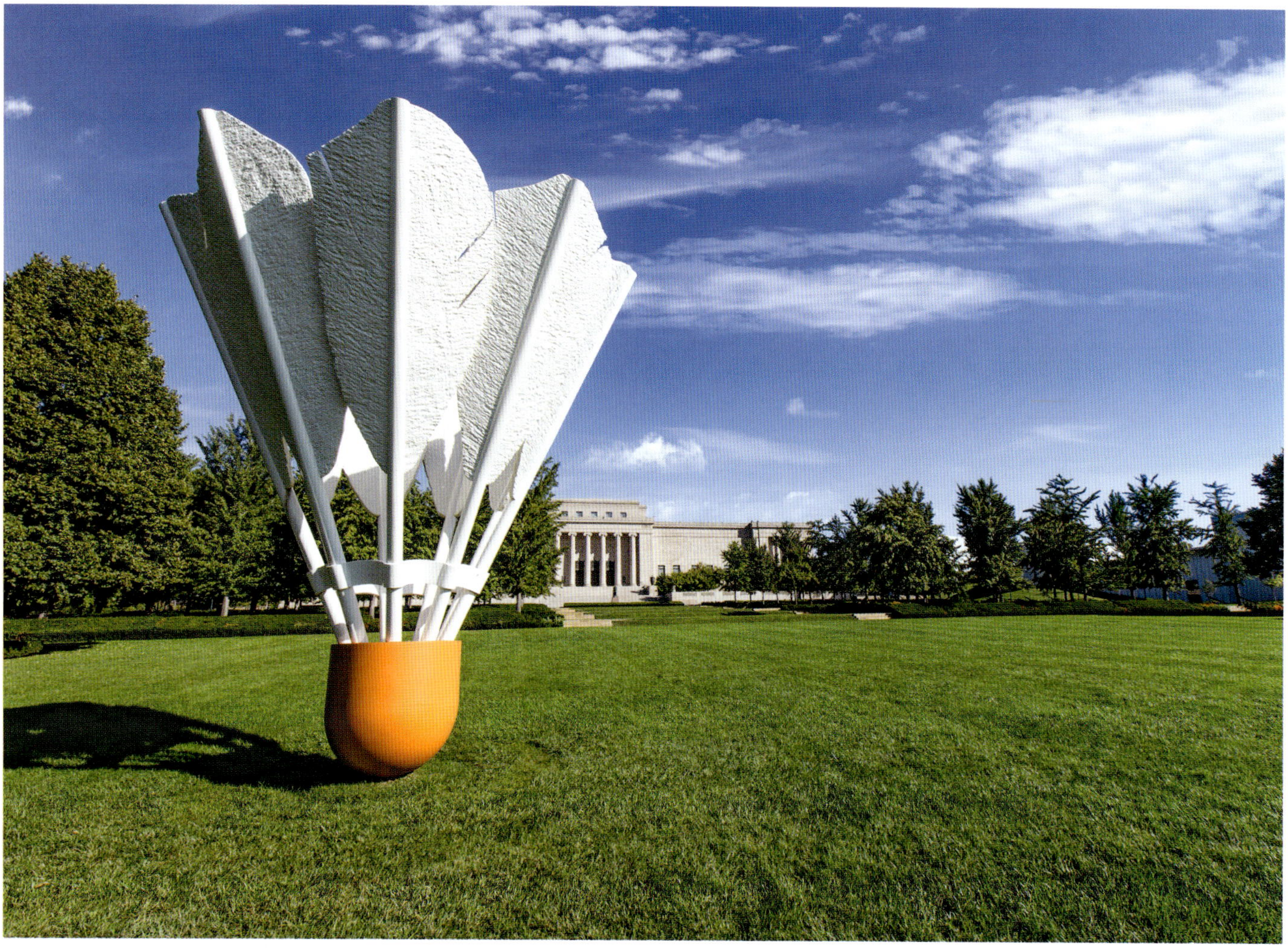

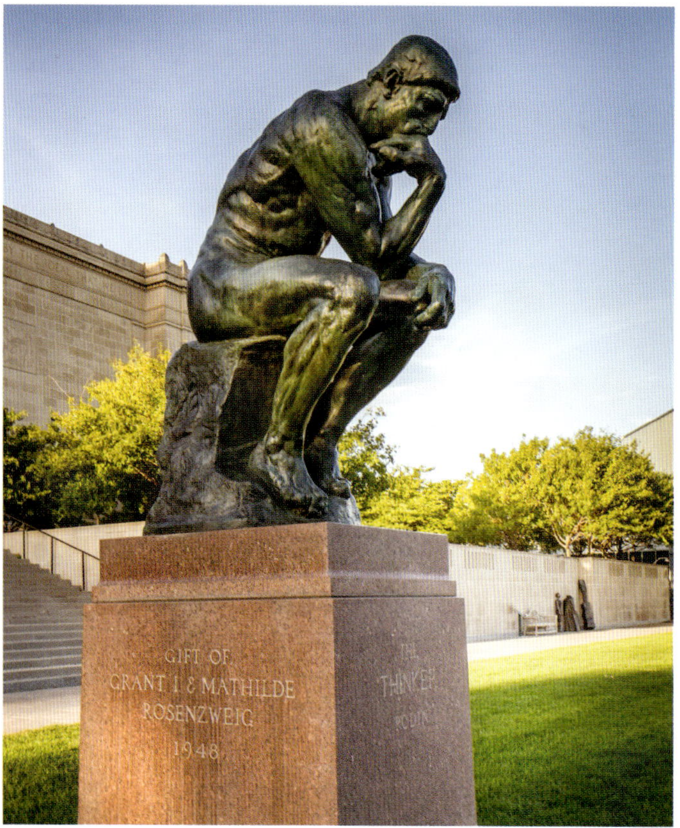

The Nelson-Atkins Museum of Art

(above and left)

This grand neoclassical building with an expansive lawn sits just east of the Plaza. Outdoors, there is a statue garden, featuring work by Rodin and Calder, and huge shuttlecocks sit on the grass. Inside, an extensive and wide-ranging art gallery is on display, for free, to the public.

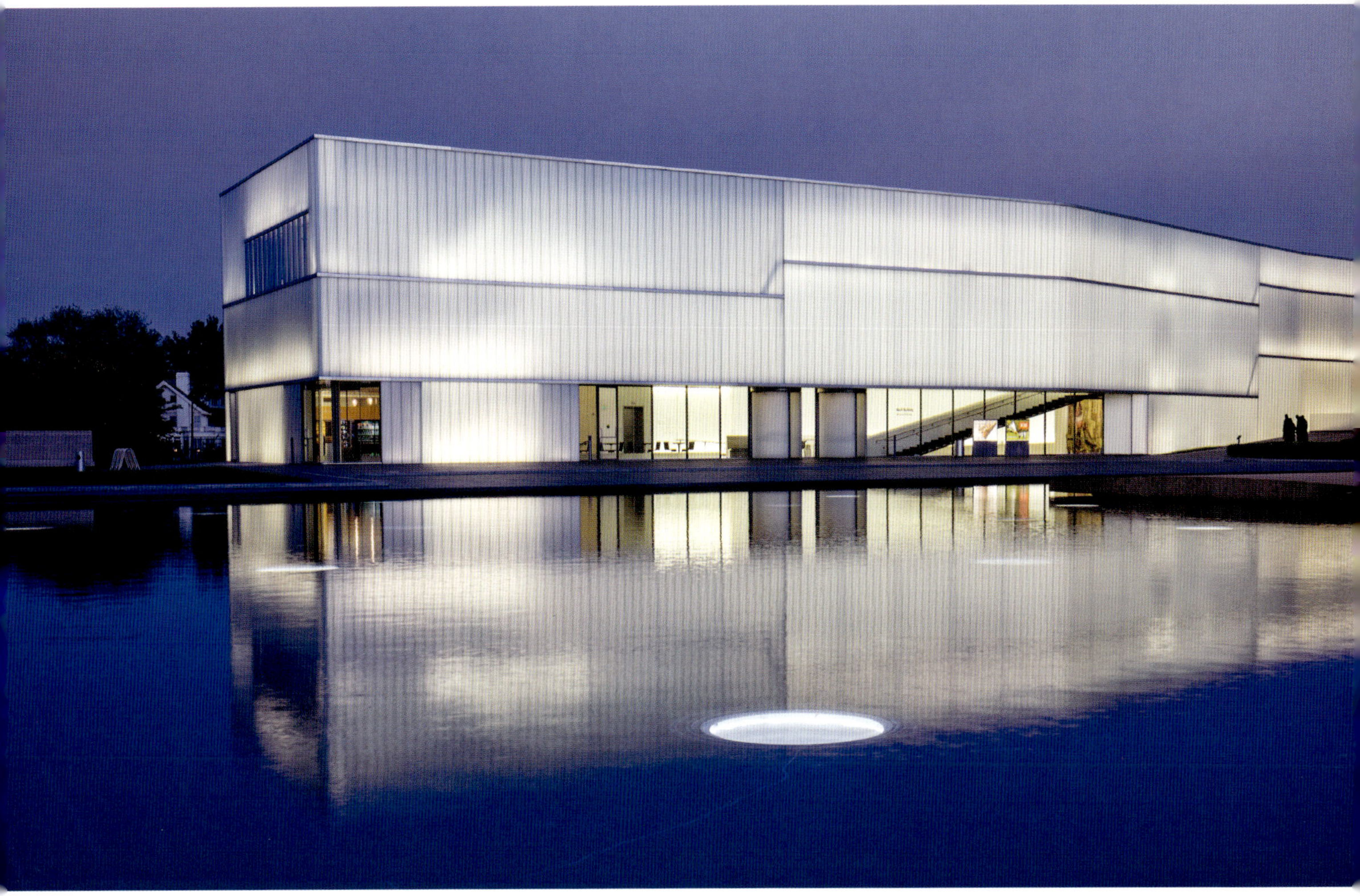

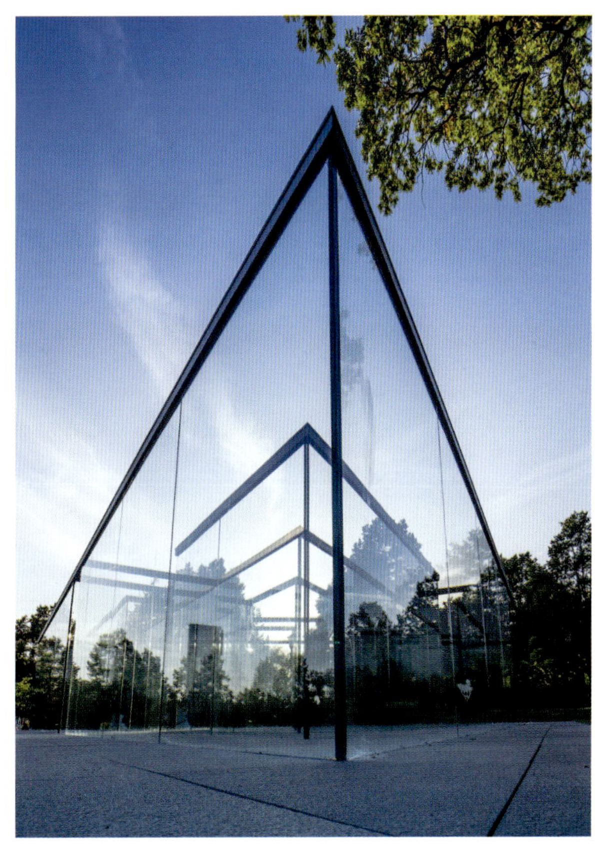

Bloch Building at the Nelson-Atkins Museum of Art *(above and right)*

This modern expansion houses some of the museum's contemporary collection, the renowned Hallmark Photographic Collection, and has space for special exhibitions. Outside the building sits a rolling garden of sculptures, including a maze with glass walls.

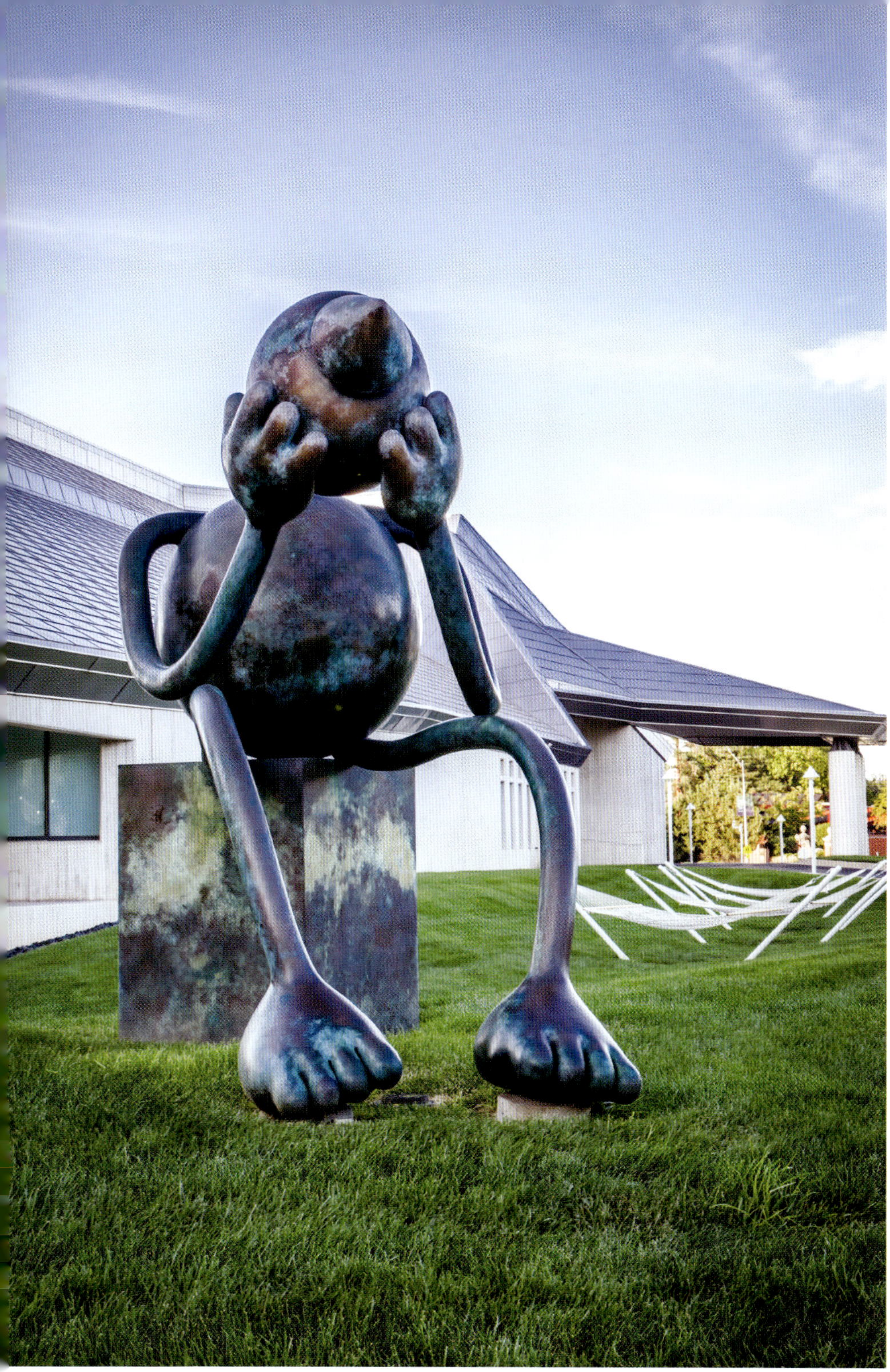

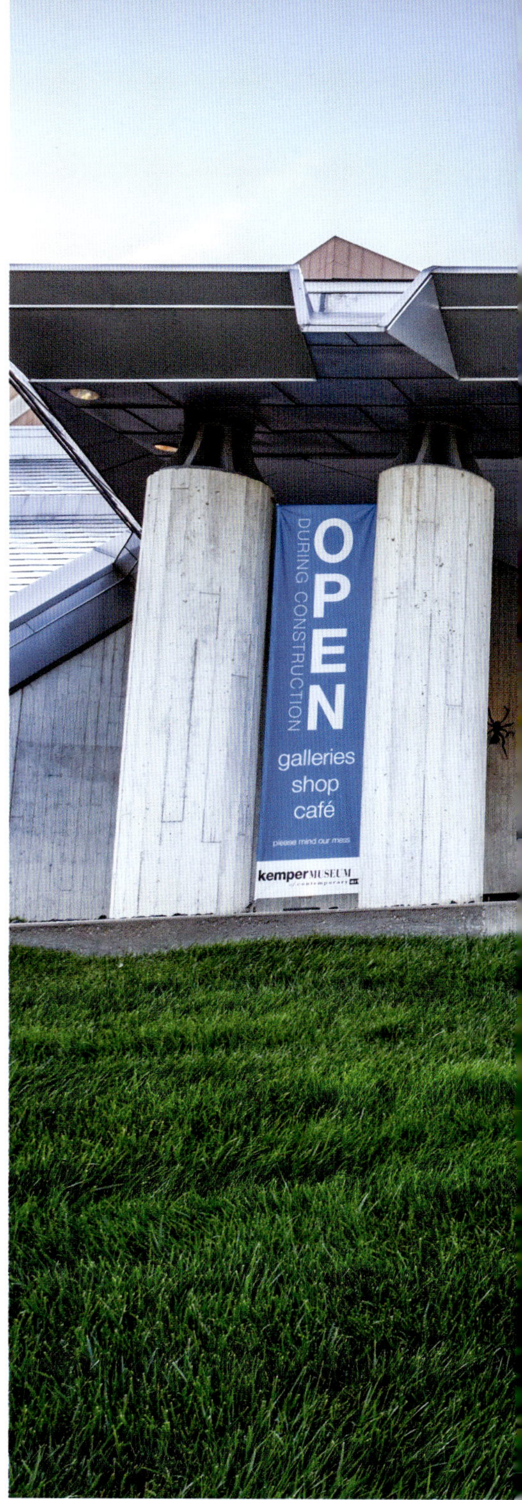

Kemper Museum of Contemporary Art

Missouri's largest contemporary art museum includes paintings, photographs, sculptures and more from many renowned contemporary artists such as Wyeth, Mapplethorpe, O'Keefe, and Johns. The museum also houses temporary exhibits each month.

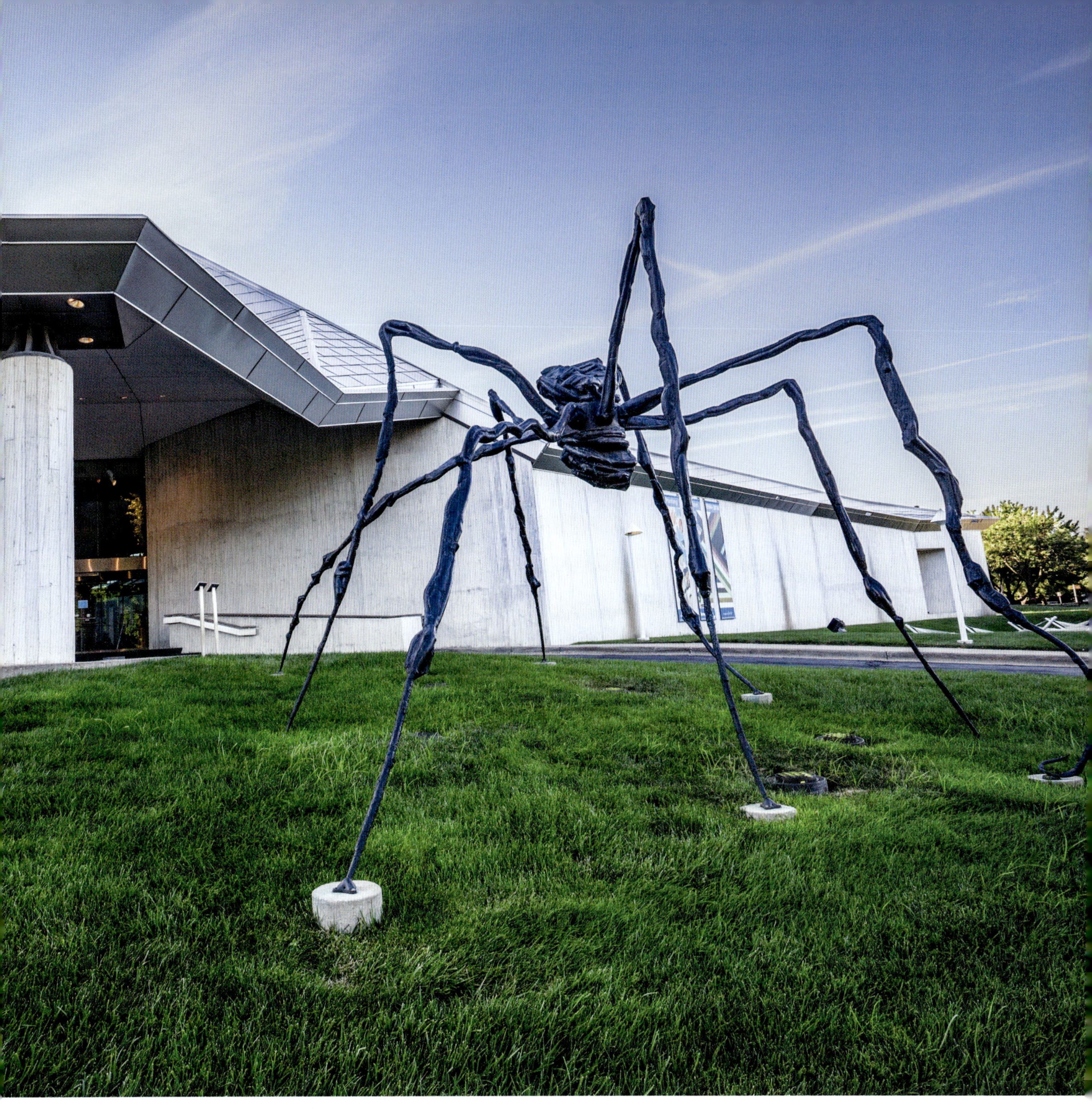

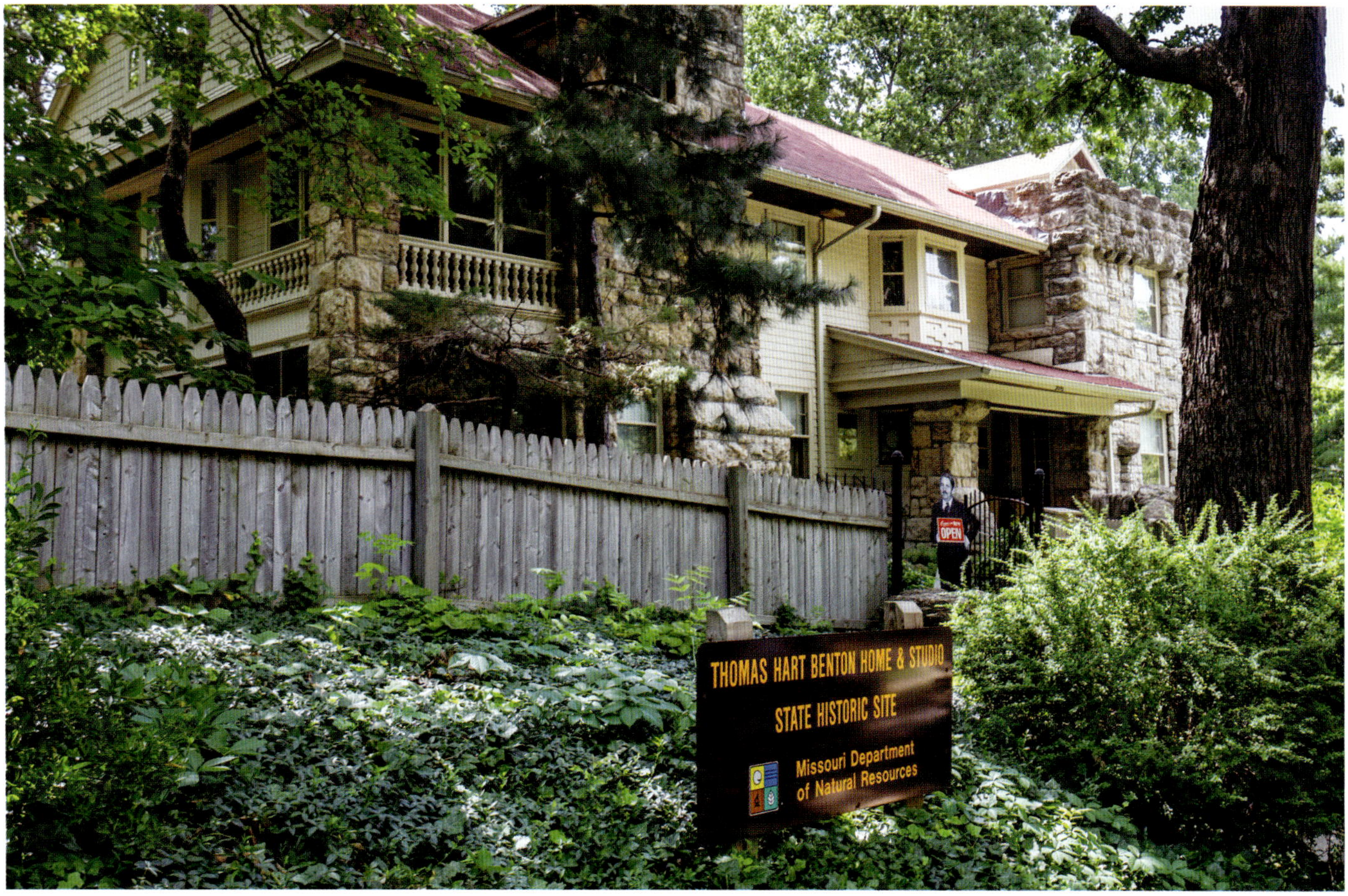

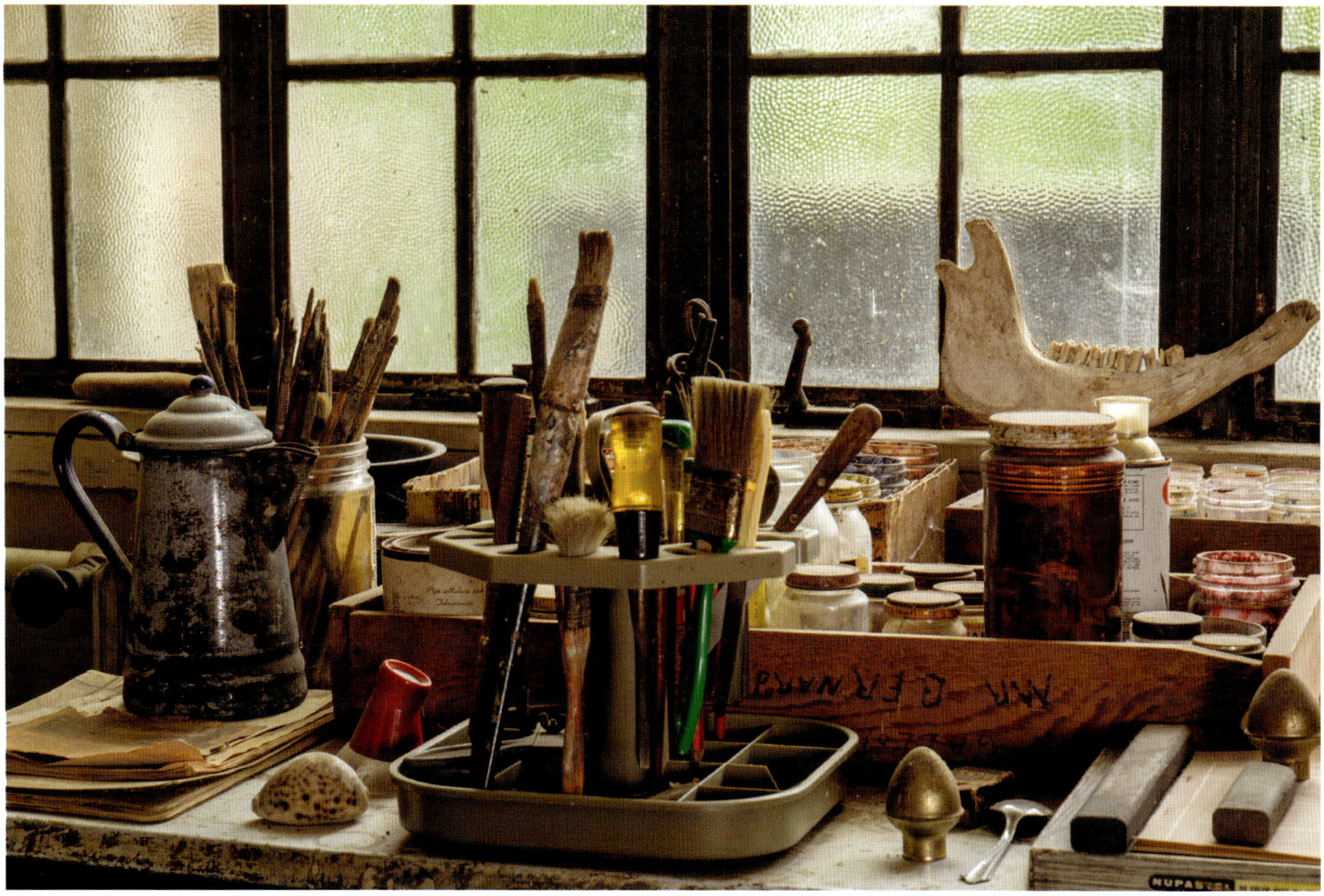

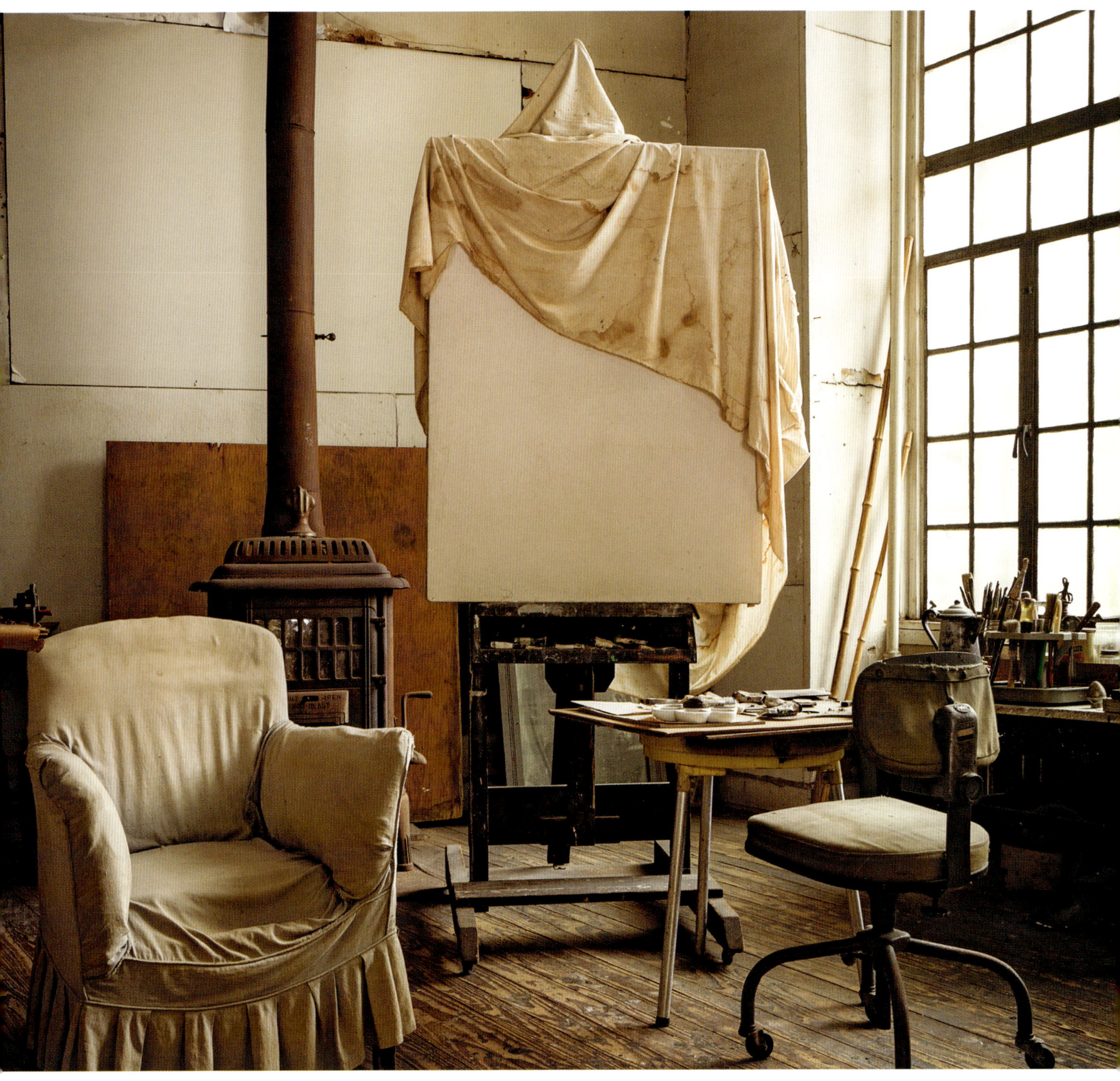

Thomas Hart Benton Historic Site

(opposite, top and bottom)

The famous painter, sculptor, and writer is Missouri's best-known artist; his work is synonymous with the Midwest. His style, part of the Regionalist art movement, depicts everyday situations and romanticizes everyday life. Now a historic site, tours are available of his home and studio.

Thomas Hart Benton Studio *(above)*

In Benton's home, visitors can take in his studio with a wall of windows and gorgeous light. Benton passed away in this room as he finished a mural for the Country Music Hall of Fame in Nashville. The studio has been preserved as when he left it.

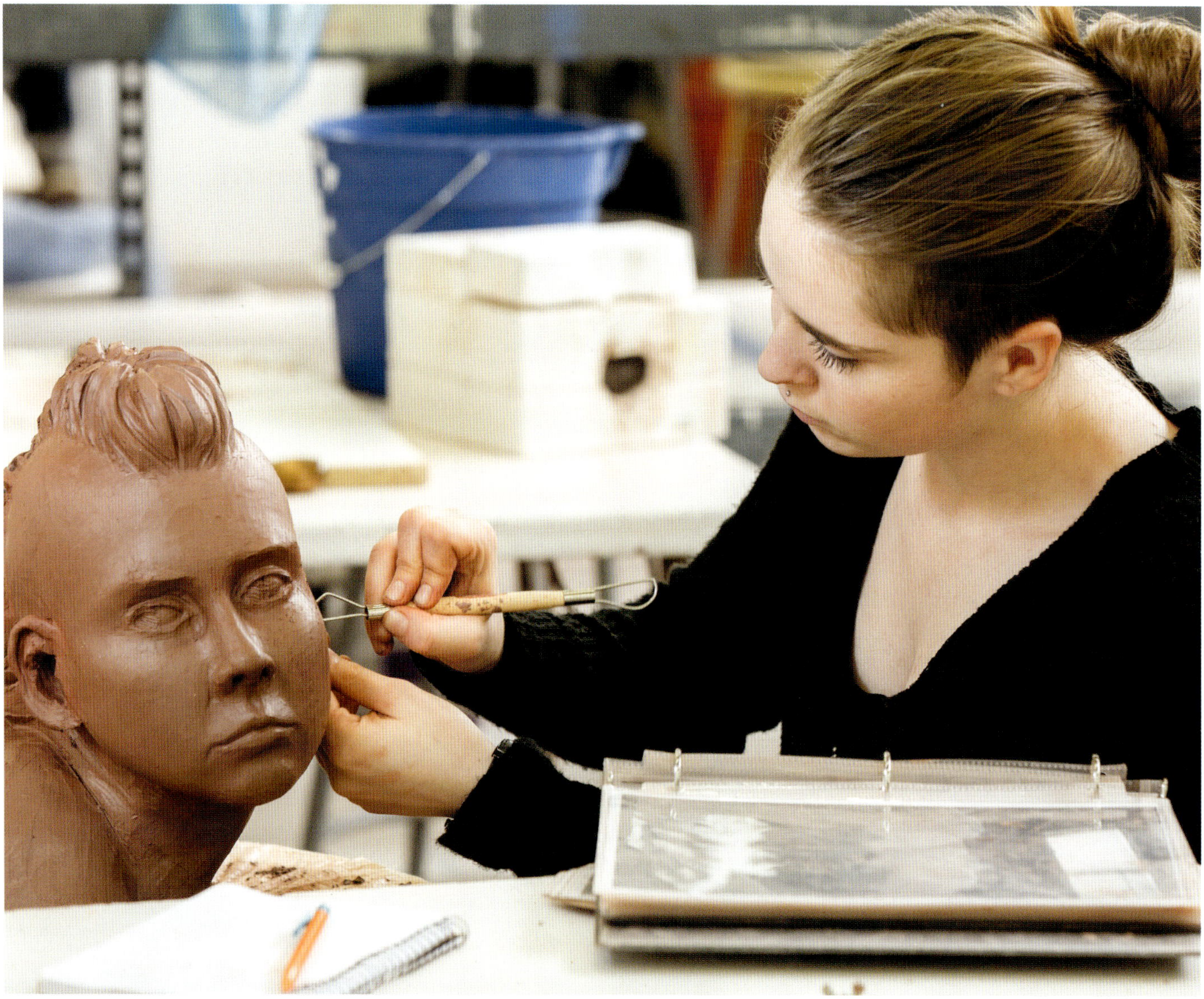

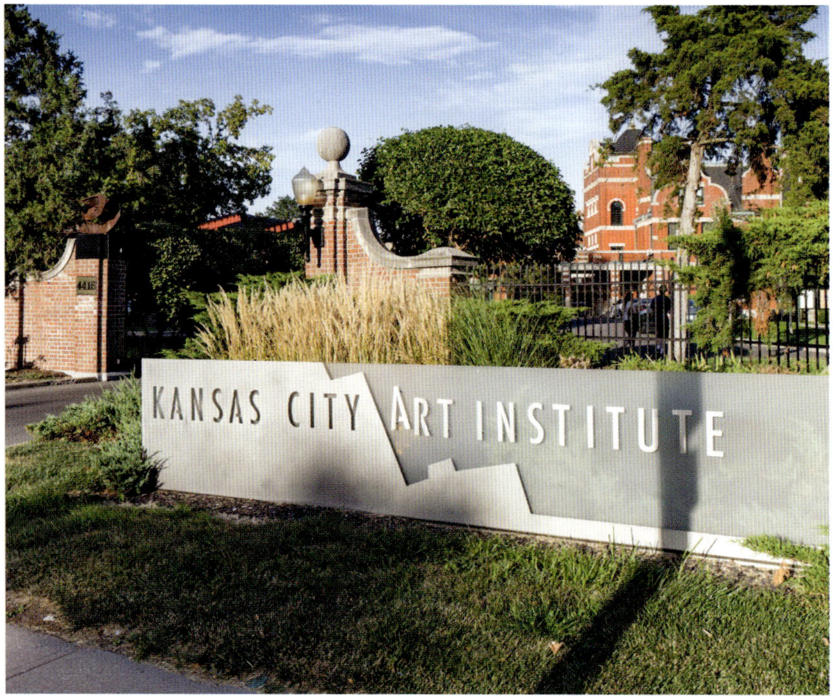

Kansas City Art Institute *(above and left)*

Walt Disney's first art classes were completed here as a child. The four-year college has offered instruction since 1885 and has an impressive list of alumni who have gone on to influence the art world. Degrees range from traditional arts to new, digital media.

Midland Theatre *(opposite)*

This theatre, built in 1927 in Baroque architecture, is immediately recognizable for its copper and gold marquee with hundreds of light bulbs. Inside, massive crystal chandeliers hang from the ceiling, along with other Renaissance Revival flourishes. The theatre showed movies for many years but is now home to live performances.

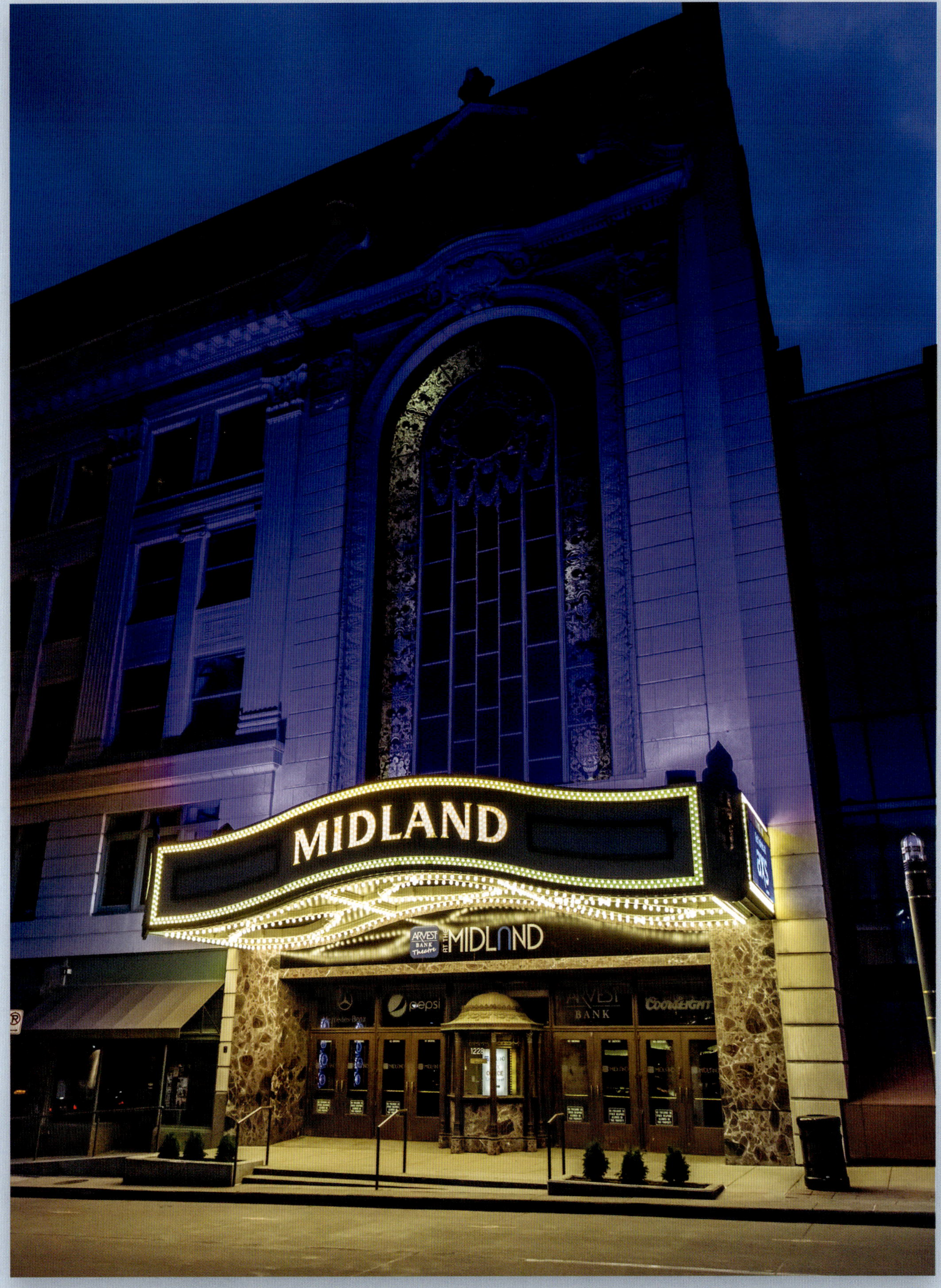
MIDLAND
ARVEST BANK Theatre
AT THE MIDLAND
pepsi
ARVEST BANK

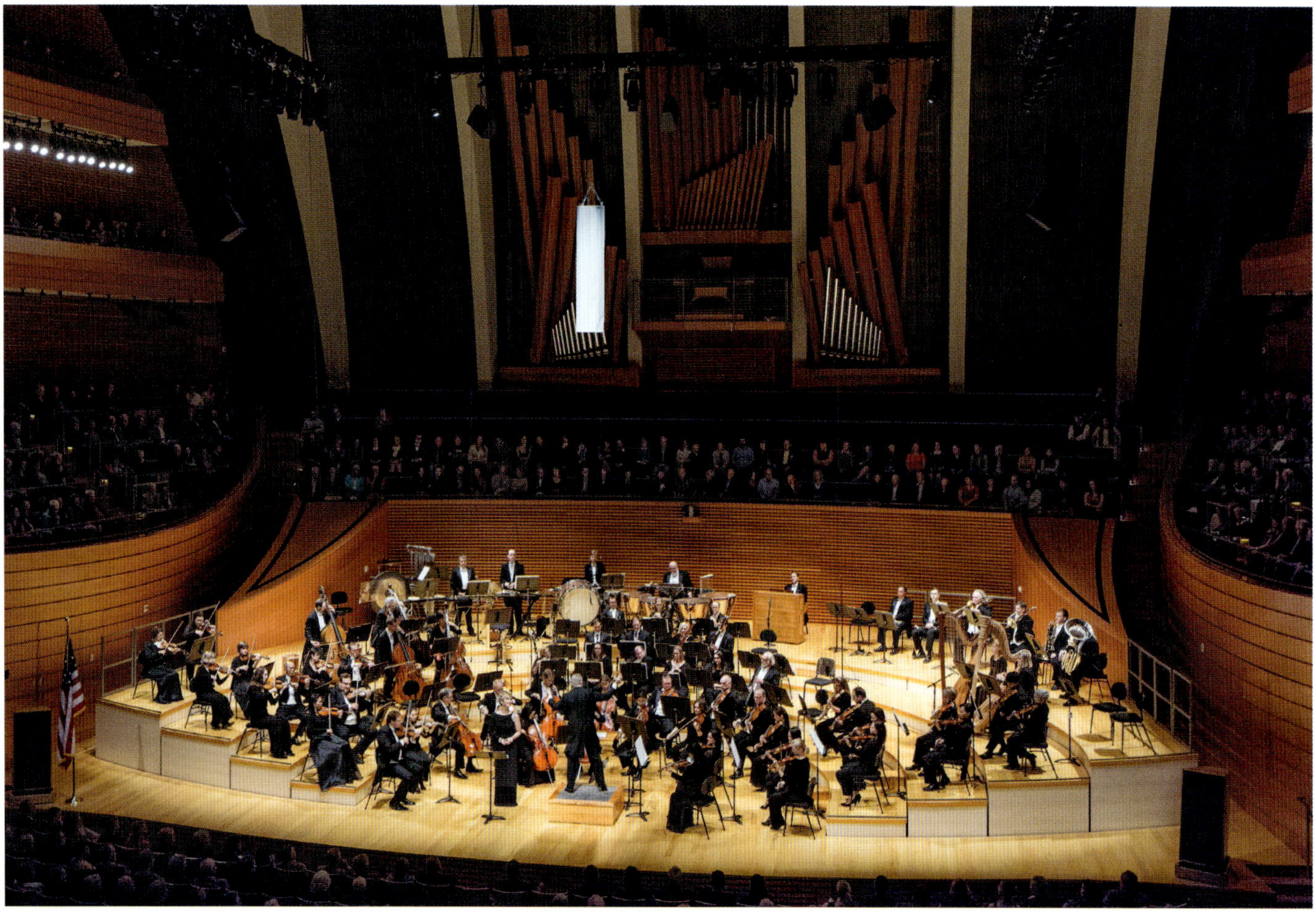

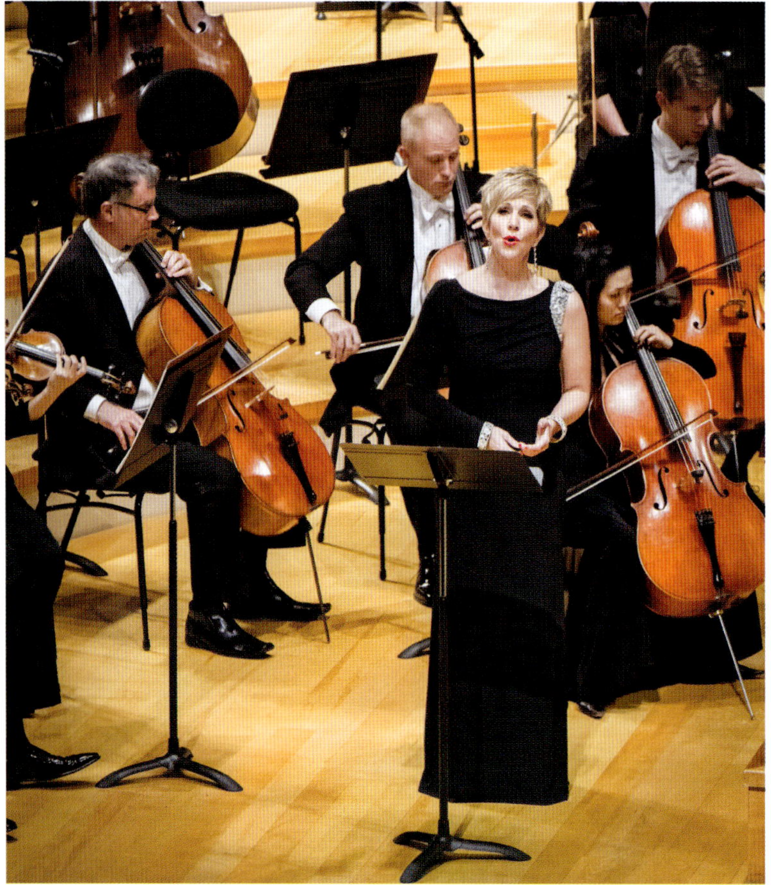

Kansas City Symphony *(above and left)*

The Symphony plays a long season, performing almost year-round. When at home in Helzberg Hall of the Kauffman Center for Performing Arts, they often feature special performers and renowned soloists. But the Symphony also takes their show on the road to outdoor venues, entertaining even larger audiences.

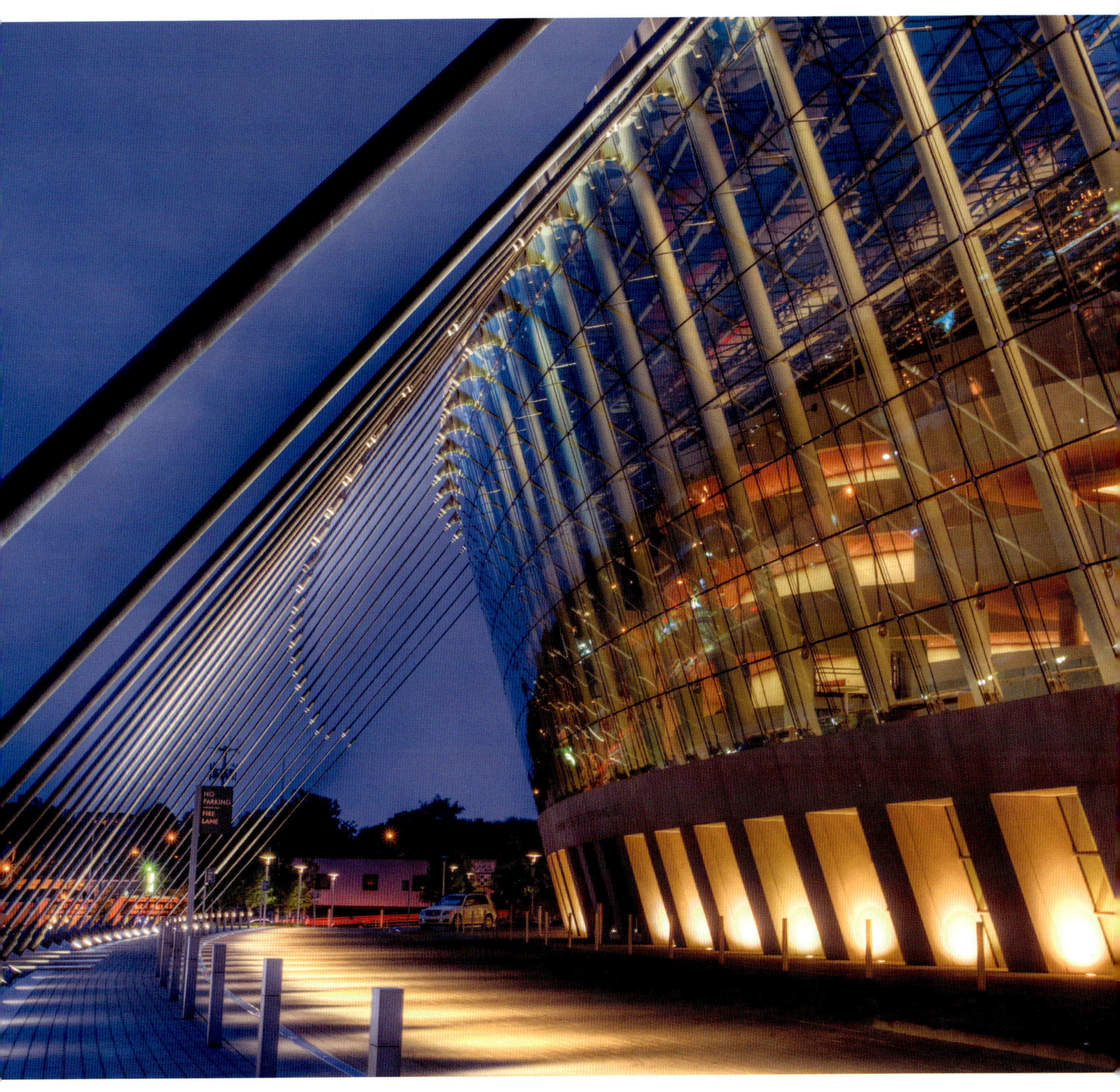

Kauffman Center for the Performing Arts *(above and pages 58 - 59)*

Kansas City's newest landmark was designed by award-winning architect Moshe Safdie. It includes two venues: Helzberg Hall, the intimate, acoustically perfect home of the Kansas City Symphony, and the larger Muriel Kauffman Theatre which hosts operas, ballet, and other performing arts.

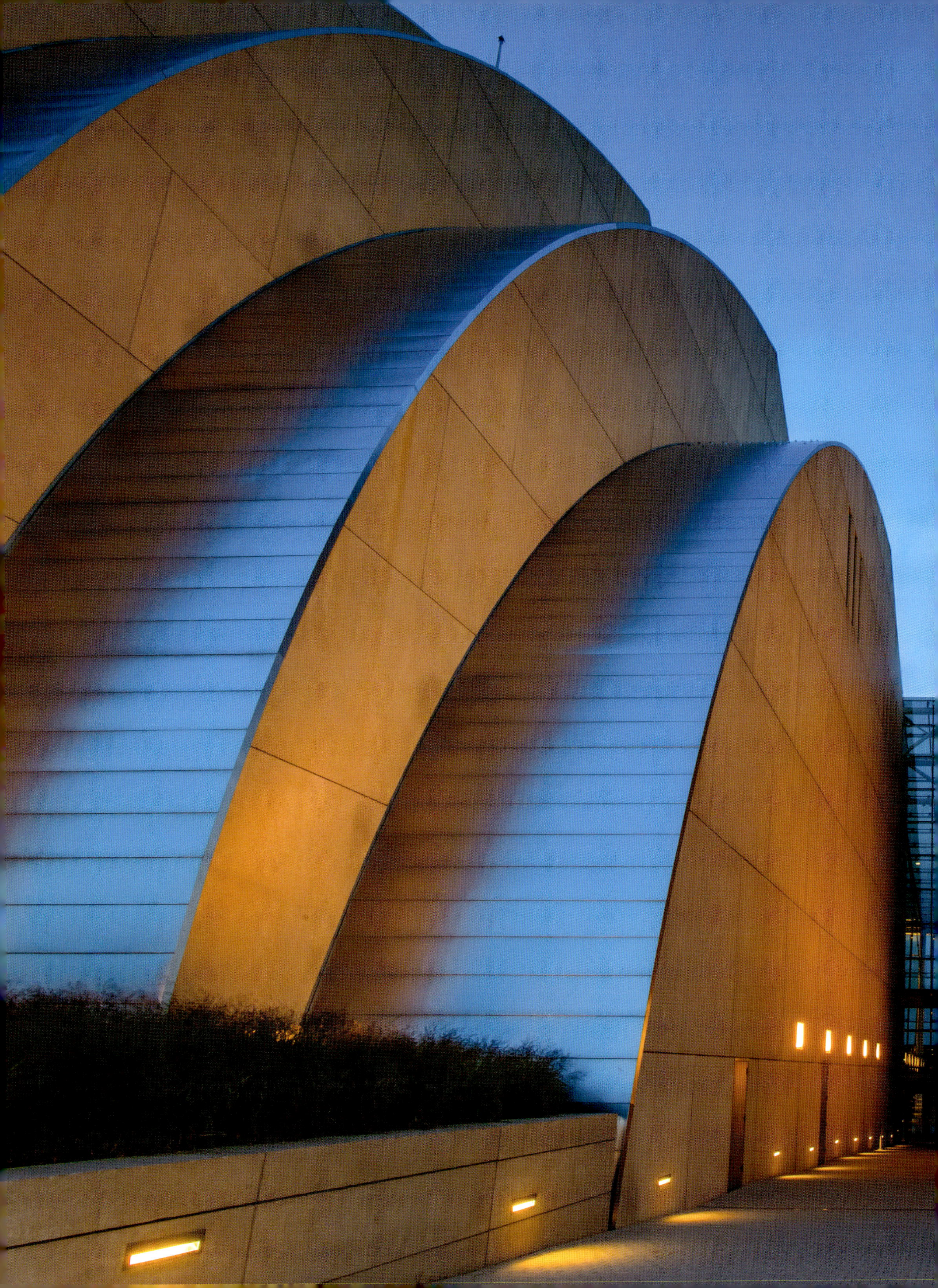

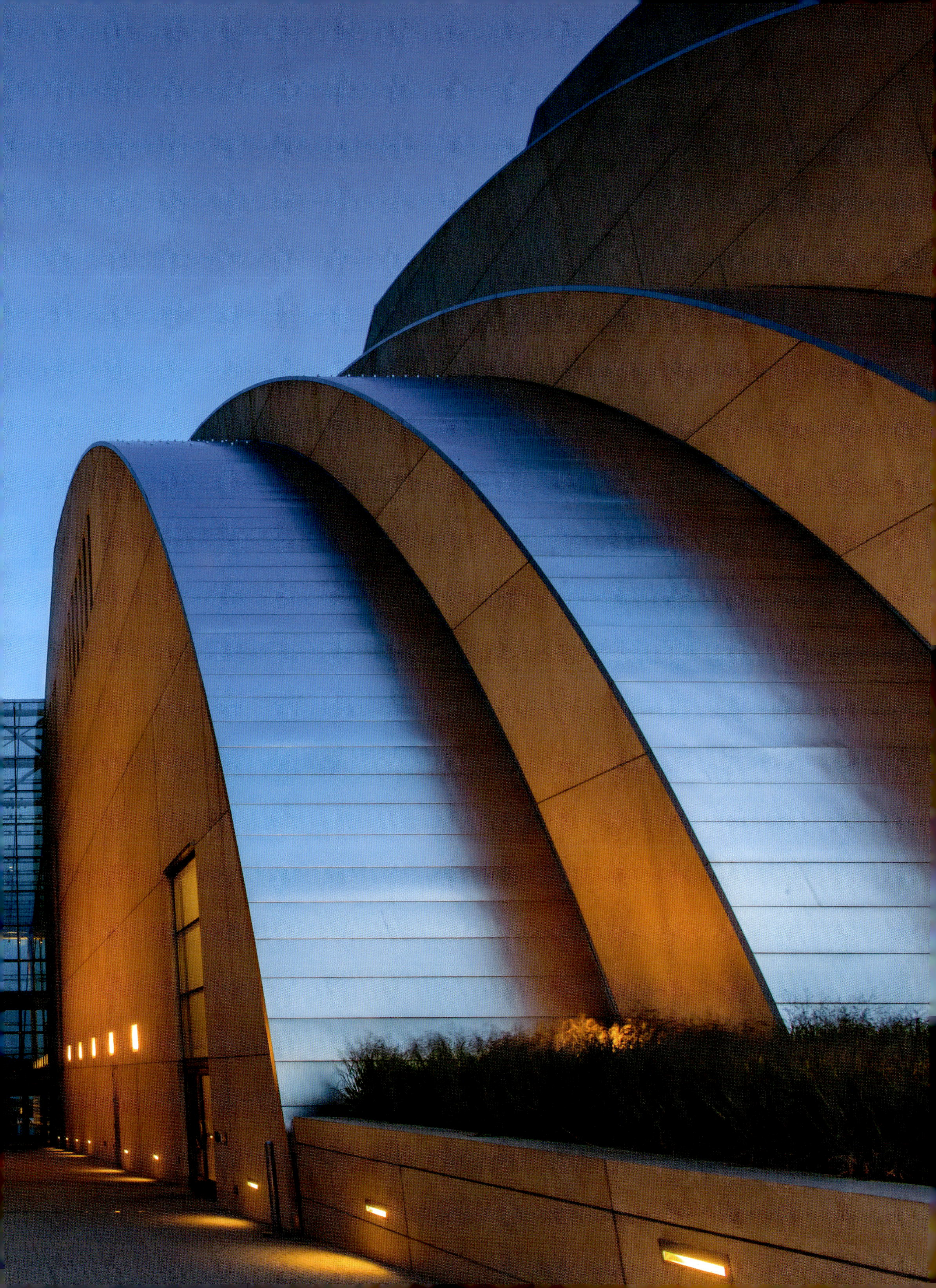

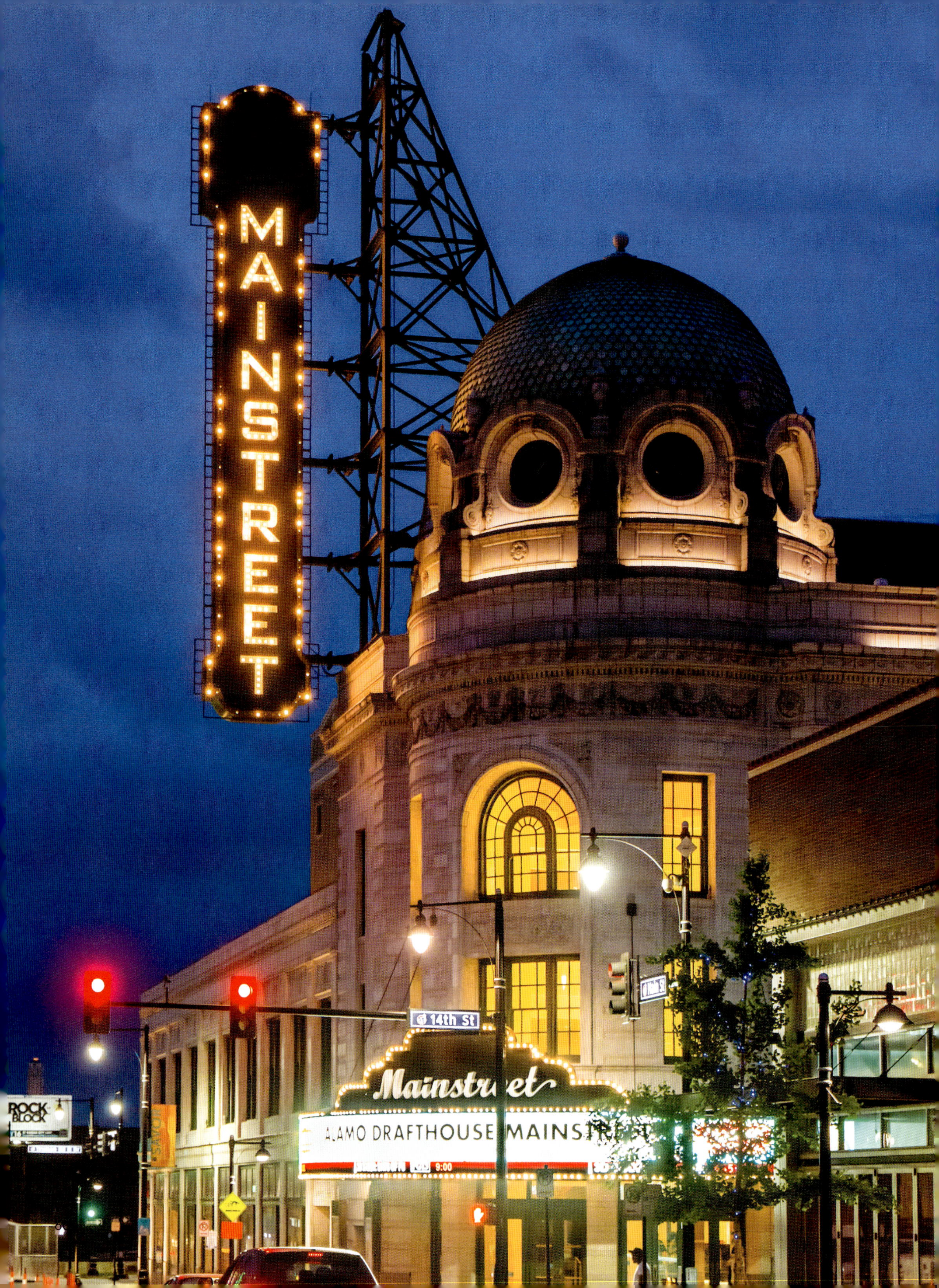
MAINSTREET
14th St
Main St
ALAMO DRAFTHOUSE
9:00
ROCK BLOCK

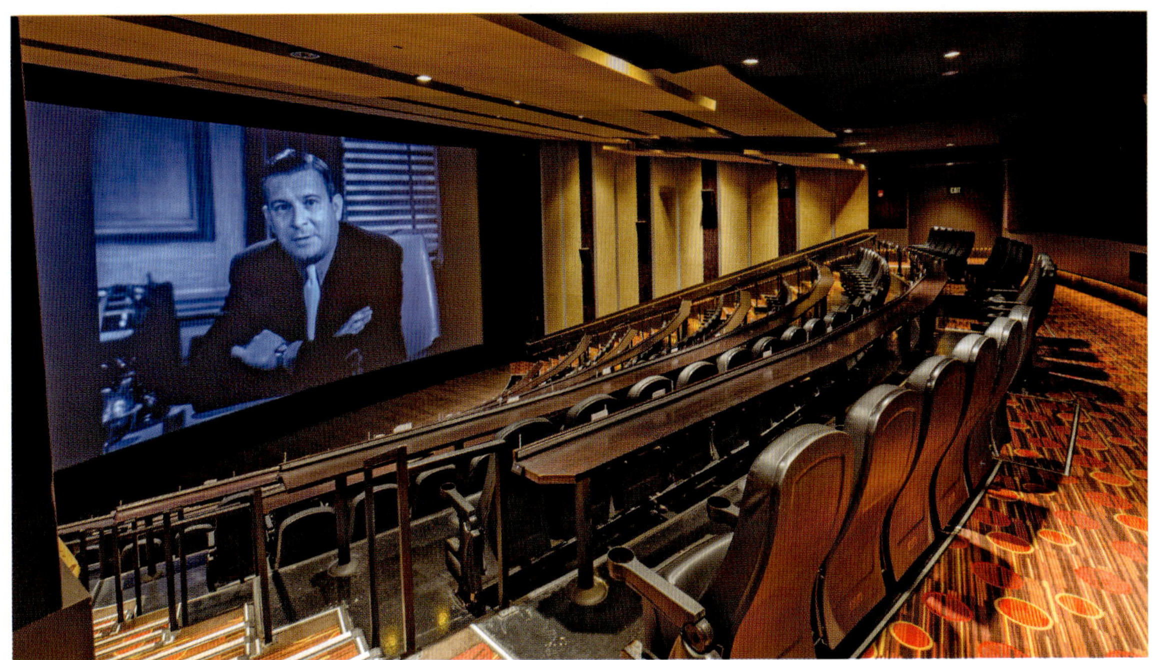

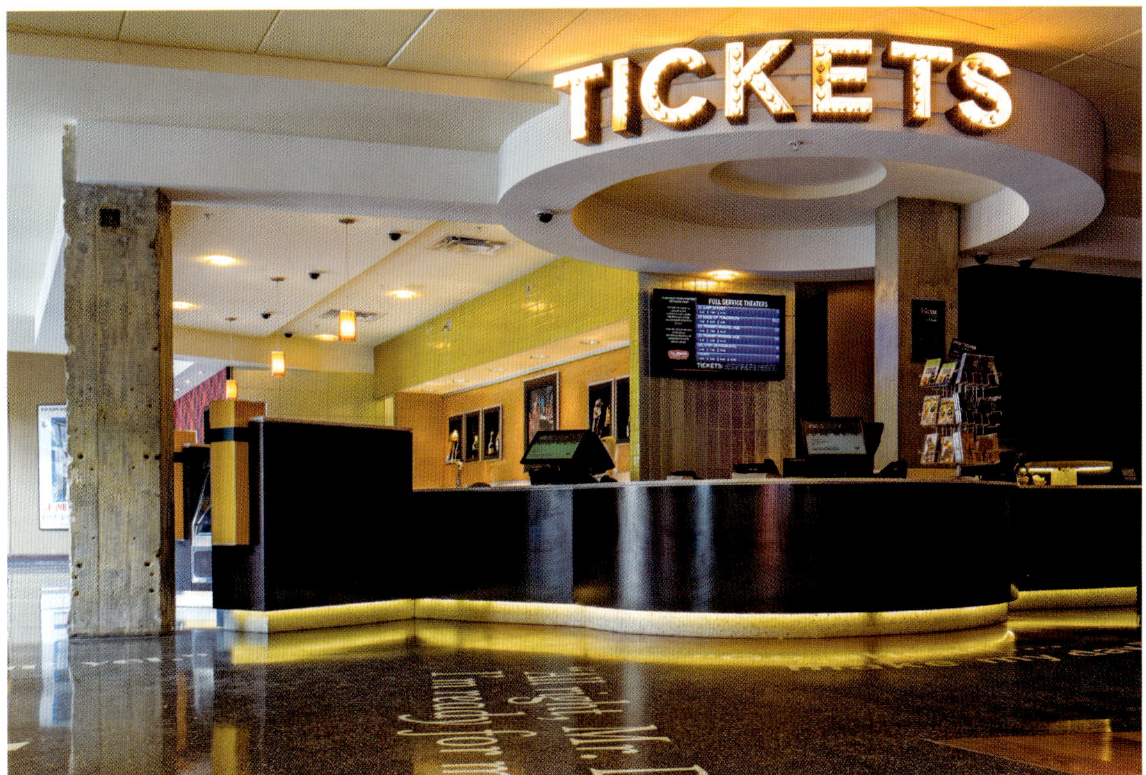

Alamo Drafthouse Cinema *(opposite)*

During the 1920s, the Mainstreet Theater was a popular venue for vaudeville acts and movies. Beneath the theater, a tunnel served as a passageway to the President Hotel and an escape for bootleggers during Prohibition. Today, the Alamo Drafthouse serves food and cocktails to patrons enjoying the latest films.

Alamo Drafthouse Cinema

(top and bottom)

The Alamo Drafthouse chain is well known for its strict behavior policy. But the theater also sponsors classic films with musical sing-alongs, quote-alongs, and other events that encourage audience participation. Along with great food and drink, the Alamo is an experience worth remembering.

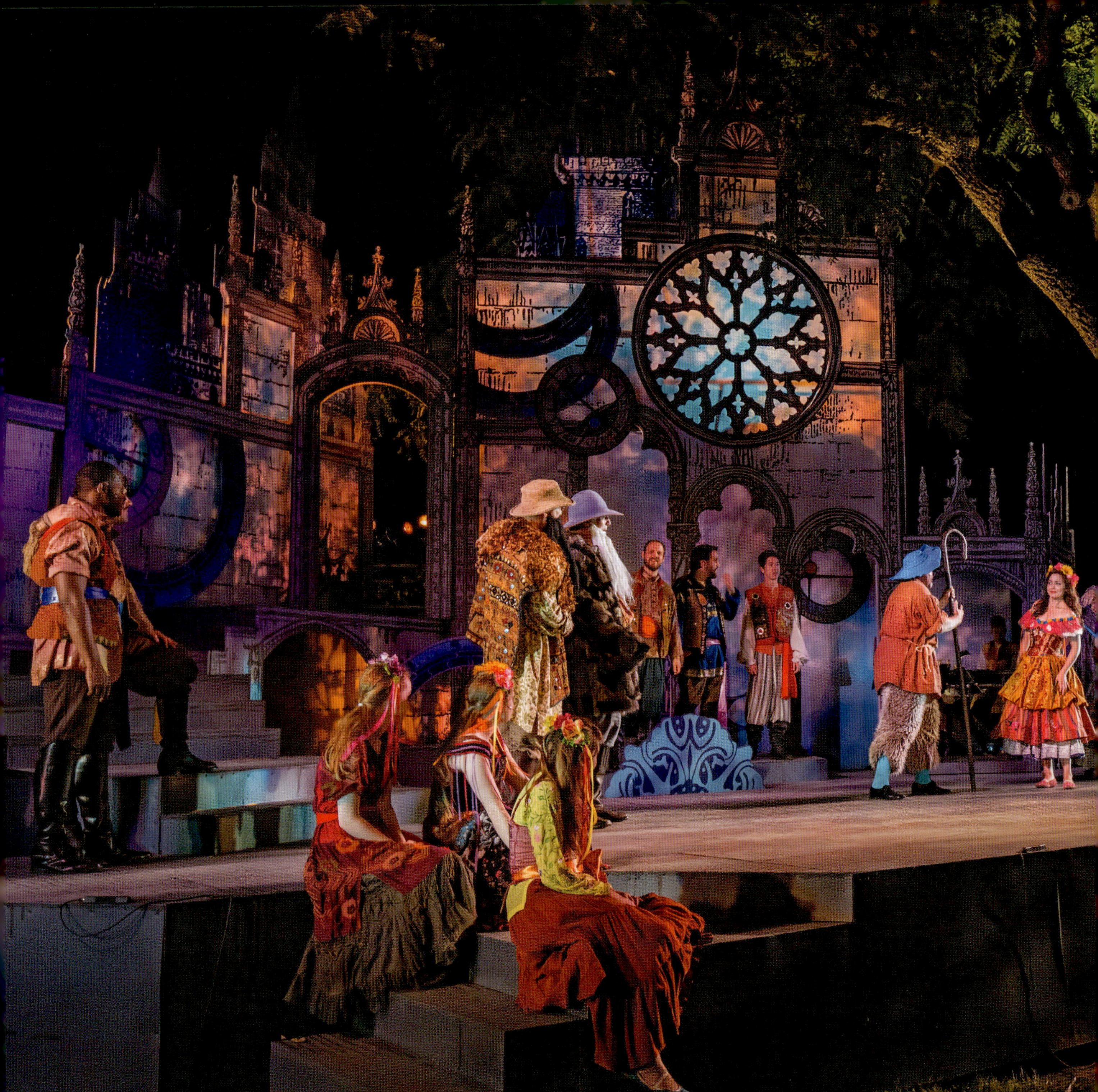

Heart of America Shakespeare Festival

In the tradition of outdoor productions of the works of William Shakespeare, Kansas City's festival has been presenting interpretations of the Bard's plays for more than two decades. Each summer, local and nationally known actors take the stage as attendees relax under the stars.

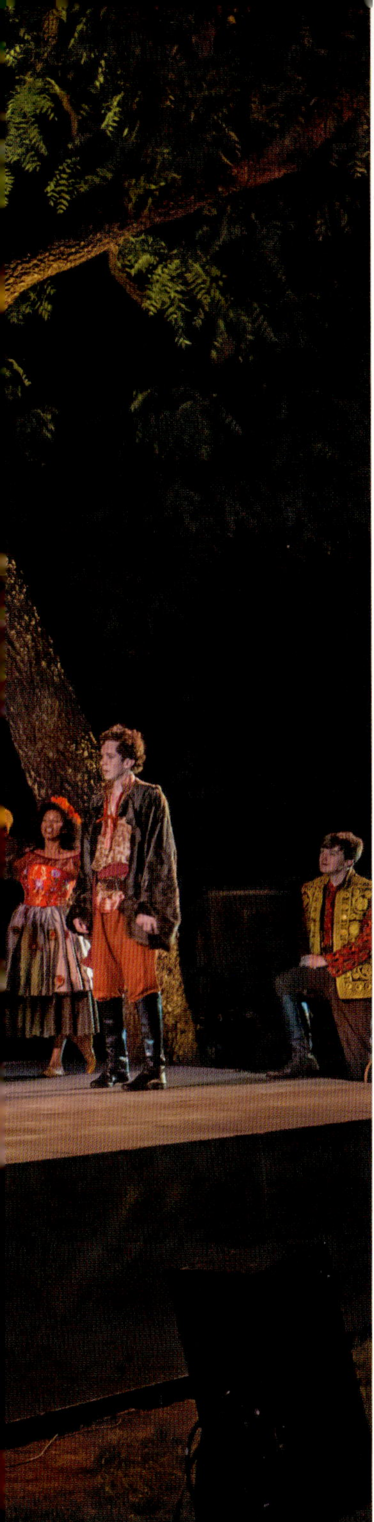

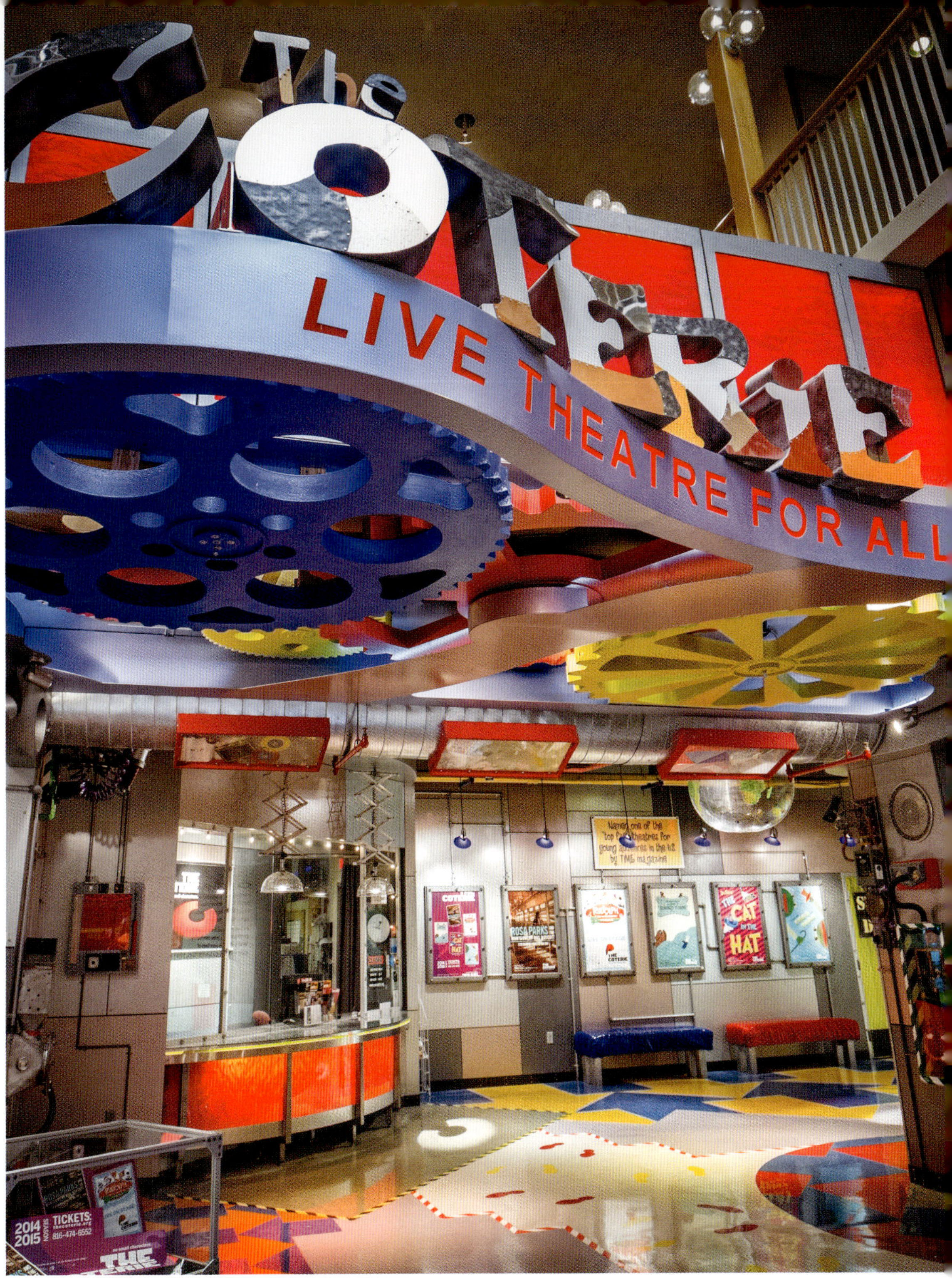

Coterie Theatre

Nationally recognized as one of the best theatres for young audiences in America, the Coterie provides unique, fun, and engaging performances year-round. The theatre often hosts school field trips, exposing new audiences to the performing arts, and also offers acting classes for children of all ages.

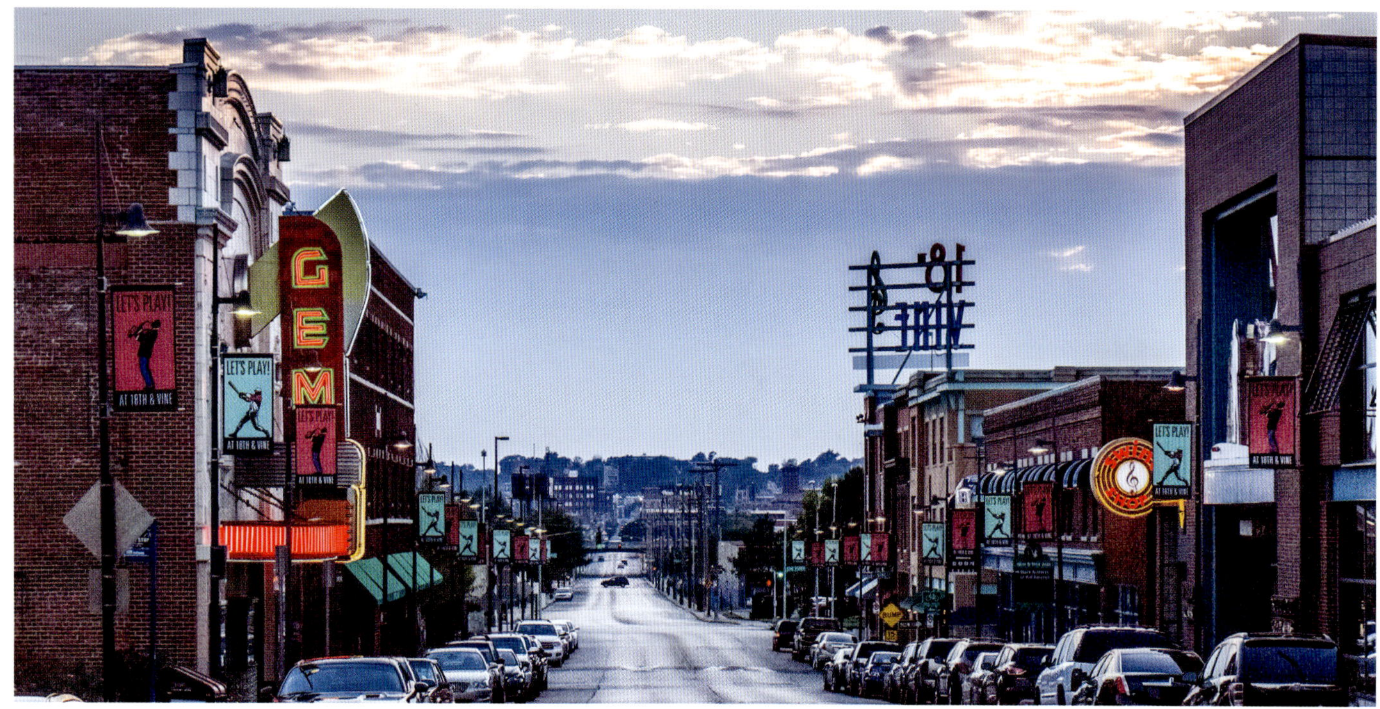

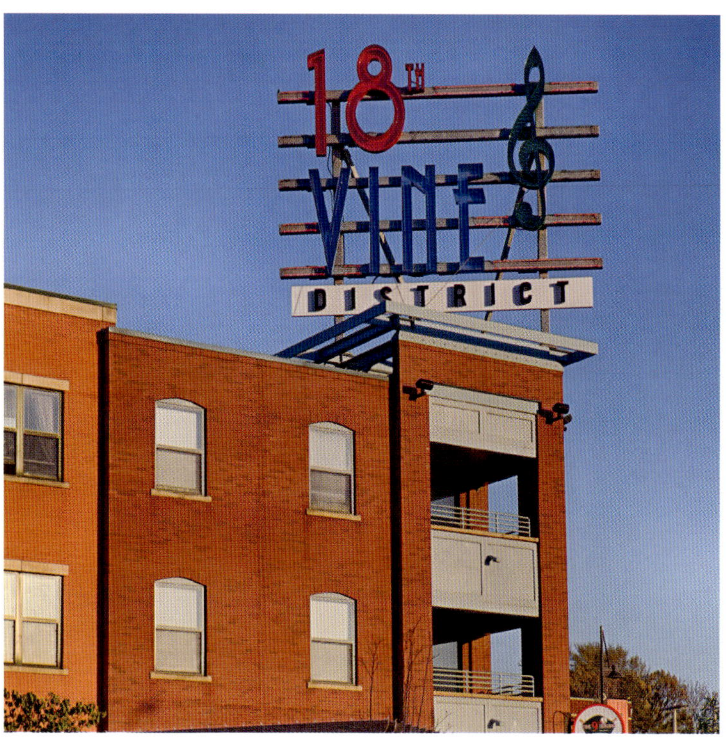

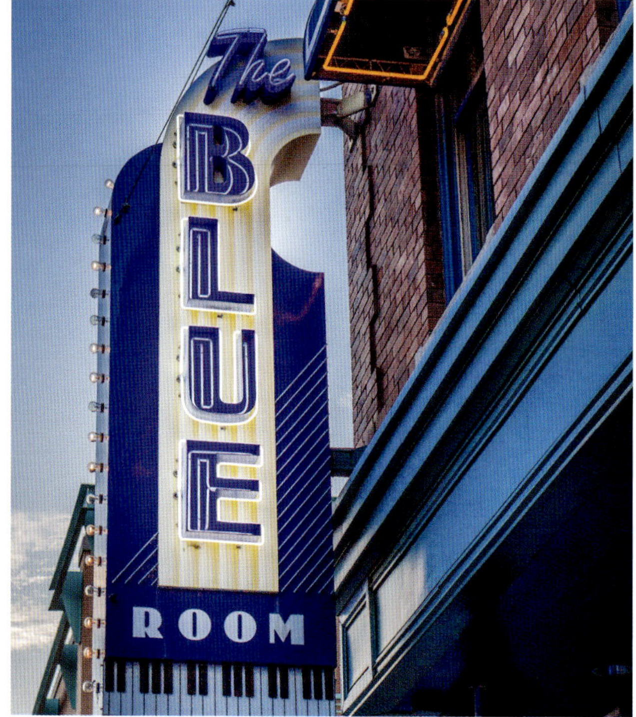

18th & Vine District

During the 1930s and 1940s, Kansas City was at the forefront of jazz music and no place was more important, no place home to more notable musicians and jazz clubs, than 18th & Vine. The district boasted crowded clubs and a "who's who" of jazz musicians, performing nightly.

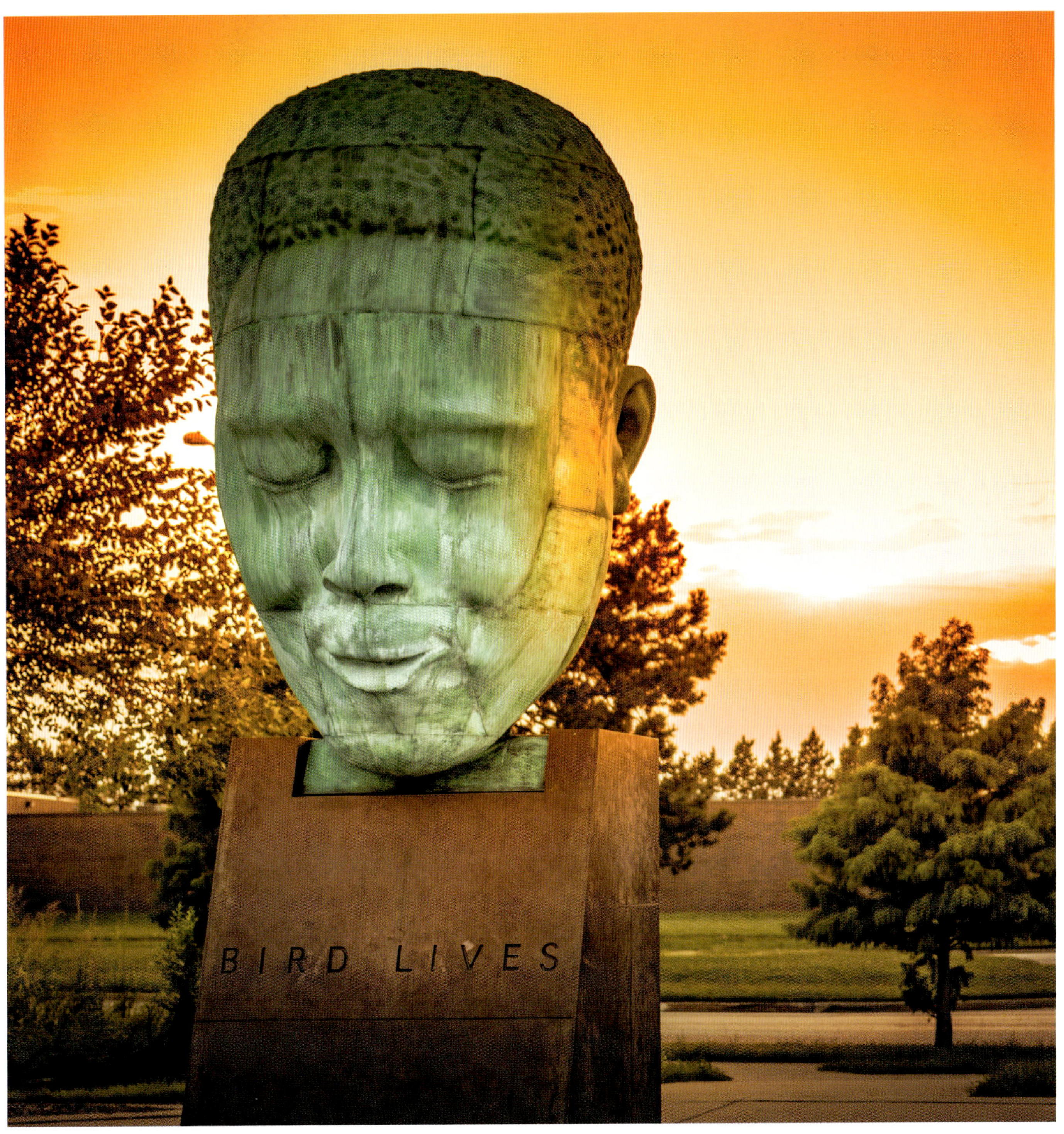

American Jazz Museum

Kansas City native, Charlie "Bird" Parker is immortalized outside the American Jazz Museum in this bronze sculpture. Parker and his saxophone were hugely influential in the development of a faster, higher tempo, jazz called bebop. Parker's career, along with hundreds of others, is detailed in the museum.

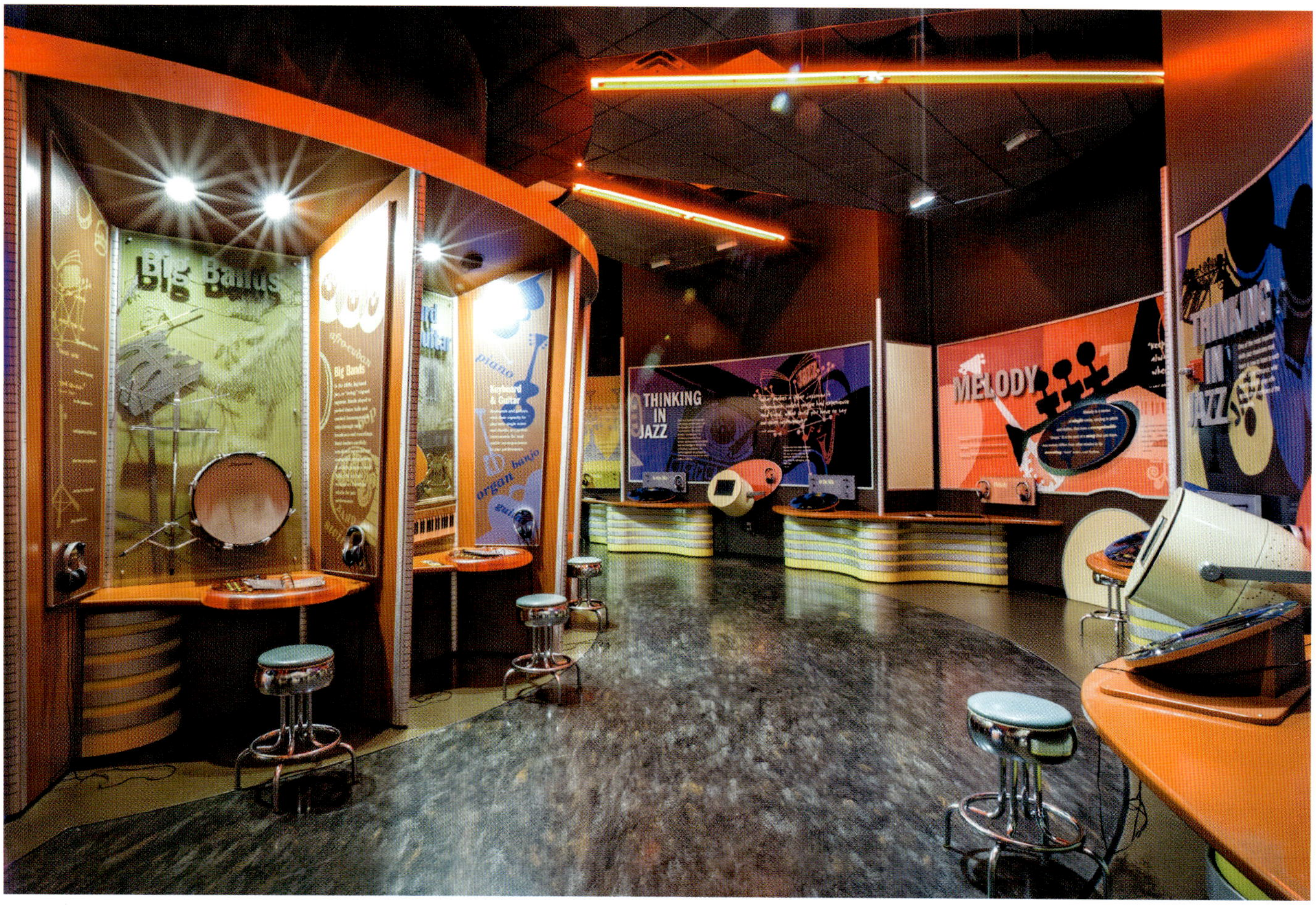

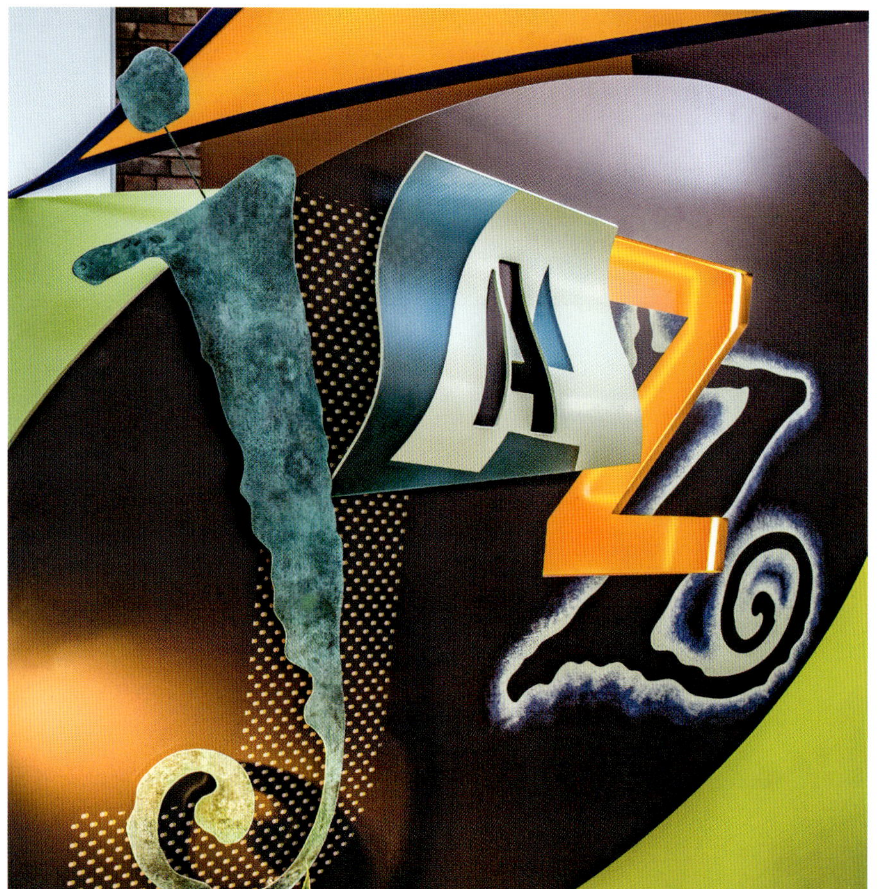

American Jazz Museum *(above and left)*

Bang out a jazz beat on a drum or tap out a melody on a saxophone — dozens of interactive exhibits help visitors understand the building blocks of jazz. Colorful displays also highlight the unique differences - from tempo to structure - between varieties in the genre in this engaging learning experience.

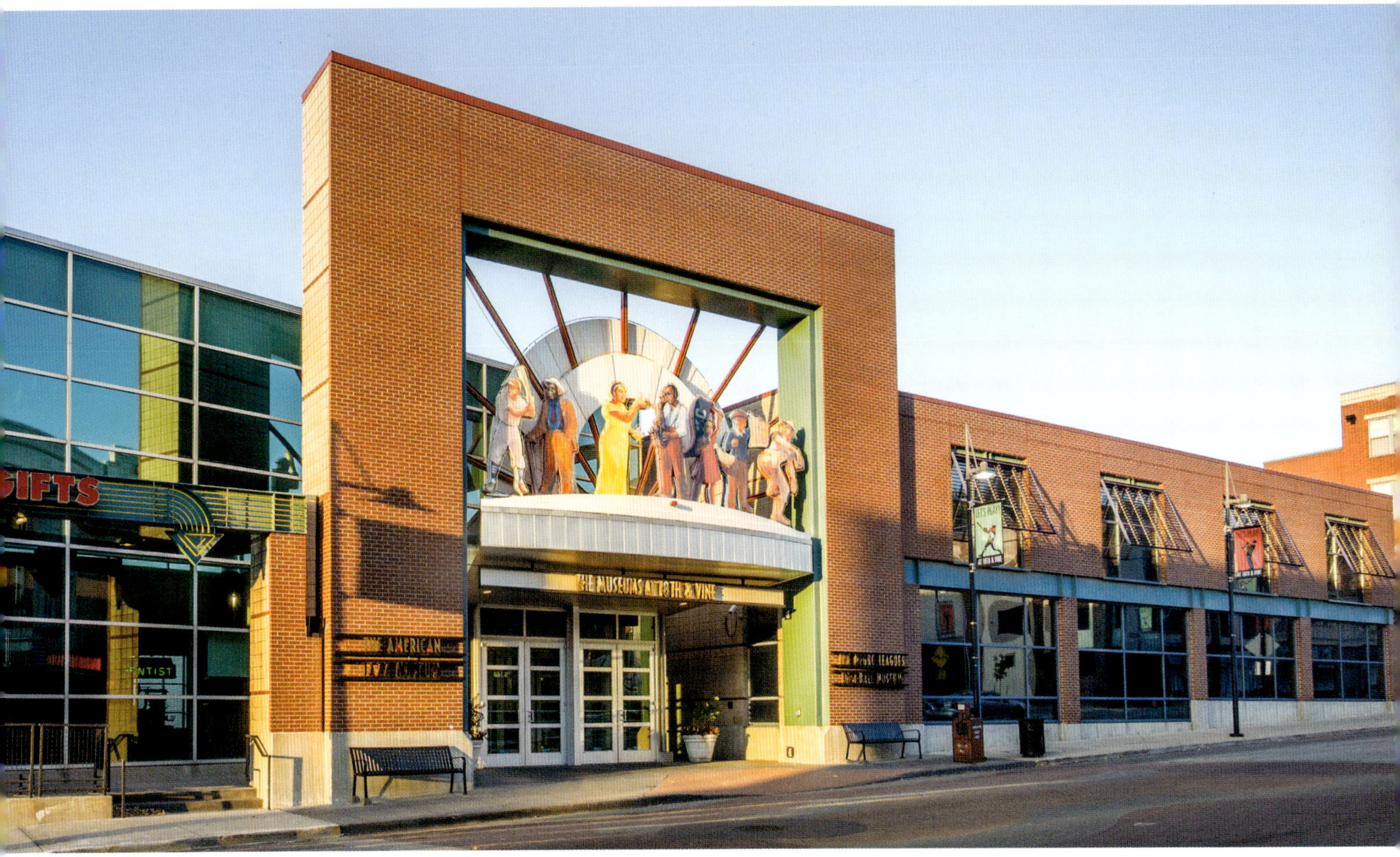

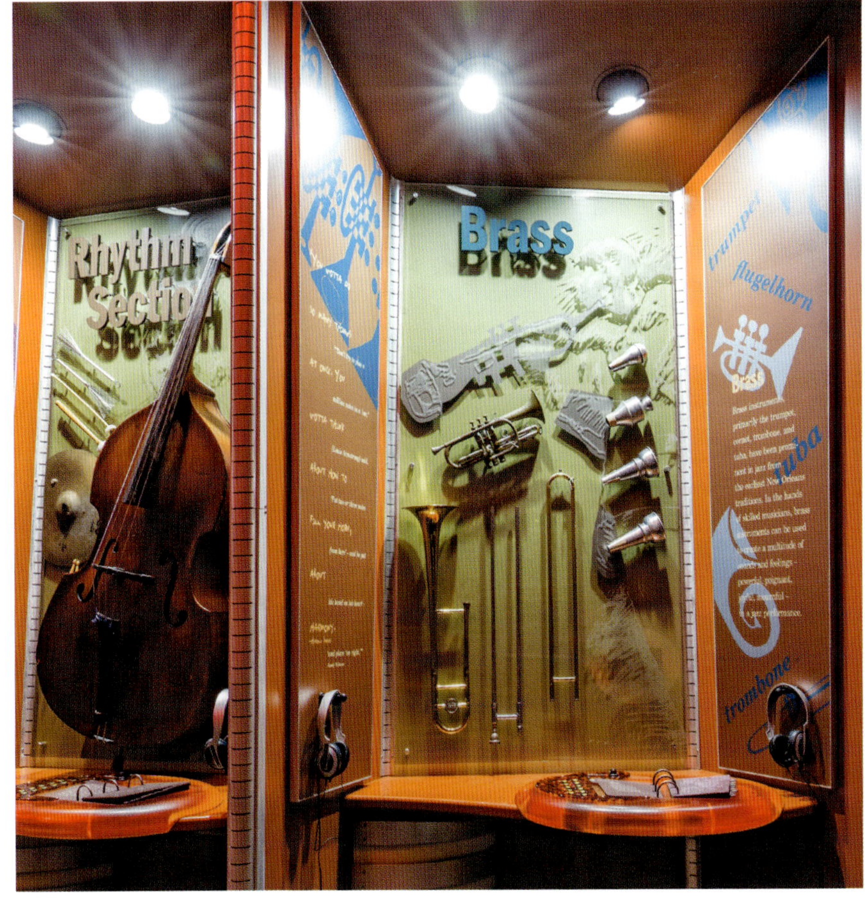

American Jazz Museum

(above and right)

Many of the masters of jazz made Kansas City their home, living near the clubs of 18th & Vine and playing their music in the crowded venues near this historic intersection. In the American Jazz Museum, many of their instruments, stage costumes, and other artifacts are on display.

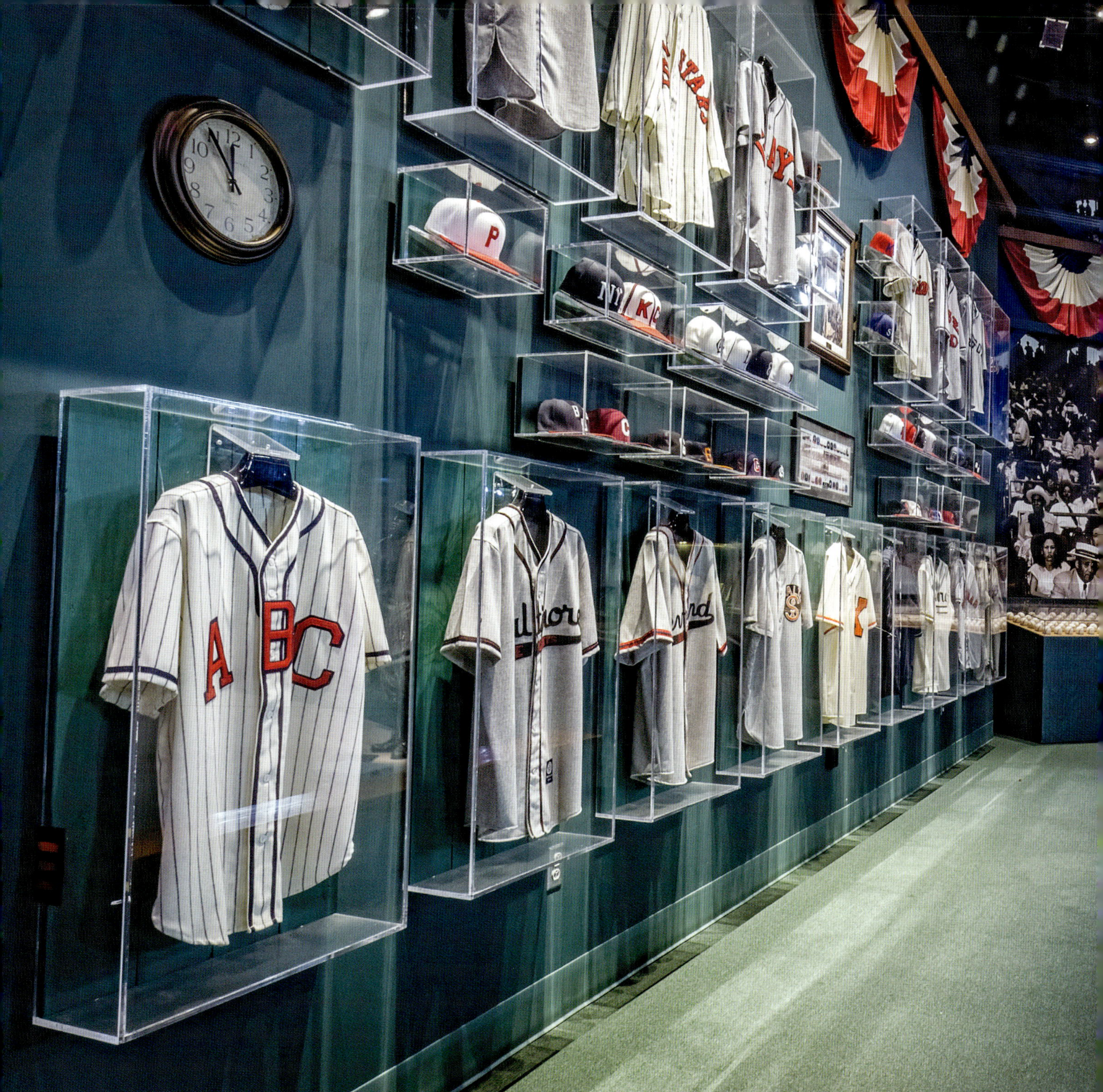

Negro Leagues Baseball Museum

Long before Jackie Robinson broke the color barrier in baseball, African Americans were playing top-notch baseball in the Negro Leagues. This captivating museum pays tribute to teams from the late 1800s through the 1960s, like the Homestead Greys and Cuban Giants, and players like Satchel Paige and Josh Gibson.

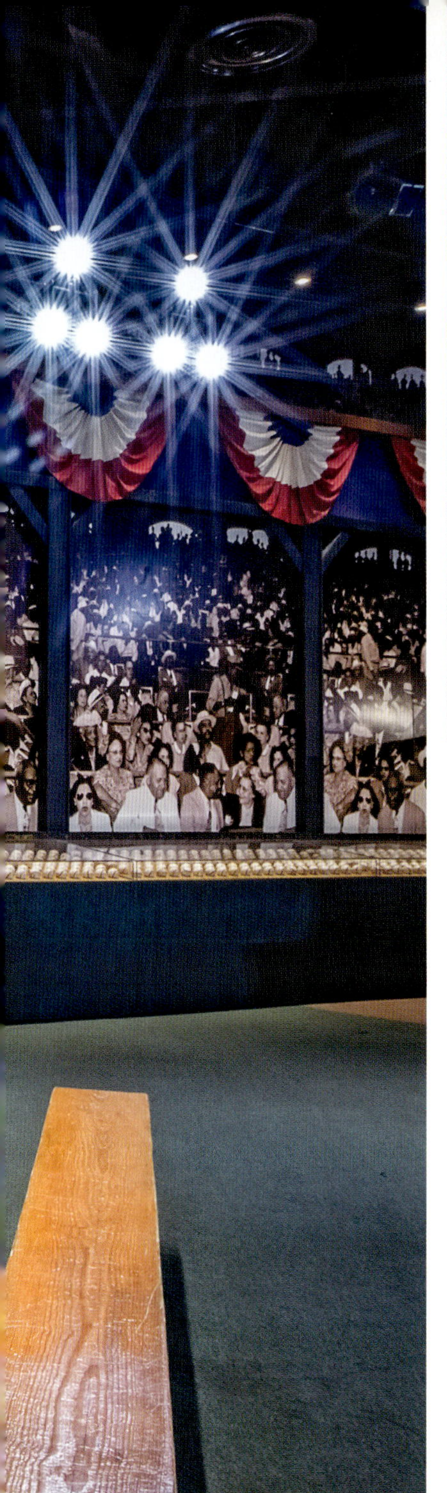

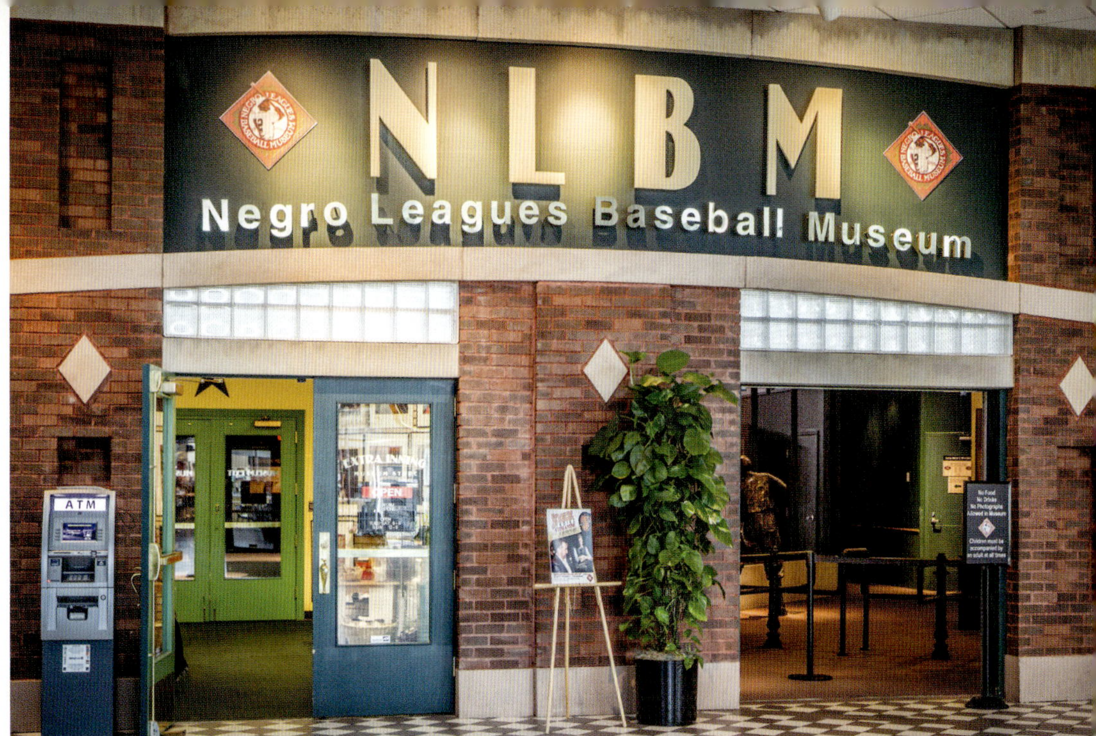

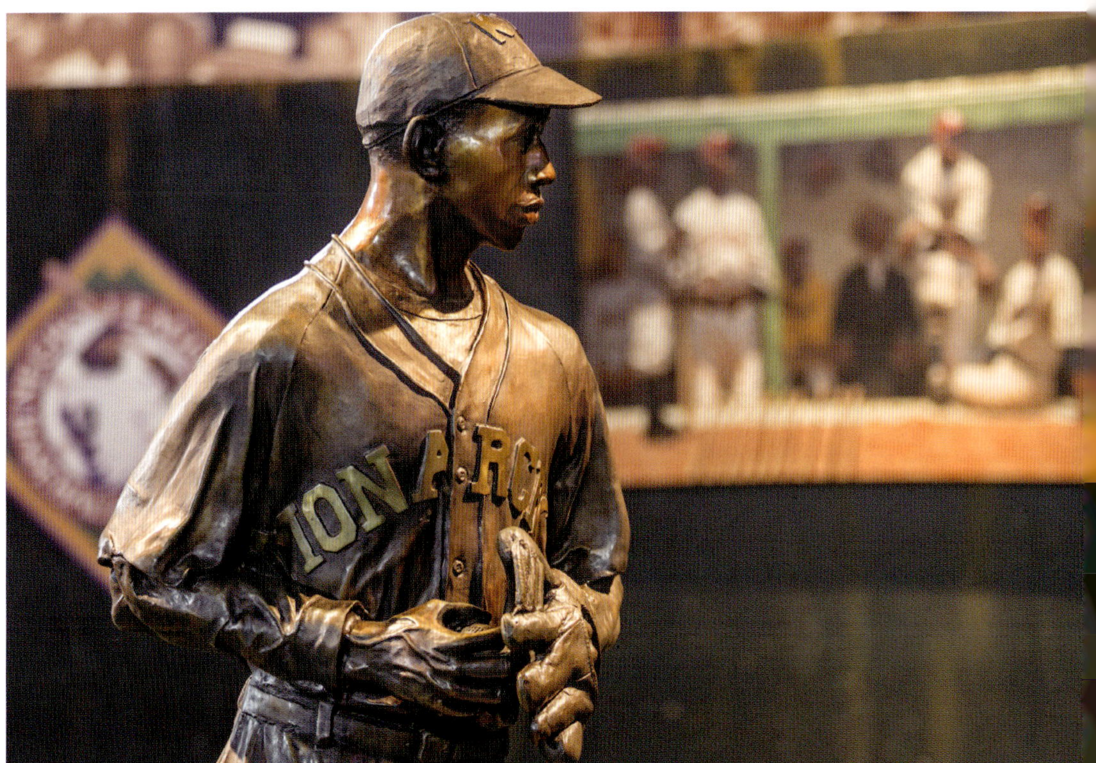

Negro Leagues Baseball Museum

(top and bottom)

It's easy to lose track of time in this museum's compelling narrative, which chronicles the traveling baseball players of the Negro Leagues. Storytelling conveys this challenging life—enduring the rigors of a long athletic season while navigating the prejudices of pre-Civil Rights America.

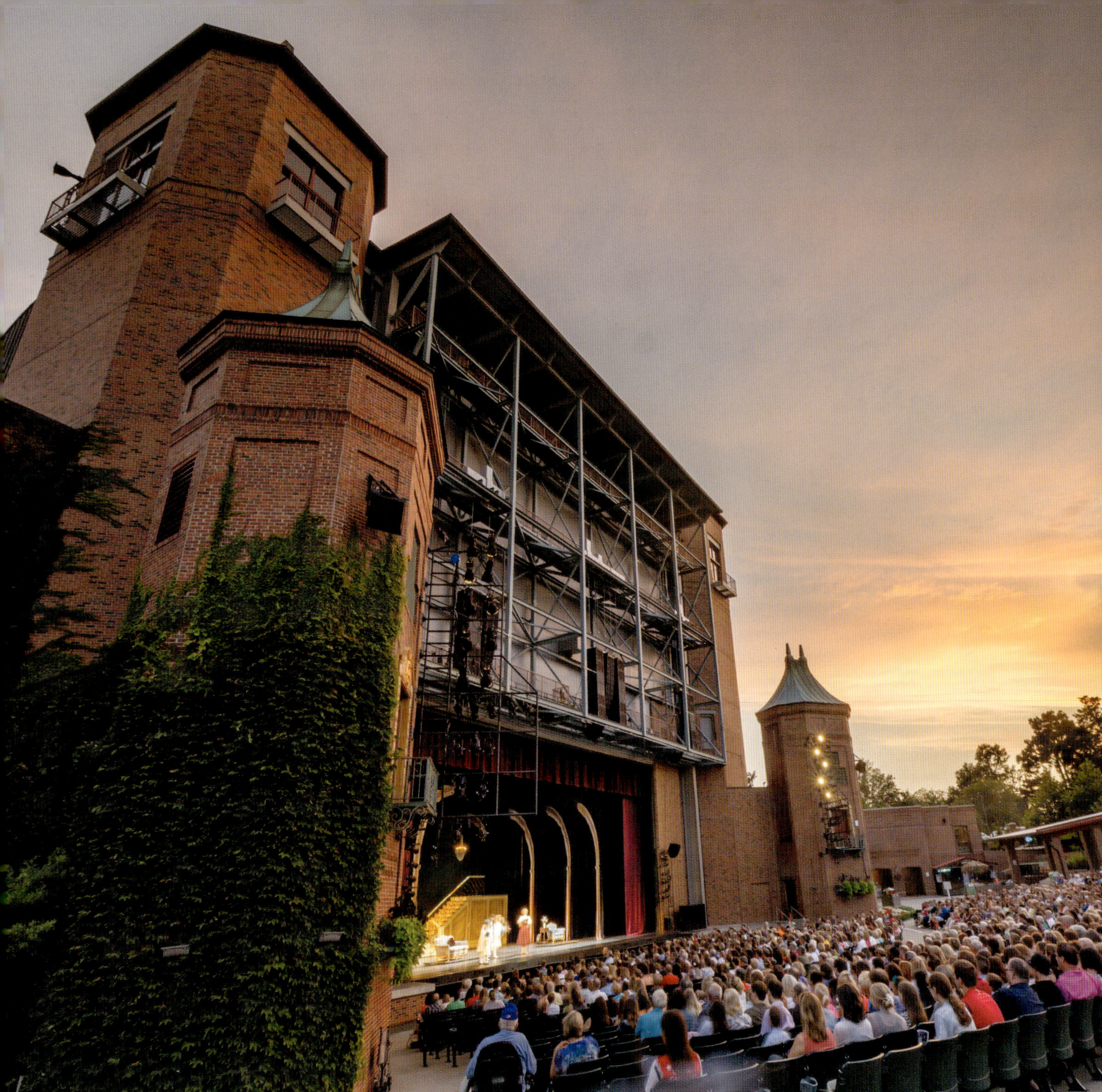

Starlight Theatre

Tucked in a valley in Kansas City's largest park, Swope Park, Starlight Theatre is an open-air venue that hosts everything from full-blown Broadway productions to rock concerts by popular performers. On warm summer nights, Kansas Citians flock to the theatre to be entertained under the stars.

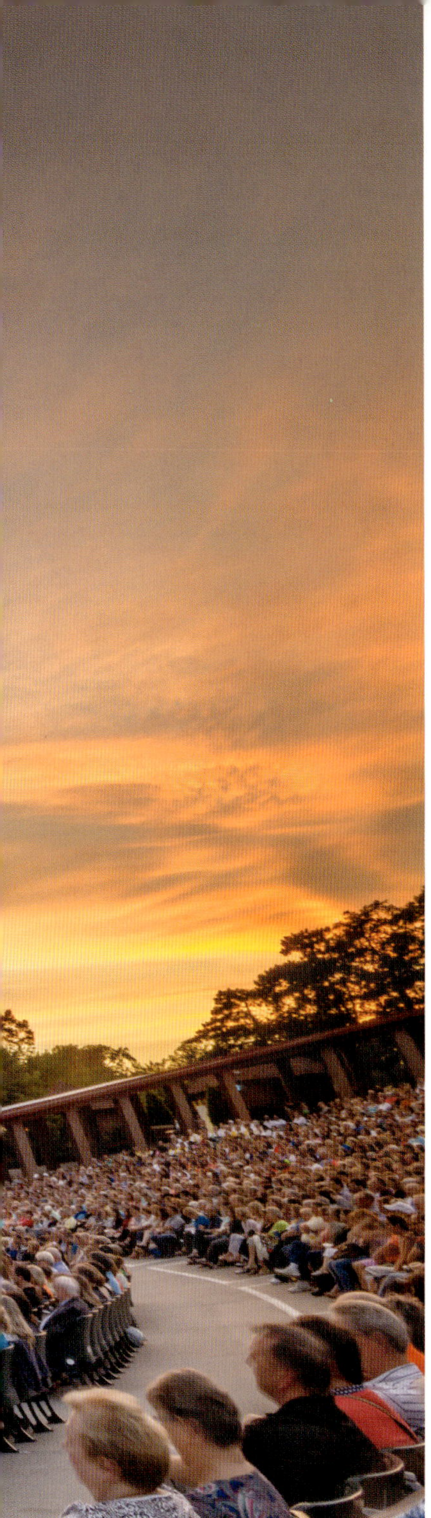

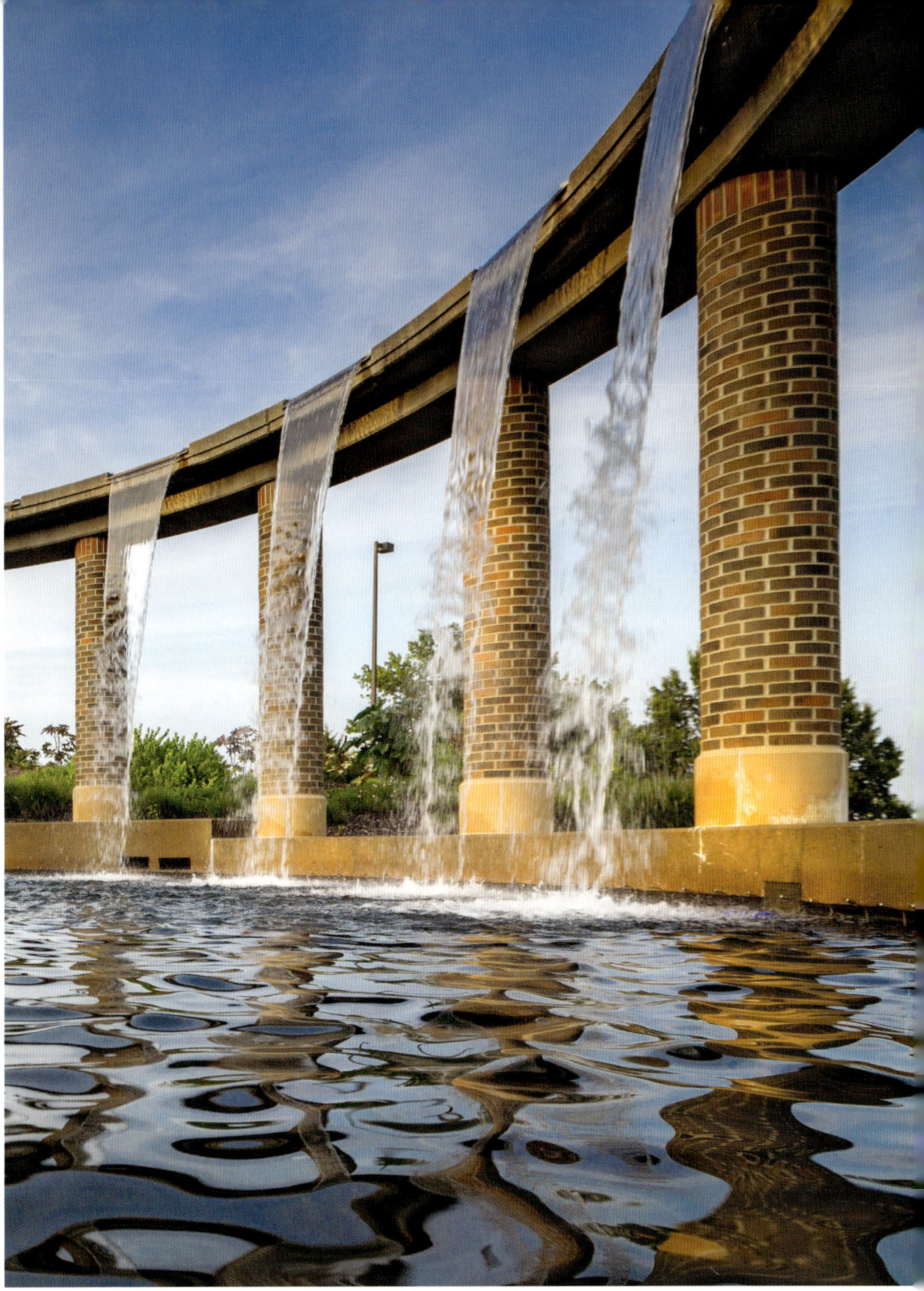

Starlight Theatre

Starlight Theatre is just one of two self-producing outdoor theatres left in the United States. This results in the freedom to attract a huge variety of fantastic shows and notable performers. A typical season at Starlight includes a half dozen theatre productions and nearly 30 concerts.

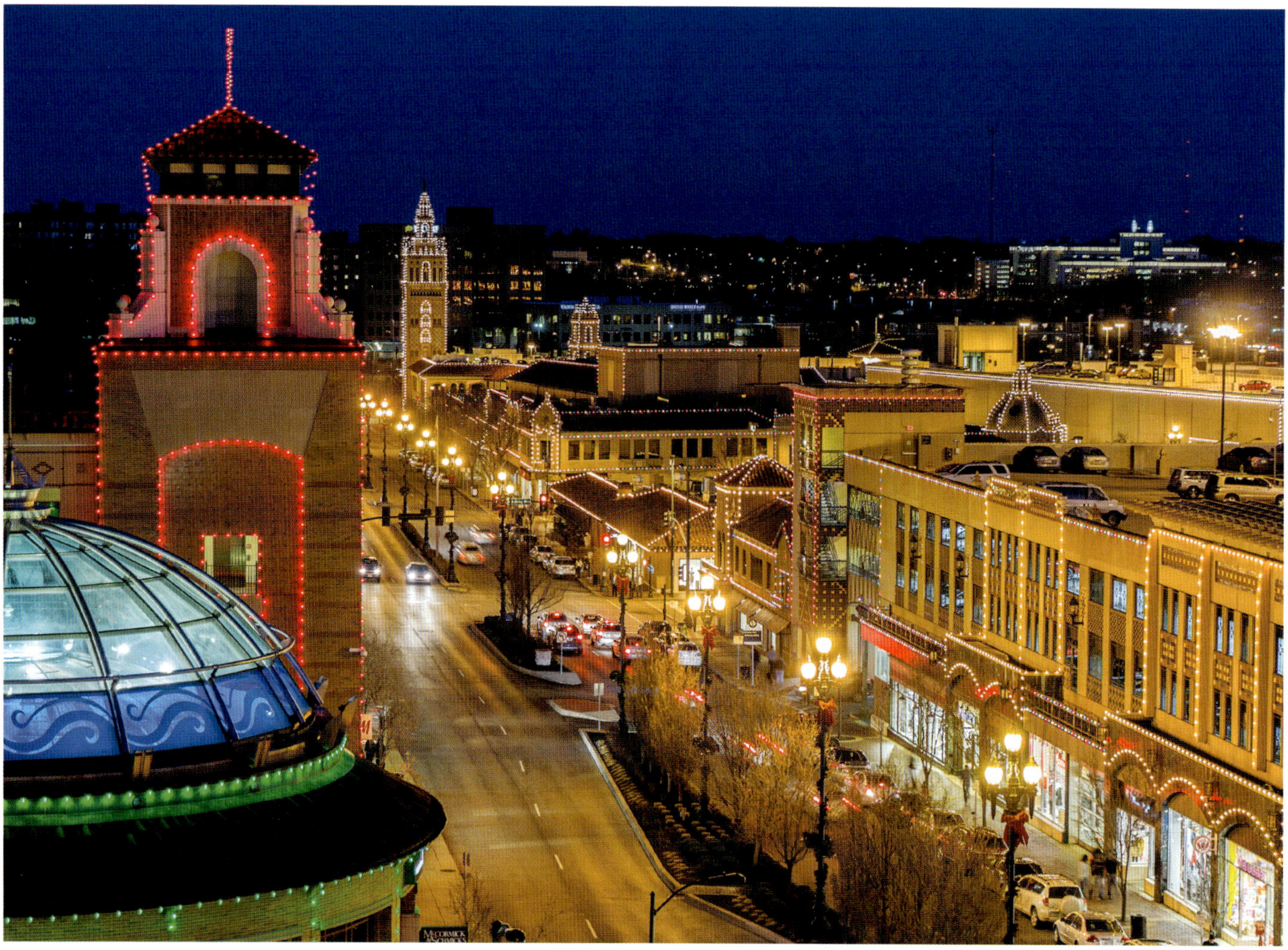

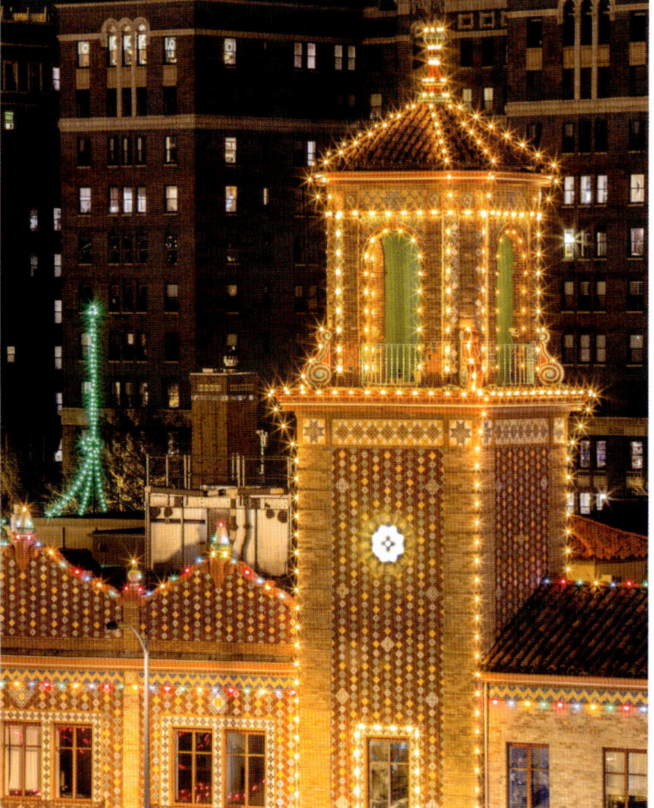

Country Club Plaza Holiday Lights

(above, left, and opposite bottom)

One of Kansas City's greatest traditions is the lighting of the Country Club Plaza on Thanksgiving night. Thousands gather to celebrate the holiday season as a countdown leads to the entire shopping district being illuminated by more than a quarter million lights. It is truly a beautiful and magical spectacle.

Mayor's Christmas Tree Crown Center *(opposite, top)*

A symbol of the Mayor's Christmas Tree Fund, a charity helping the city's less fortunate, the Mayor's Christmas Tree stands in the plaza of Crown Center each year. The tree often reaches more than 100 feet tall, and wood from the tree is recycled into ornaments for the following year.

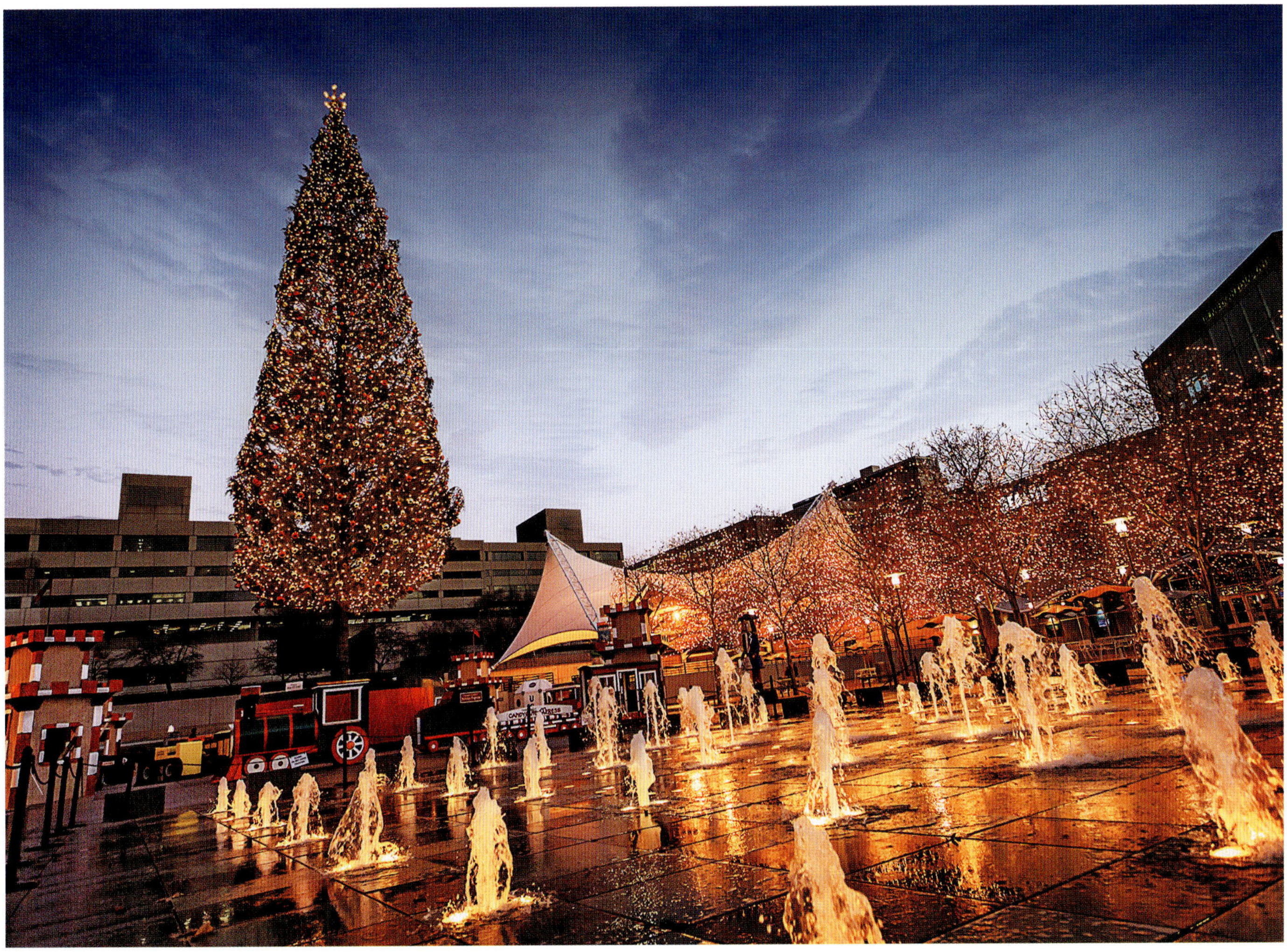

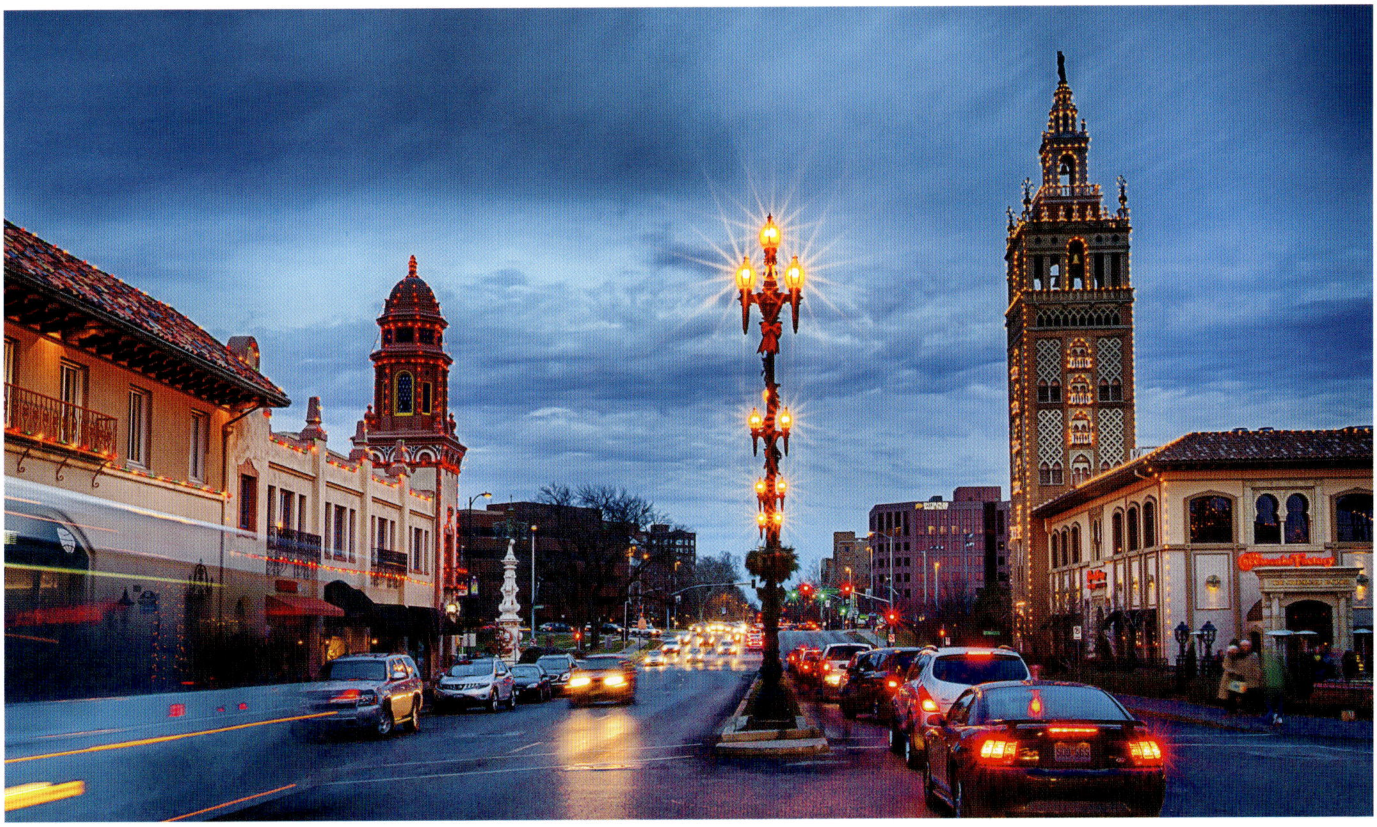

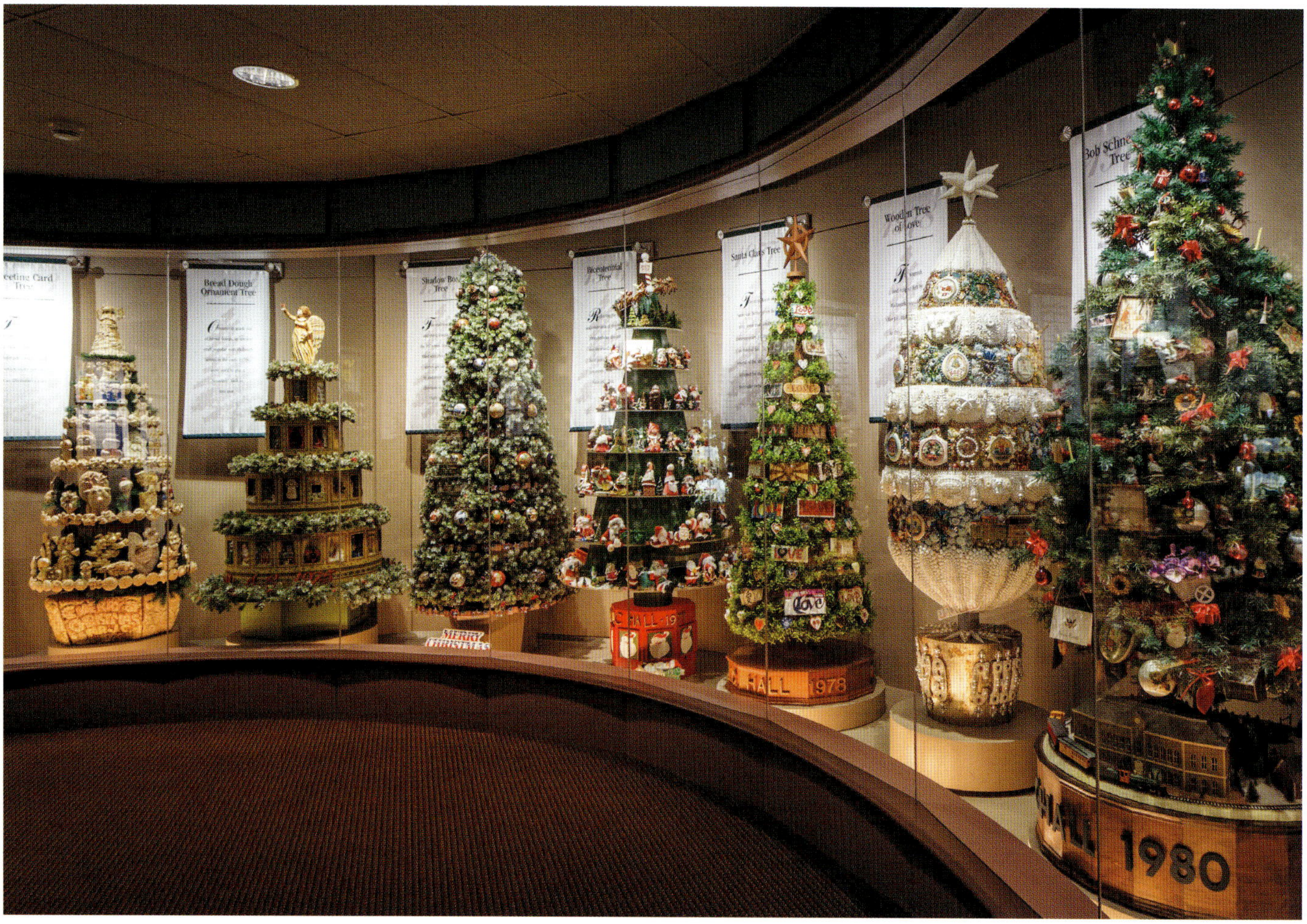

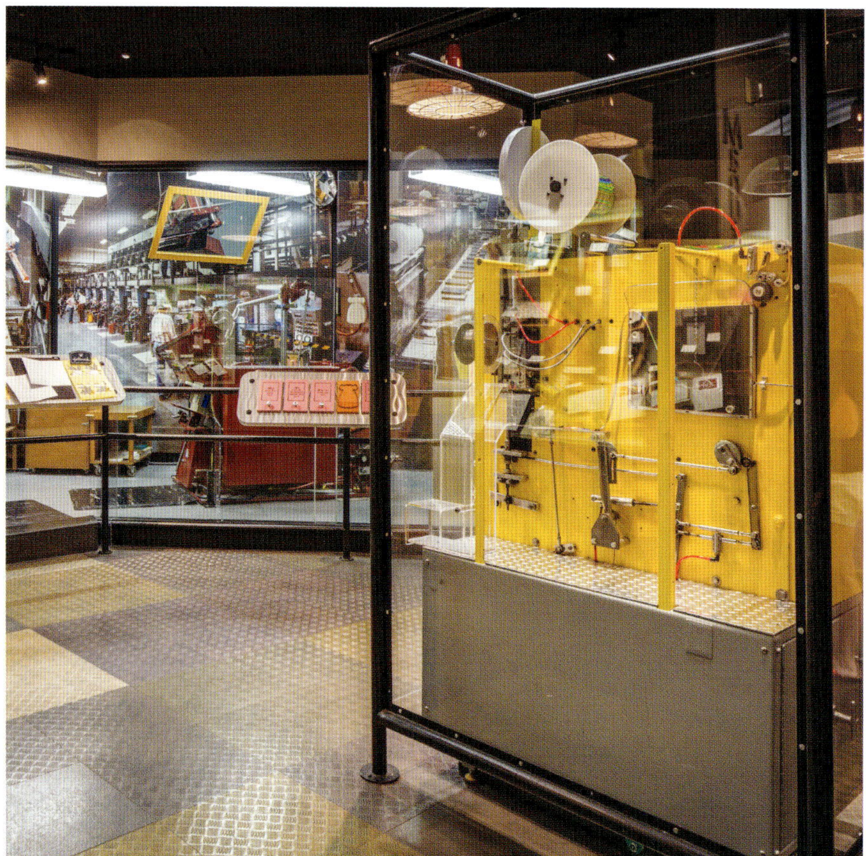

Hallmark Visitor's Center

(above and left)

At the headquarters of Hallmark, the nation's largest greeting card producer, you can meet the creators of some of the company's most popular products, make your own shiny bow for placing atop a package, and walk through a museum of their famous and festive Christmas tree ornaments.

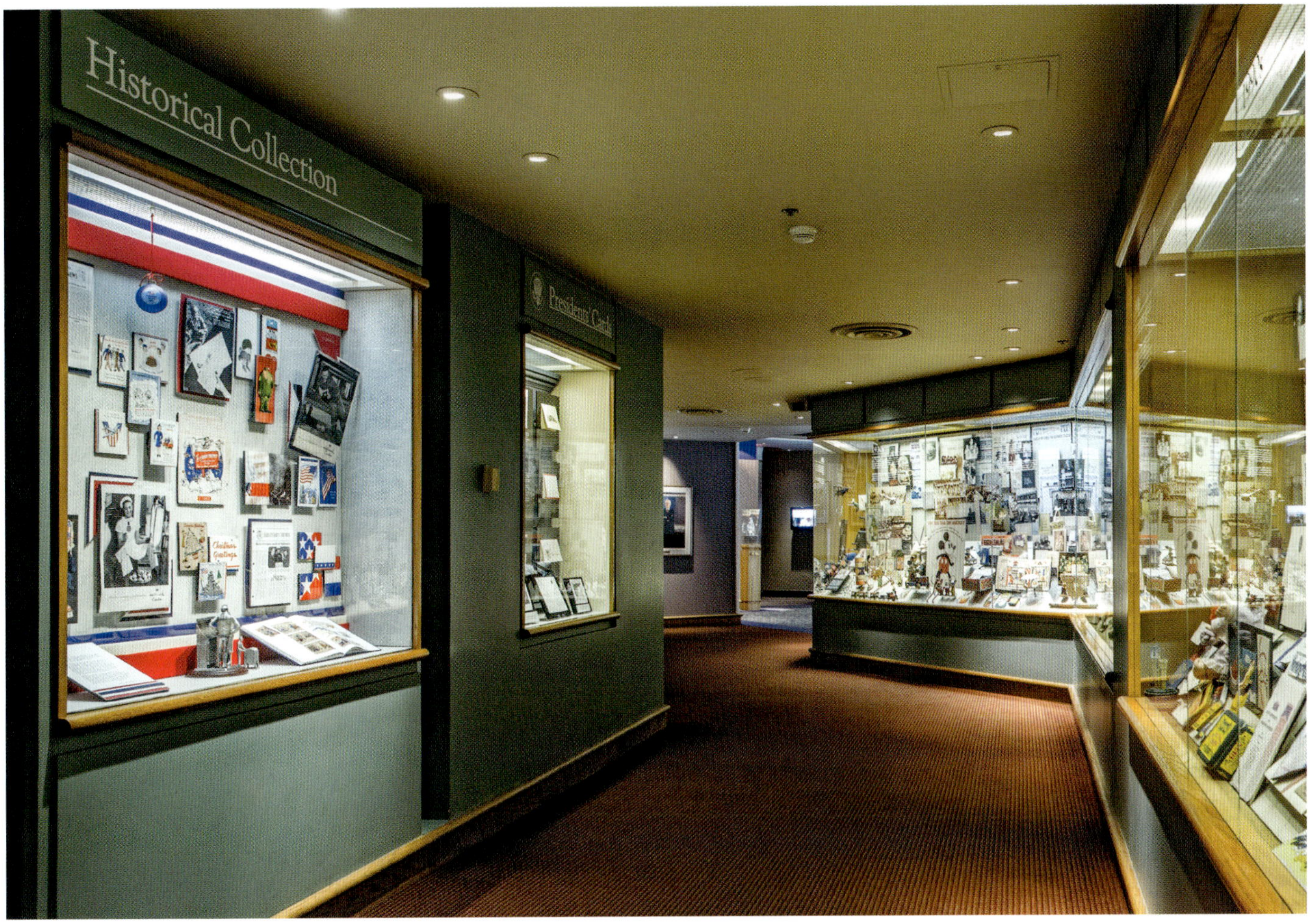

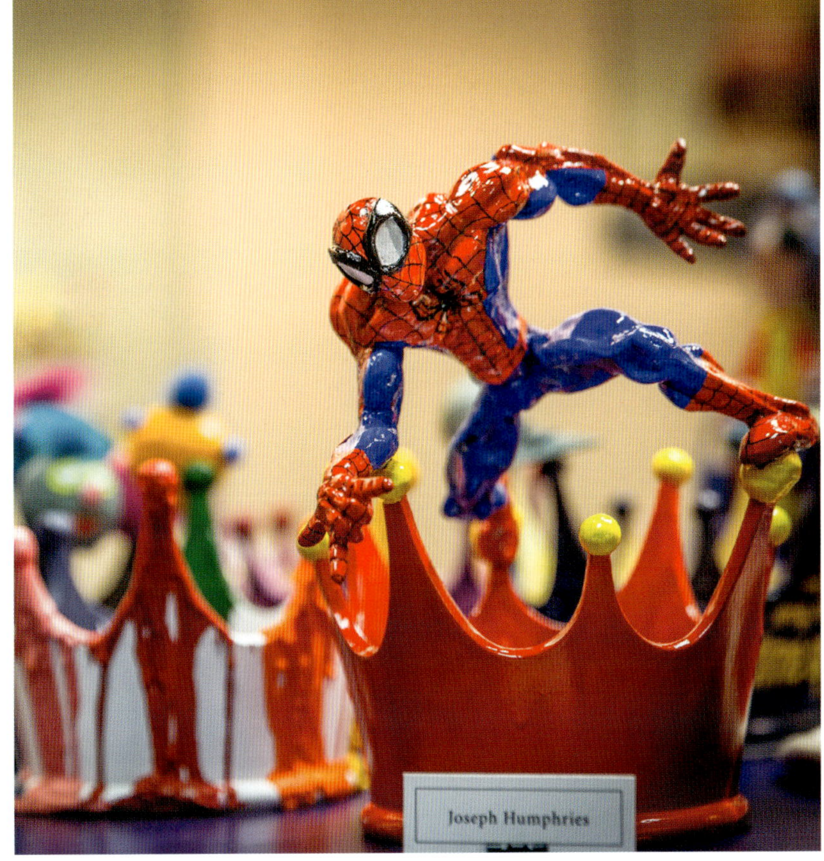

Hallmark Visitor's Center

(above and right)

Hallmark has sold greeting cards, wrapping paper, ribbon, and more for more than a century. Their products are made extra special with the addition of popular licenses like the Peanuts, Marvel, Disney, and Star Wars. A free tour includes many of these customer favorites from over the years.

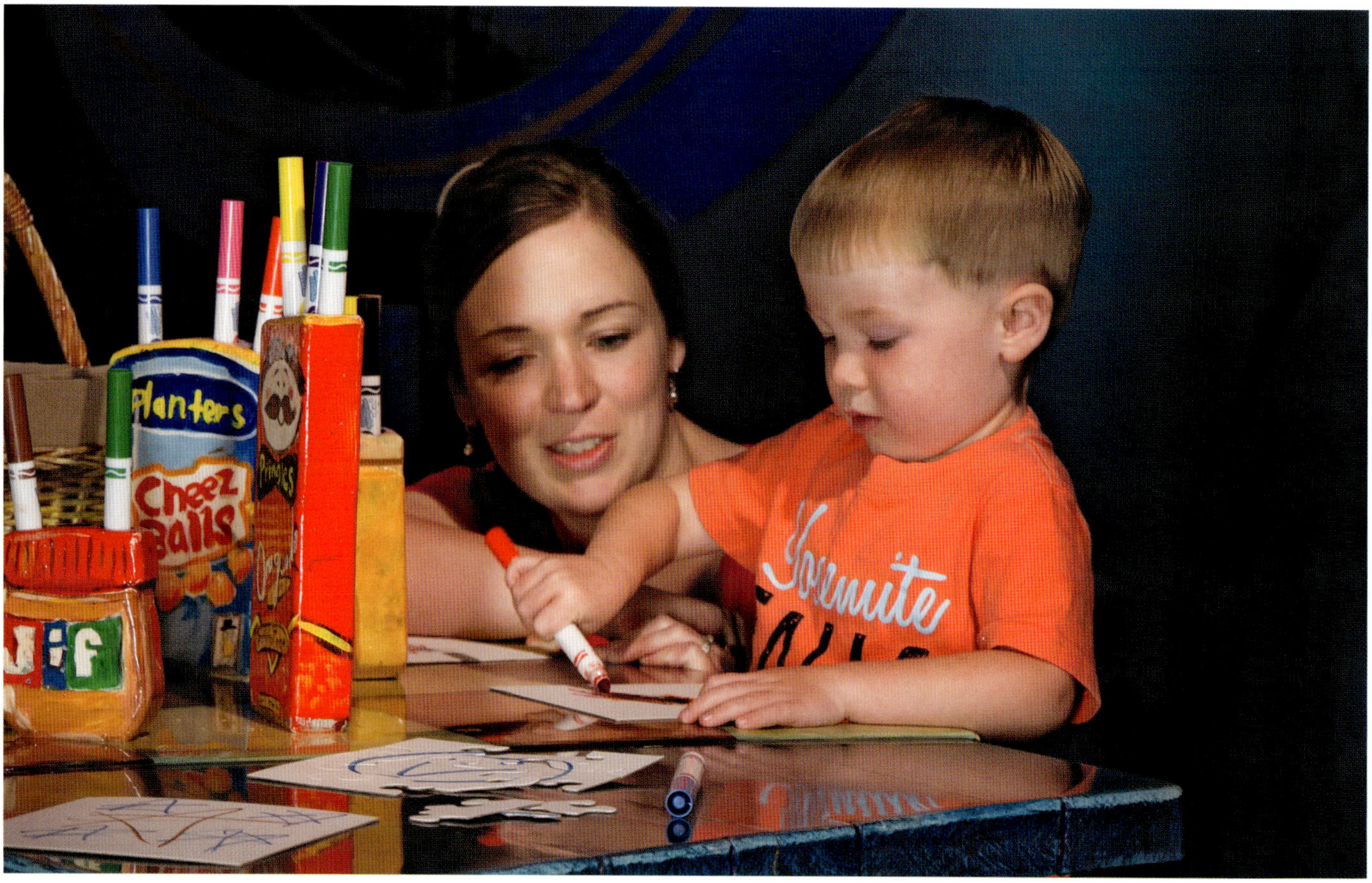

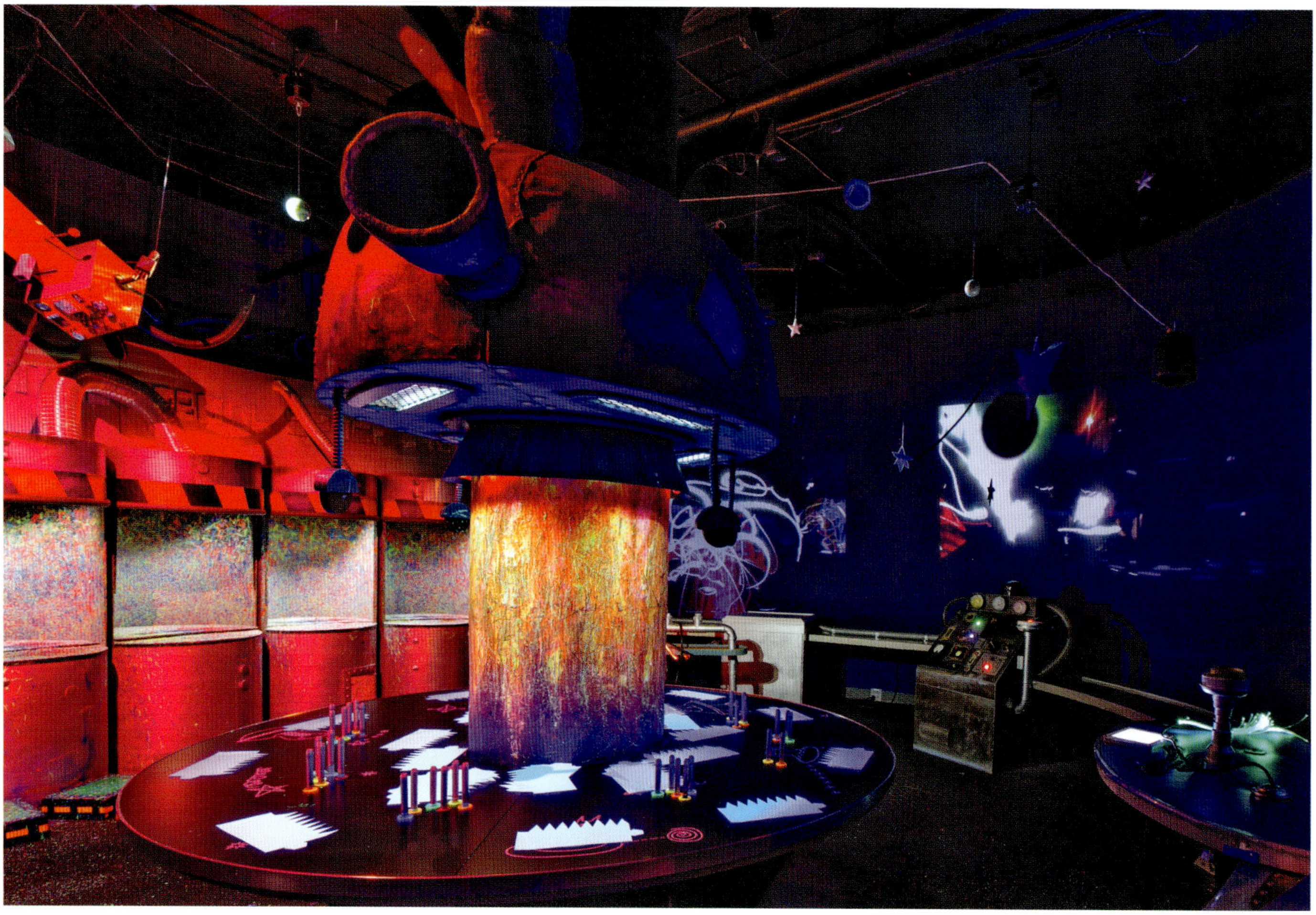

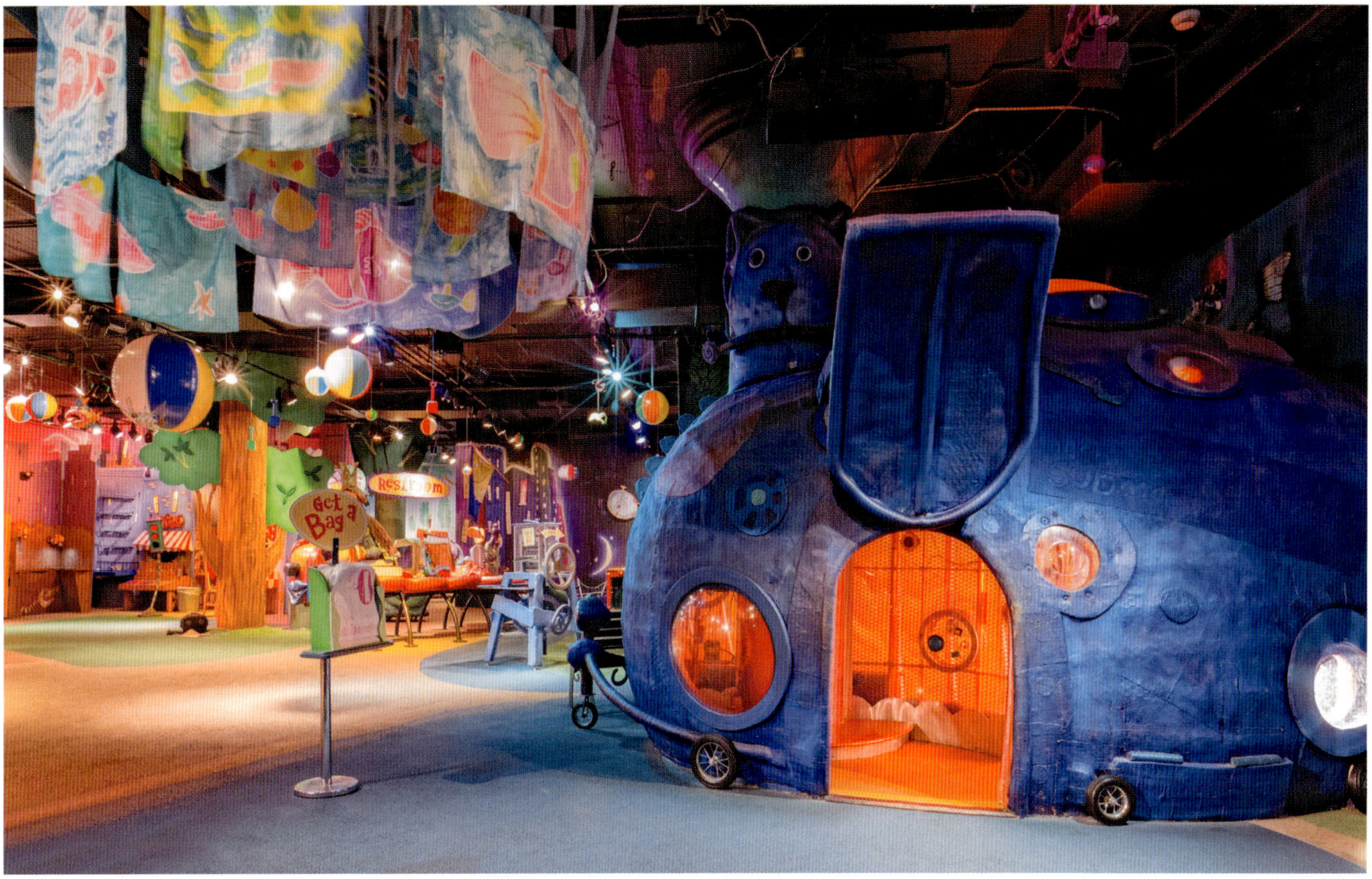

Kaleidoscope *(above and right)*

This activity center for kids was built to challenge, nourish, and bring out a child's creativity. The free arts and crafts program leans heavily on imaginations and making. The materials at Kaleidoscope are donated from Hallmark's production processes and kids are allowed to take home all of their creations.

Kaleidoscope *(opposite, top and bottom)*

Comical sculptures and fanciful nooks abound in Kaleidoscope, providing children with lots of inspiration. There are bright colors and exaggerated, cartoonish art everywhere. Kids can be kids at the activity center and, given the freedom to express their feelings through art, they can create wondrous and amazing art.

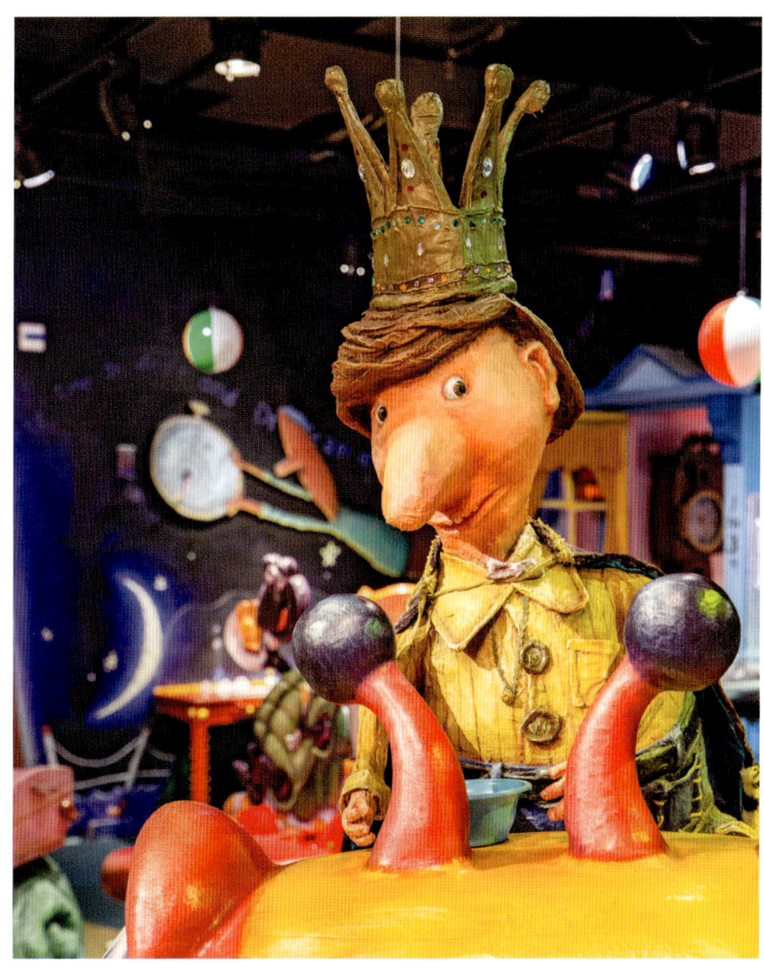

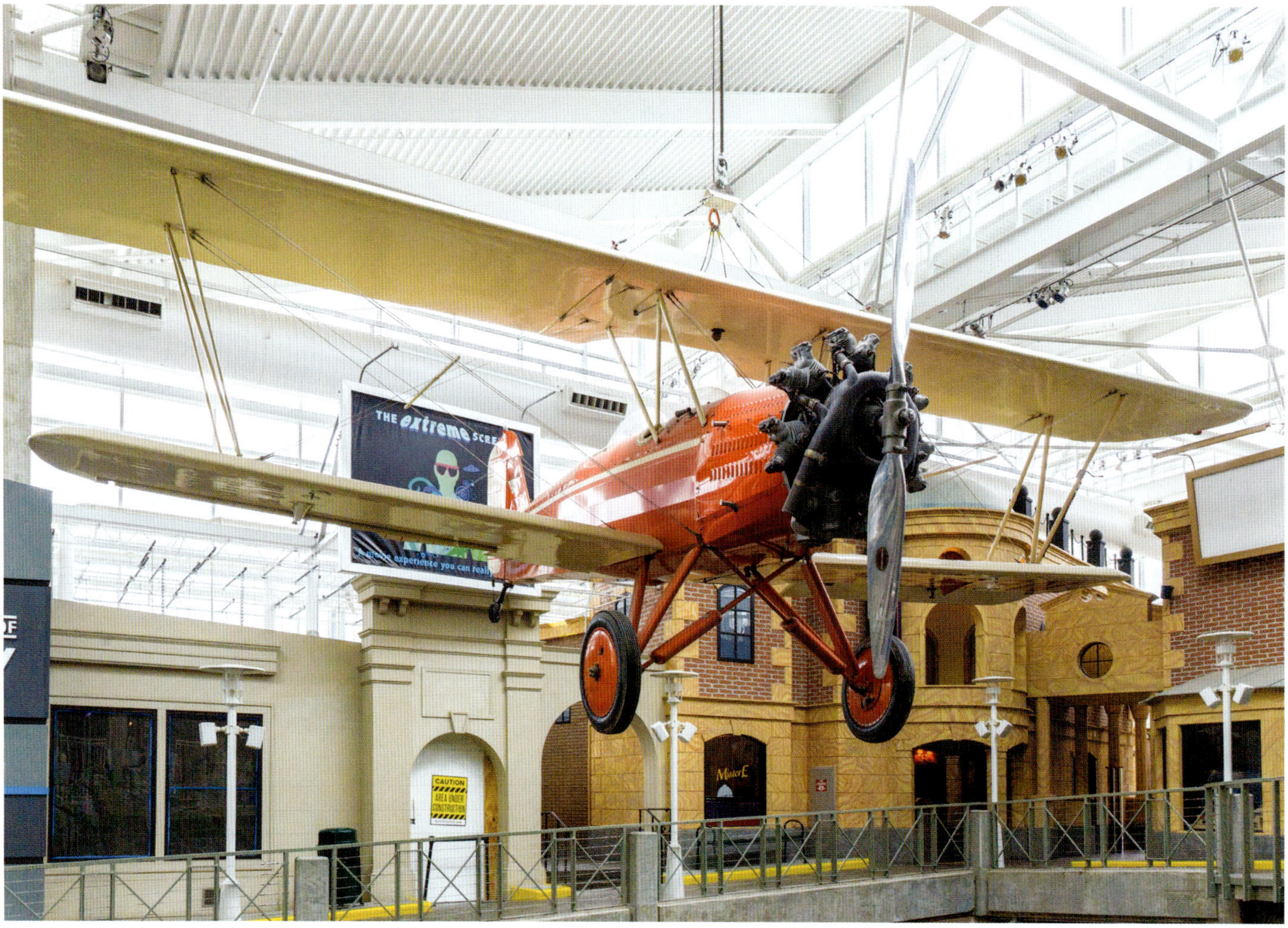

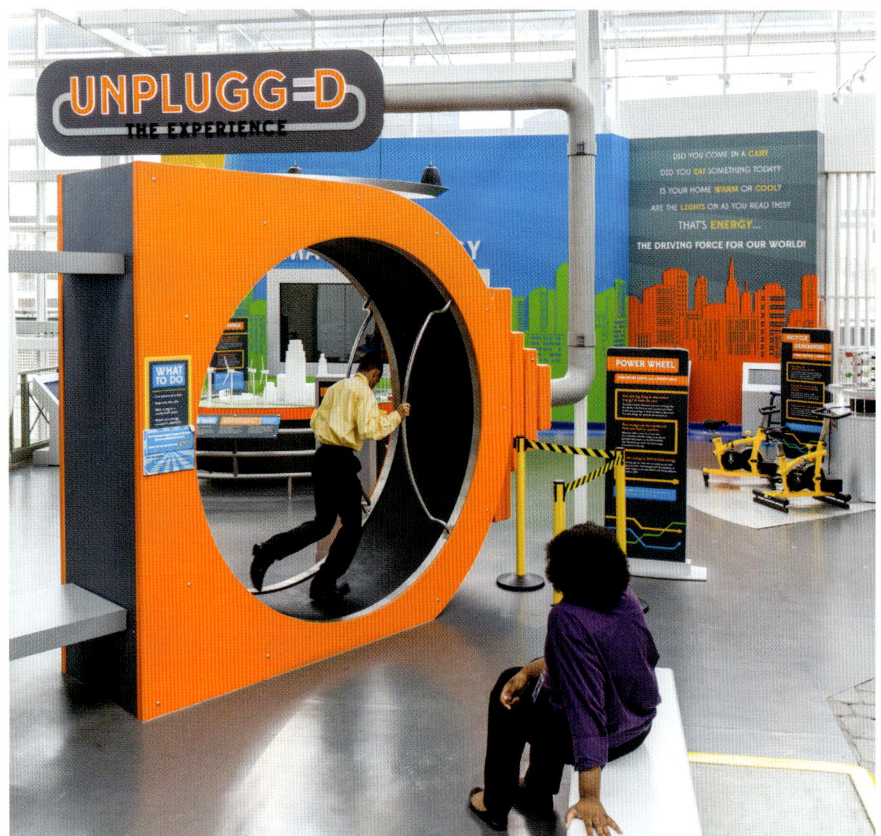

Science City *(above, left, and opposite)*

This engaging and interactive science center is a place of wonder. Kids and families get hands-on as they learn about all manner of scientific principles. Education comes by means of exploration, experimentation, and discovery. Before leaving, head over to the planetarium and enjoy a thought-provoking astronomical presentation.

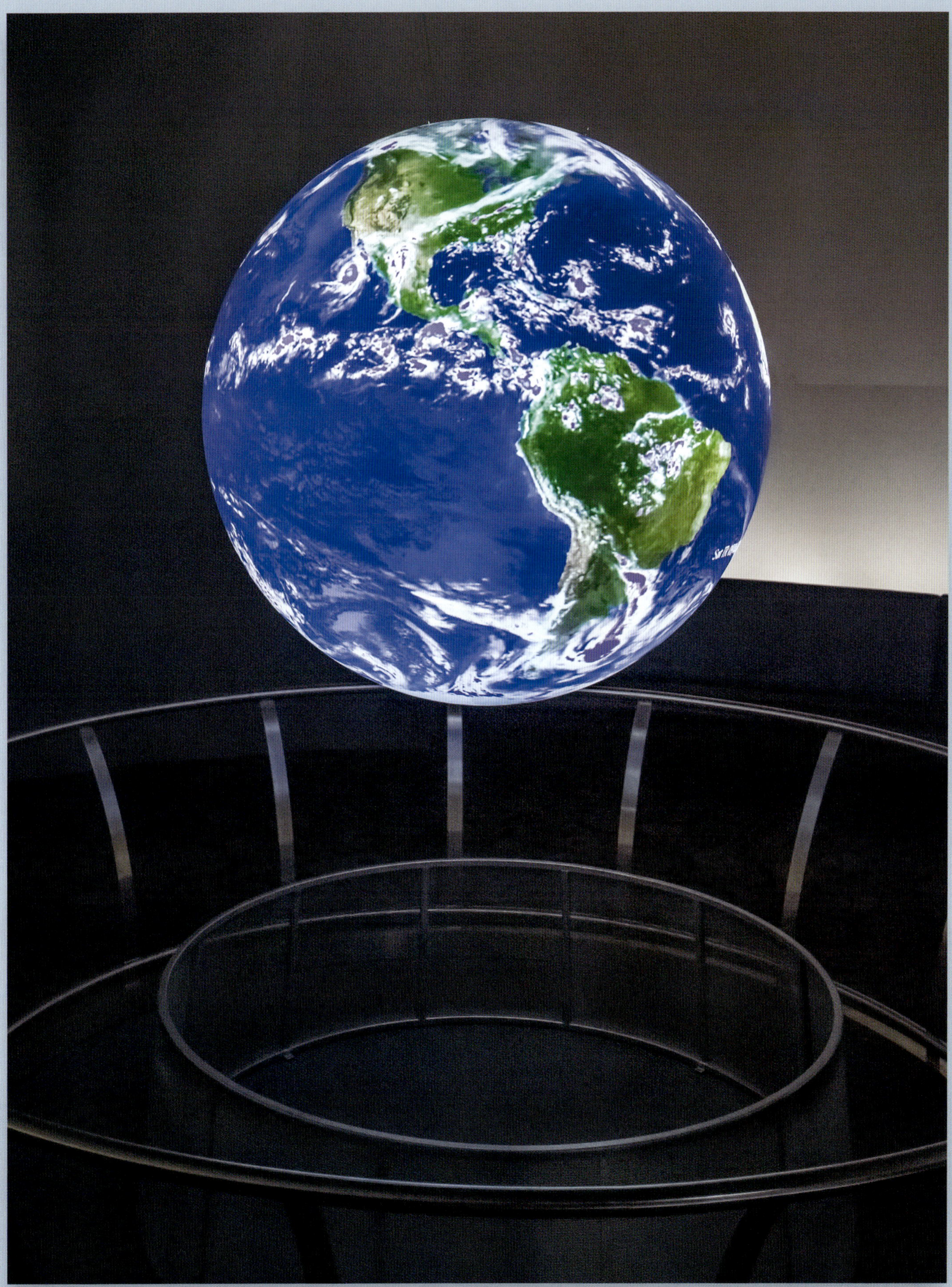

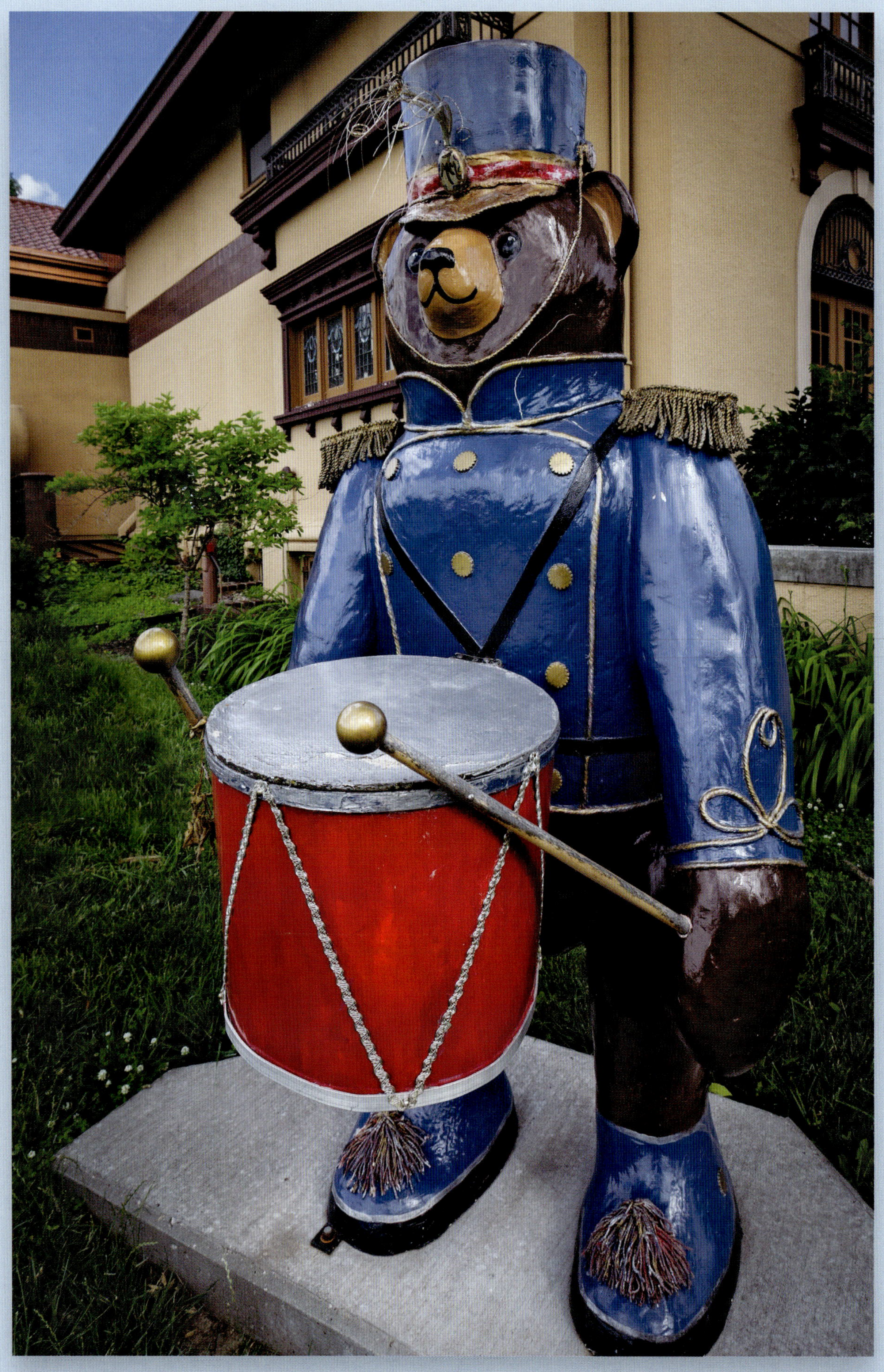

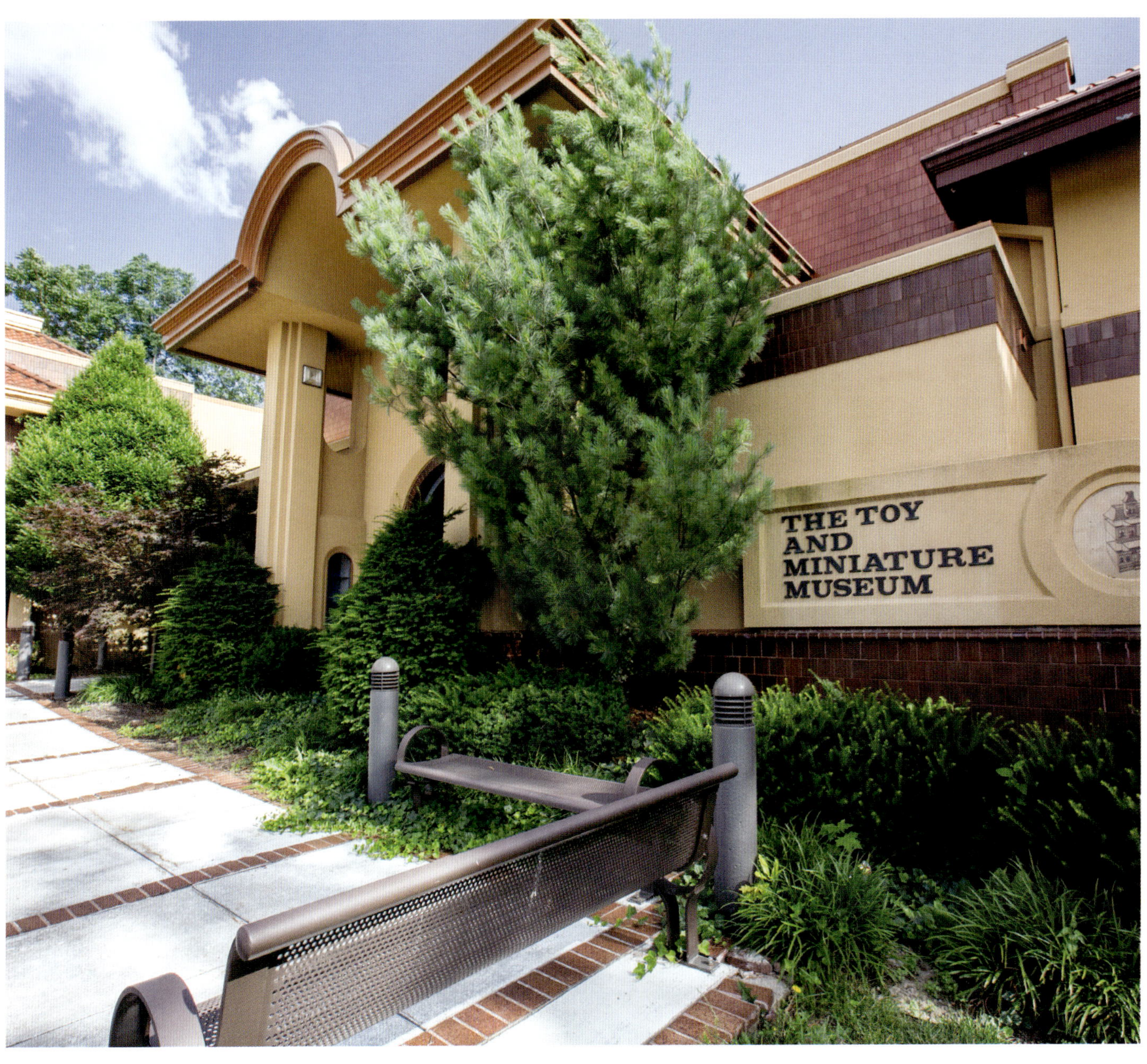

National Toy and Miniature Museum

(above and opposite)

The newly renovated museum is a must-see for kids of all ages. Before the days of disposable plastic, kids played with toys that lasted. An extensive collection of nostalgic amusements are housed here including elaborate doll houses and the world's largest collection of marbles.

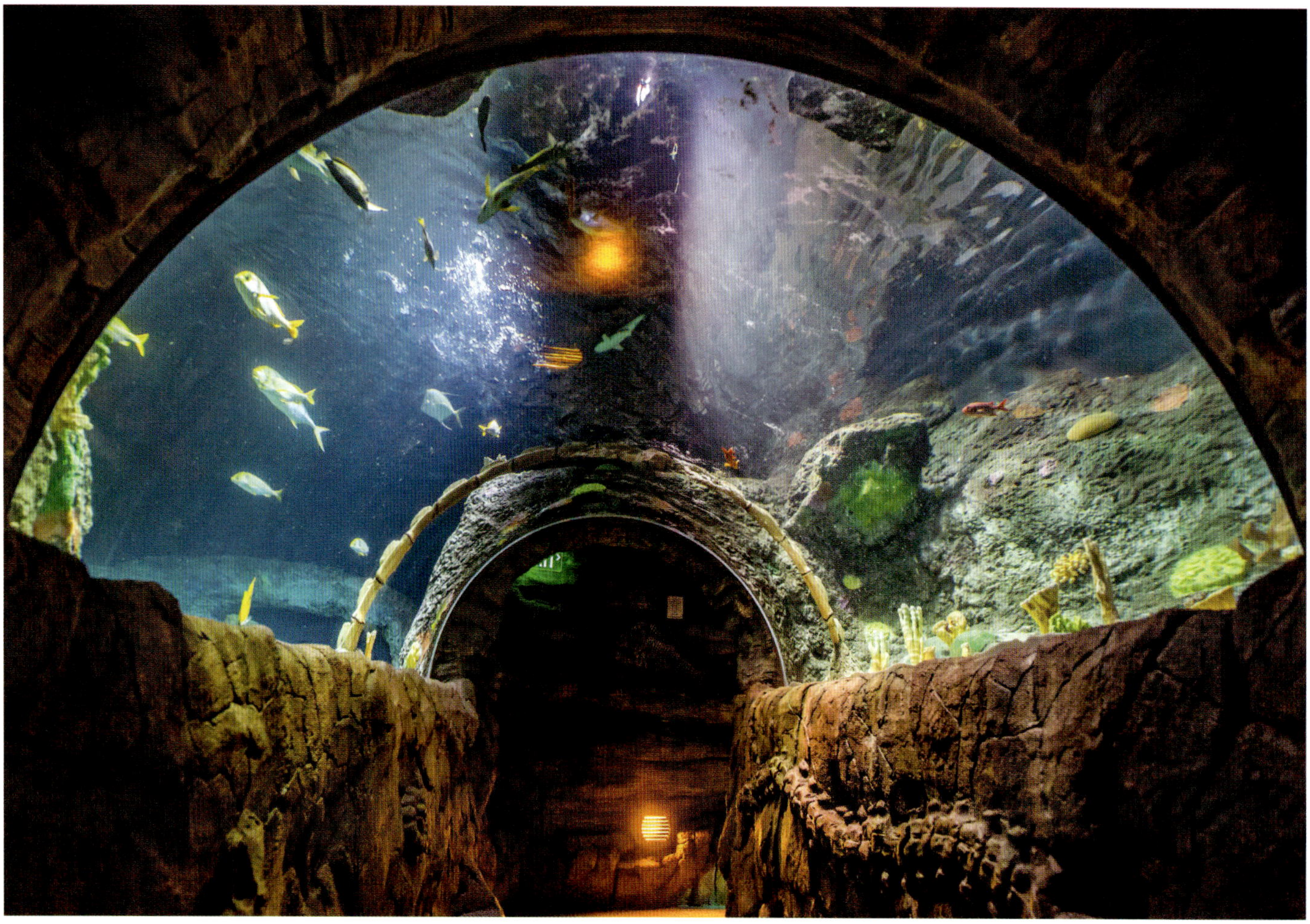

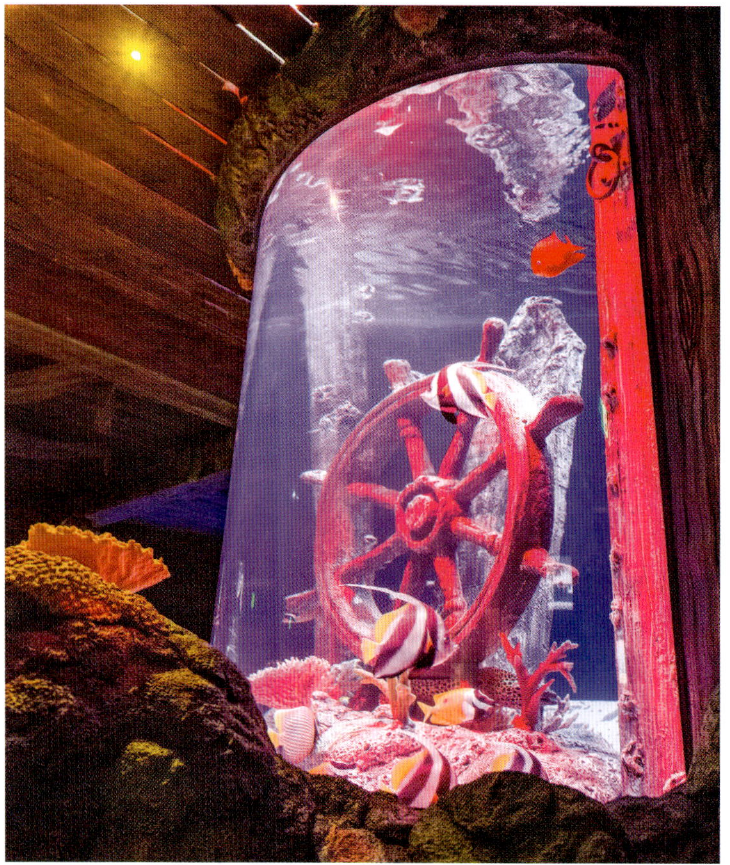

SEA LIFE Aquarium *(above and left)*

Kansas City is about as far as you can get from the ocean, however you can still get close to sharks, octopus, jellyfish, and lots of other sea creatures at the SEA LIFE Aquarium. The displays are geared toward kids and many allow for up-close encounters with marine life.

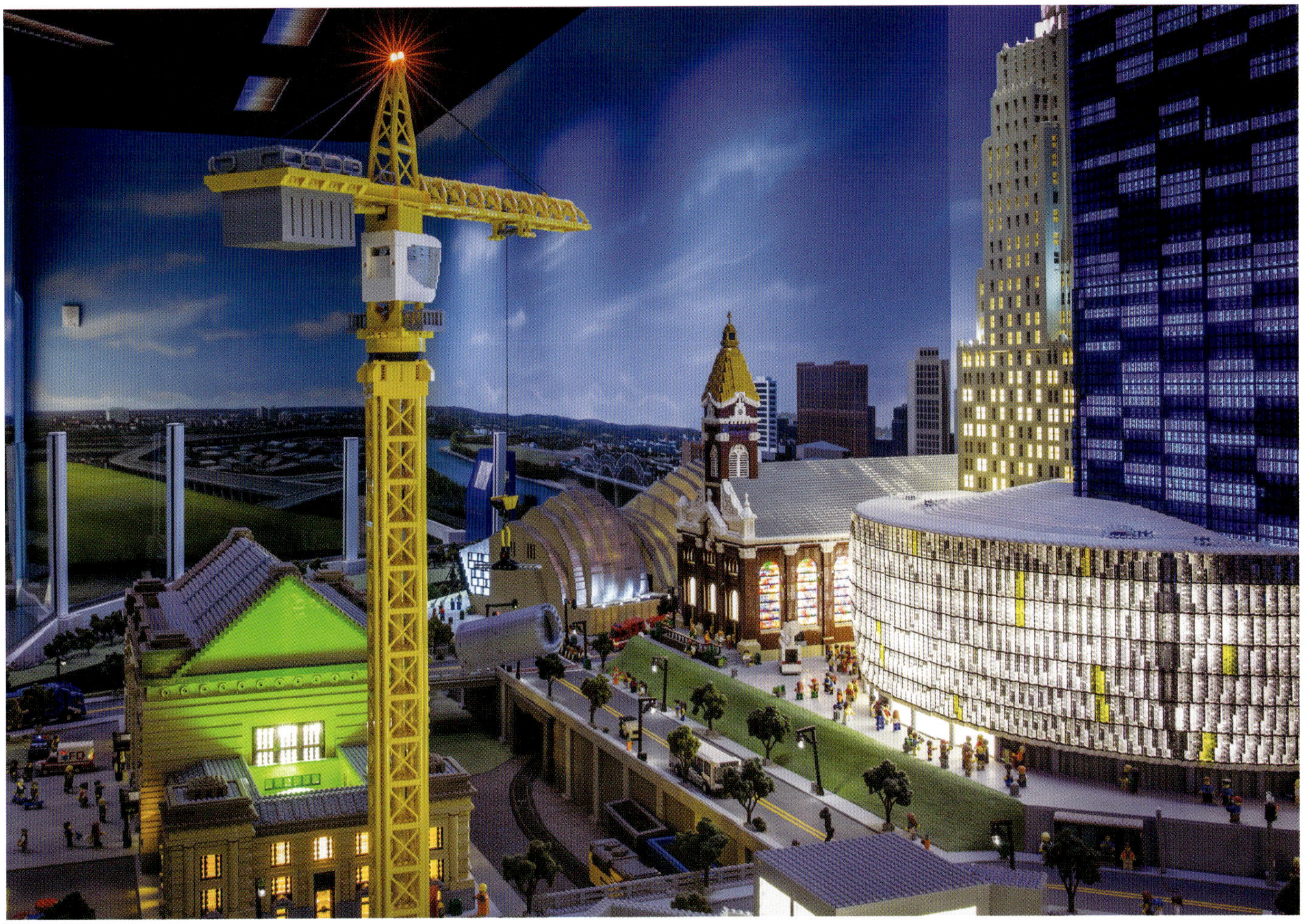

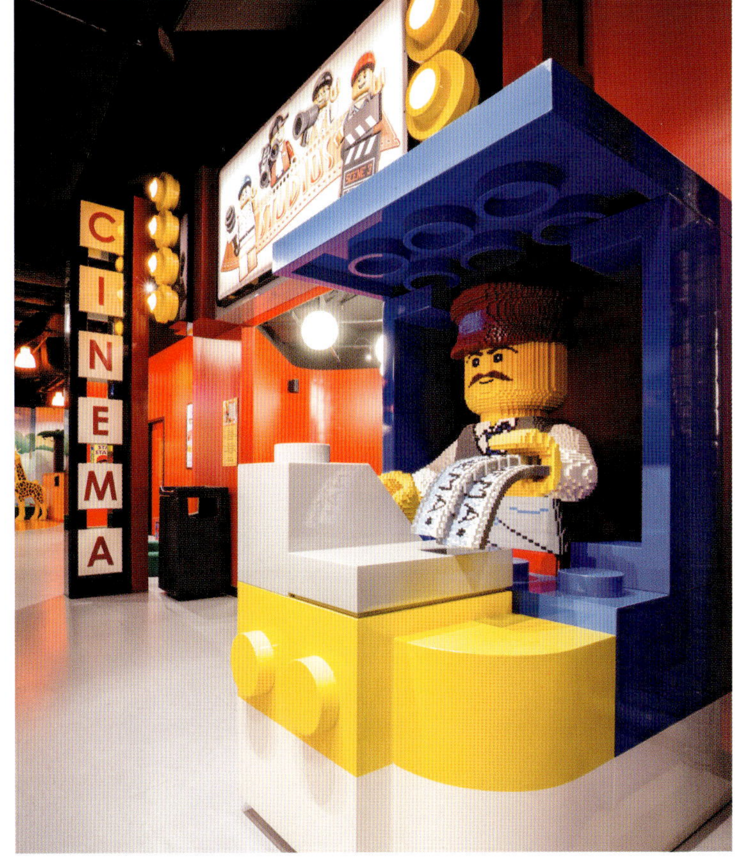

LEGOLAND® Discovery Center

(above and right)

There's plenty to see and do at the indoor Discovery Center. Kids can build and race fantastical cars, ride a roller coaster, watch a 4D movie, or create a building to withstand an earthquake. A popular attraction is the miniature replica of Kansas City's landmarks made with LEGO bricks.

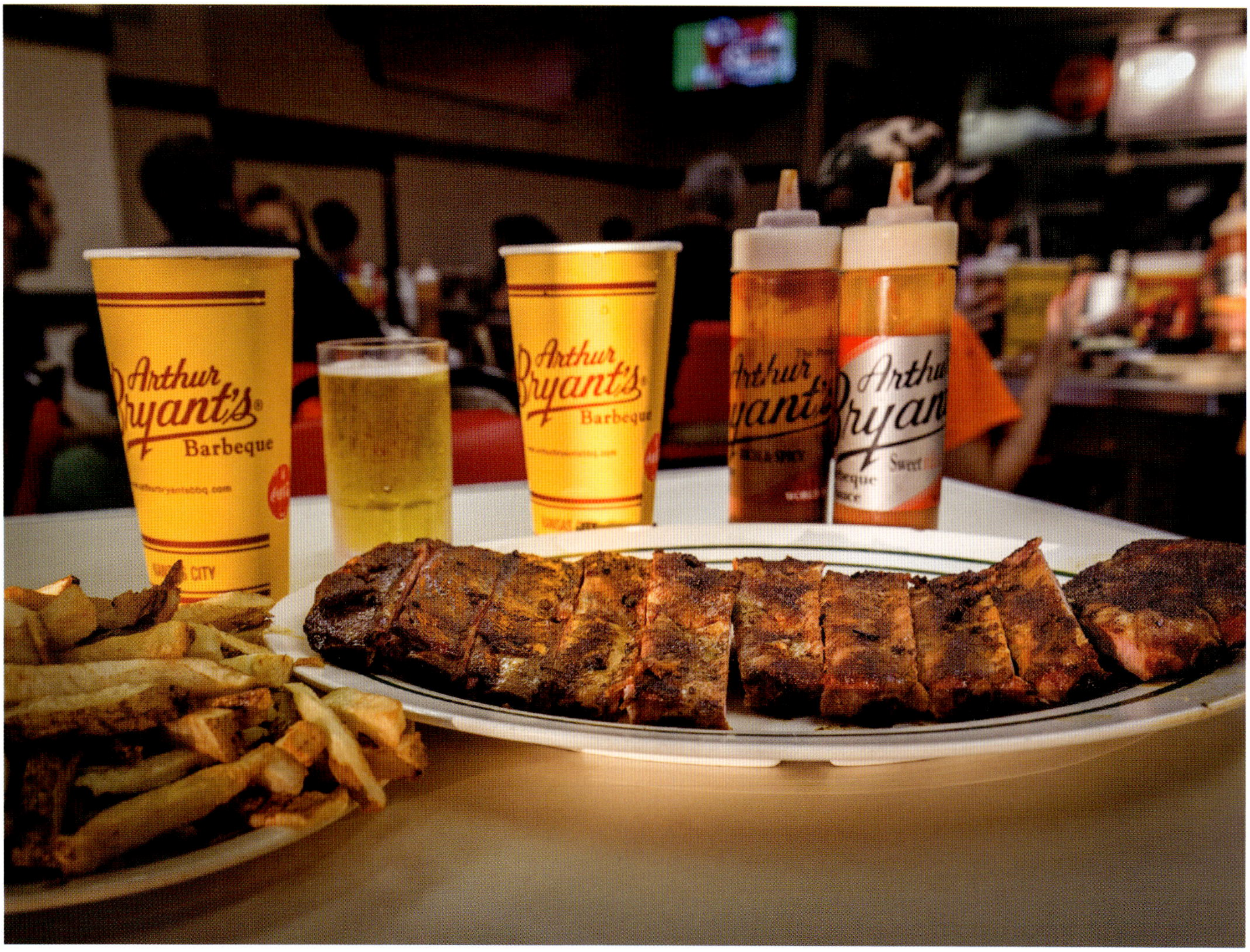

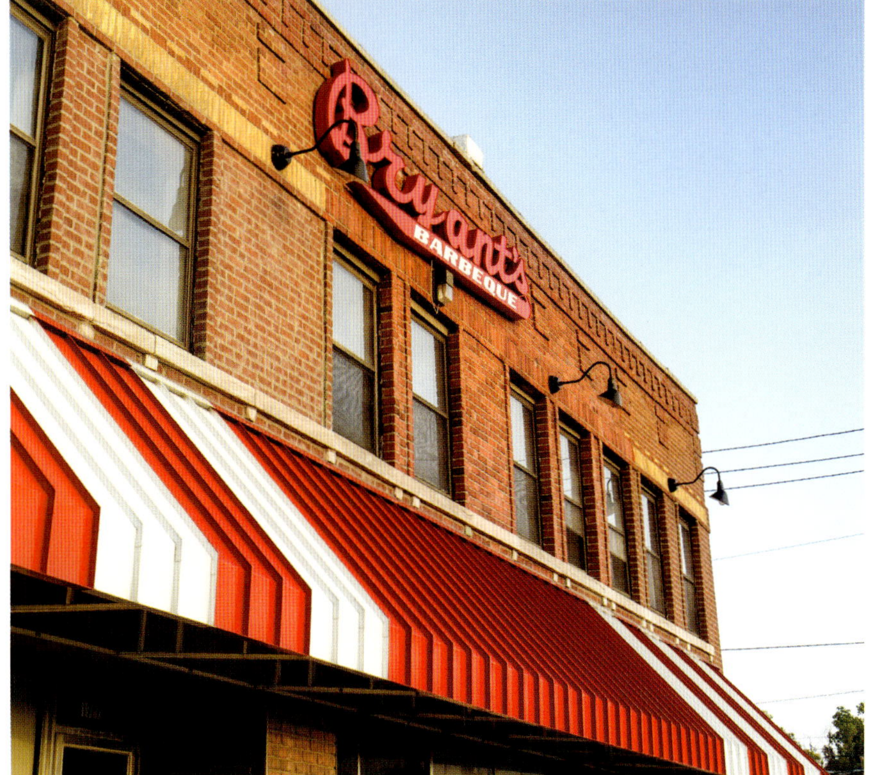

Arthur Bryant's Barbeque *(above and left)*

In a city full of world-class barbecue restaurants, Arthur Bryant's stands tall. The legendary and unpretentious eatery is considered by many to be the most famous barbecue restaurant in the world. A very long list of presidents and celebrities have dined on Bryant's ribs and tall-stacked sandwiches.

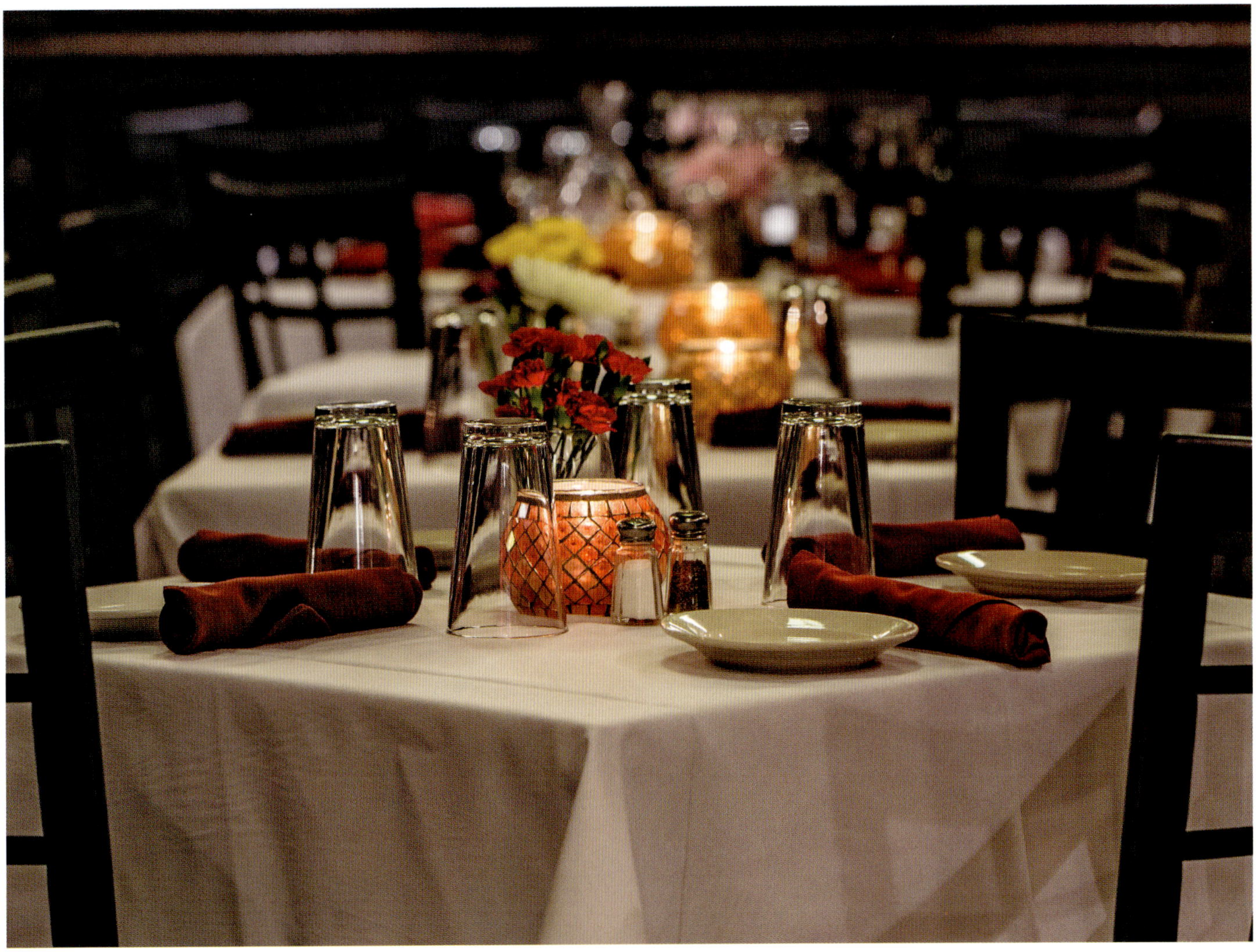

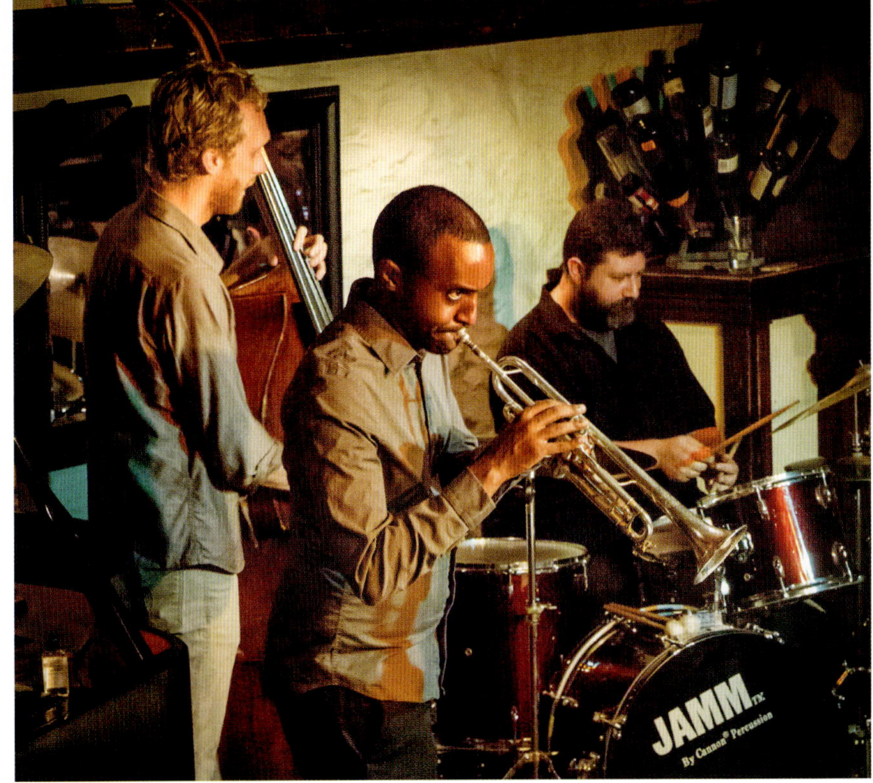

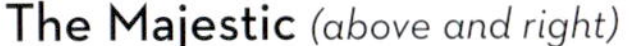

The Majestic *(above and right)*

Not far from Kansas City's historic stockyards sits one of the finest steakhouses in a city that loves its red meat. When making a reservation, ask for a downstairs table to enjoy some live jazz with your meal. The Majestic is also a hotspot for weekend brunch.

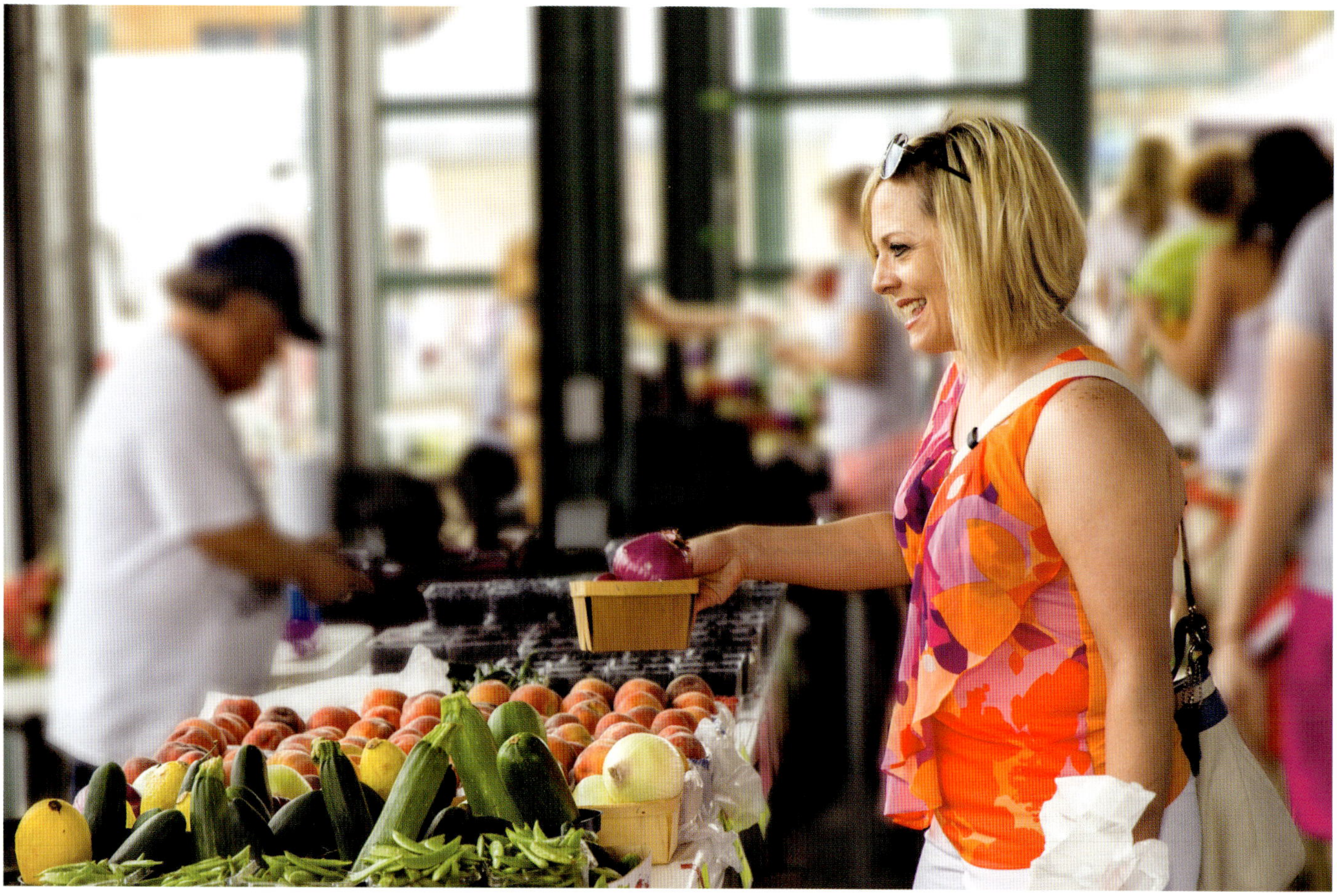

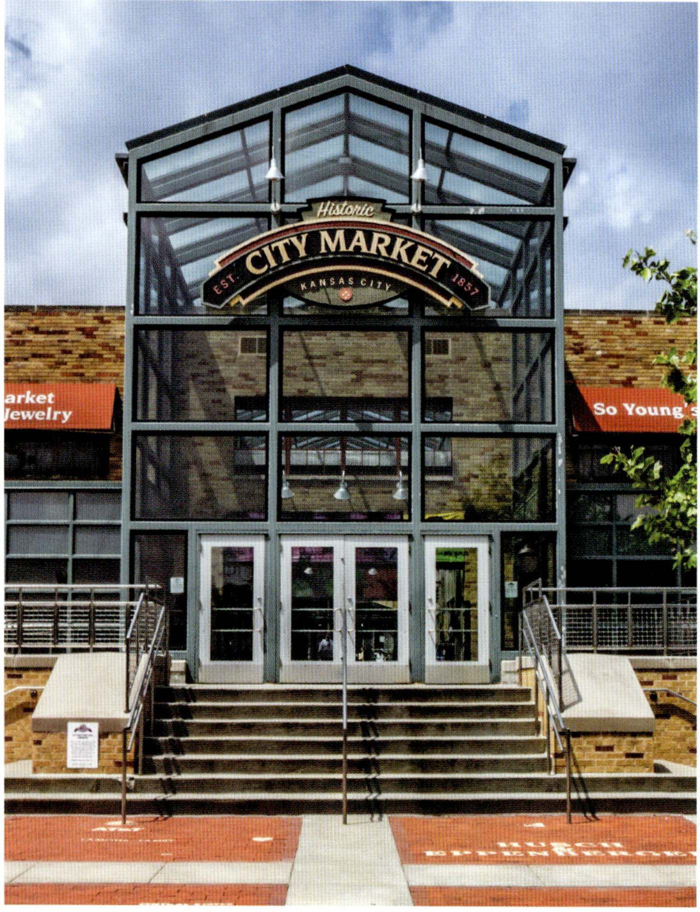

City Market *(above and left)*

For more than 150 years, the City Market has been the place for farmers and growers to offer their fare to the public. Walking the outdoor stalls, you'll be treated to a savory and fragrant mix of farm-fresh seasonal fruits, vegetables, flowers, meats, specialty groceries, and more.

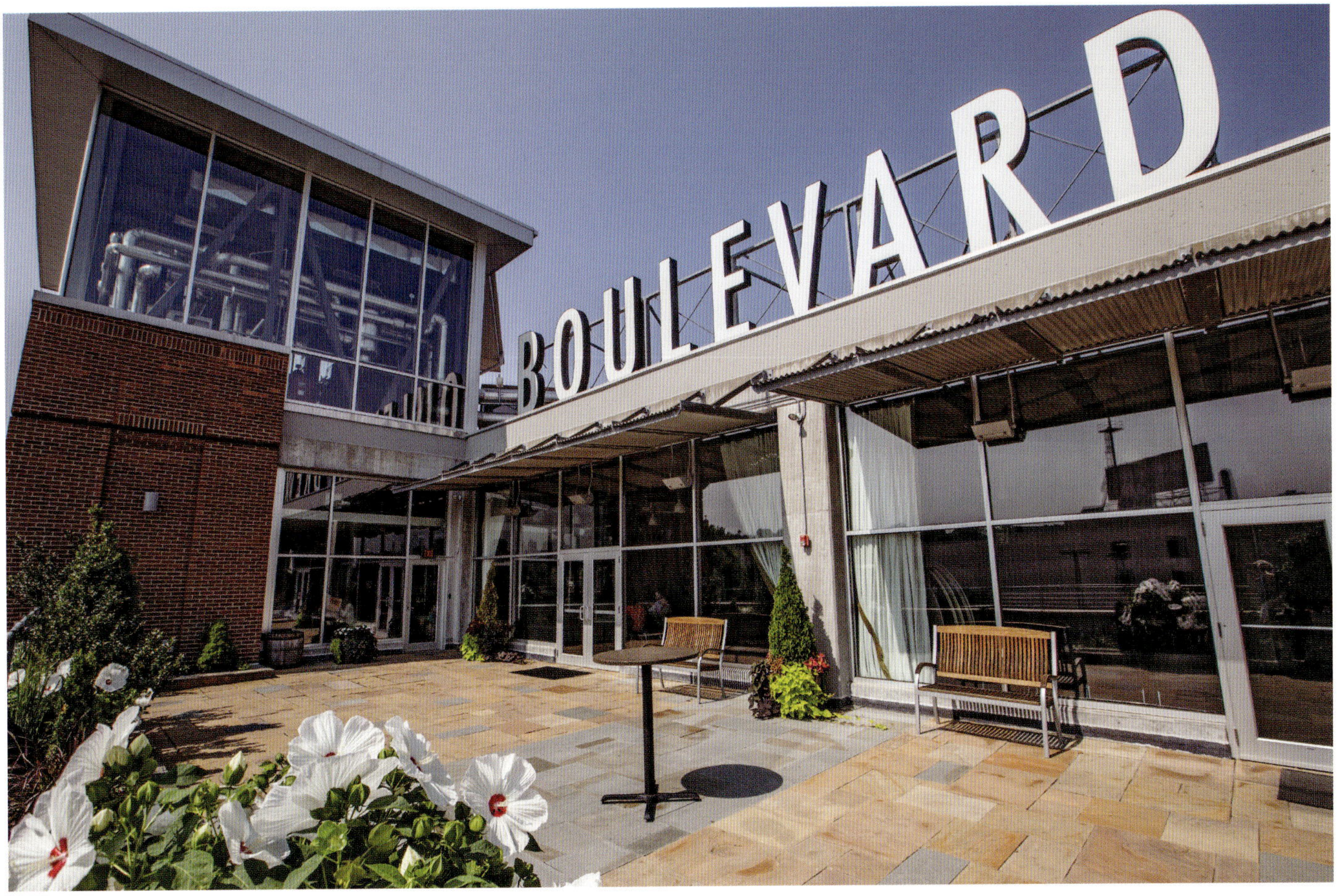

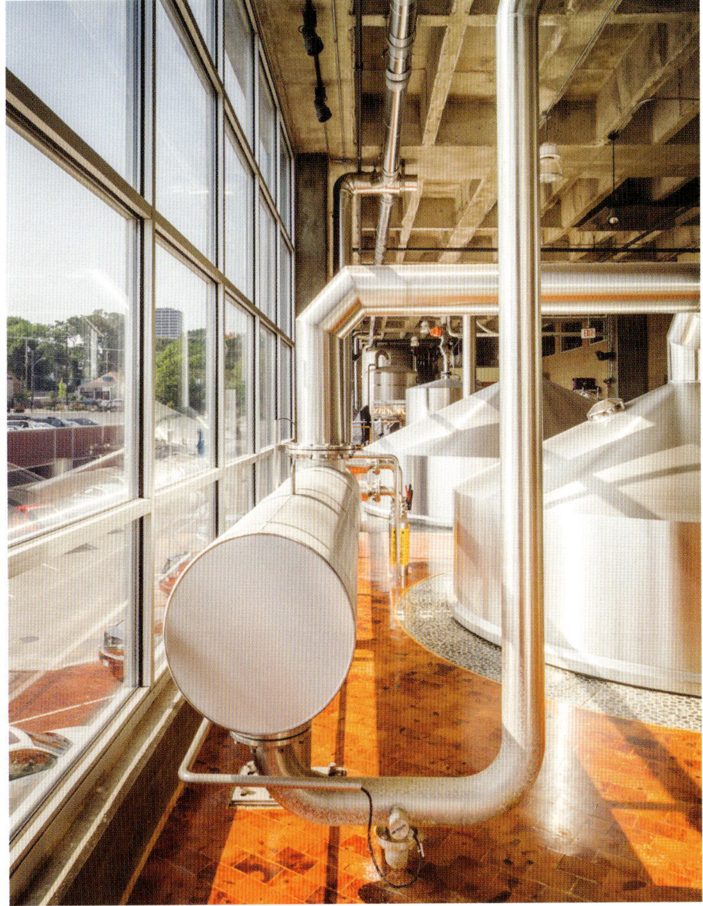

Boulevard Brewing Company

(above and right)

Boulevard is one of the largest craft brewers in the nation with more than a dozen flavorful year-round beers and a large offering of seasonal brews. Their Chocolate Ale is so sought after, it's not unusual to see customers following delivery trucks when it's released. Tours are available daily.

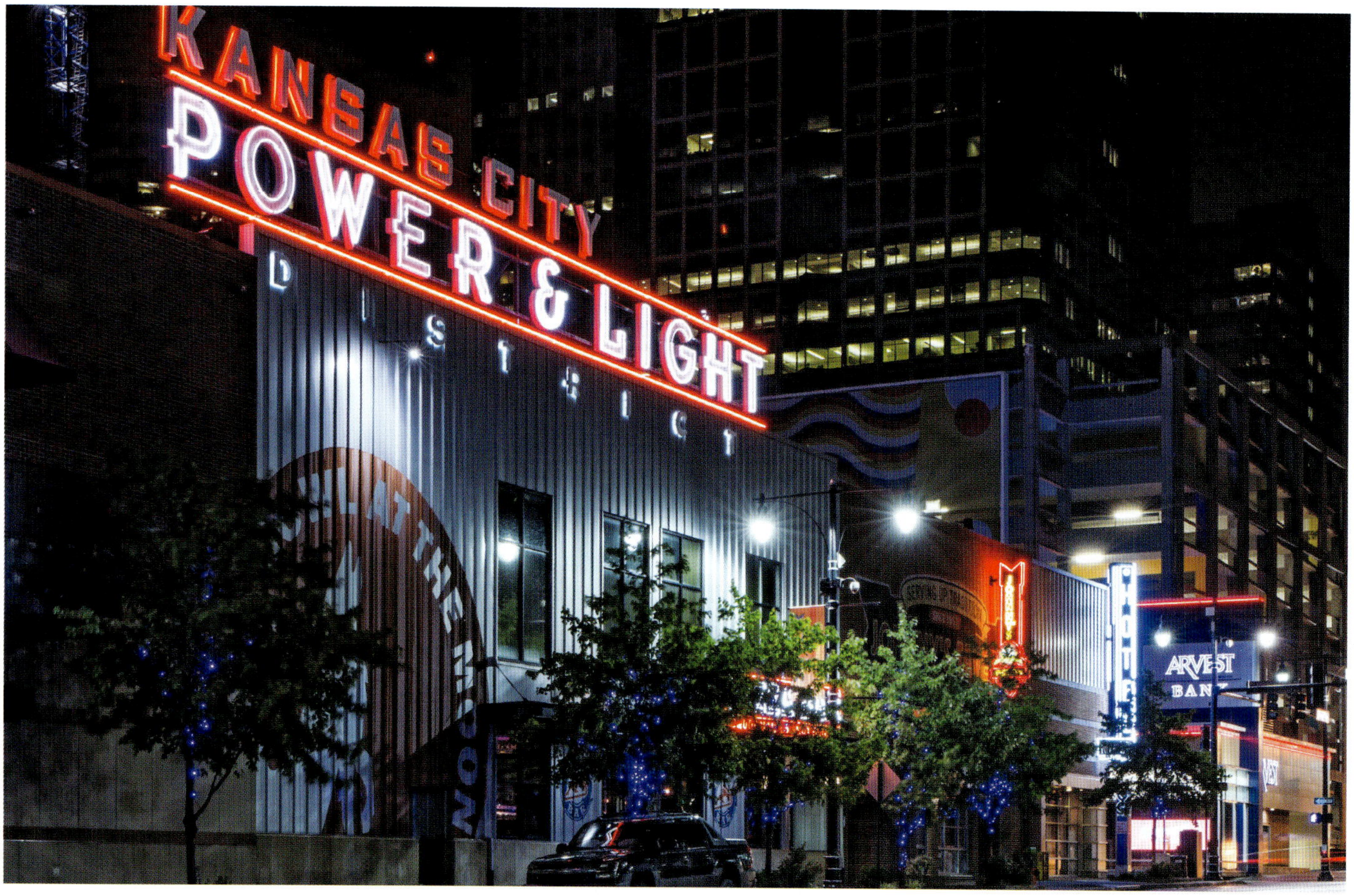

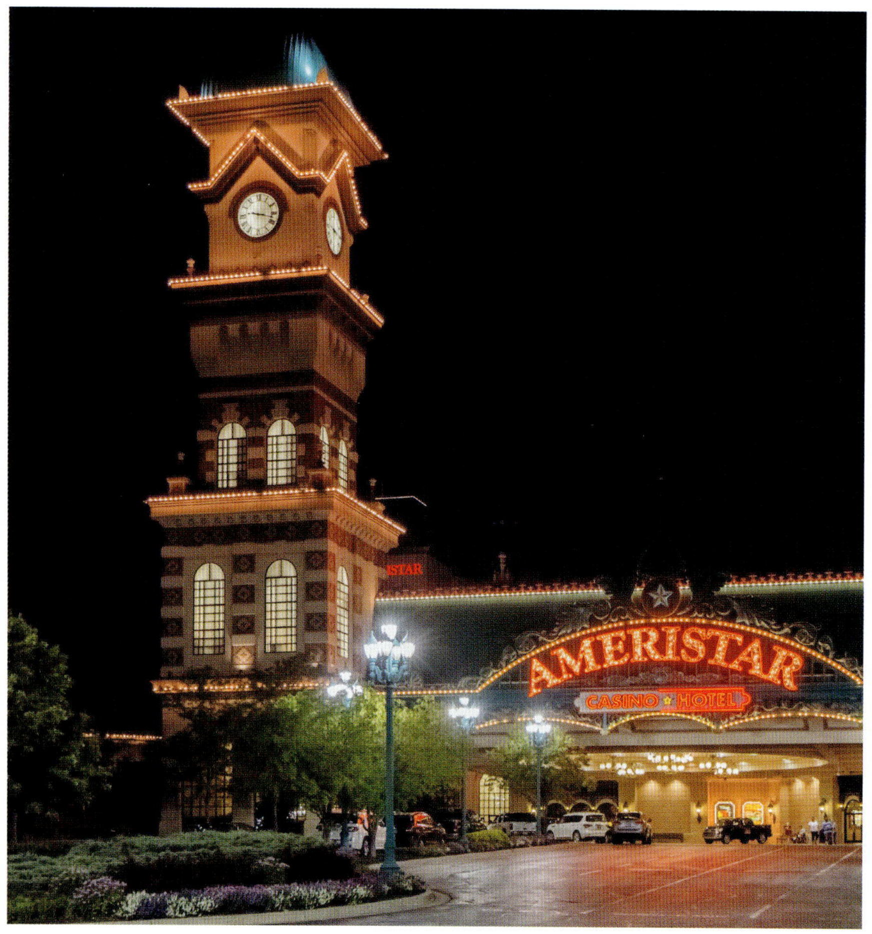

Power & Light District *(above)*

At the center of downtown and one of the hottest spots for nightlife, the "P&L" is home to a bounty of bars and restaurants. Most are just a short walk from KC's largest arena, offering lots of choices for a quick drink or bite before a game or concert.

Riverboat Casinos *(left and opposite)*

Riverboat casinos used to ply their entertainment up and down the rivers that cut through Kansas City. They still do, but the boats are perpetually docked. Fine dining, entertainment, and nightlife are other opportunities if gambling's not your thing. If you're feeling lucky, head on out "to the boats."

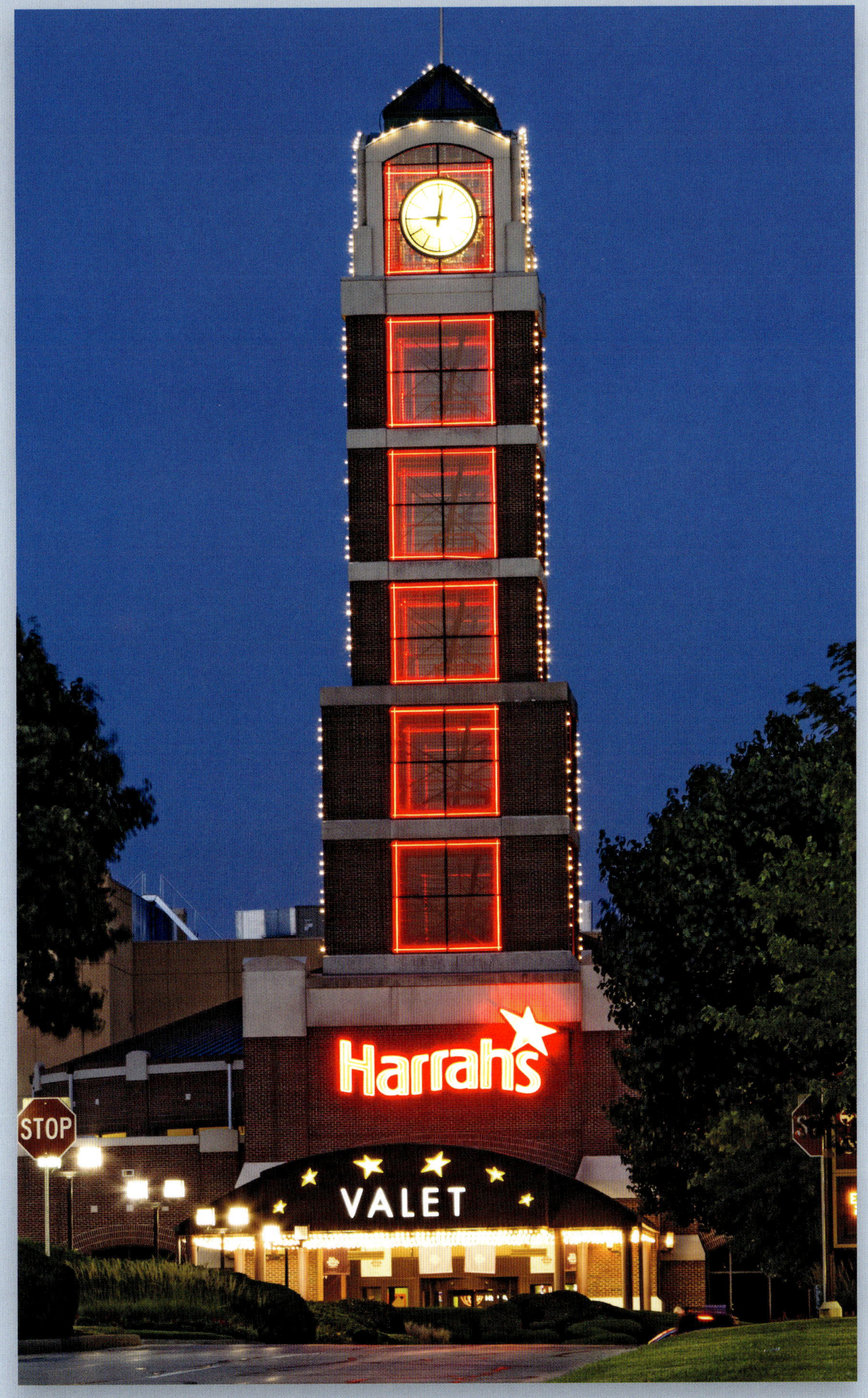
Harrah's
VALET
STOP

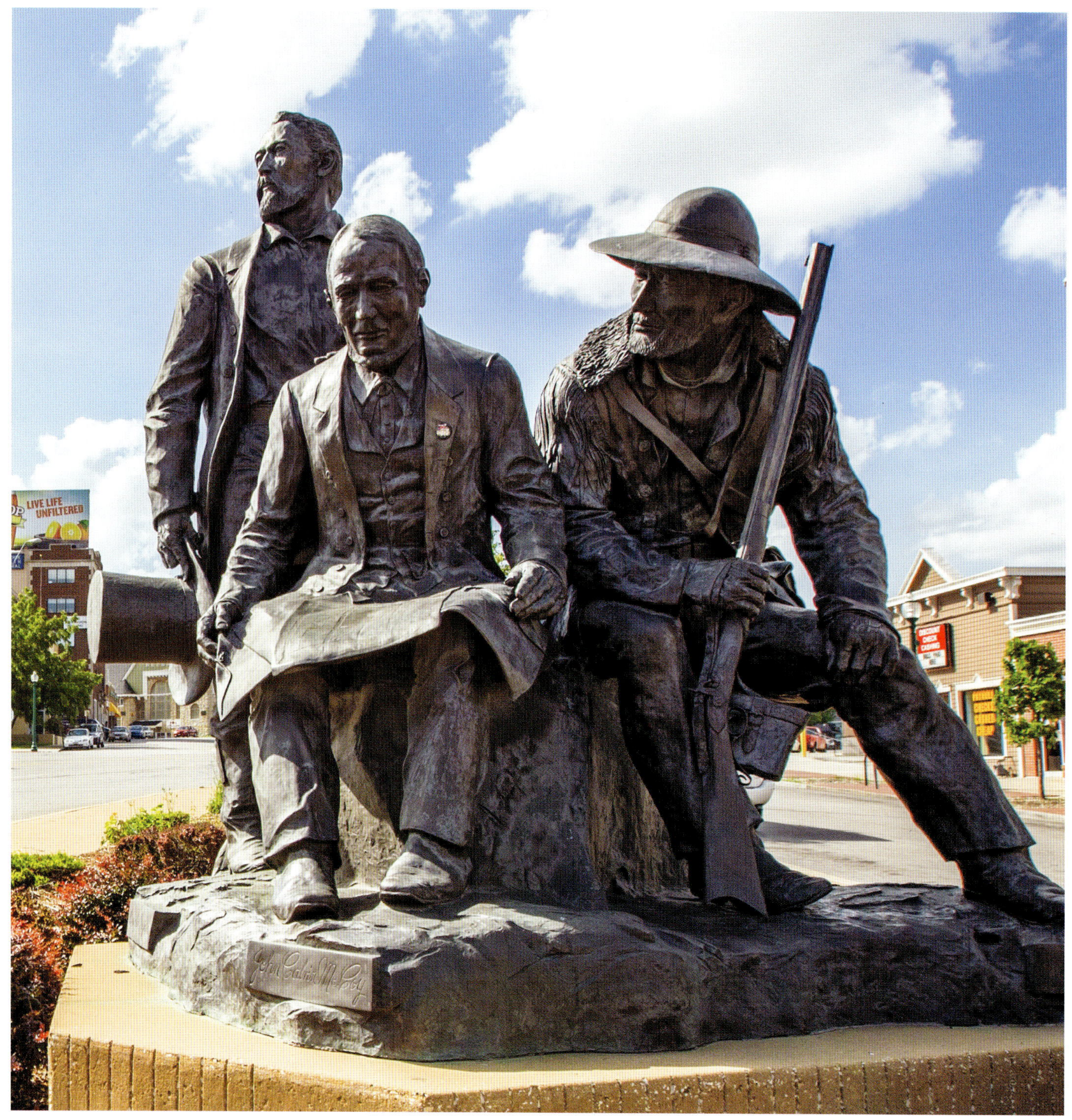

Westport and Pioneer Park

Westport was a supply stop for three westward trails—the Santa Fe, California, and Oregon. This statue commemorates frontiersman Jim Bridger (right) and businessmen John C. McCoy and Alexander Majors (left), who ran Westport's saloons and dance halls. You can still drink and dance in Westport's many bars and nightclubs.

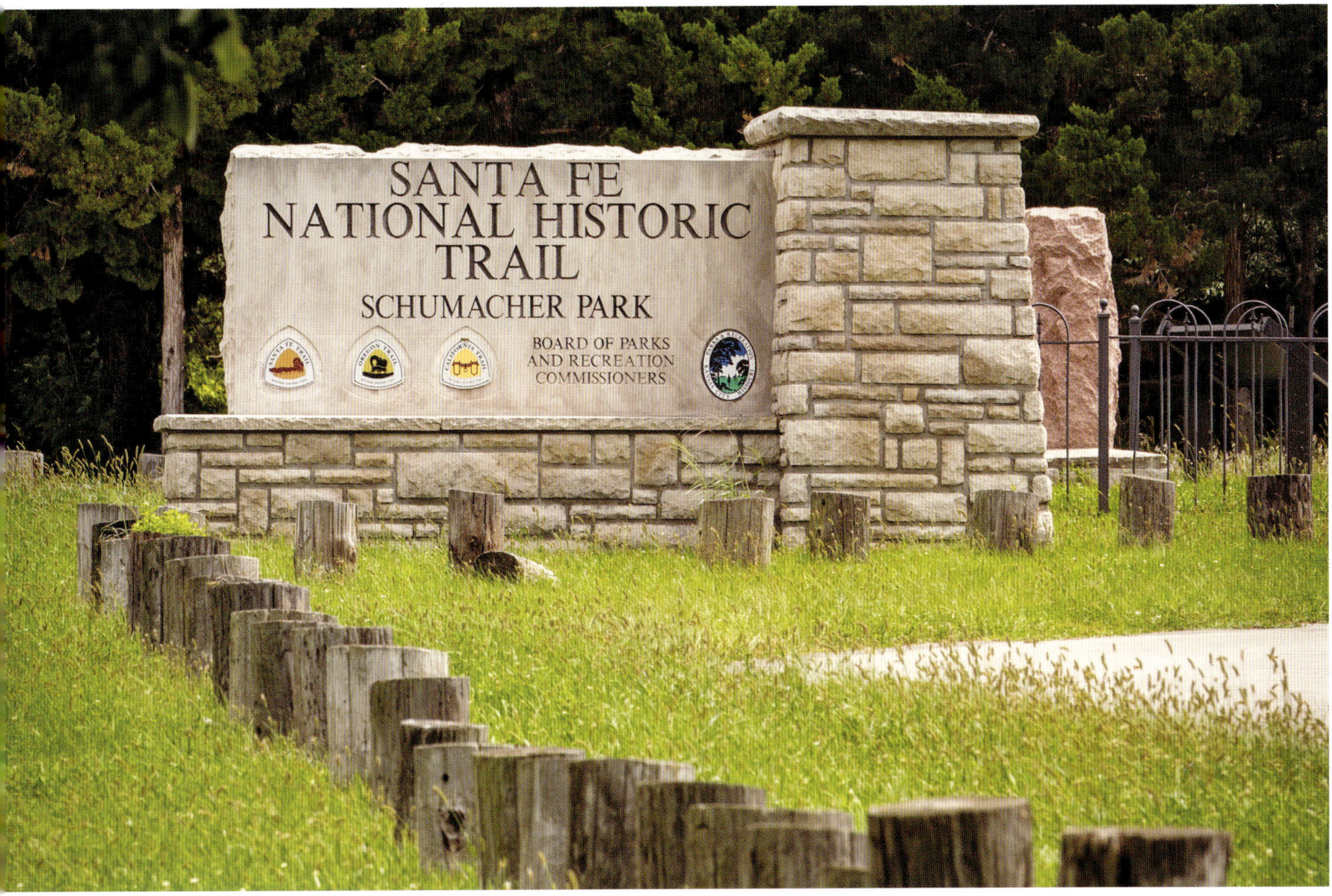

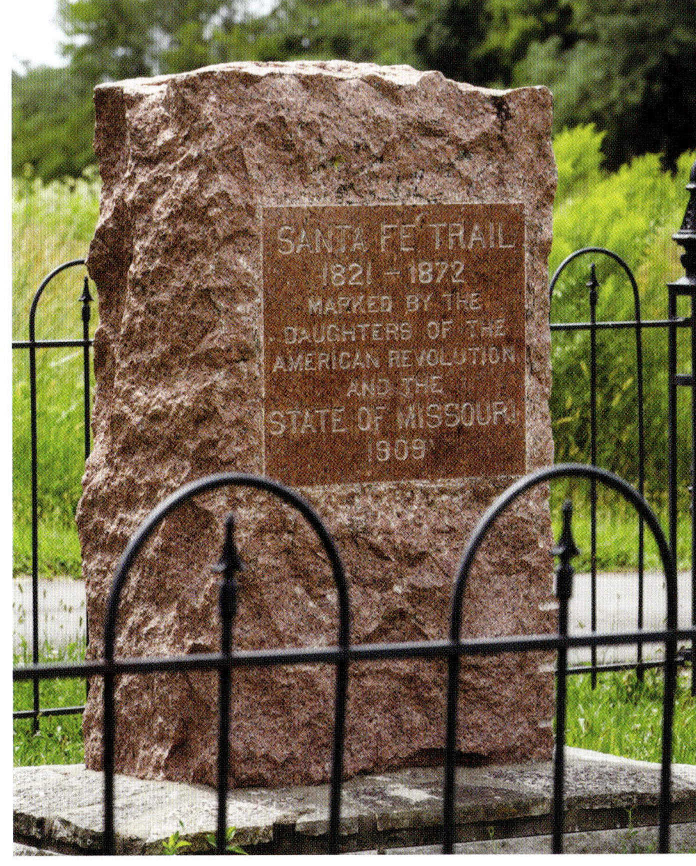

Oregon Trail and Santa Fe Trail

(above and right)

Kansas City was a starting point to western destinations. Travelers secured goods and made final plans before heading off on two famous trails. Both departed from Independence, Missouri, headed east through KC via Westport, before splitting toward Santa Fe, New Mexico and Oregon City, Oregon.

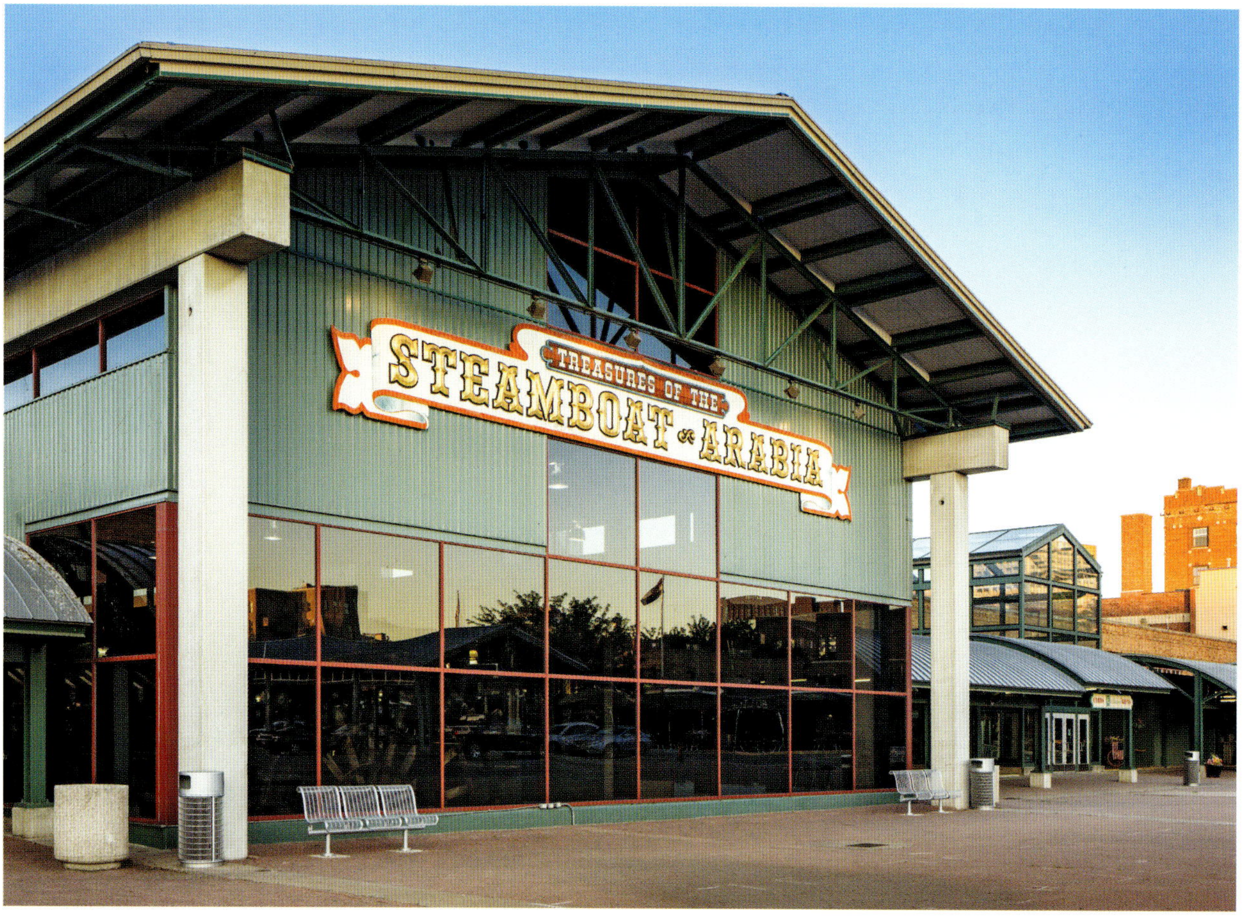
TREASURES OF THE
STEAMBOAT
ARABIA

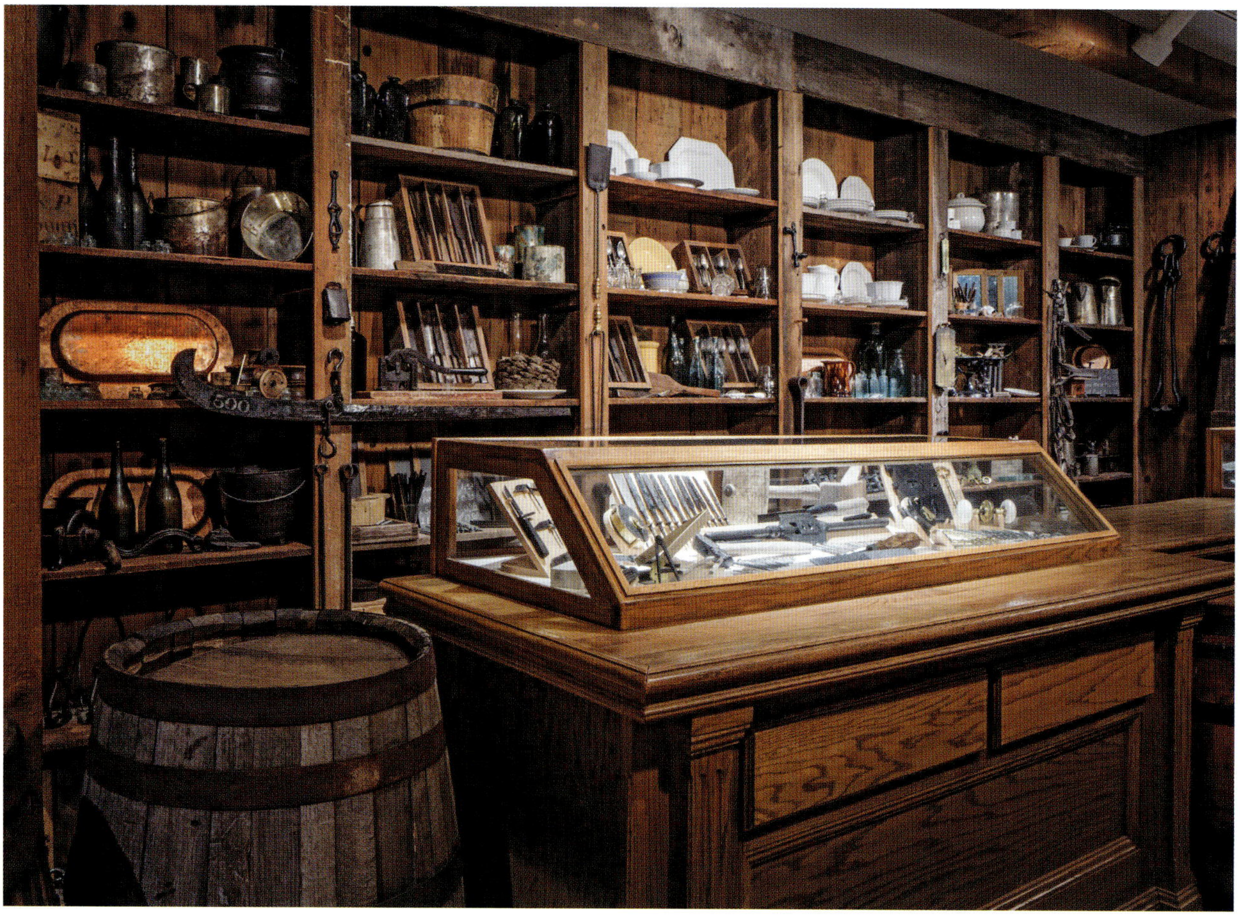

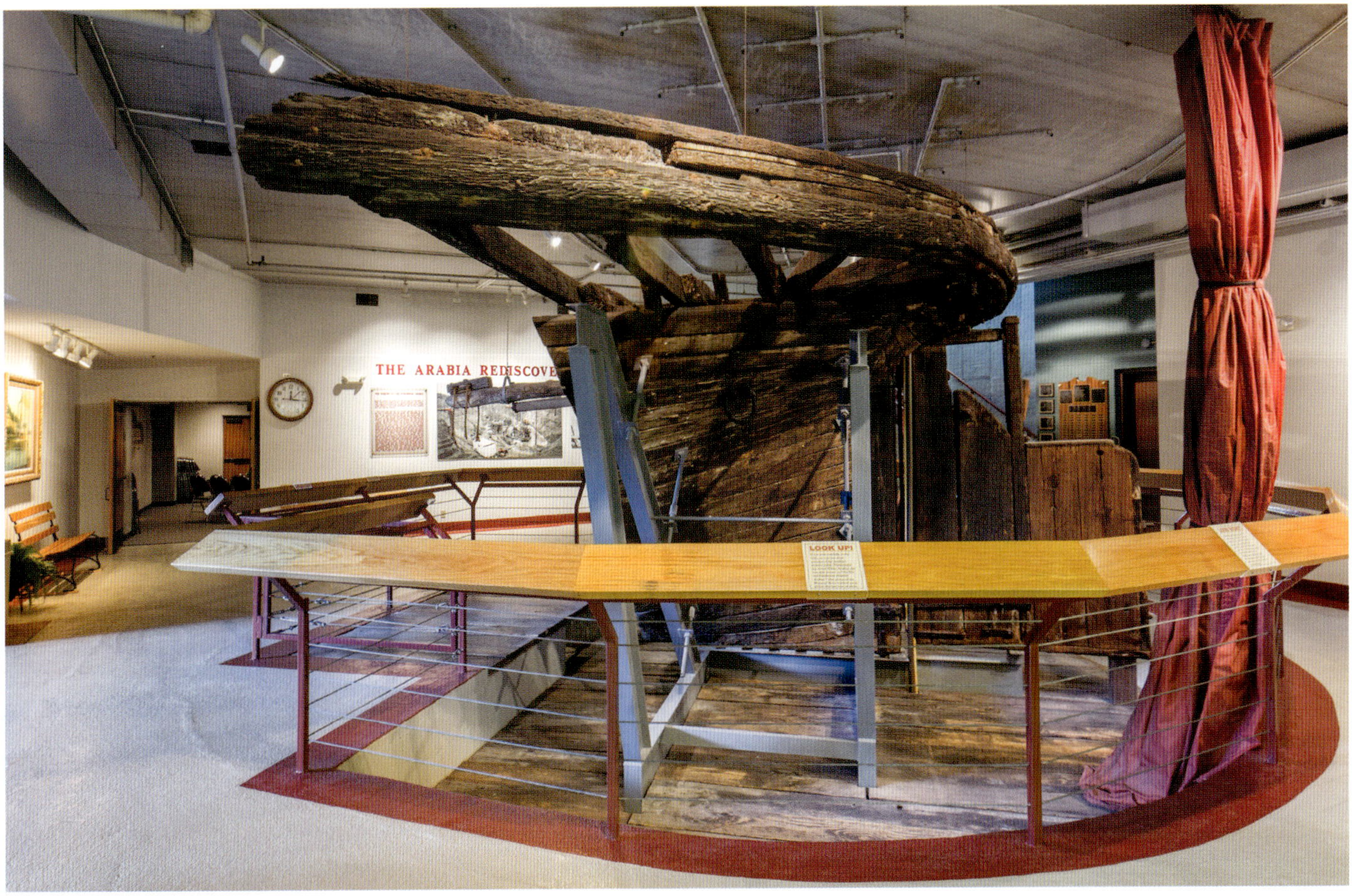

Arabia Steamboat Museum

(above and opposite bottom)

Loaded with 200 tons of supplies, the Steamboat *Arabia* sunk just outside Kansas City. One hundred fifty years later, the boat was discovered and what is a time capsule of pre-Civil War America was recovered and put on display. Just observing the impressive ongoing restoration is worth the price of admission.

Arabia Steamboat Museum

(opposite, top and right)

One of the challenges in displaying the artifacts of the Steamboat *Arabia* was finding a home large enough to display all the goods, the ongoing salvage, and the huge paddle wheel. Just the space was found in the City Market, where the museum has been for more than two decades.

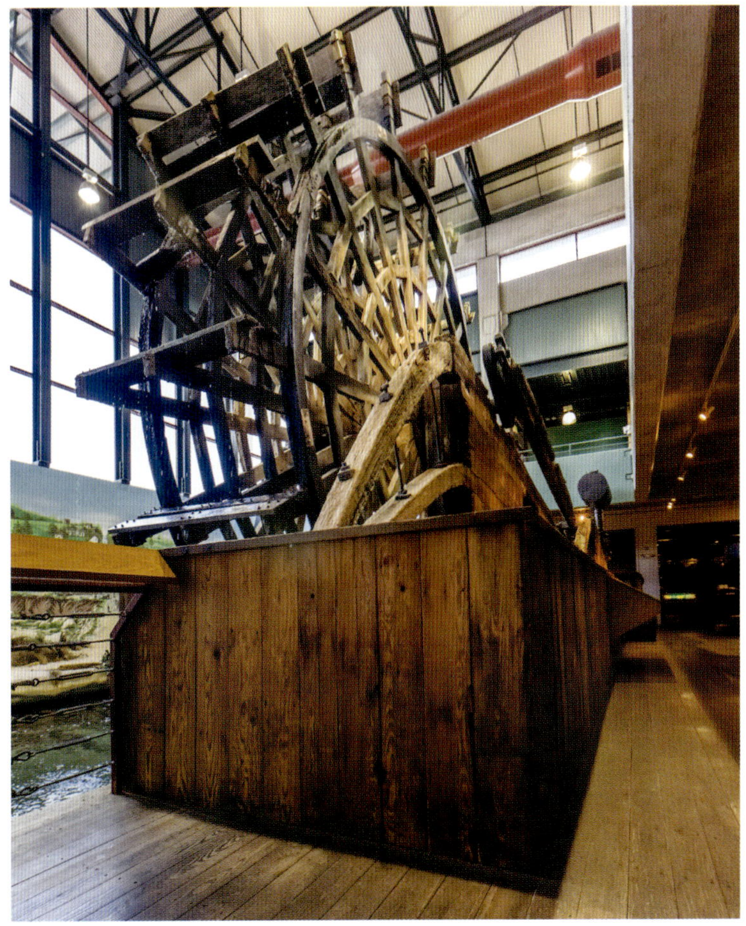

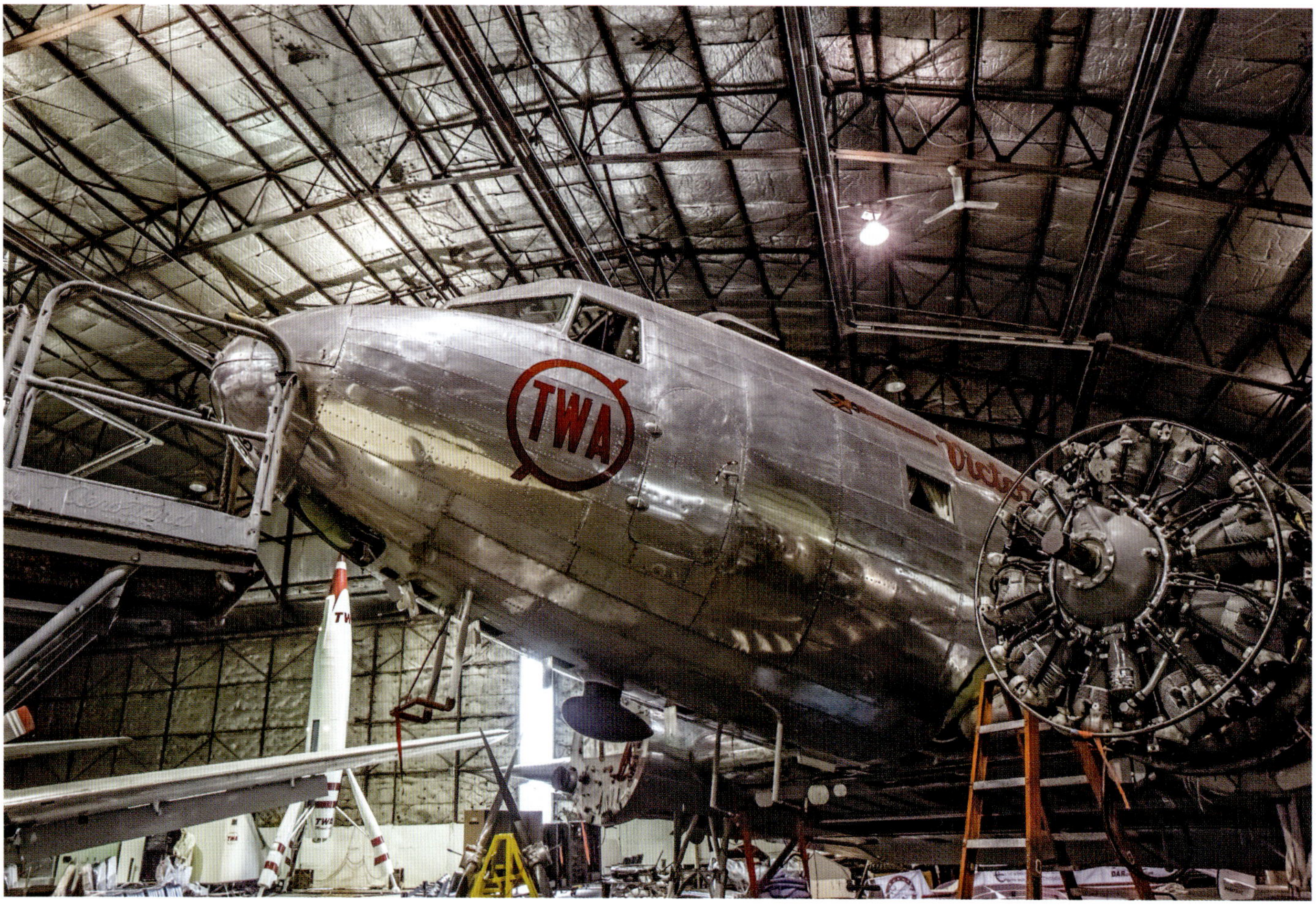

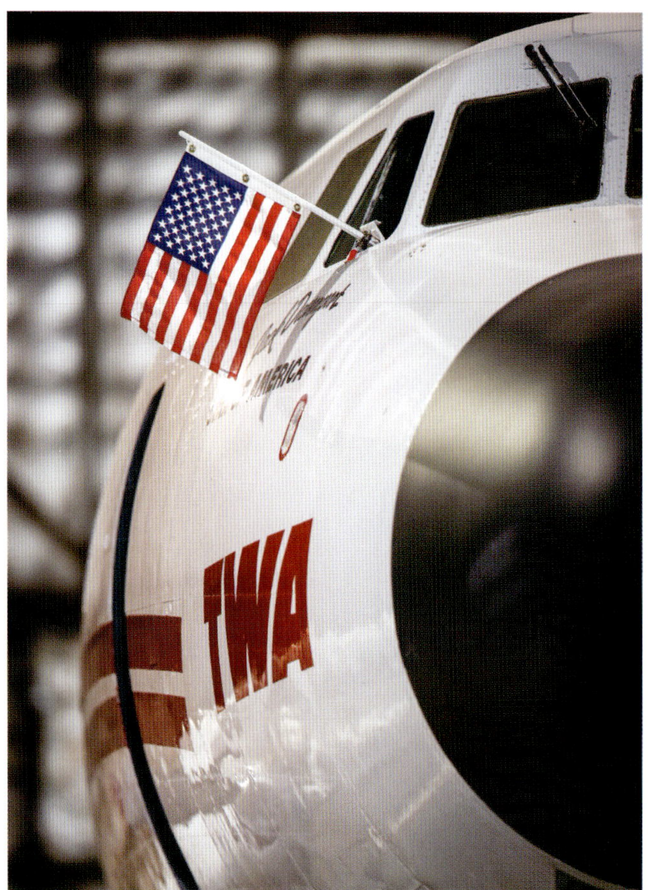

National Airline History Museum

(above and left)

This museum, located in the Downtown Airport, was originally devoted to propeller-driven commercial aircraft, but now includes jet aircraft, too. For 25 years, they've been restoring old planes to factory line condition and showing them off to the public. The passionate staff makes tours memorable and enjoyable.

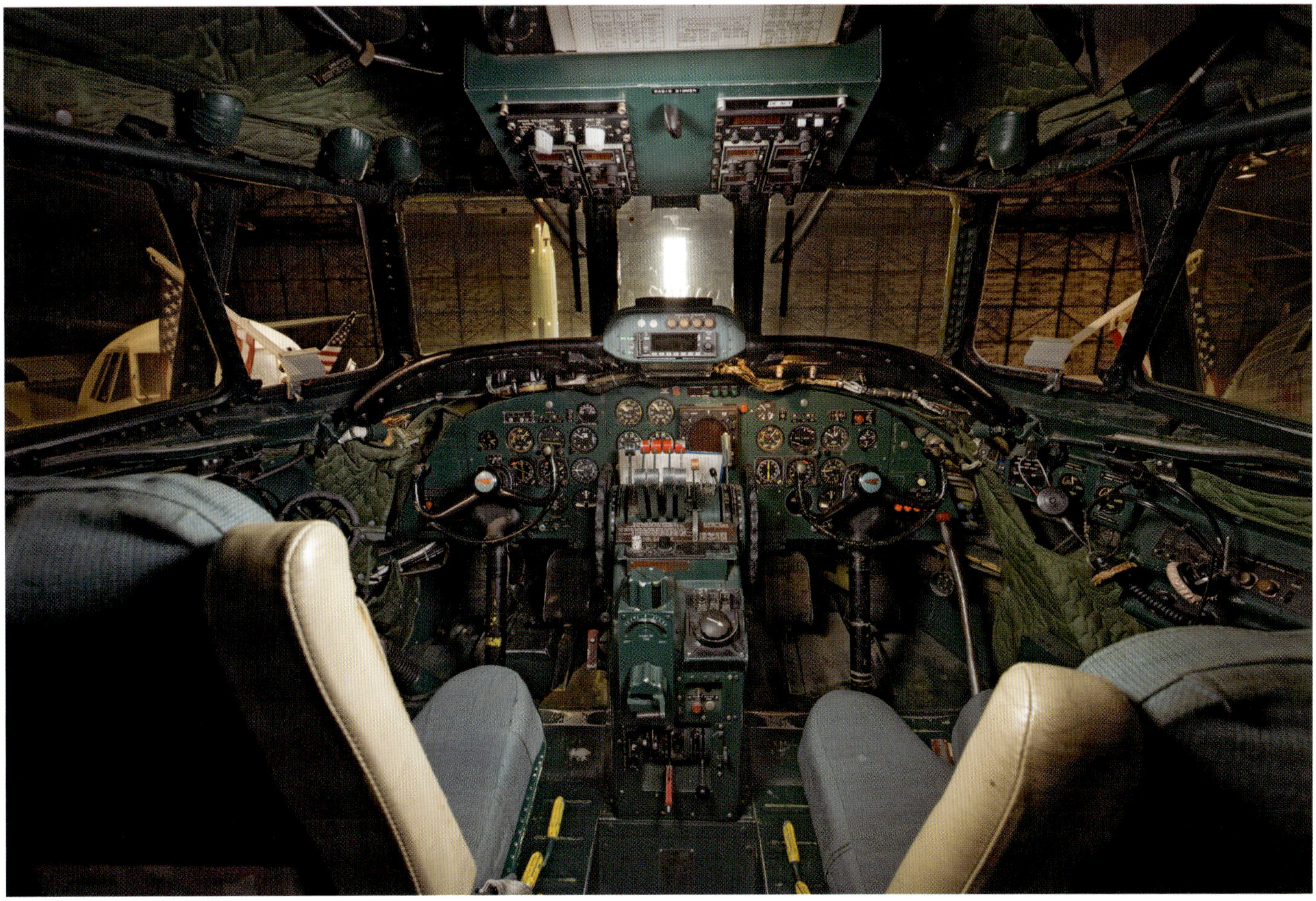

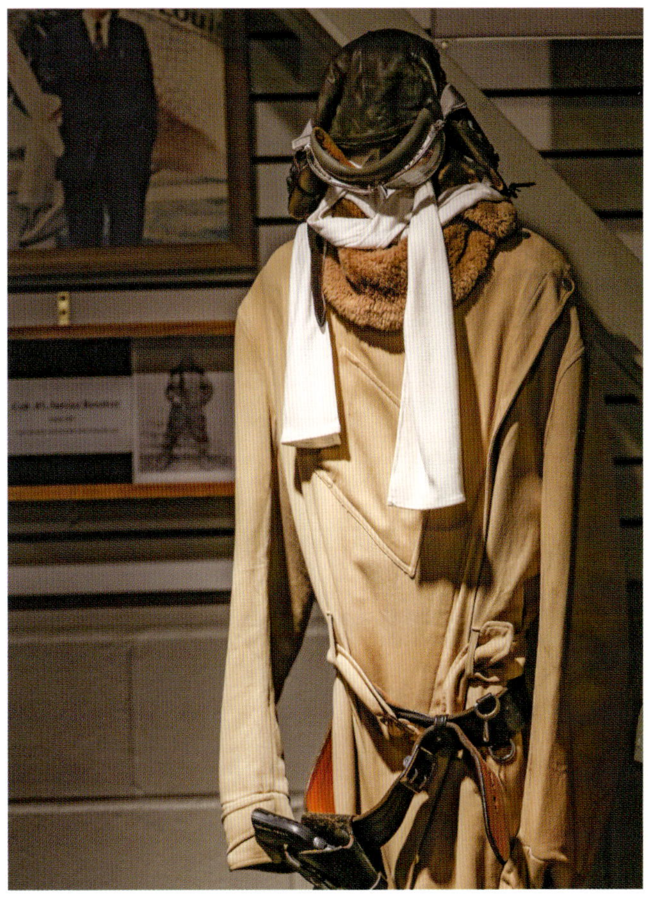

National Airline History Museum

(above and right)

Alongside a hanger of aircraft that you can explore, the National Airline History Museum also exhibits clothing and memorabilia from the history of commercial flight. Flight souvenirs, vintage airline posters, airplane models, and stewardess uniforms are catalogued and displayed, along with photographs from the history of flight.

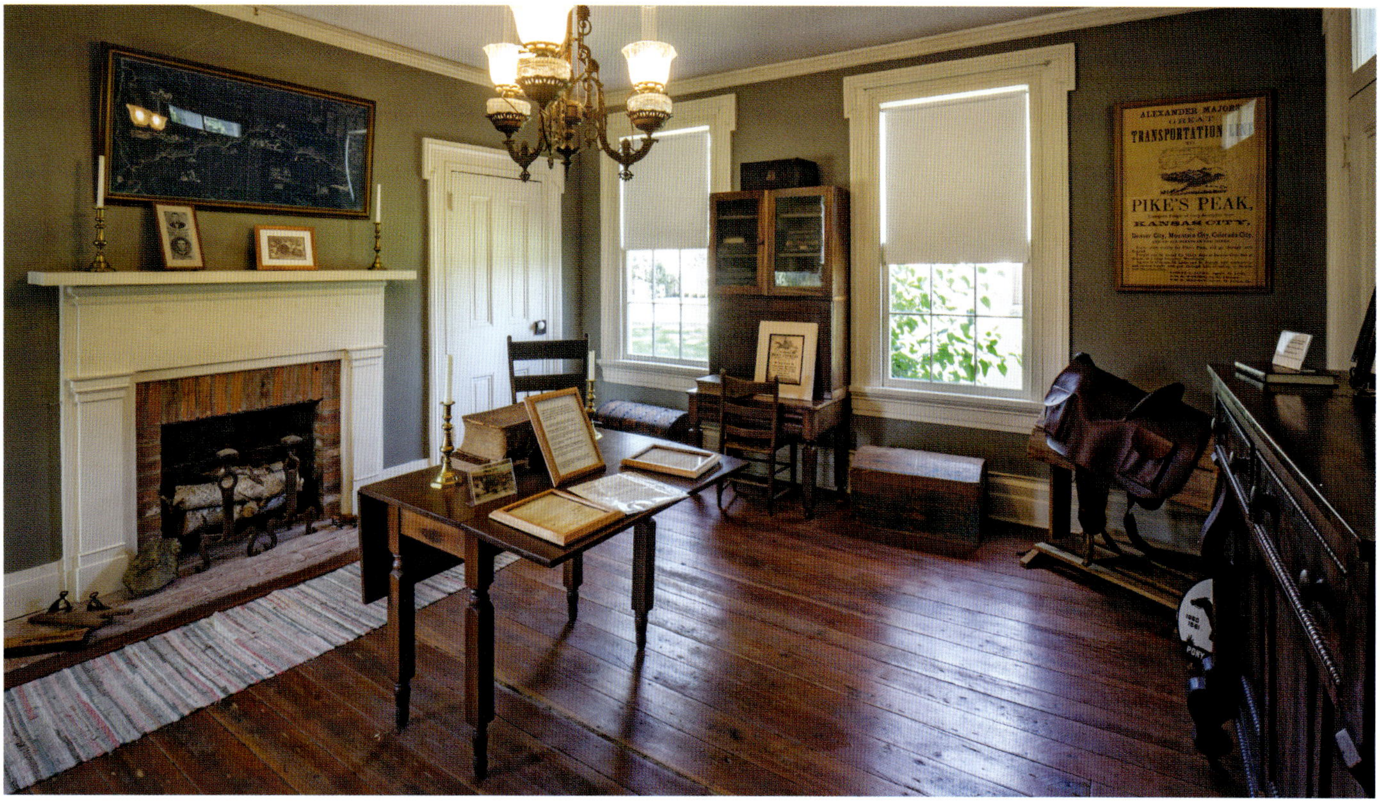

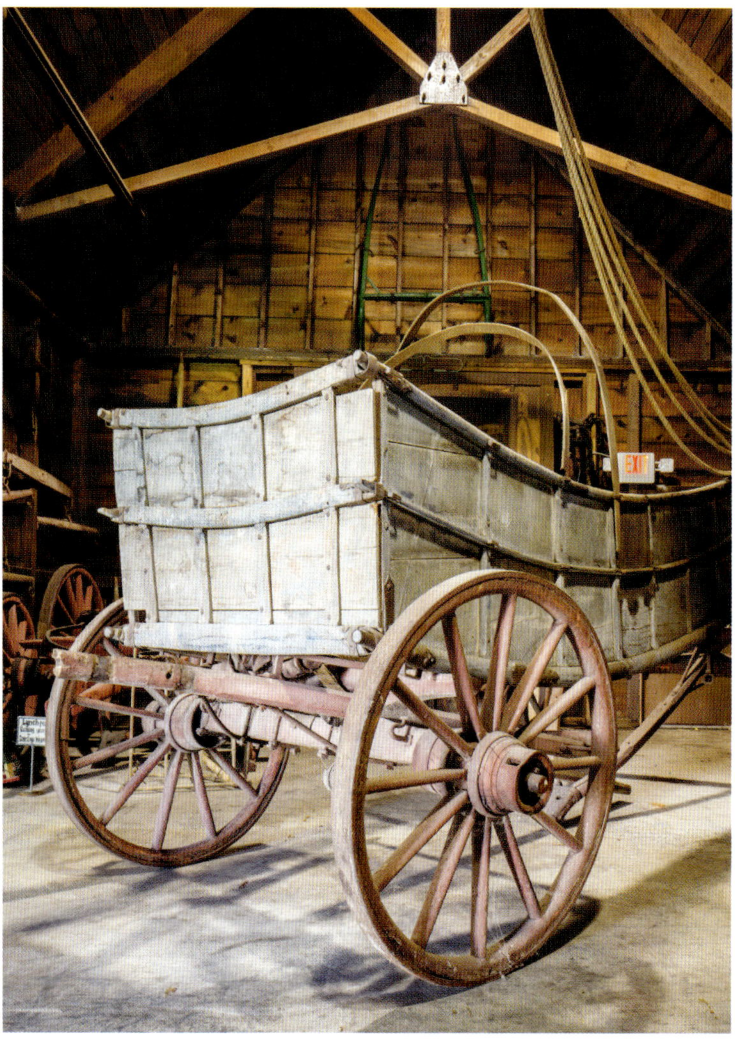

Headquarters for Westward Expansion *(above and opposite)*

Built on what was then the edge of the United States, the Alexander Majors house served as headquarters for his freight business, the Overland Stagecoach line, and the Pony Express. The house sat on 300 acres of farm, horse pens, and outbuildings that prepped settlers, freight, and mail for journeys west.

Alexander Majors Barn *(left)*

In the barn on the Majors' property, wagons and stagecoaches were repaired before being loaded in Westport to carry people and goods westward. Outside his front door, a dirt path led north a short distance to the famous trading post, West Port Landing, and waypoint for the important trails west.

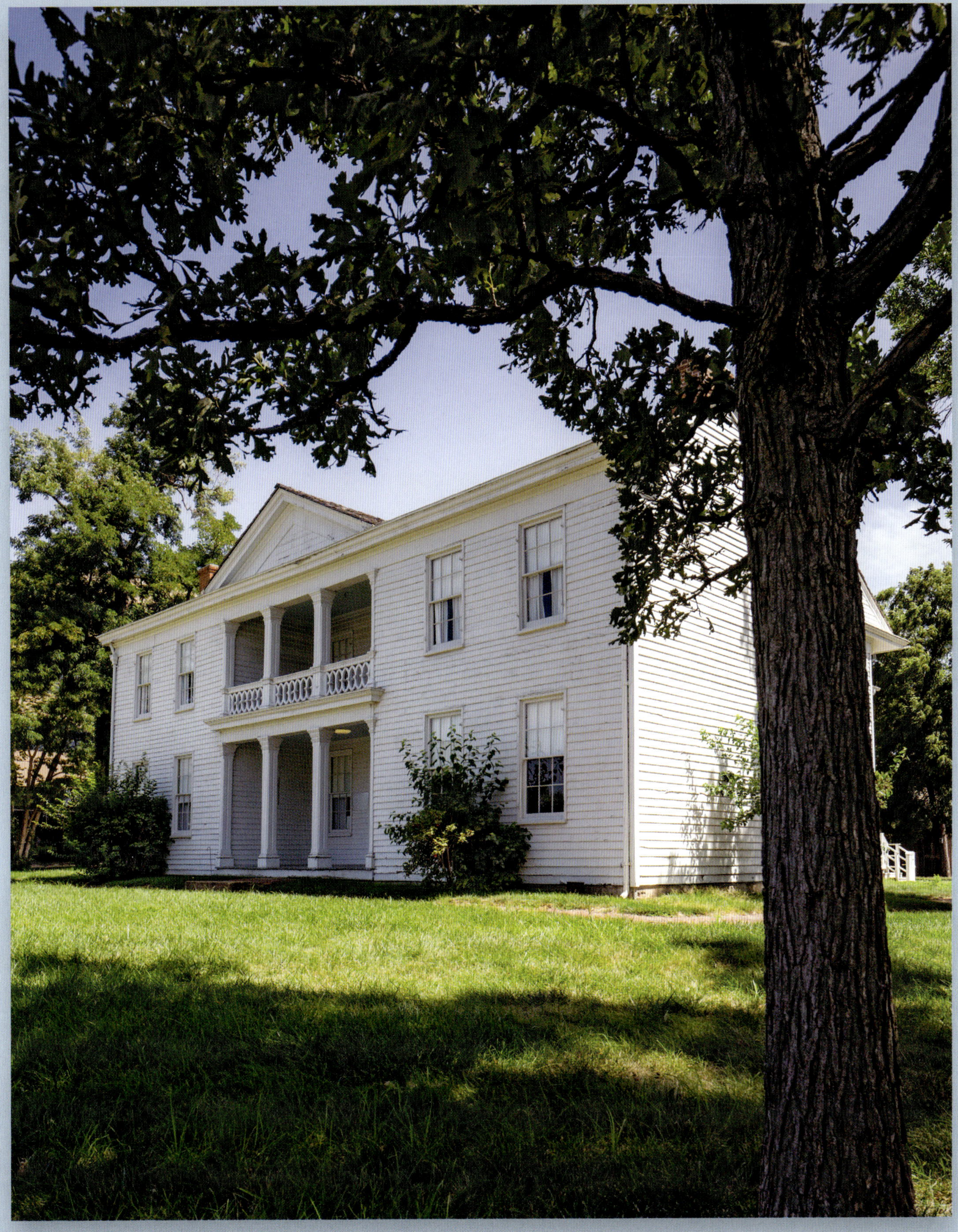

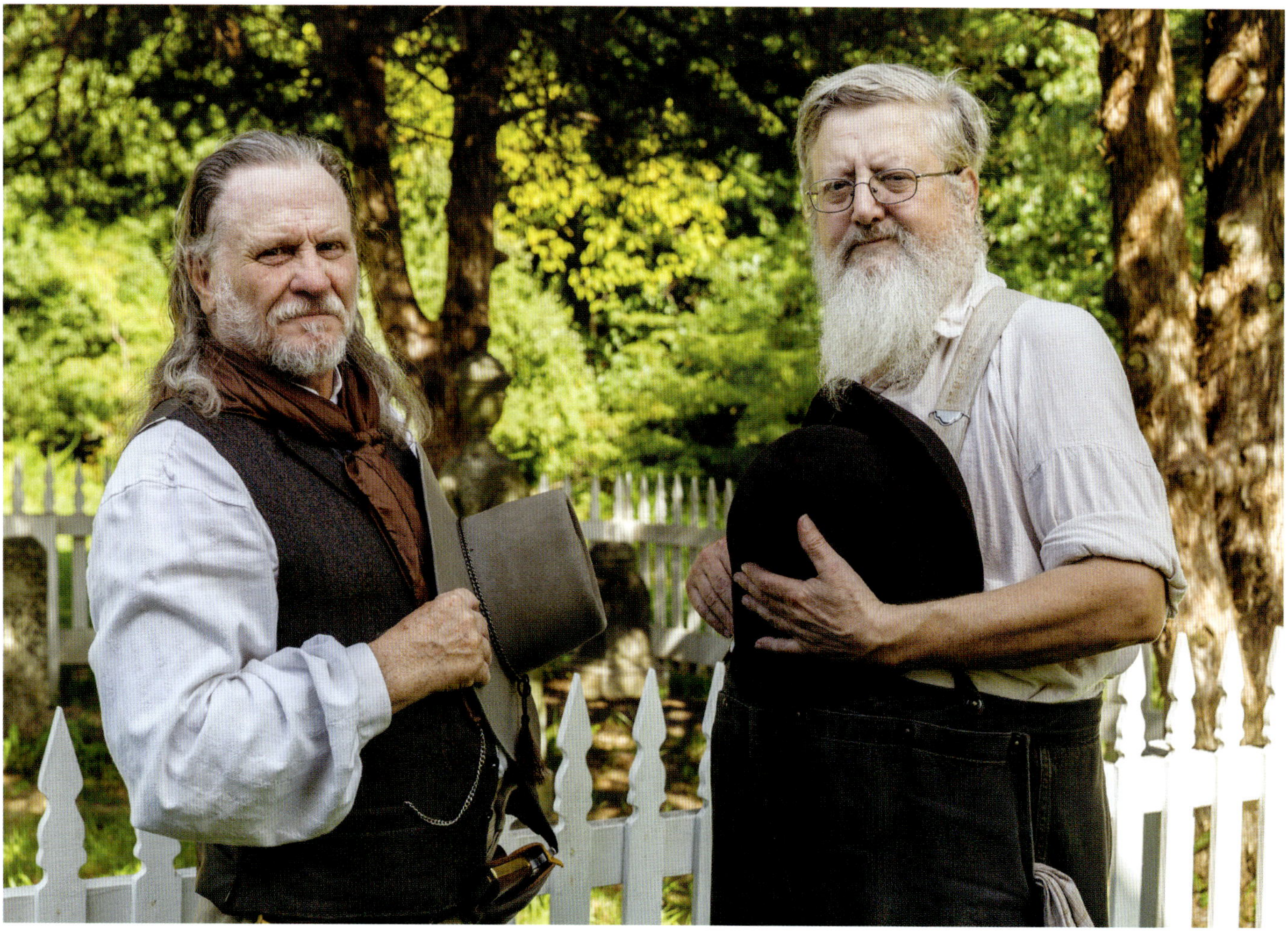

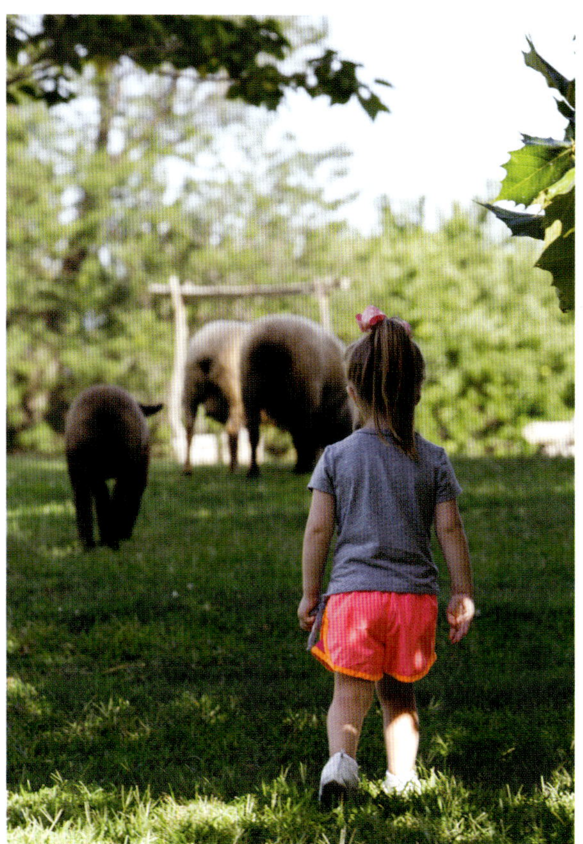

Missouri Town 1855 Museum

(above and left)

Historical interpreters in period clothing roam 30 rolling acres of farmland in this living museum just outside Kansas City. The past comes to life in this working antebellum village as farmers tend to crops, care for livestock, and tradesmen go about their crafts.

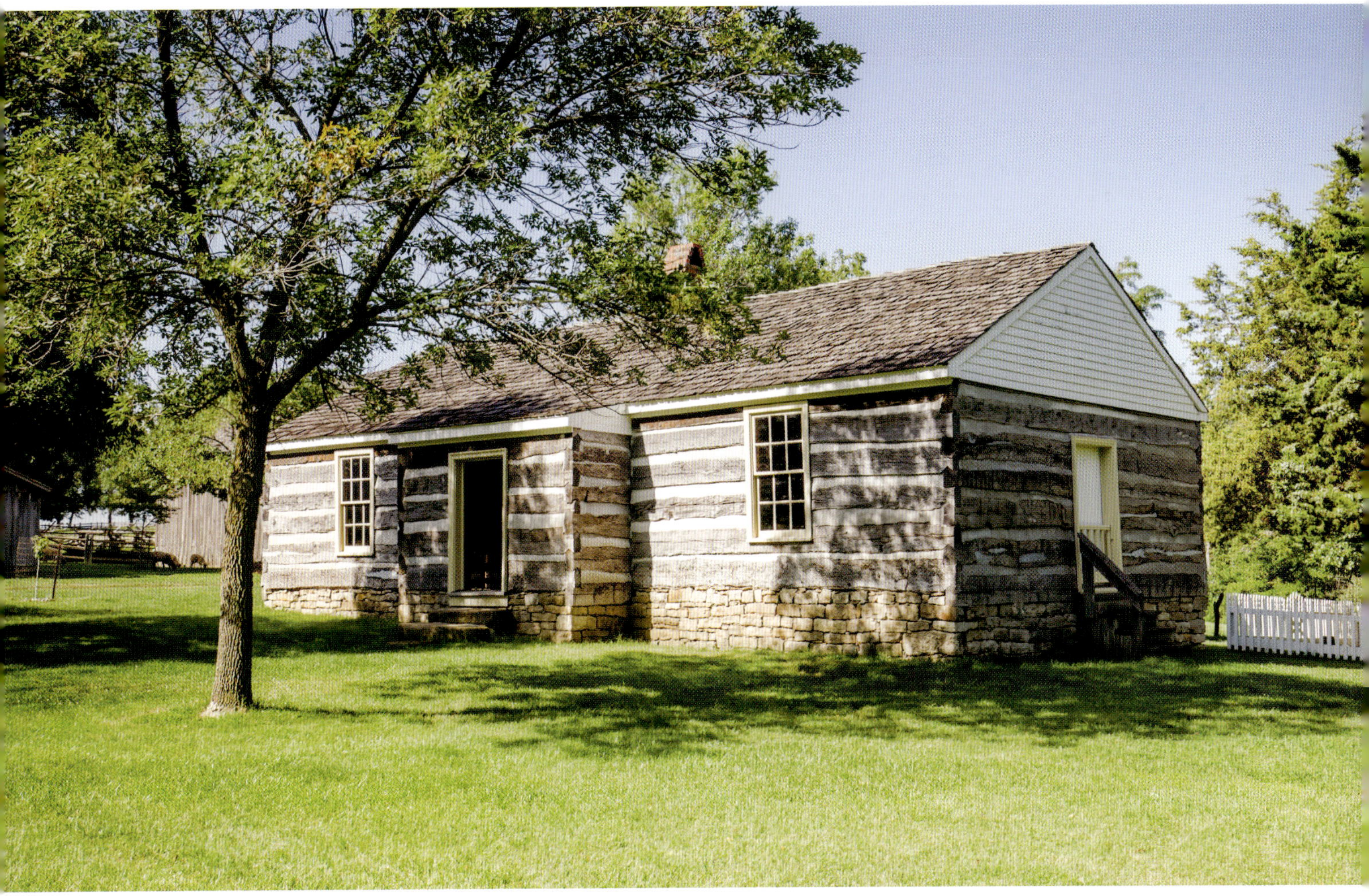

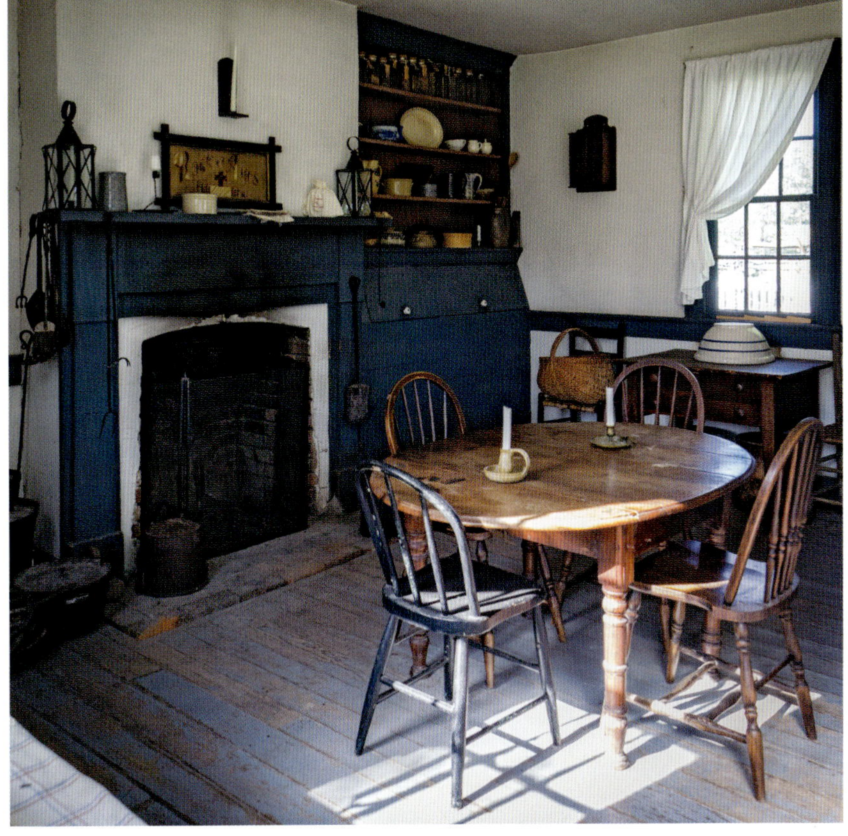

Missouri Town 1855 Museum

(above and right)

More than 25 original period buildings are located on the museum grounds, each filled with authentic furniture and equipment. Get a sense of what life was like in a farming community just years before the Civil War. The museum is a constant bustle of activities and frequent festivals.

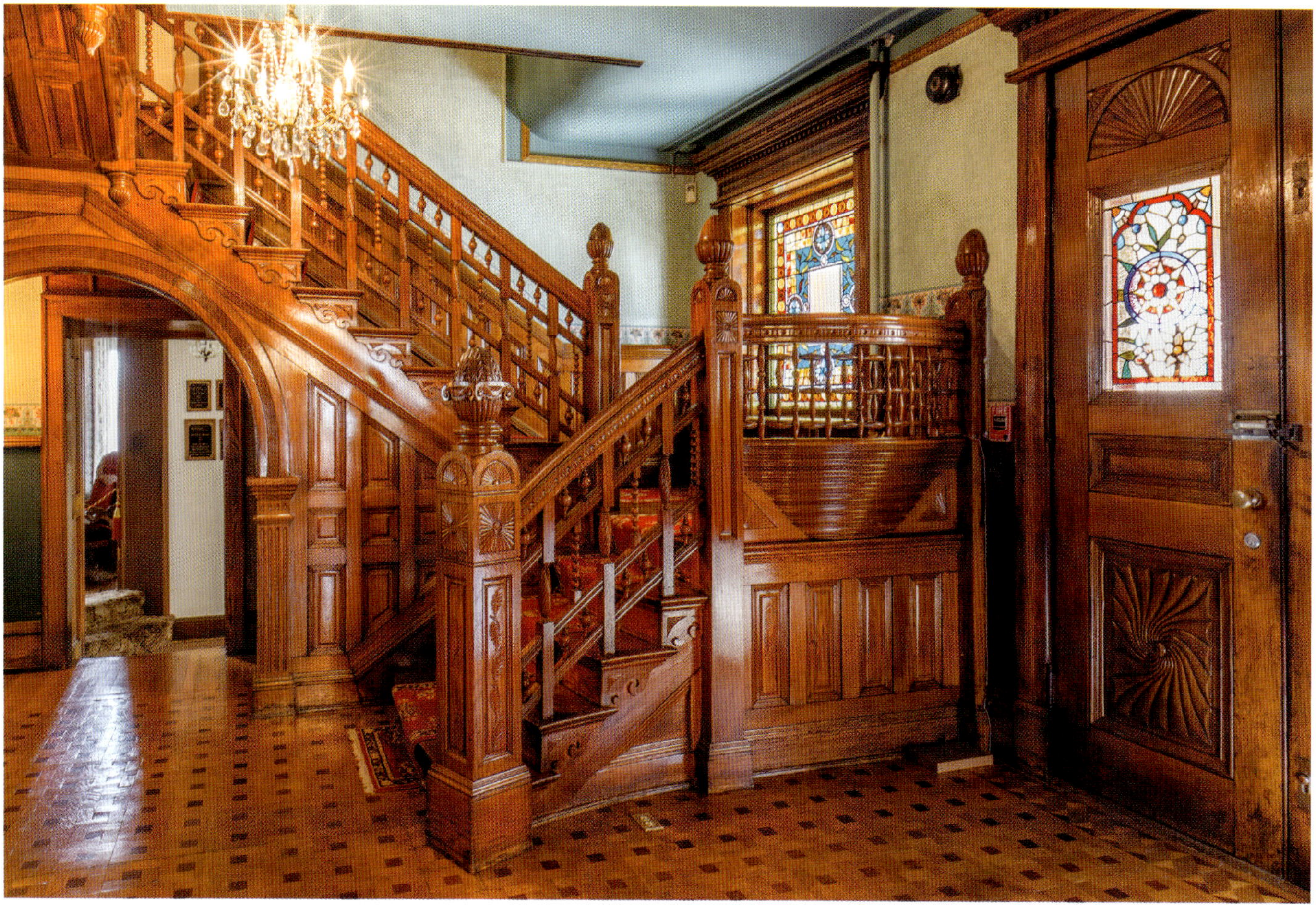

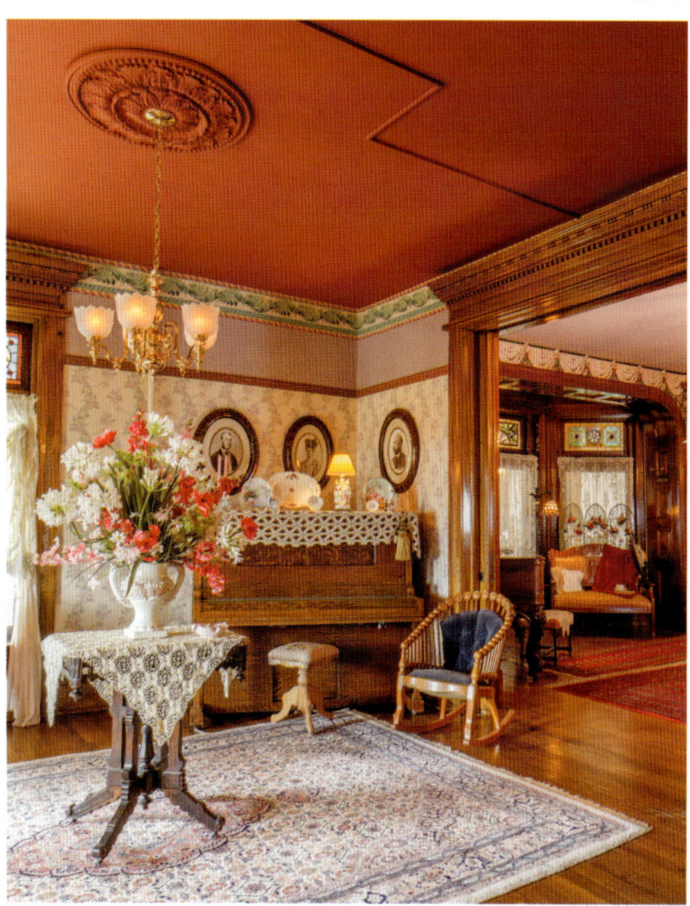

Strawberry Hill Museum

(above, left, and opposite)

The Strawberry Hill neighborhood of Kansas City has long been home to Eastern European immigrants, as seen in the museum's Cultural Center. The museum is also an example of elegant and majestic Victorian craftsmanship. Beautifully decorated, it is the city's finest Queen Anne style home.

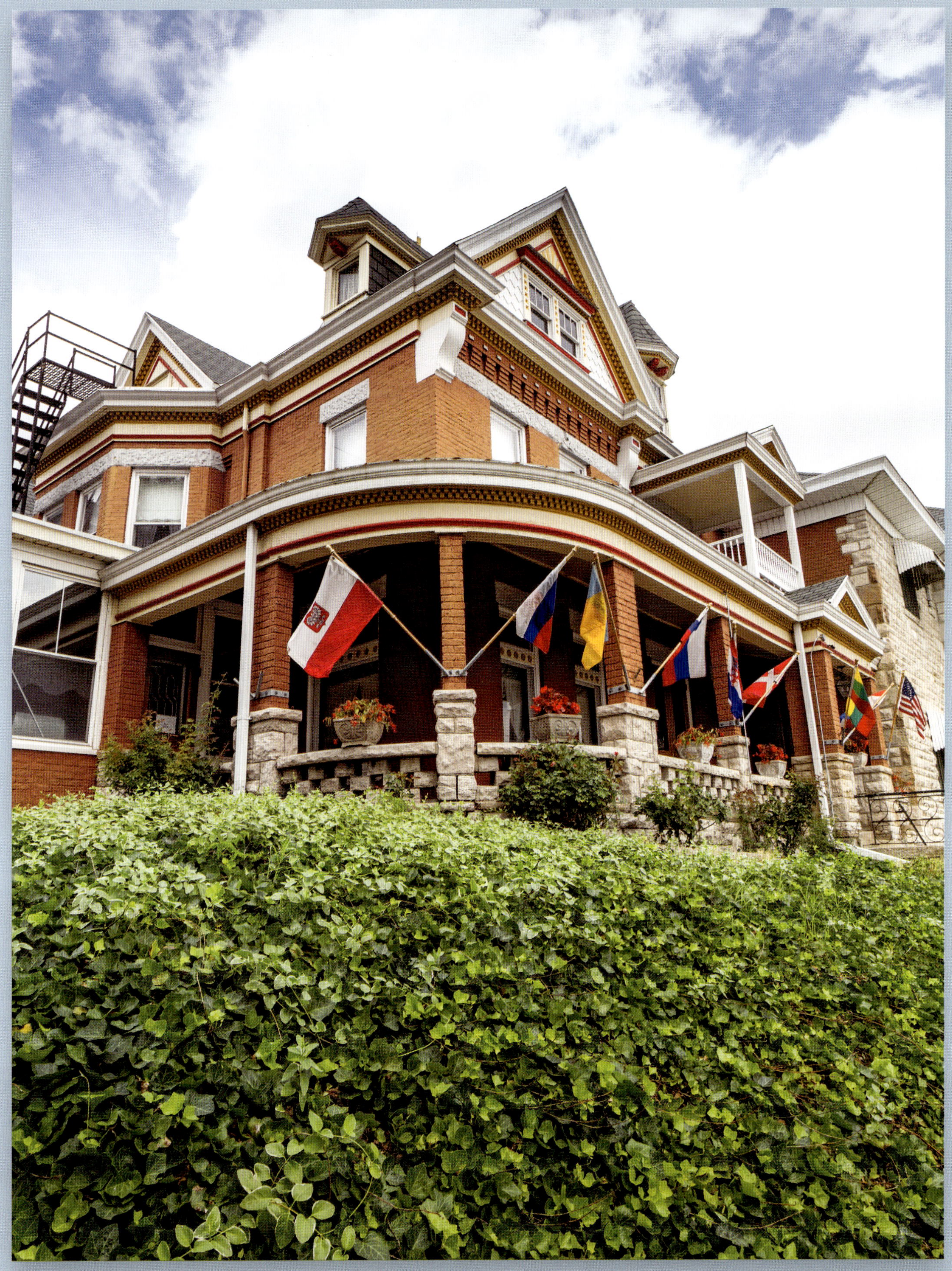

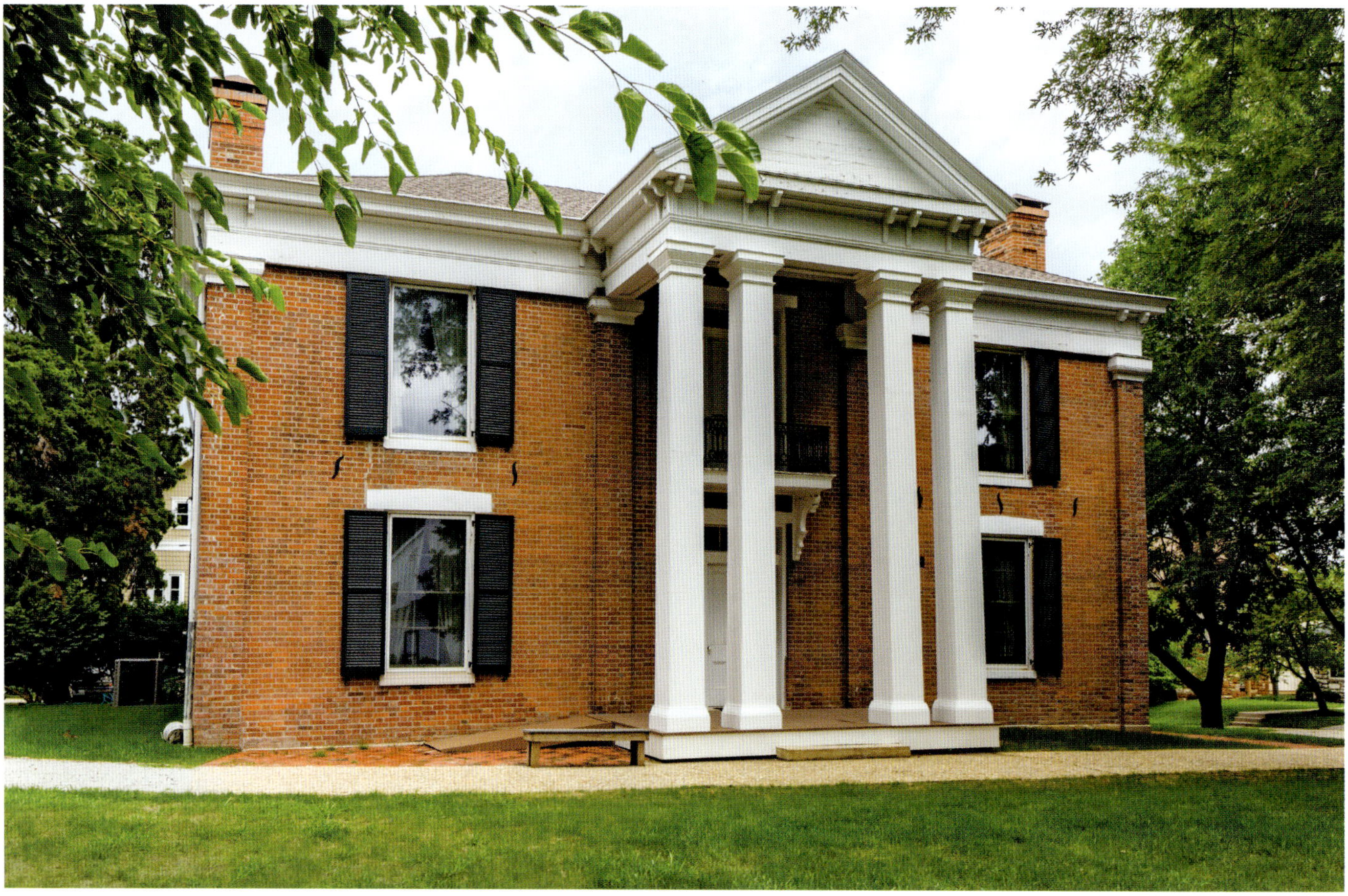

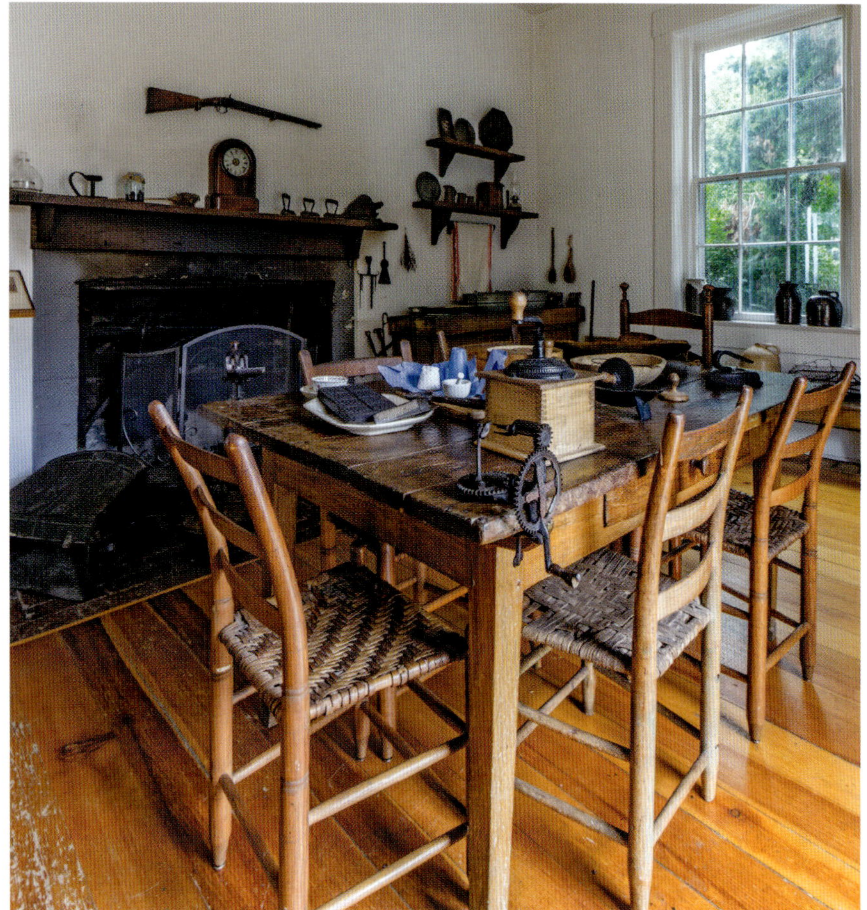

John Wornall House *(above and left)*

John Wornall was one of the most prosperous farmers in Kansas City before becoming a banker and highly influential in the city. His home, built to be pretentious with 25-foot columns and a showcase location near a main road, evoked images of his native home of Kentucky.

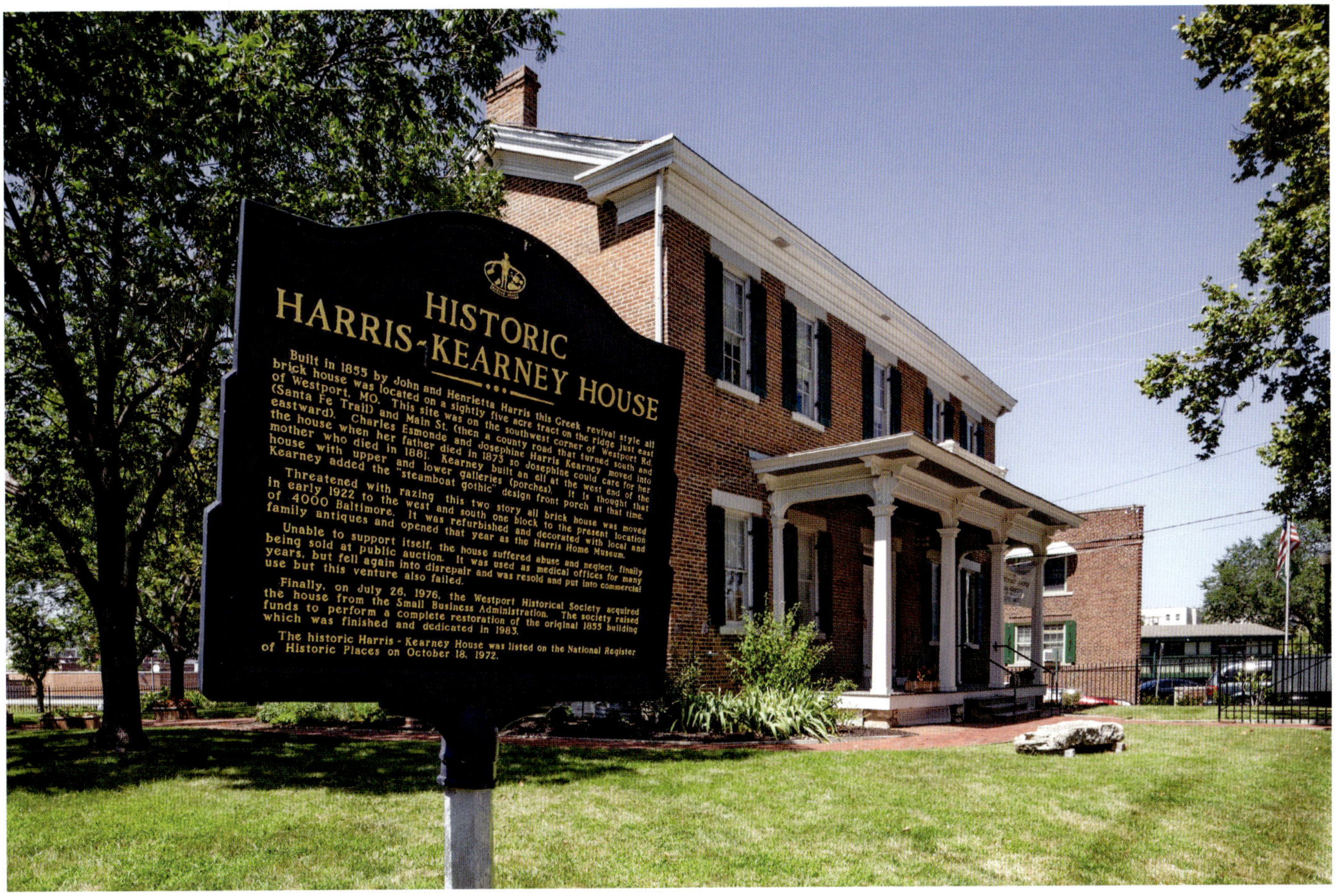

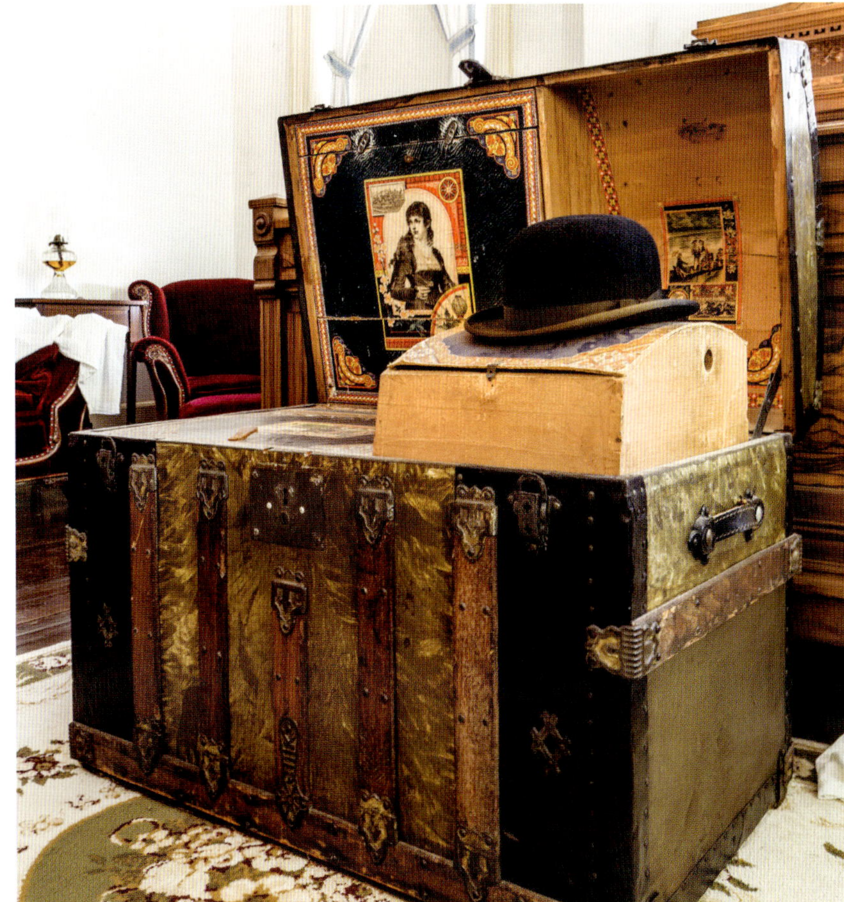

Harris-Kearney House *(above and right)*

For years, the Harris-Kearney home, situated just north of Westport, saw a near constant flow of trappers, traders, and pioneers headed westward. Later, the home was occupied by Union forces during the bloody Battle of Westport. Today, the city's oldest brick residence is home to a fascinating historical museum.

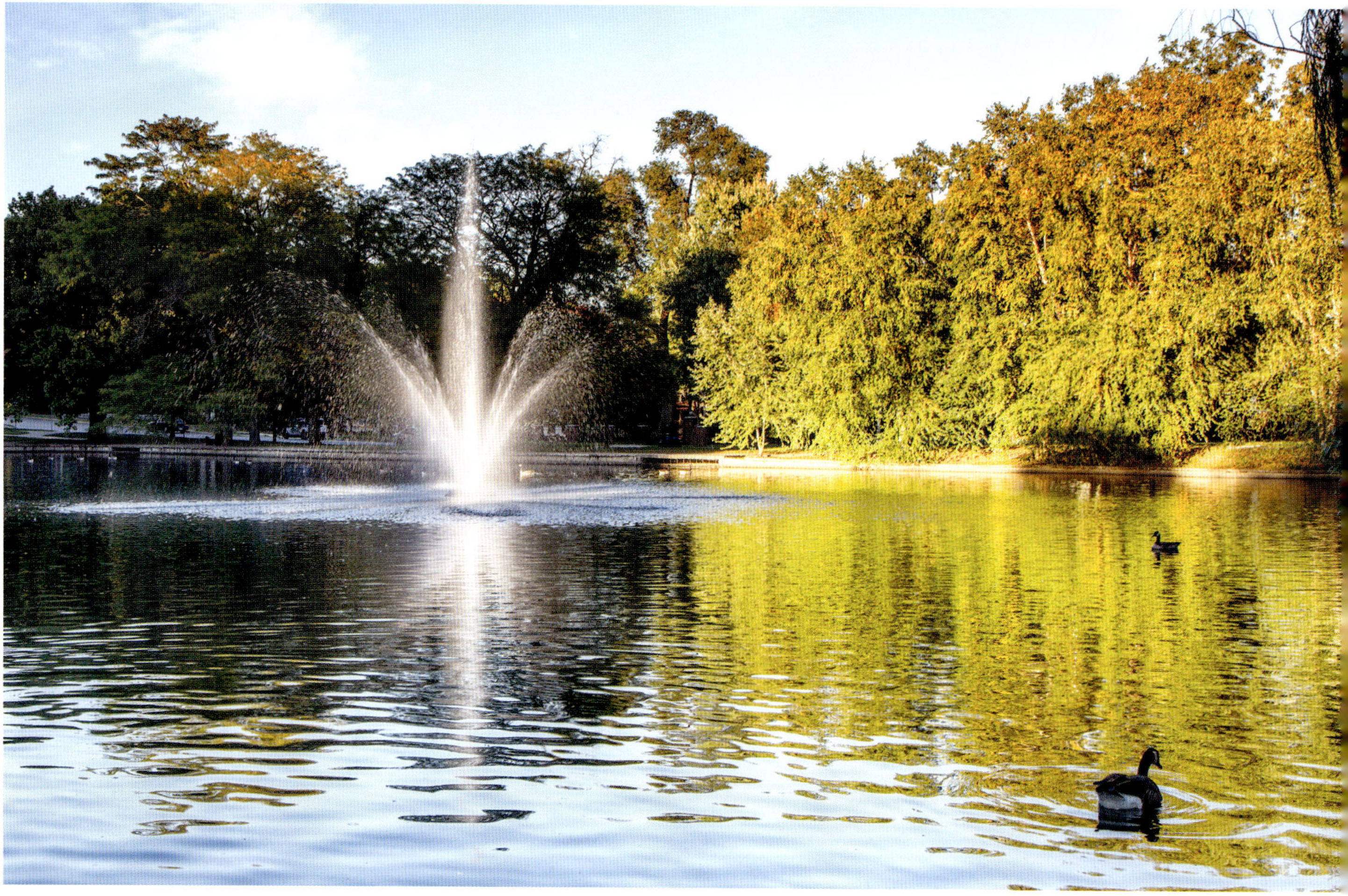

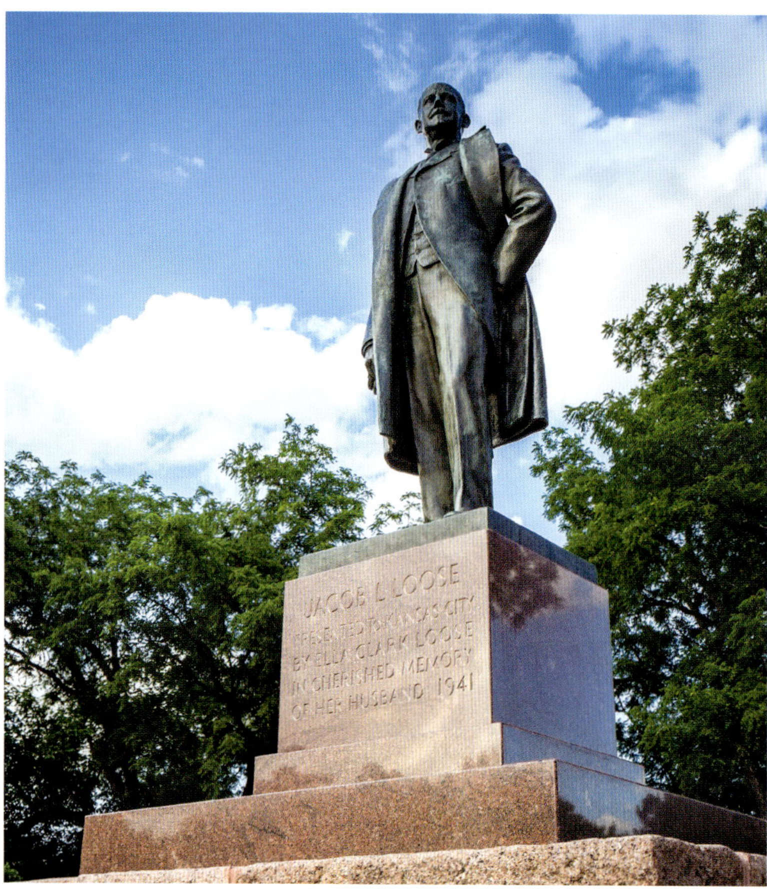

Loose Park *(above and left)*

The 75-acre park, memorializing prominent citizen Jacob Loose, is well known for being the main site of the Battle of Westport. Later, it was home to Kansas City's first golf course. For nearly a century, the land has operated as a city park and is a popular place to enjoy the outdoors.

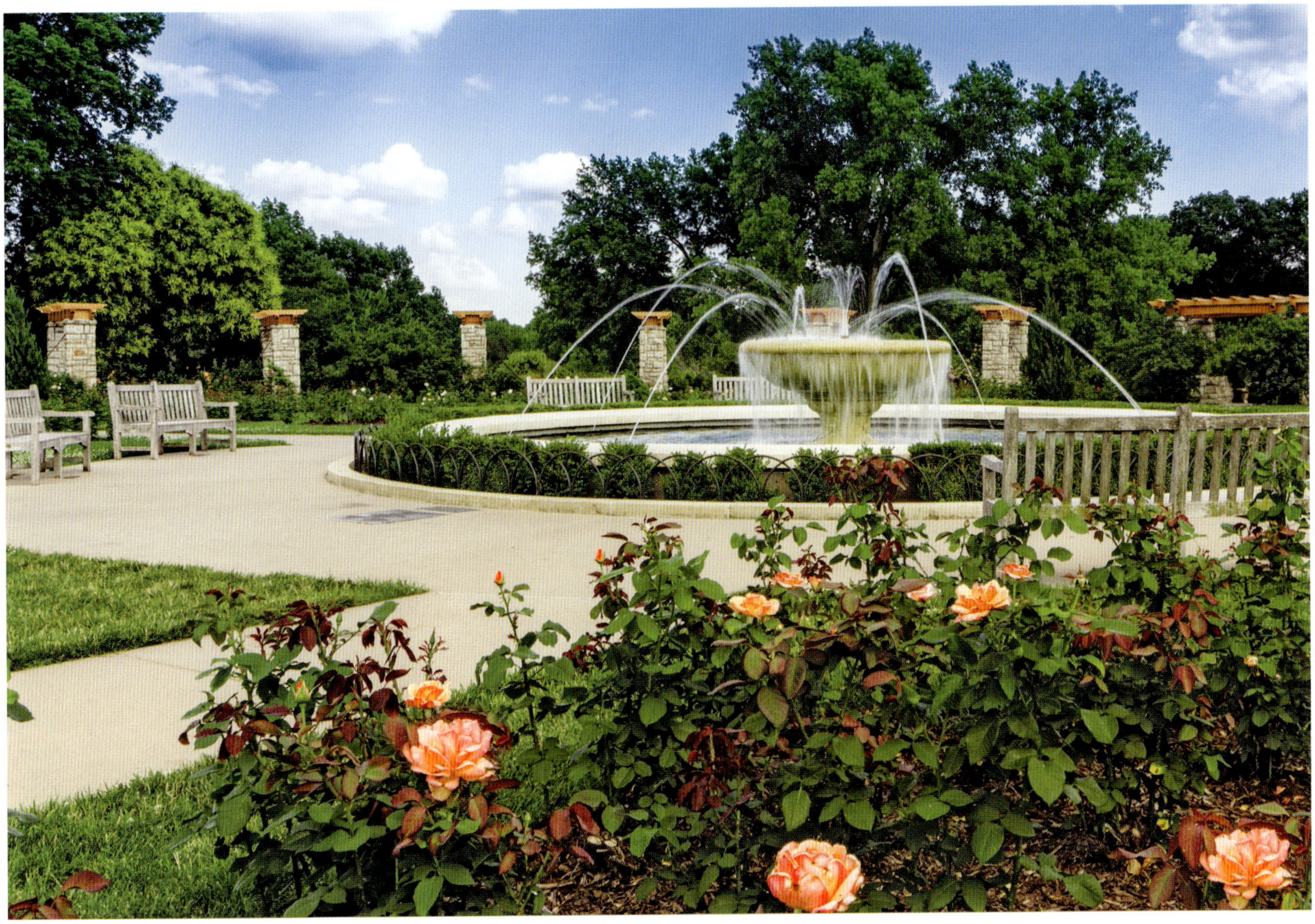

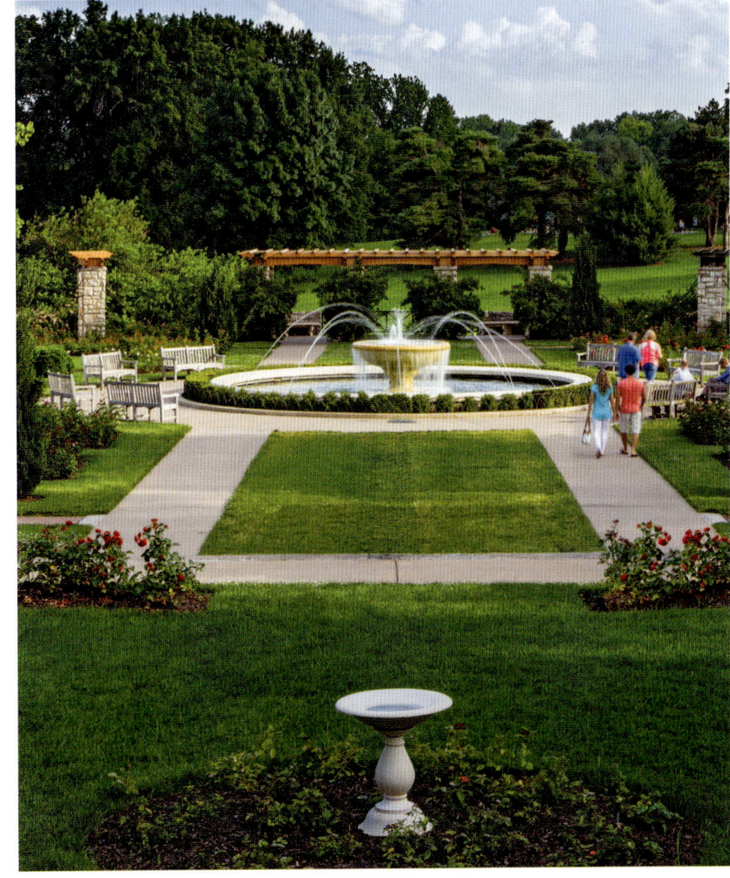

Loose Park Rose Garden

(above and right)

This sweeping, circular garden boasts more than 4,000 roses representing nearly 170 different varieties. Strolling along the gravel path beneath the garden's 33 pillared pergolas stimulates the senses with a bounty of fragrances. The garden is a popular spot and venue to hundreds of weddings.

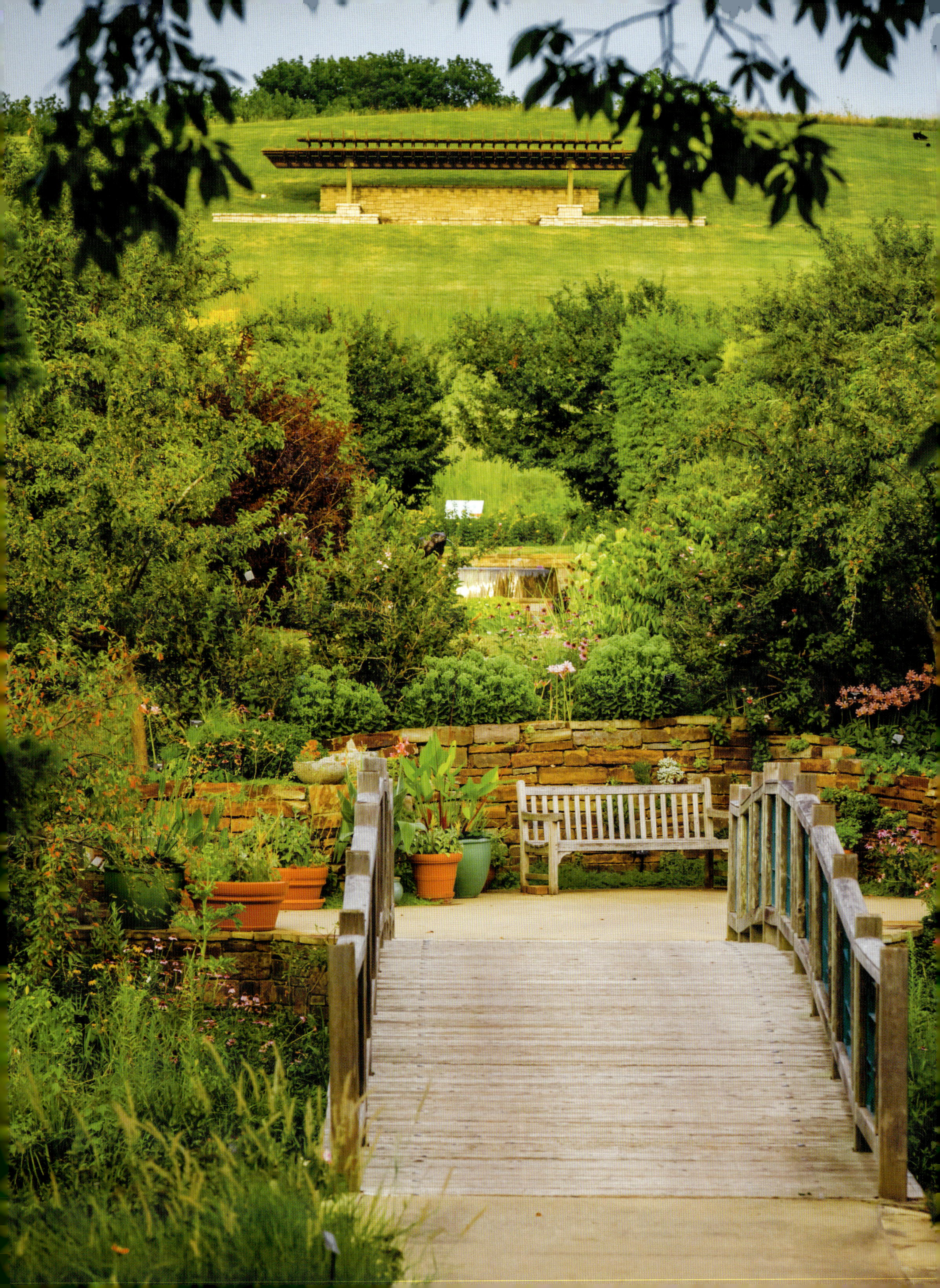

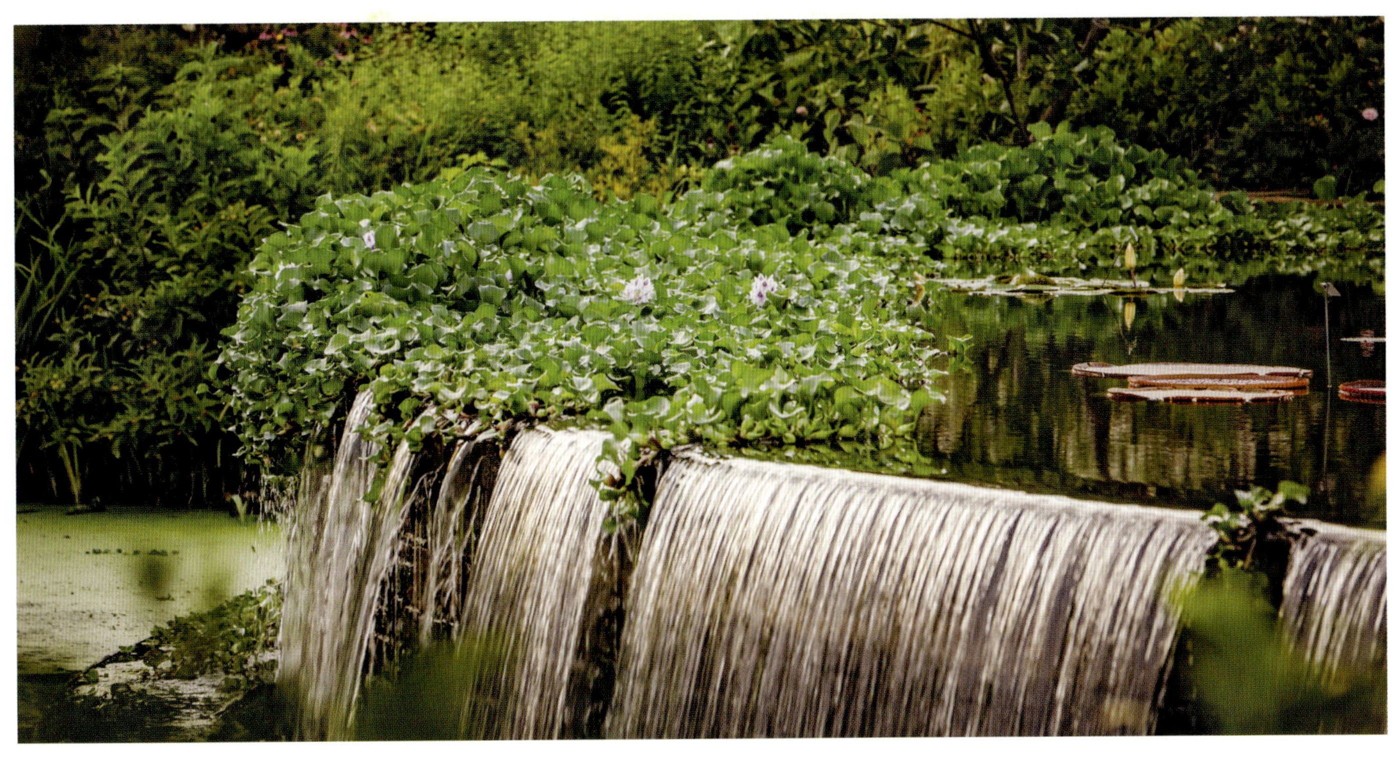

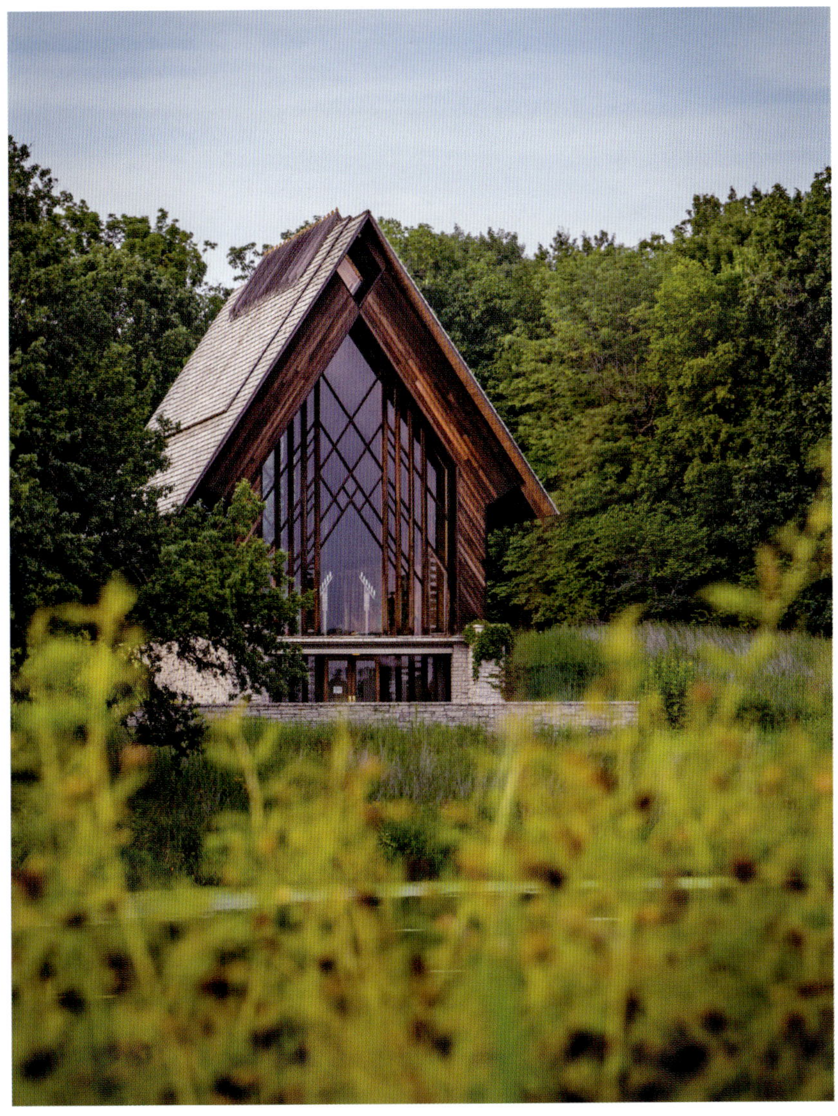

Powell Gardens *(above and right)*

These sweeping gardens are situated on more than 900 acres of rolling hills and forested plains. Dozens of gardens are planted along curving paths that wind their way through ponds, waterfalls, and terraced walls. Among the buildings on the property is a nondenominational chapel, a beautiful setting for weddings.

Powell Gardens Pavilion *(opposite)*

Take a break from the manicured and shaped gardens beneath the shade of this redwood pavilion, which sits near the crest of a hill. A peaceful vista lies before you. Wildflowers grow among native grasses all around the pavilion, reflecting the beauty and diversity of the "fruited plains."

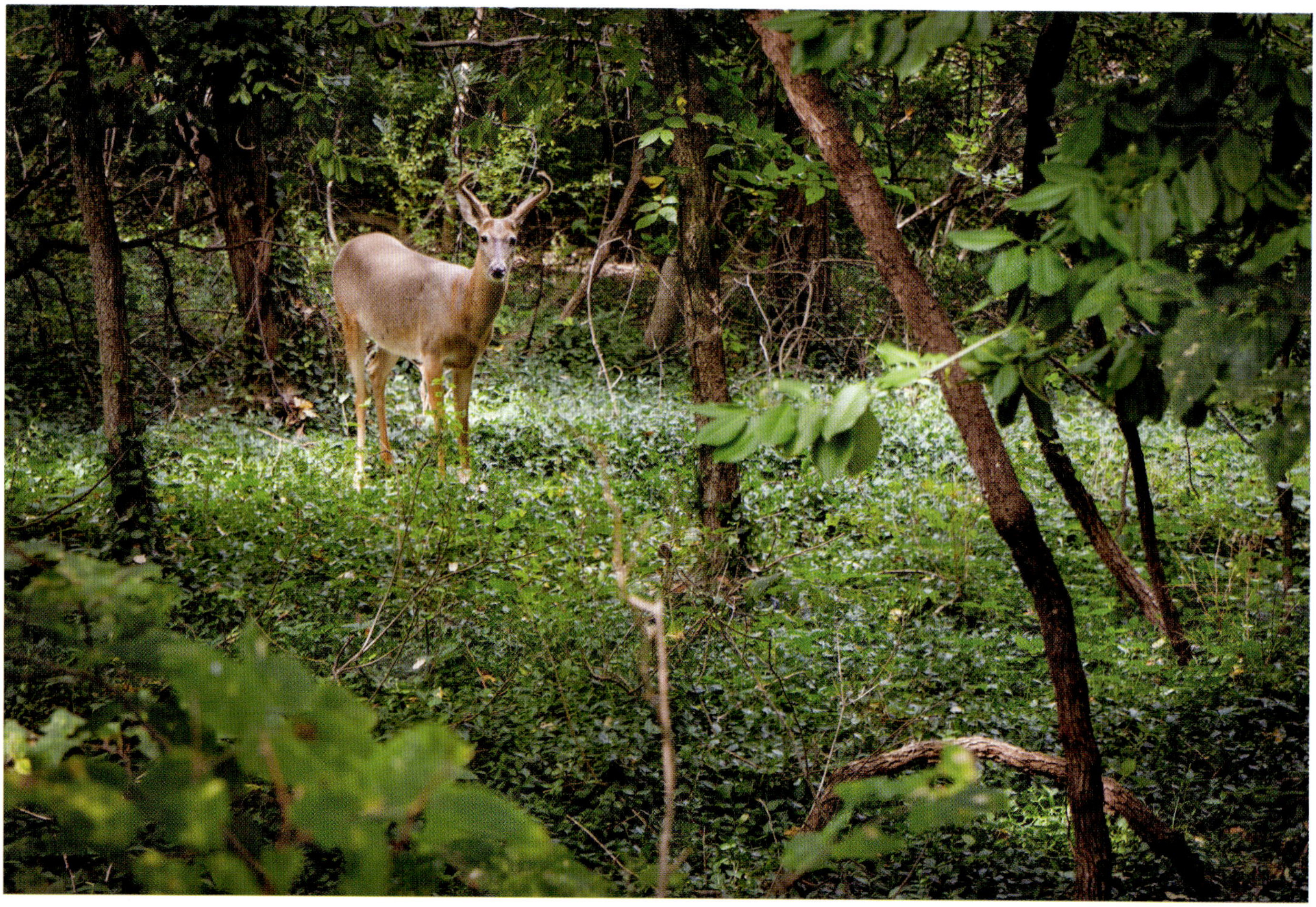

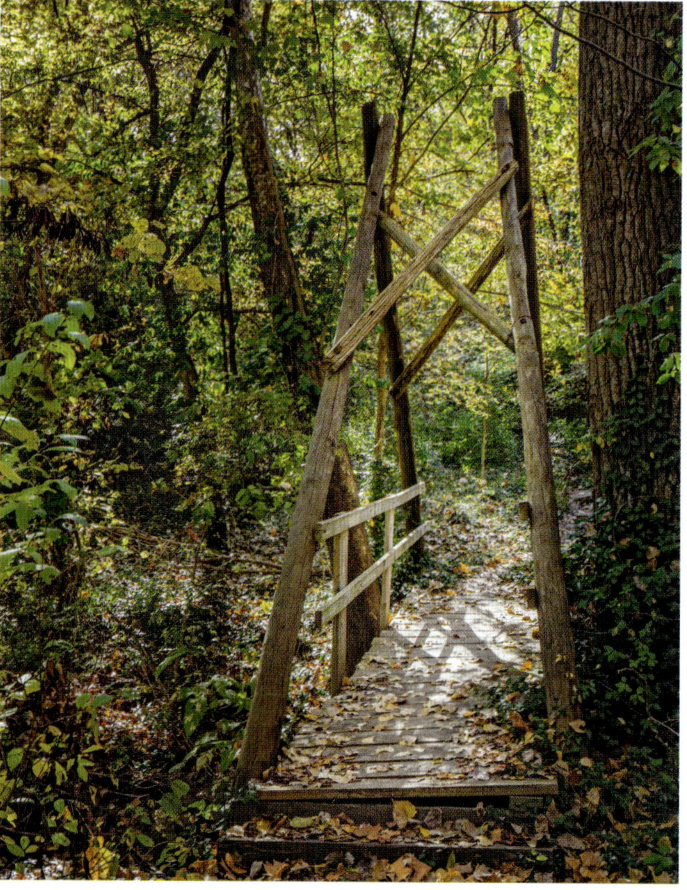

Cave Spring Interpretive Center
(above and left)

The wooded Cave Spring area was a stopping point for travelers on the Santa Fe, Oregon, and California trails. Pioneers camped and pastured their livestock, while securing water from a spring in a nearby cave. At the time, the spring produced over one million gallons of water a day.

Cave Spring Interpretive Center
(opposite)

Walking the trails of this 36-acre historic site, hikers are likely to come across the remains of a number of cabins that once stood in these wooded hills. The site has six miles of trails and is an outdoor educational facility, attracting thousands of area school children each year.

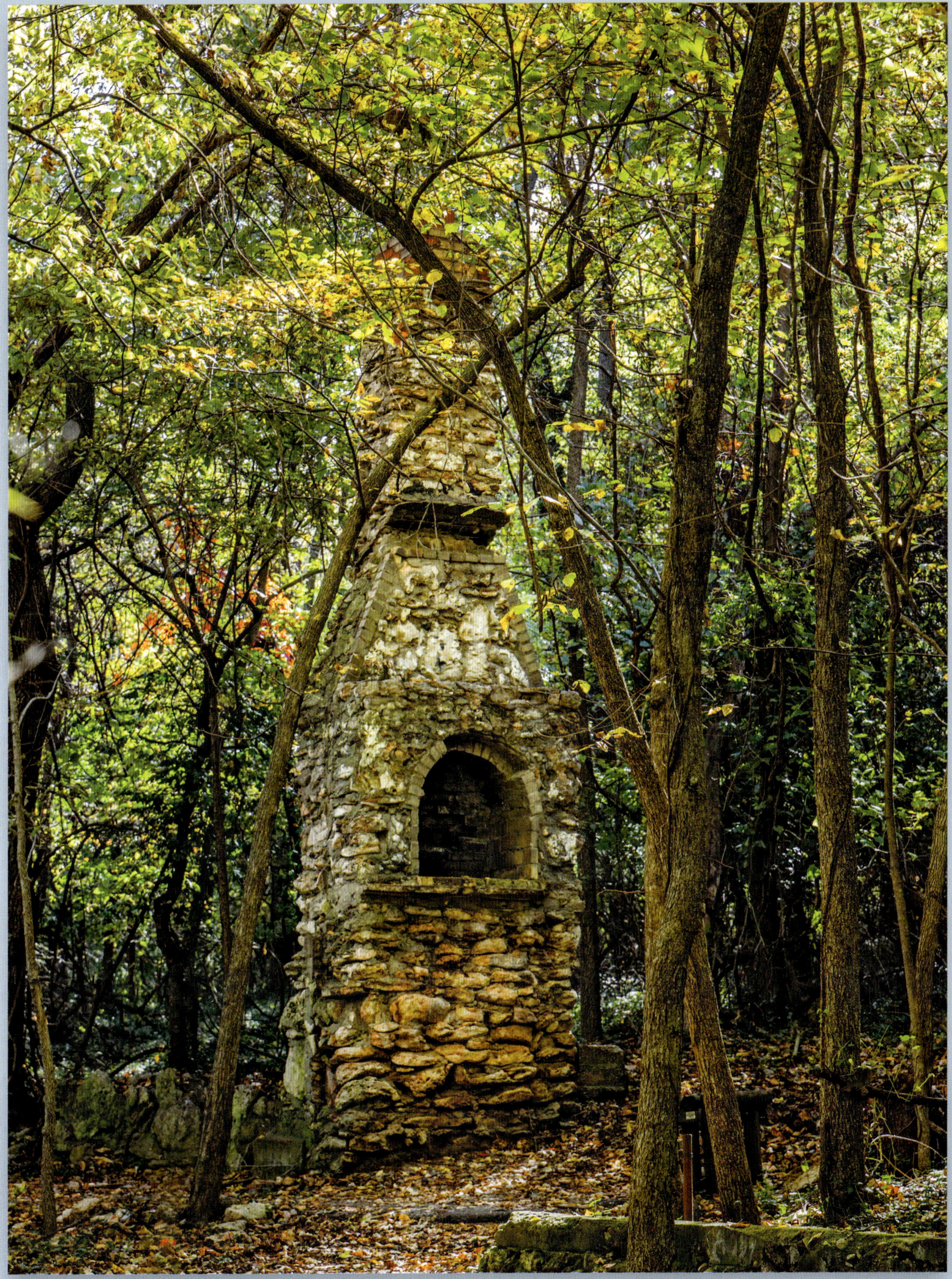

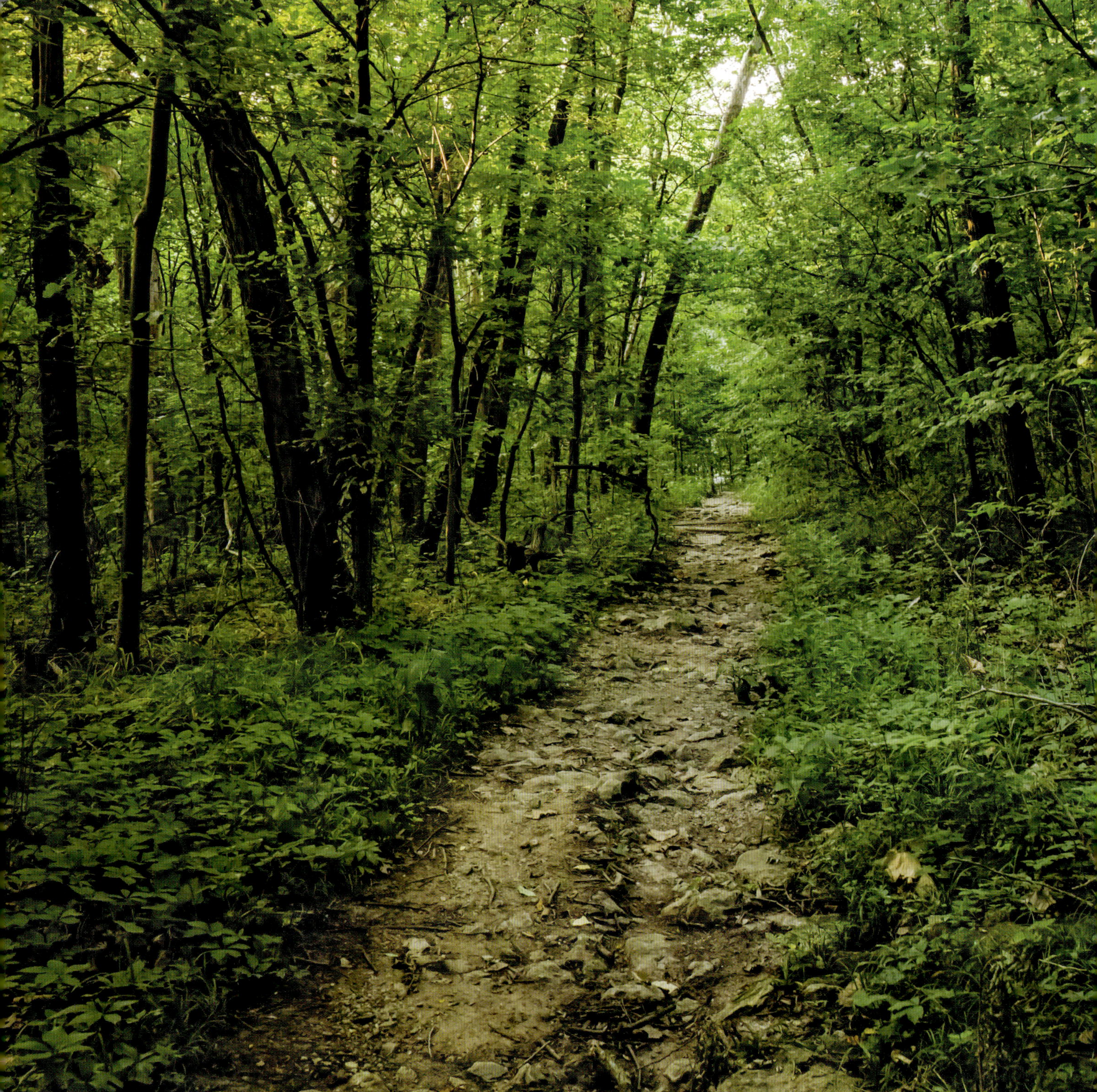

Maple Woods Nature Preserve

This remnant, old-growth forest gives visitors a sense of what the area looked like hundreds of years ago. Mature black maples and a variety of oak trees offer an abundance of shade to hikers walking the preserve's trails. The area is especially gorgeous in the fall when leaves change color.

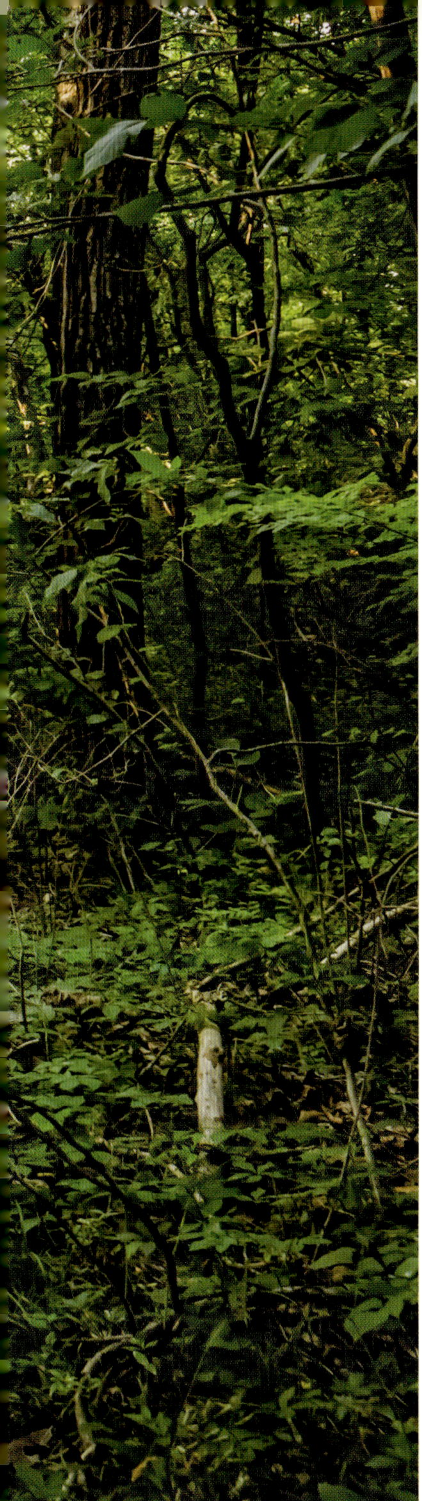

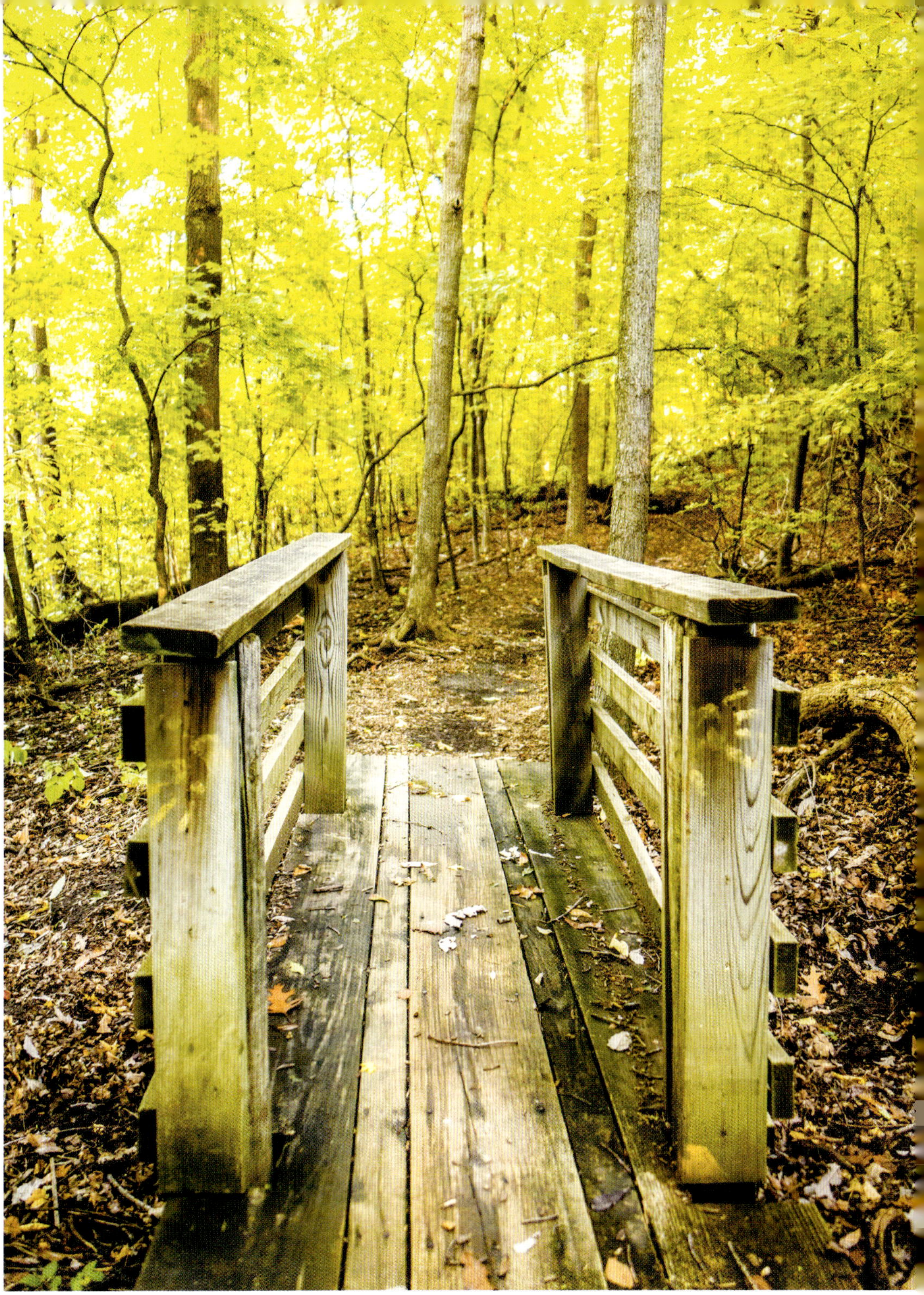

Maple Woods Nature Preserve

At the entrance to the Maple Woods trail, possibilities await. Wildflowers and wildlife are in abundance and the trail is a popular destination for bird watchers. Migrating songbirds can be found in the spring and fall, while native forest birds can be seen in the preserve year-round.

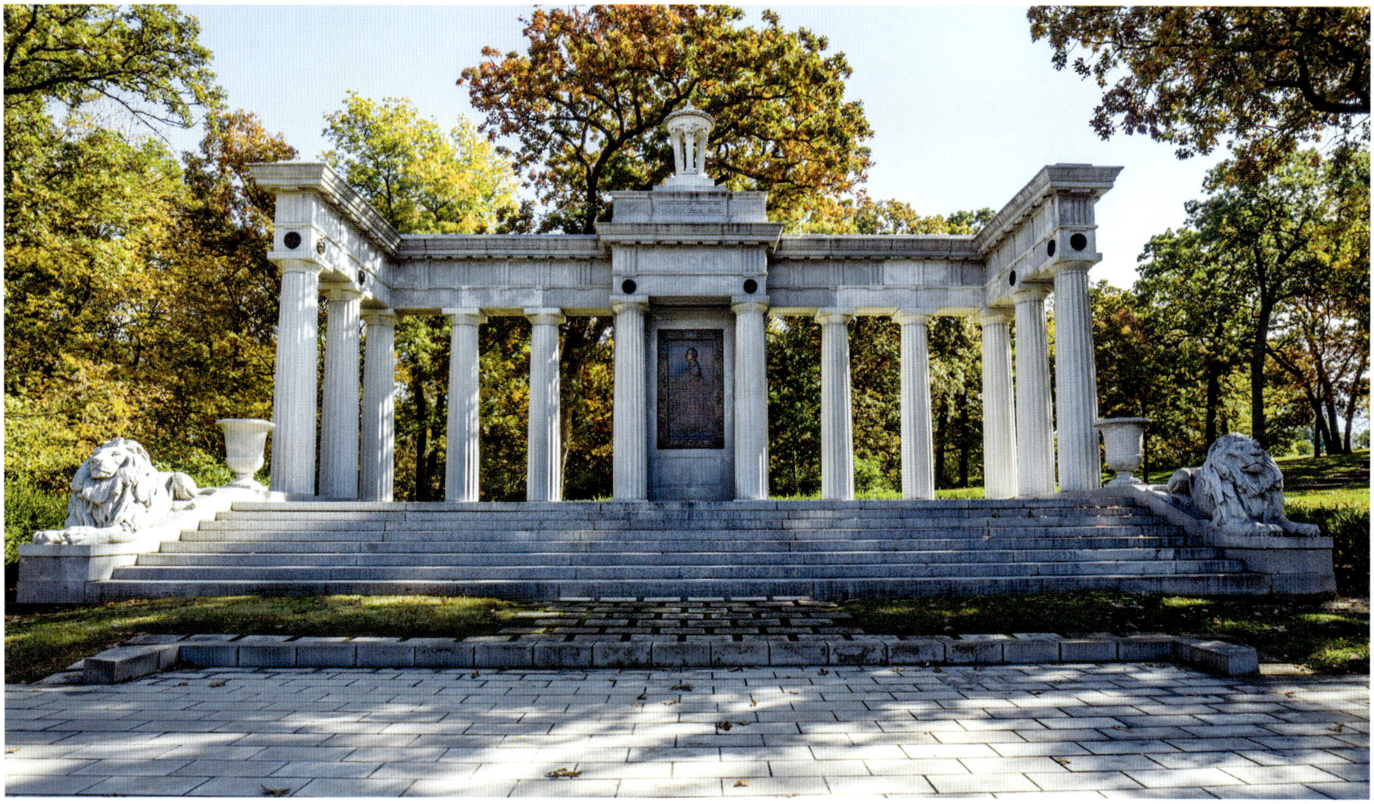

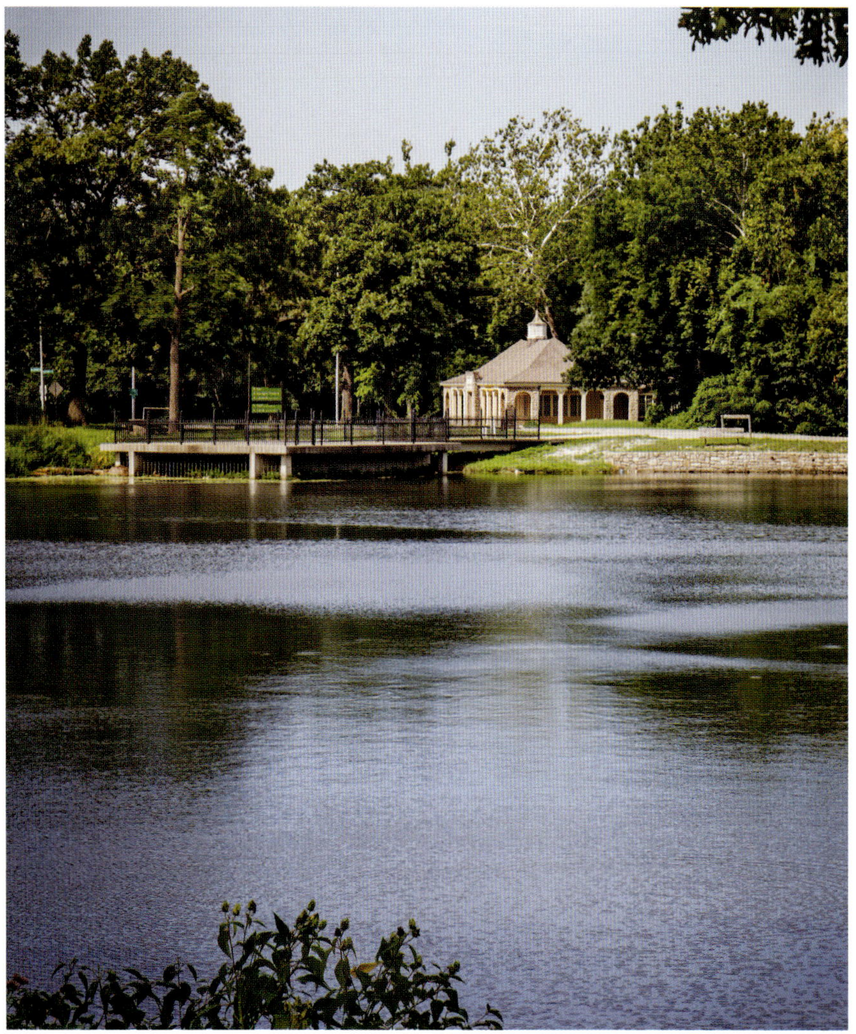

Swope Park *(above and left)*

With 1800 acres of forests, hills, and open spaces, Swope Park is one of the largest urban parks in America. The park contains some of the city's biggest attractions and hosts millions of visitors a year. A colonnade memorial to the park's benefactor sits on a hill overlooking the park.

Swope Park *(opposite)*

Swope Park is home to the zoo, an outdoor amphitheater, golf course, athletic fields and sport courts, nature center, miles of trails for horses, hiking, and biking, plus the training facilities for the city's soccer team. There's lots to do, but it's also a nice place to sit and relax.

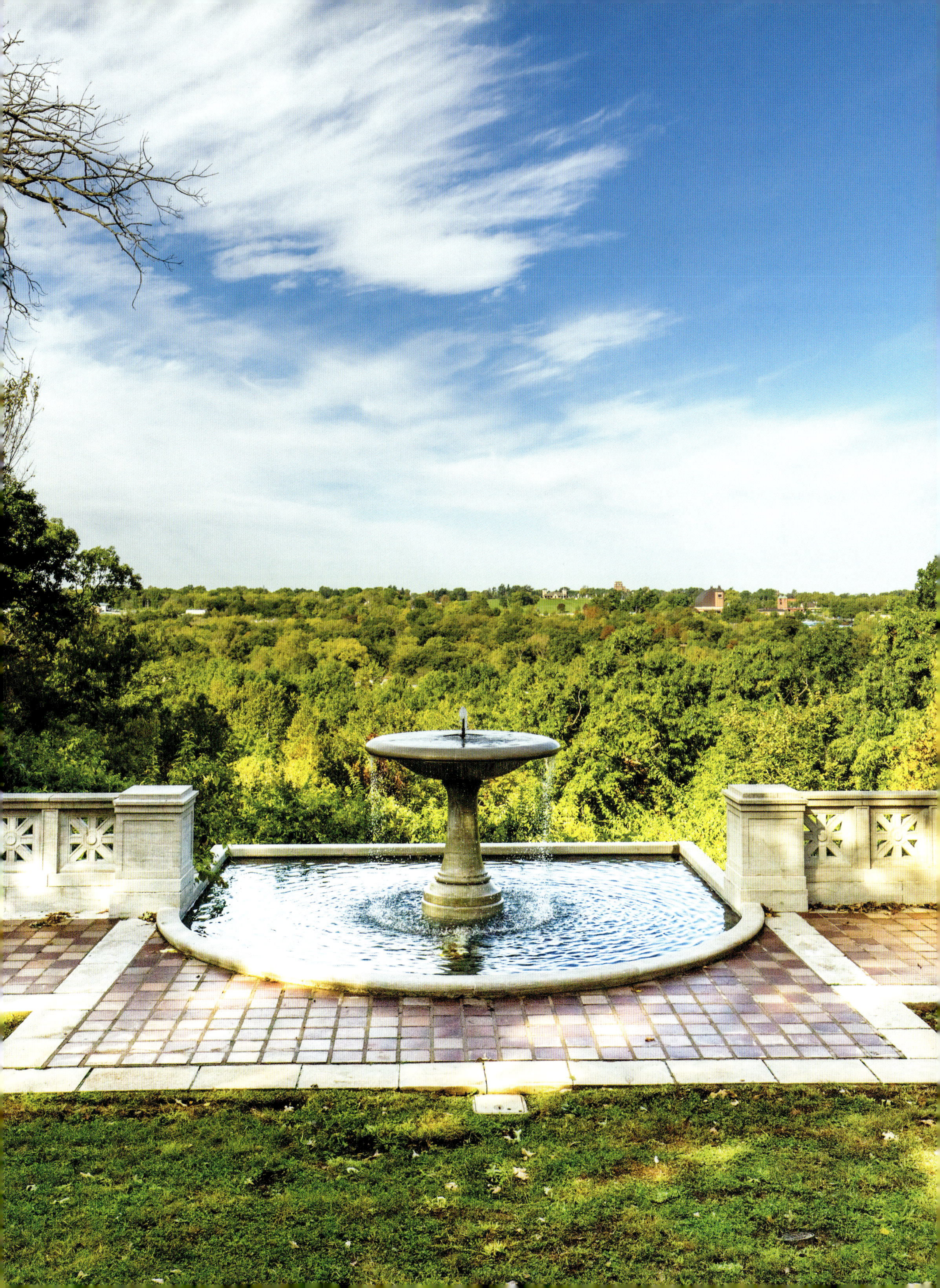

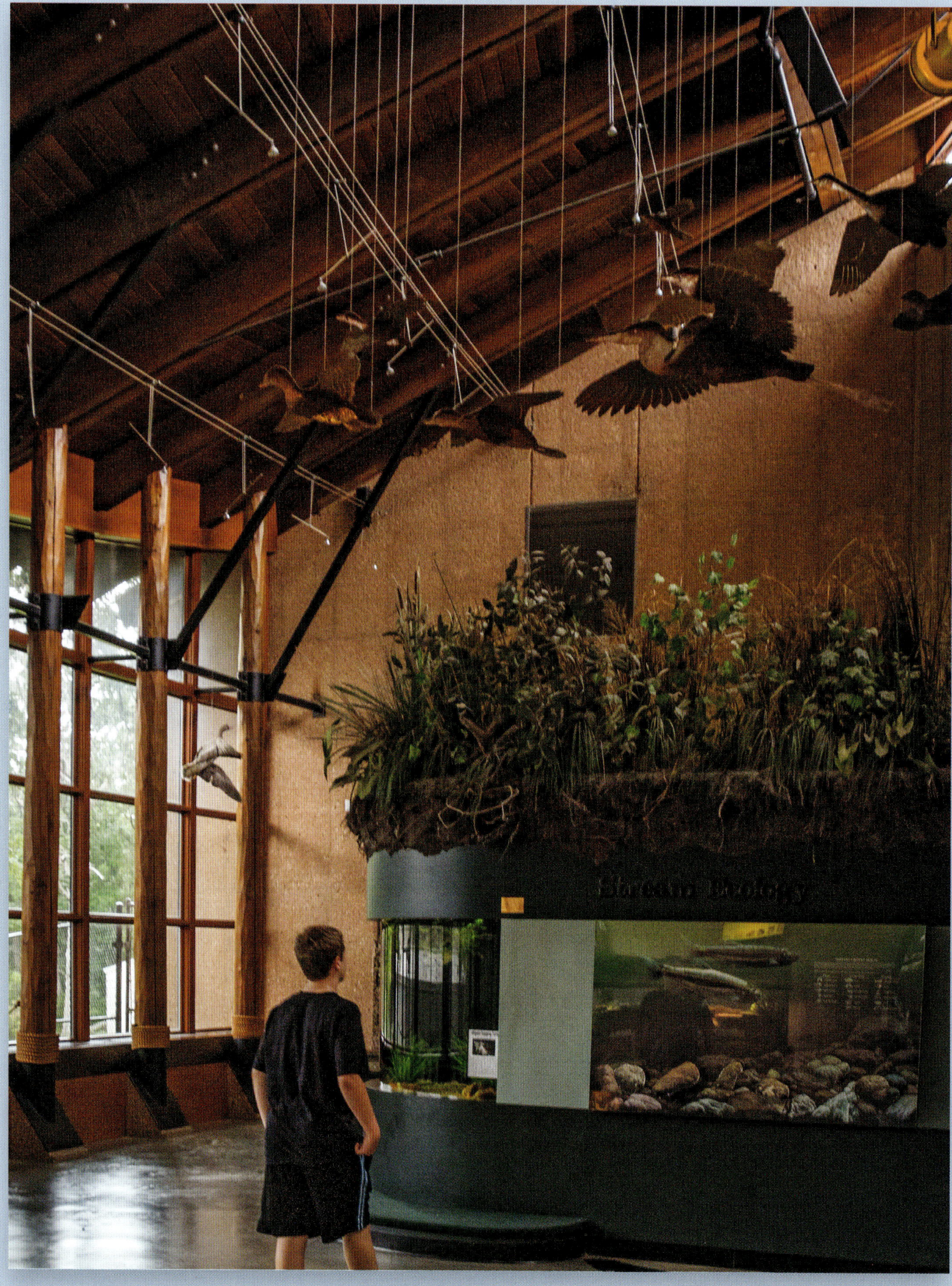

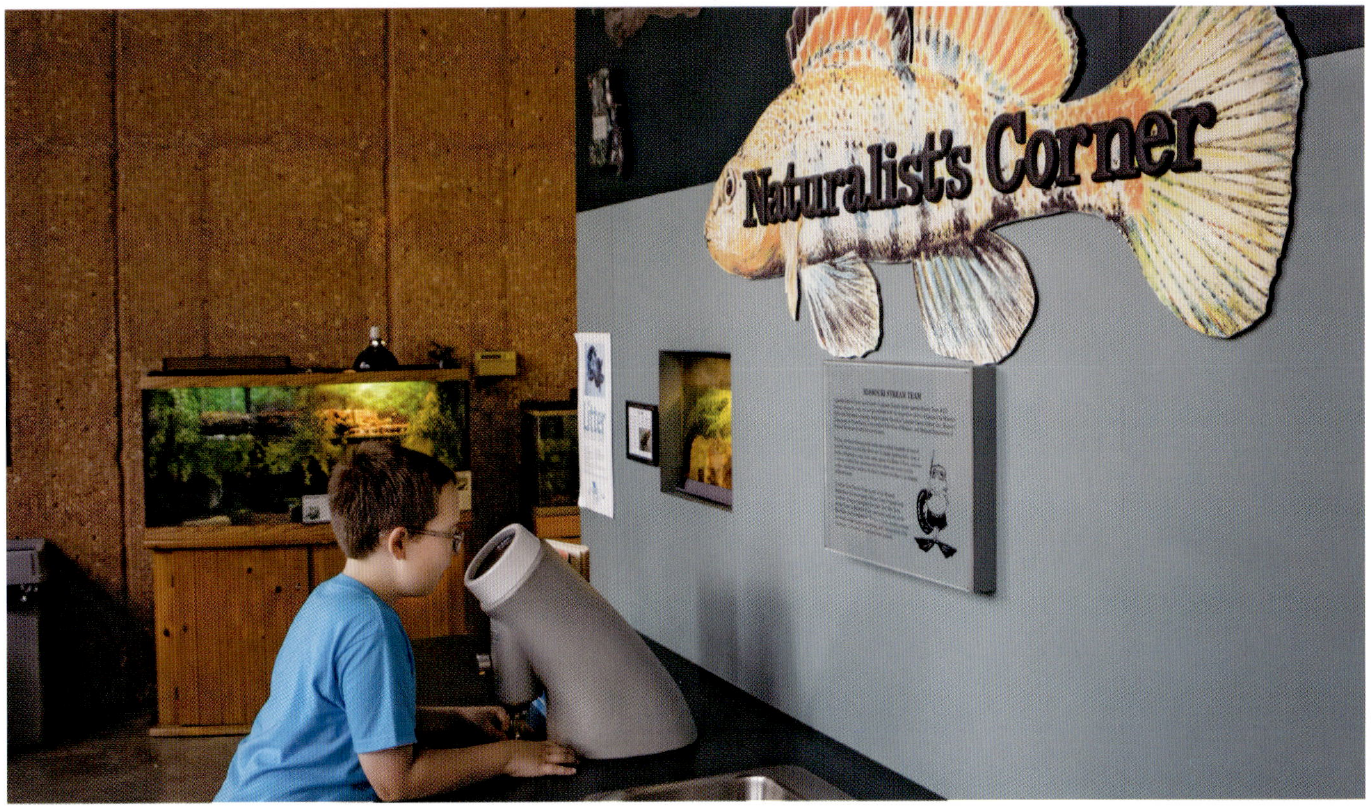

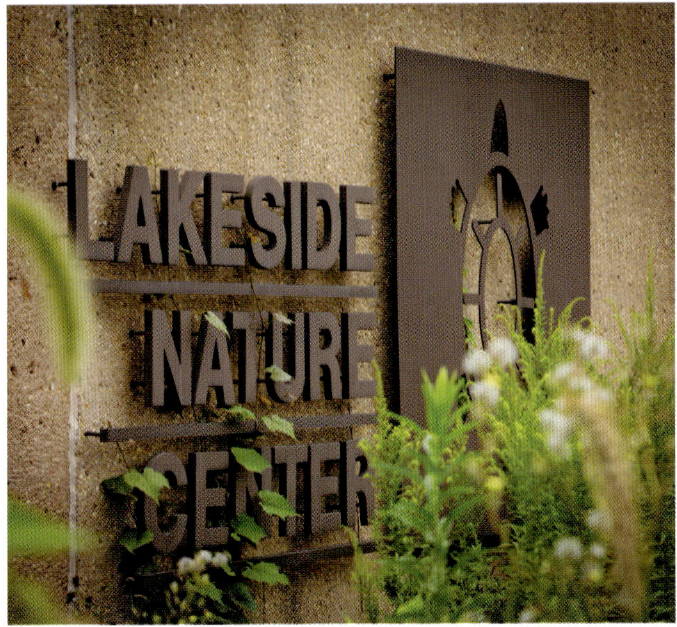

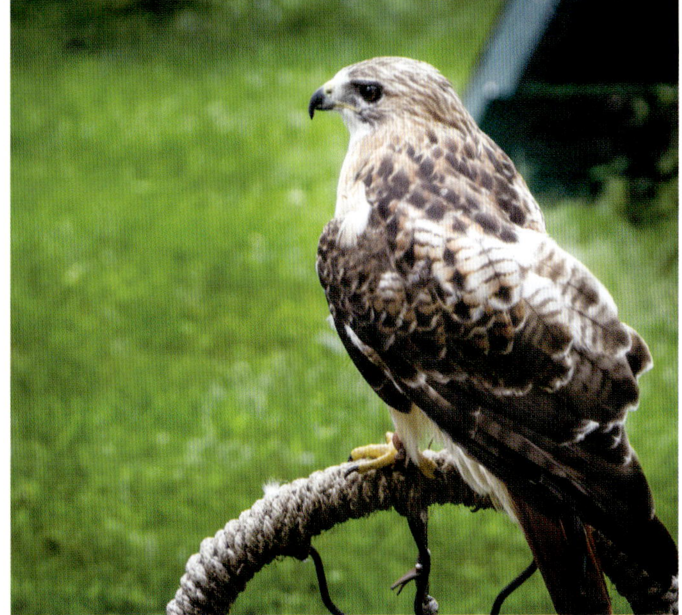

Lakeside Nature Center *(opposite)*

The area's wildlife is on display at the Lakeside Nature Center. Fish from local rivers and lakes swim in large aquariums, while snakes, turtles, and opossums can also be seen. Birds like owls, hawks, and even bald eagles are often being cared for at the center, as well.

Lakeside Nature Center *(top, bottom left and right)*

The educational facility provides many opportunities to learn about local wildlife. Exhibits and trails bring our living environment into focus and provide a base for many conservation projects. The center is also home to Missouri's largest animal rehabilitation program, nursing sick animals back to health.

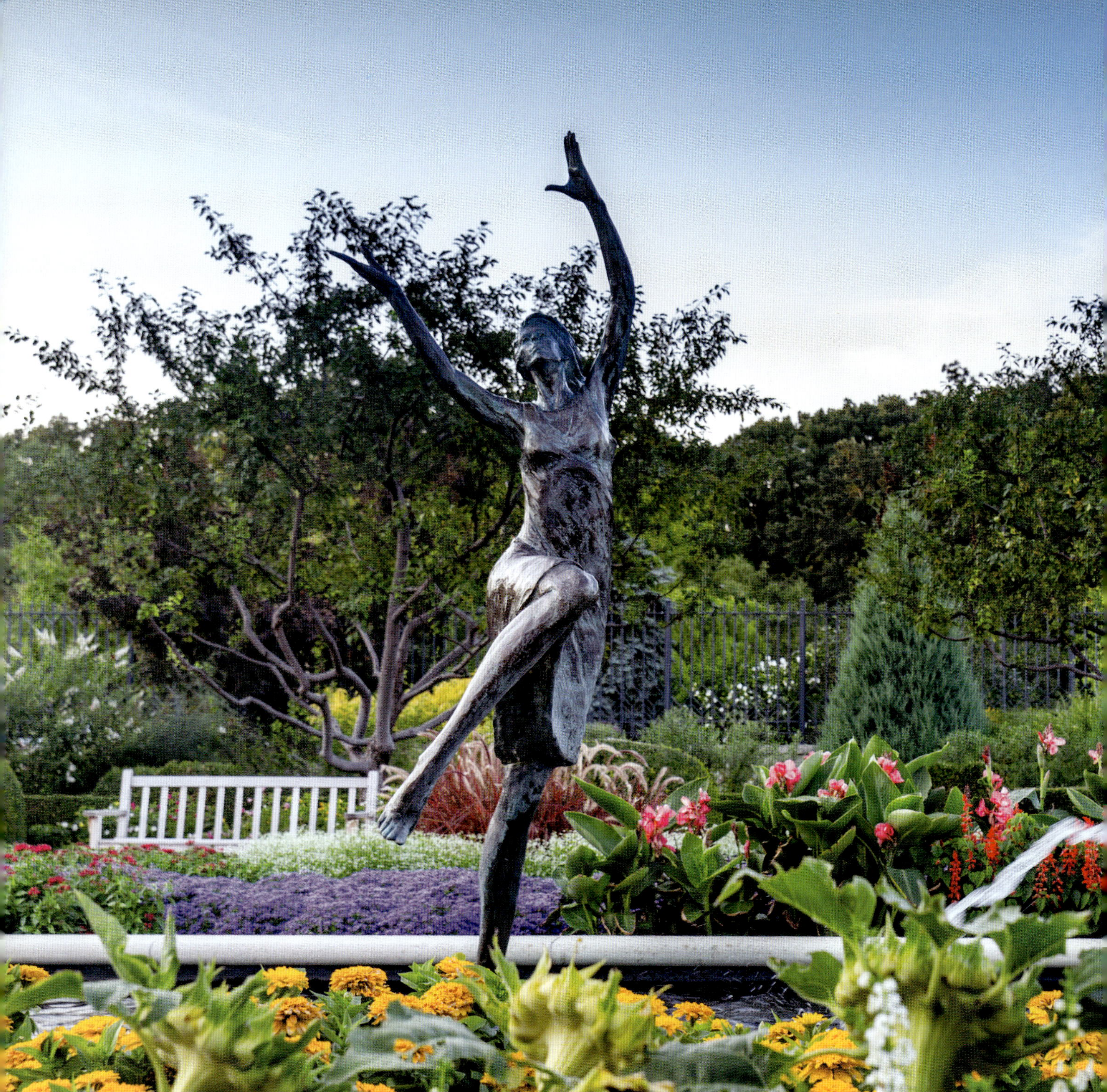

Kauffman Memorial Garden

With seasonal flowers, perennials, and frequently updated beds, Kauffman Memorial Garden is a joy to the senses; fragrant blossoms fill the air, while colorful petals seem to represent the entire spectrum of color. It's a fitting tribute to the Kauffmans, a couple who worked tirelessly to make Kansas City beautiful.

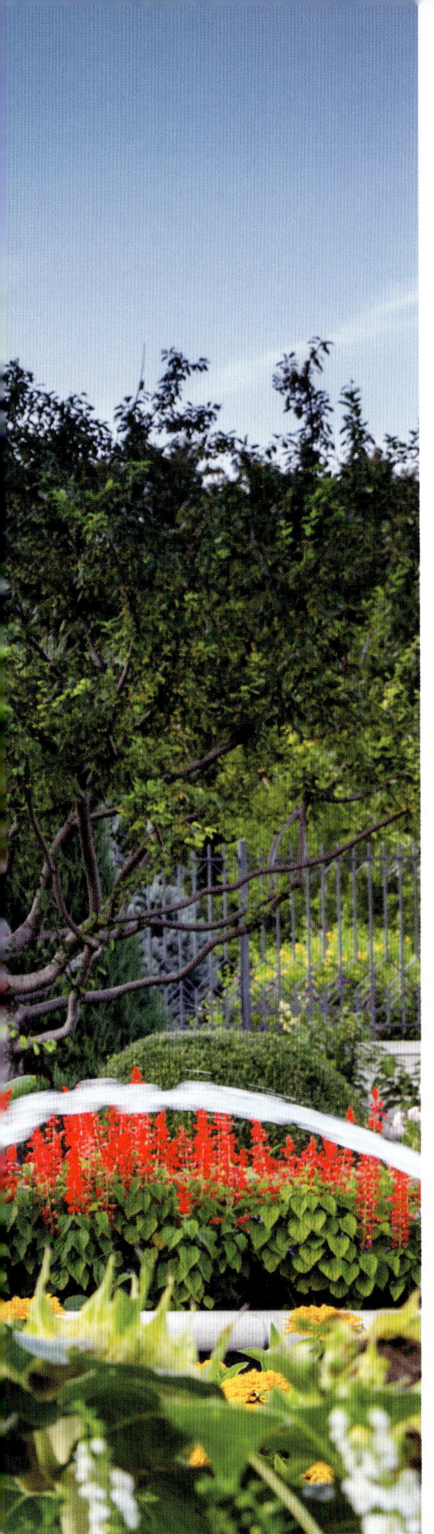

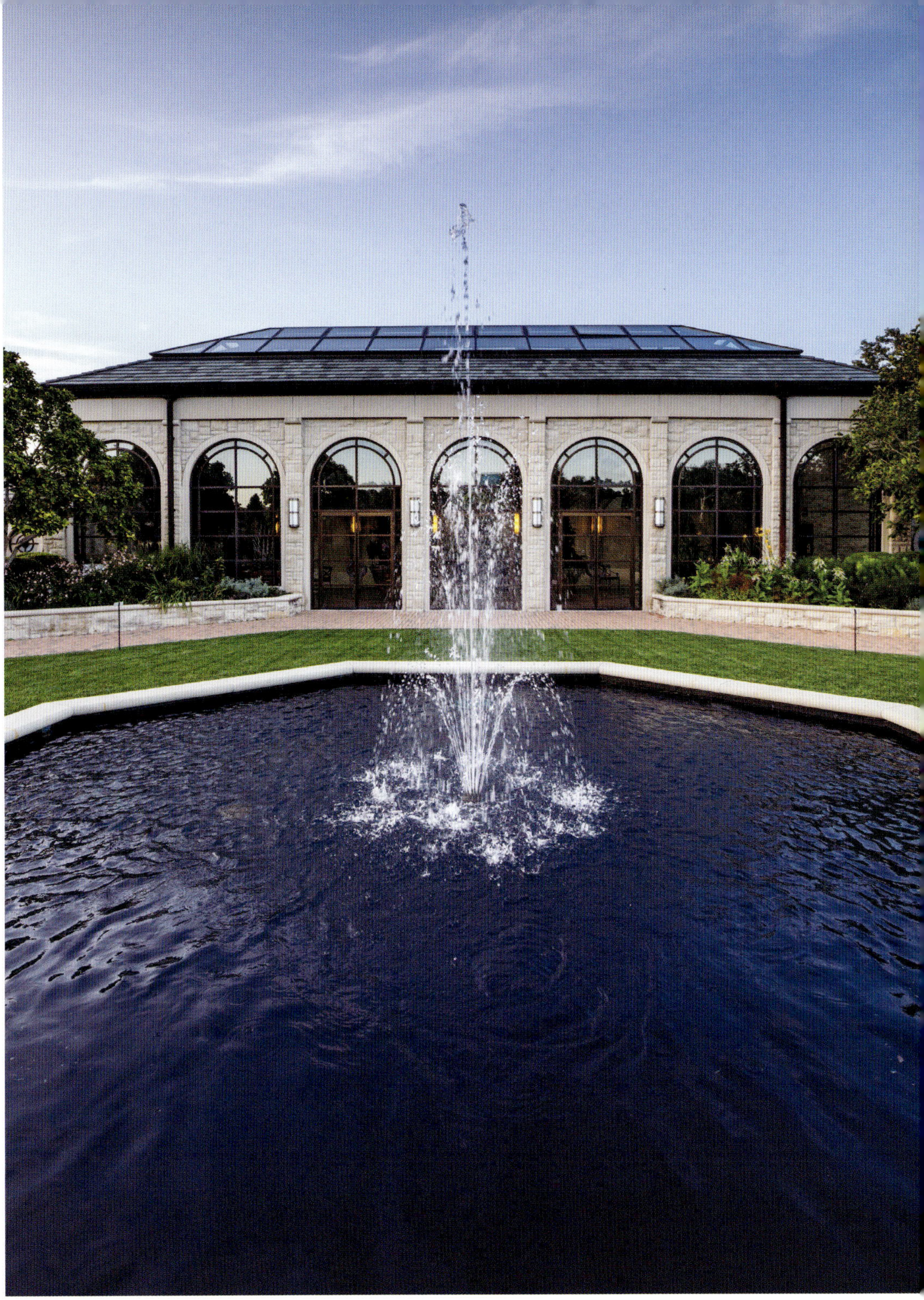

Kauffman Memorial Garden

The garden is open year-round so, even if it's cold outside, it's possible to appreciate tropical flowers like orchids and palms in the orangery. This greenhouse also offers respite during the summer months when the building is air conditioned. During the holidays, don't miss the Christmas display inside.

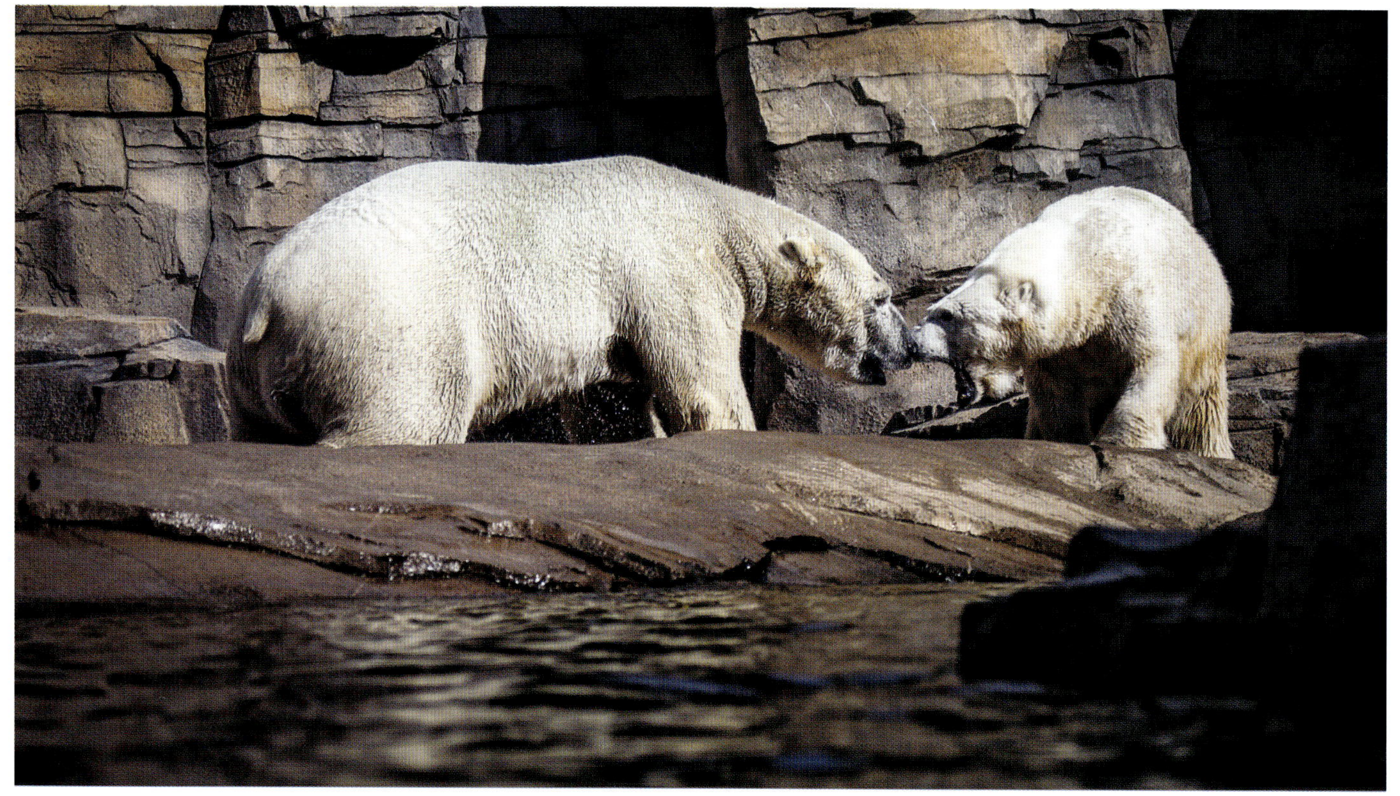

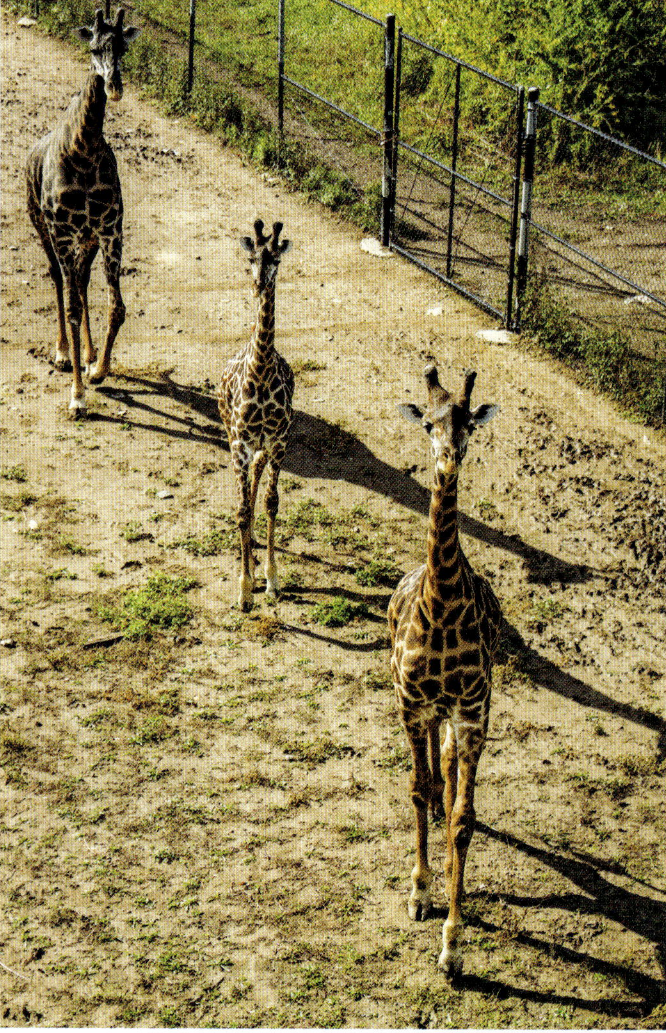

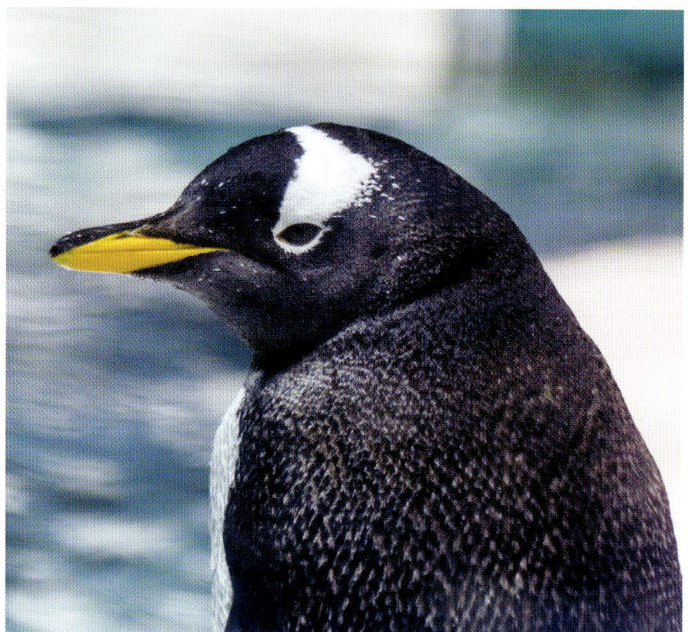

Kansas City Zoo

There are few zoos in America that are any better for viewing elephants, rhinos, hippos, or kangaroos. In fact, Jane Goodall said Kansas City's zoo has "one of the finest chimpanzee exhibits in North America." The lively zoo is constantly improving with recent additions of polar bear and penguin exhibits.

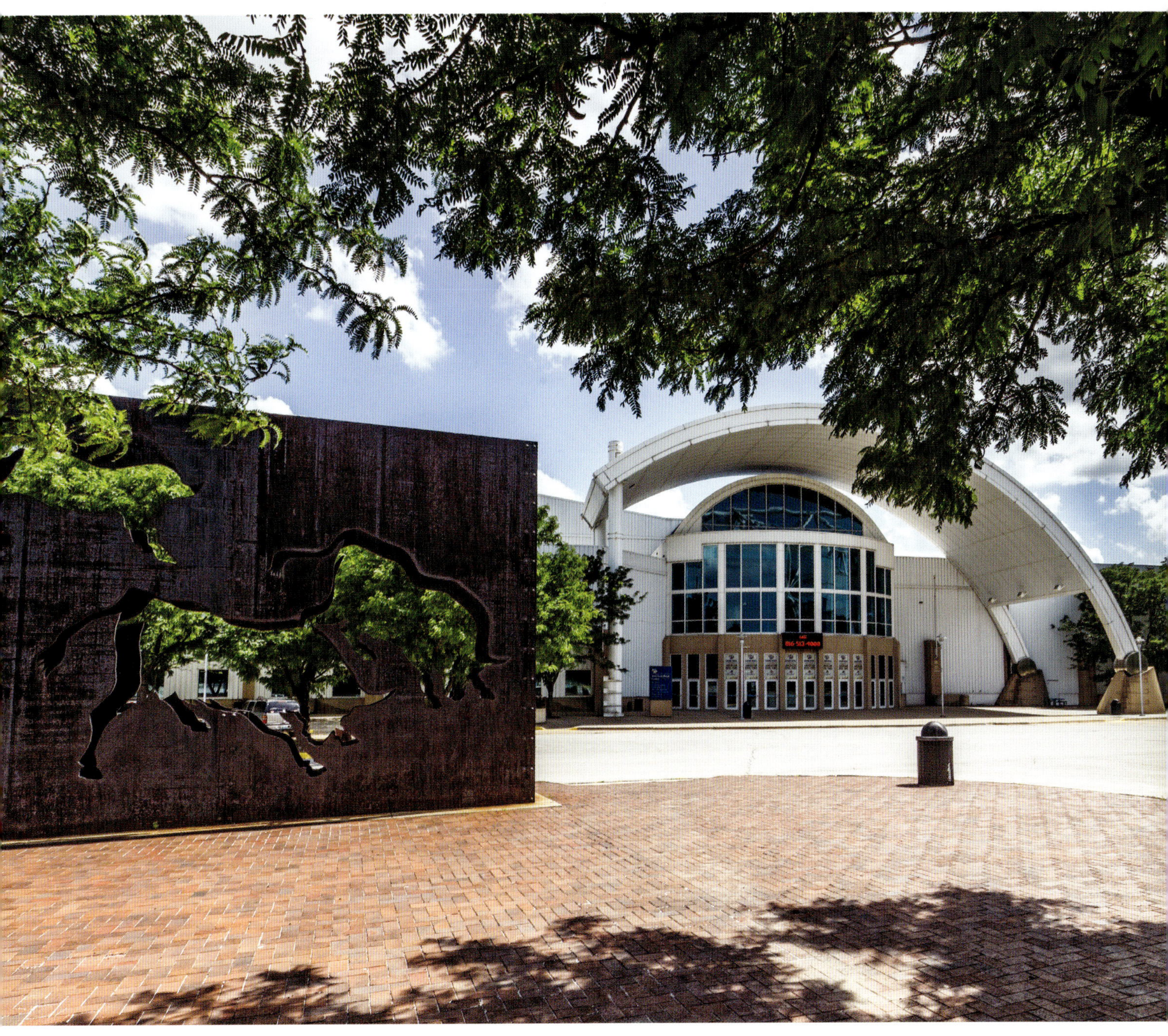

American Royal

Touching on Kansas City's roots, every fall "The Royal" includes a livestock show, rodeo, parade, and the world's largest barbecue competition. The organization's headquarters sits near the site of the old stockyards in the West Bottoms where millions of cows, pigs, and other livestock were once shipped and processed.

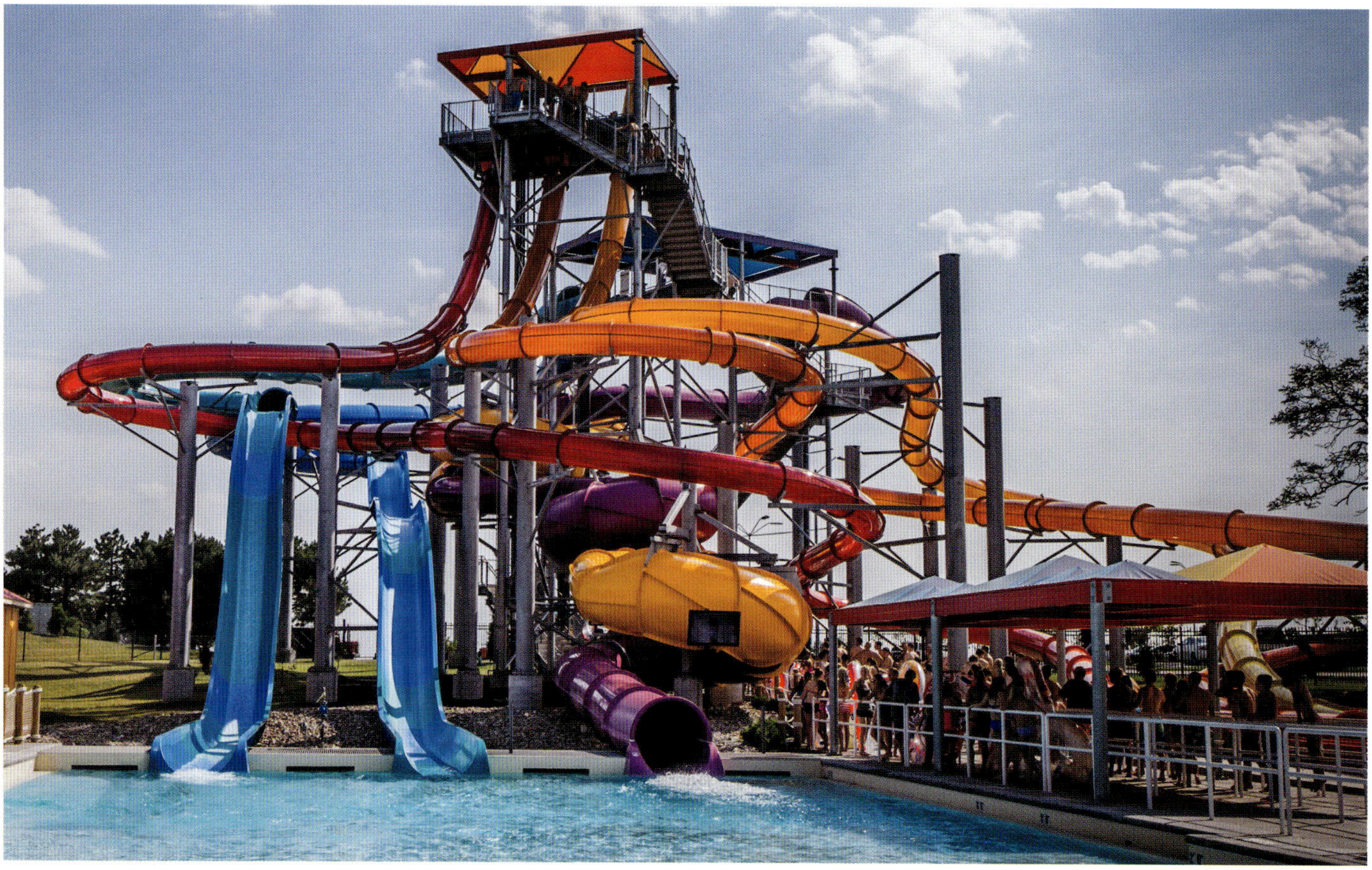

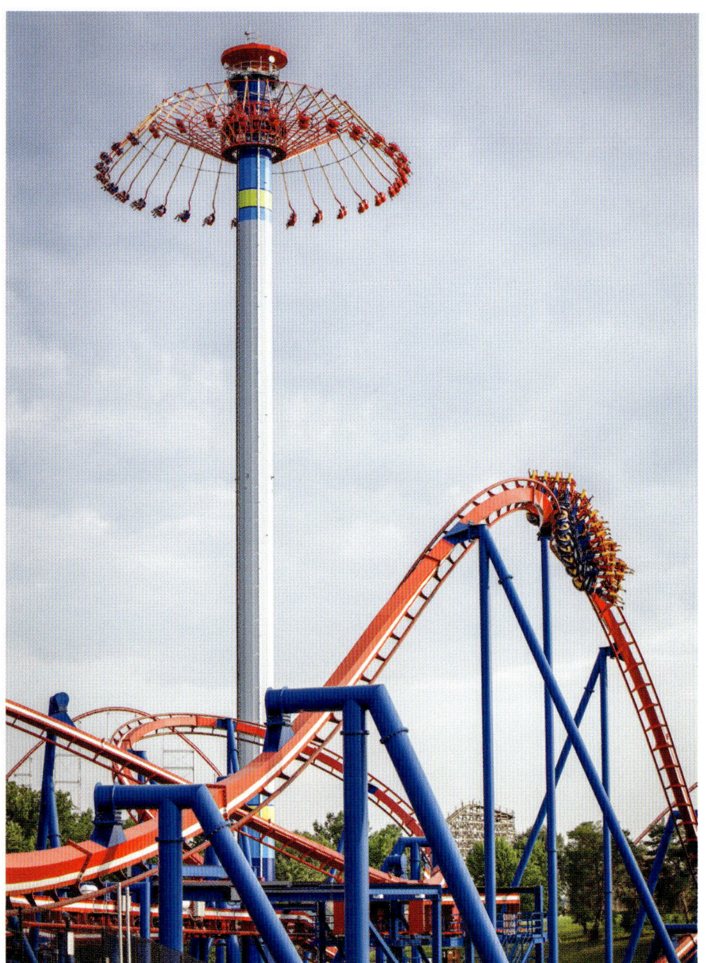

Worlds of Fun and Oceans of Fun

(above and left)

Kansas Citians know where to go to get their fix for thrills and laughter. Worlds of Fun is an amusement park with more than 40 rides and seven roller coasters. During the warm summer months, when the mercury rises, the Oceans of Fun waterpark is a great place to cool off.

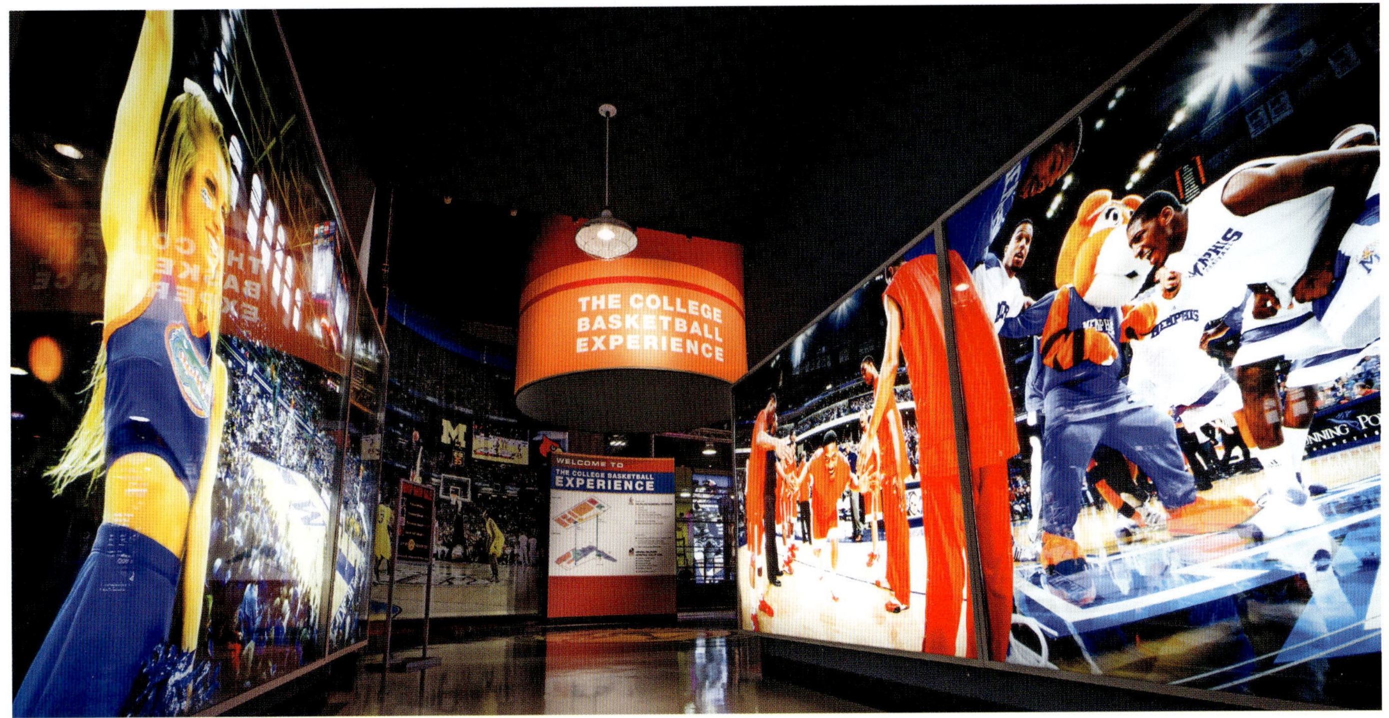

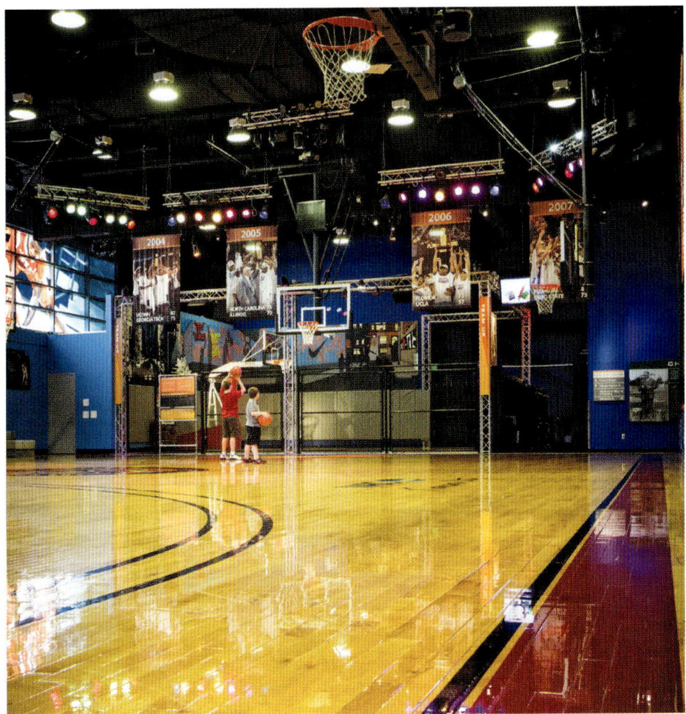

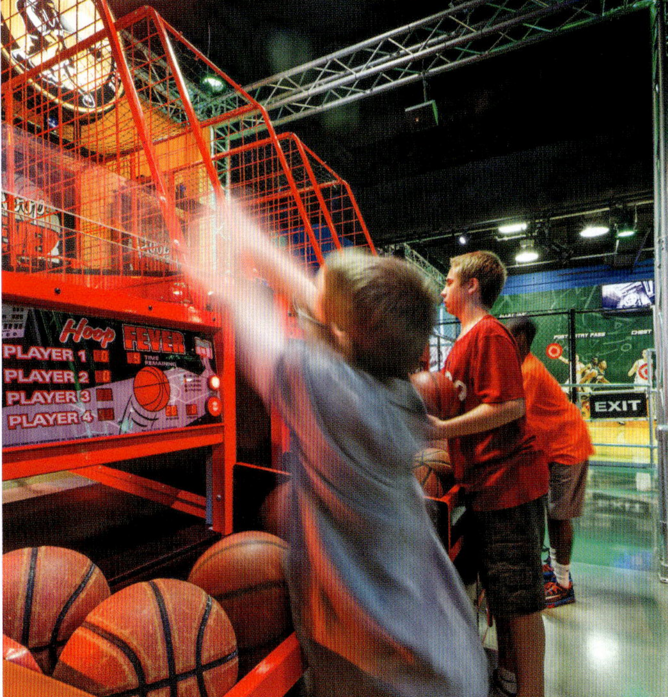

College Basketball Experience

(top, bottom left and right)

It doesn't have to be March to get excited about college basketball. The CBE is a hands-on experience where future basketball stars can practice three point shots, precision passing, and even give play-by-play a try. It's also home to the National Collegiate Basketball Hall of Fame.

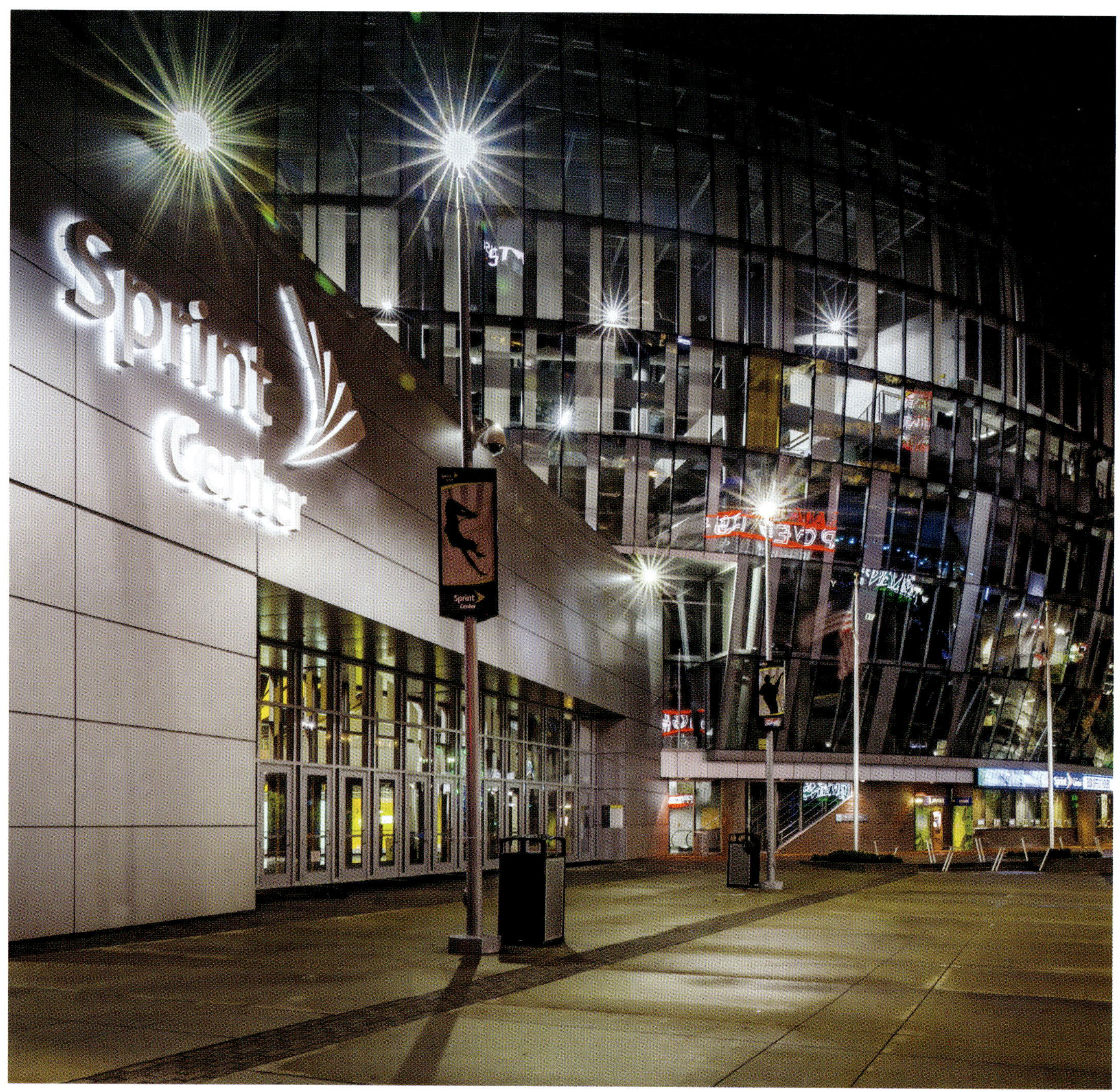

Sprint Center *(above and opposite)*

The largest arena in Kansas City, the Sprint Center seats more than 19,000 and has 72 suites. The building opened in 2007 by featuring nine consecutive sold out shows by Garth Brooks. The facility routinely hosts major concerts, unique theatrical performances, and a wide range of sporting events.

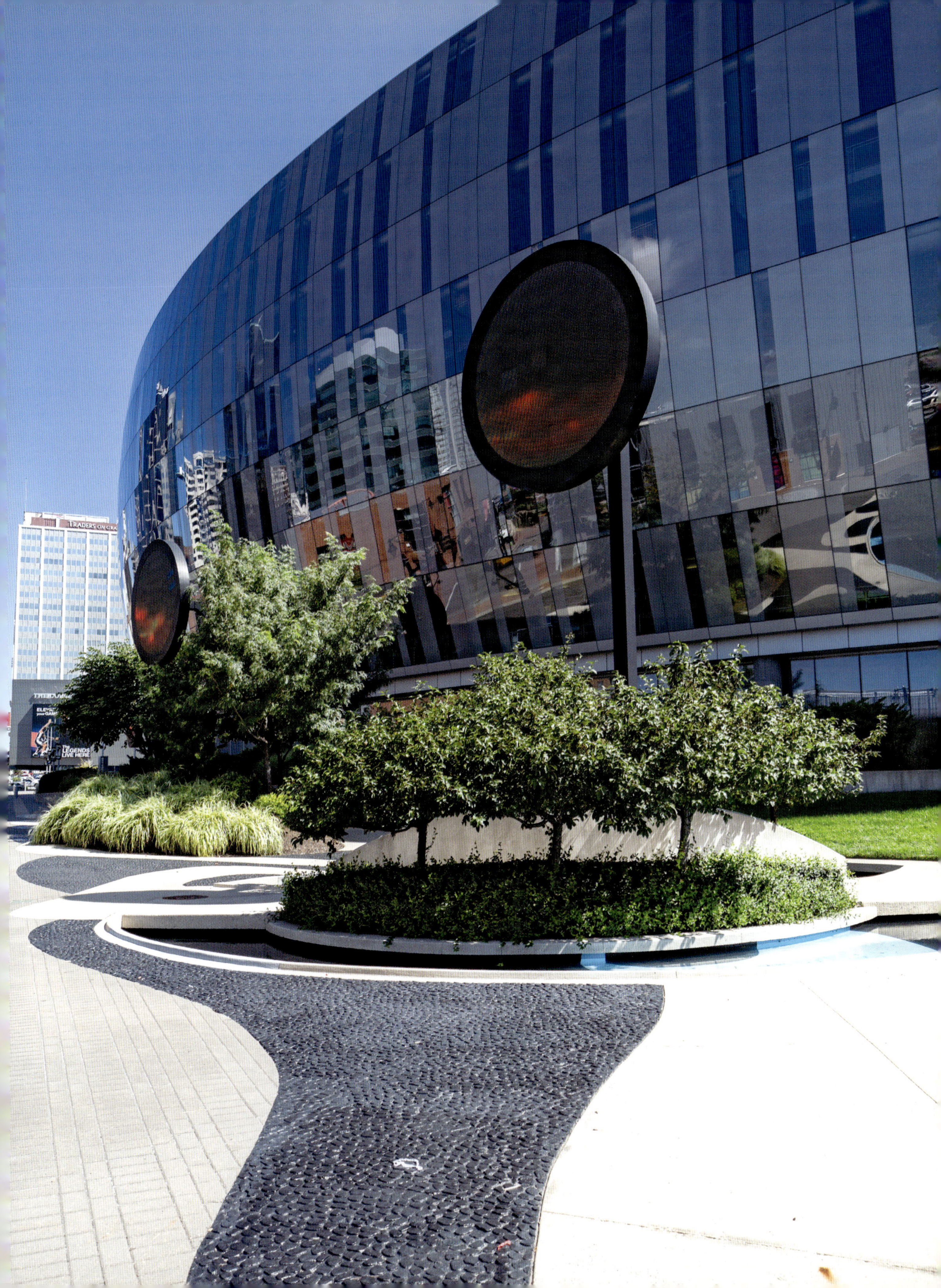

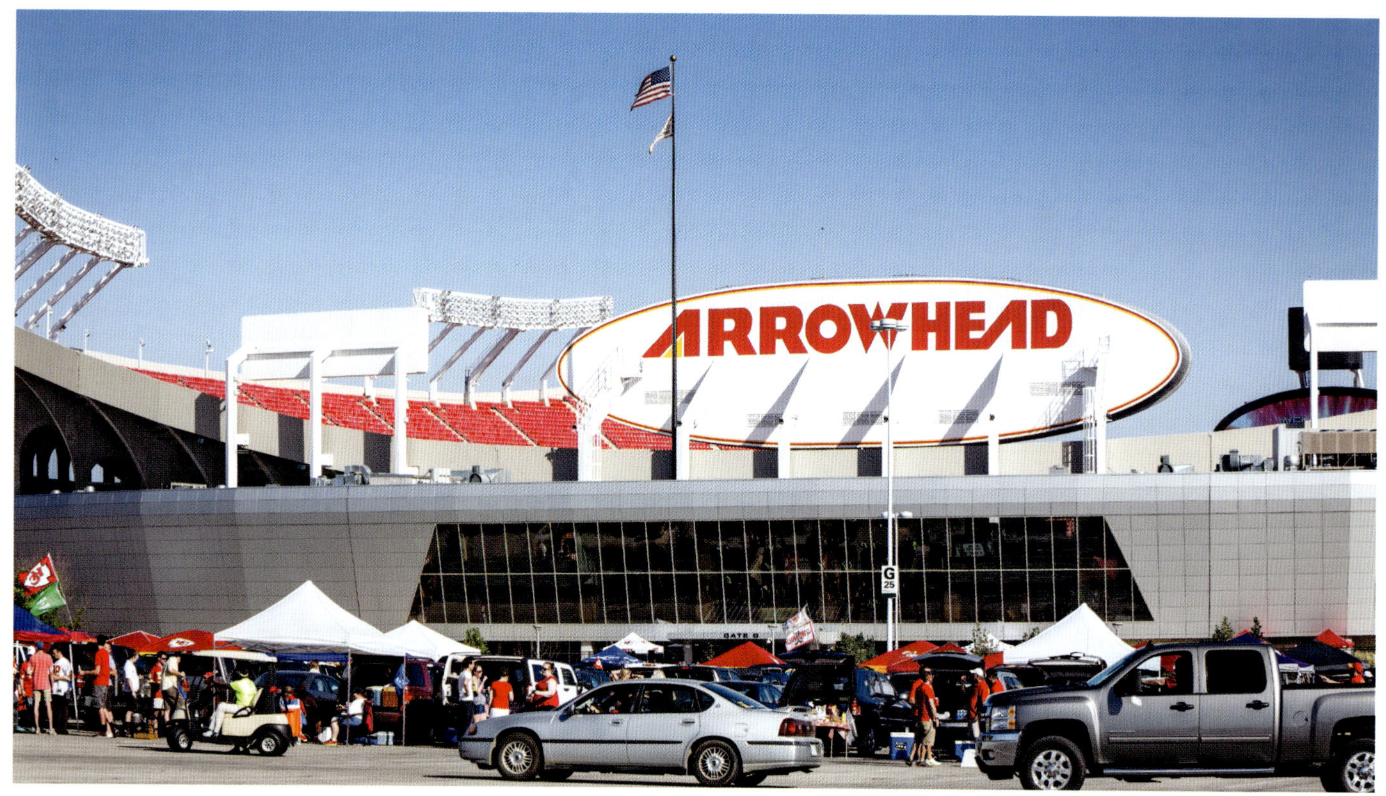

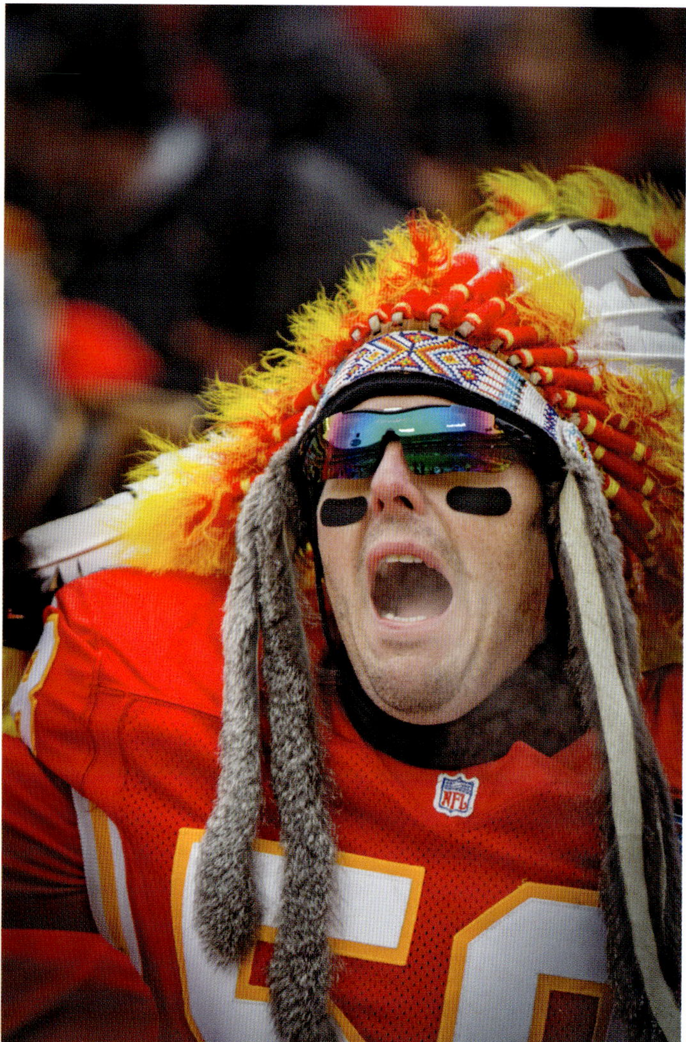

Arrowhead Stadium *(above)*

On Sundays in the fall, Arrowhead is a sea of red, as Chiefs fans watch their team battle it out on the grid-iron. Prior to games, fans arrive early by the thousands to tailgate, and soon the expansive parking lots are covered in a smoky haze of aromatic barbecue smoke.

Arrowhead Stadium *(left)*

Powered by nearly 80,000 screaming fans, Arrowhead holds the world record as the loudest stadium in the world. The venue hosts occasional college and high school football games and has seen major outdoor concerts, as well. Arrowhead is primarily home to the NFL's Kansas City Chiefs.

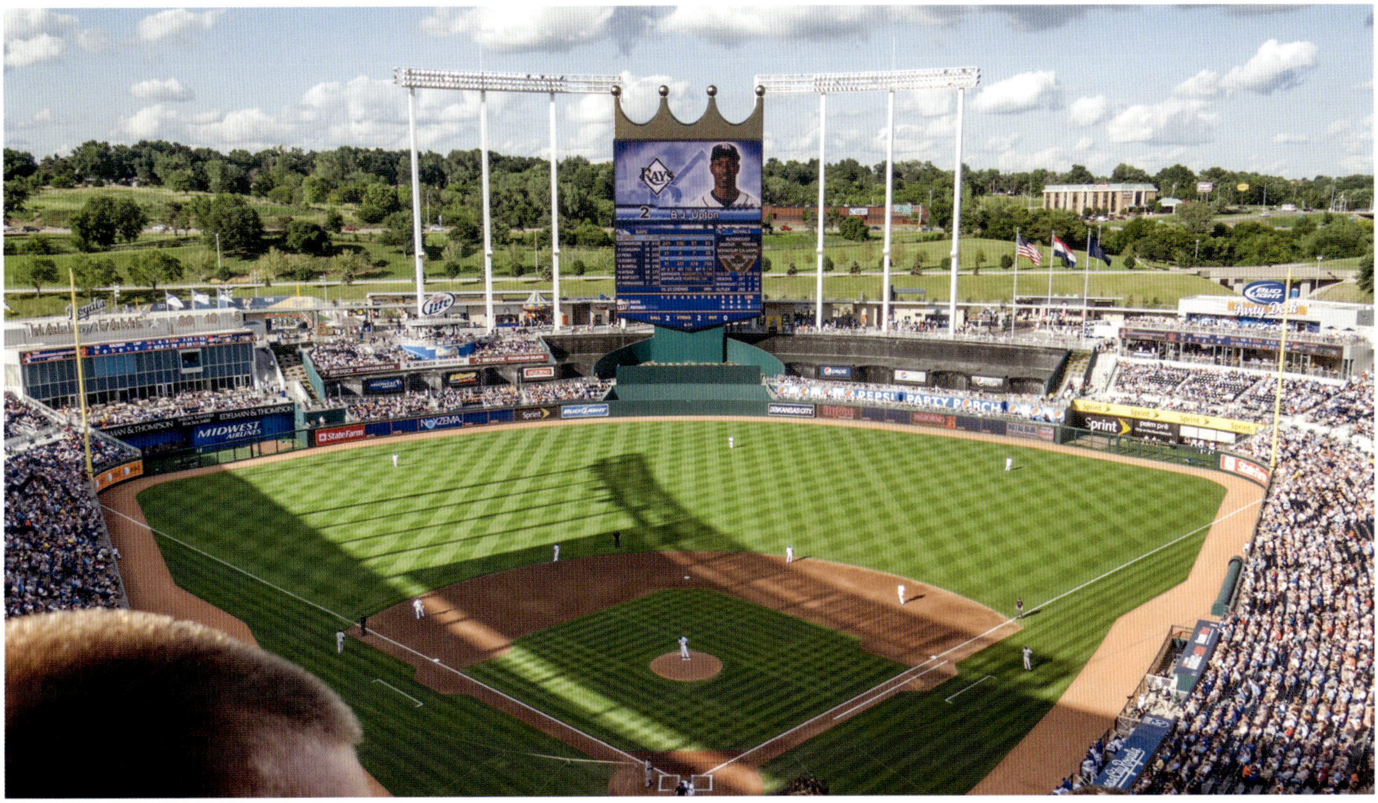

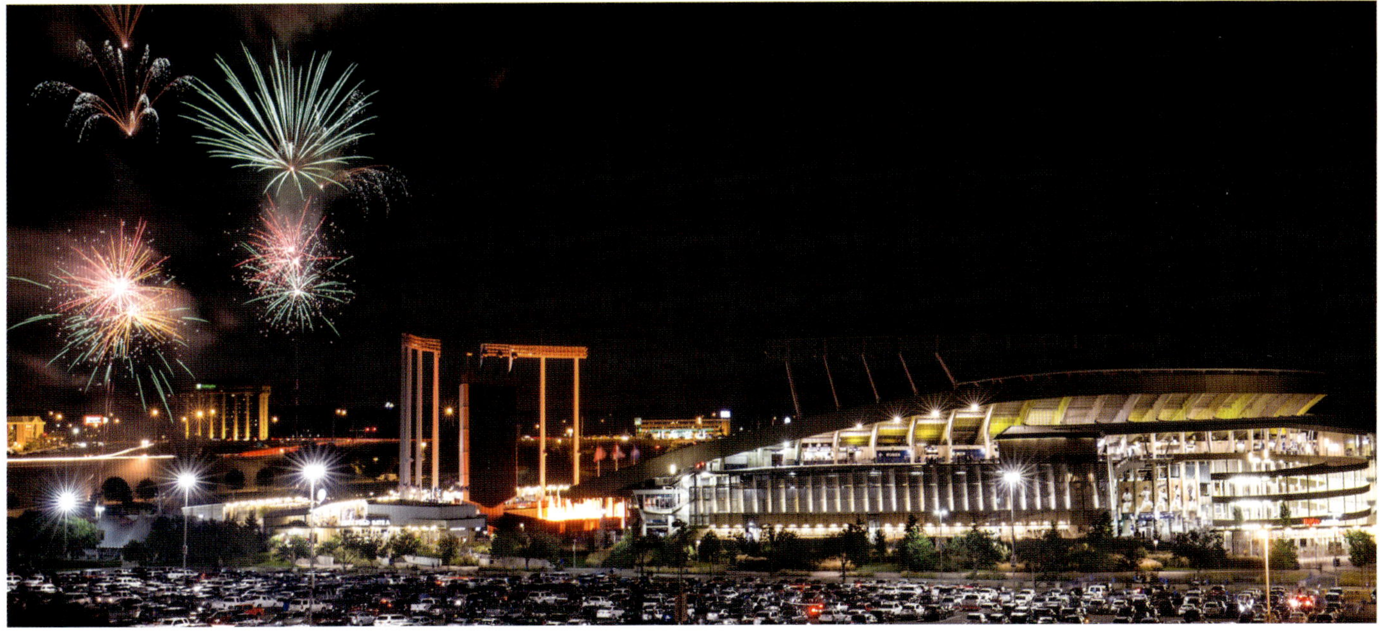

Kauffman Stadium *(top and bottom)*

Located next door to Arrowhead, "The K" is home to MLB's Royals. The stadium has the second largest outfield in all of baseball and, just beyond right field, a huge fountain display runs between innings. The massive scoreboard in center field is topped with a crown, punctuating the team's name.

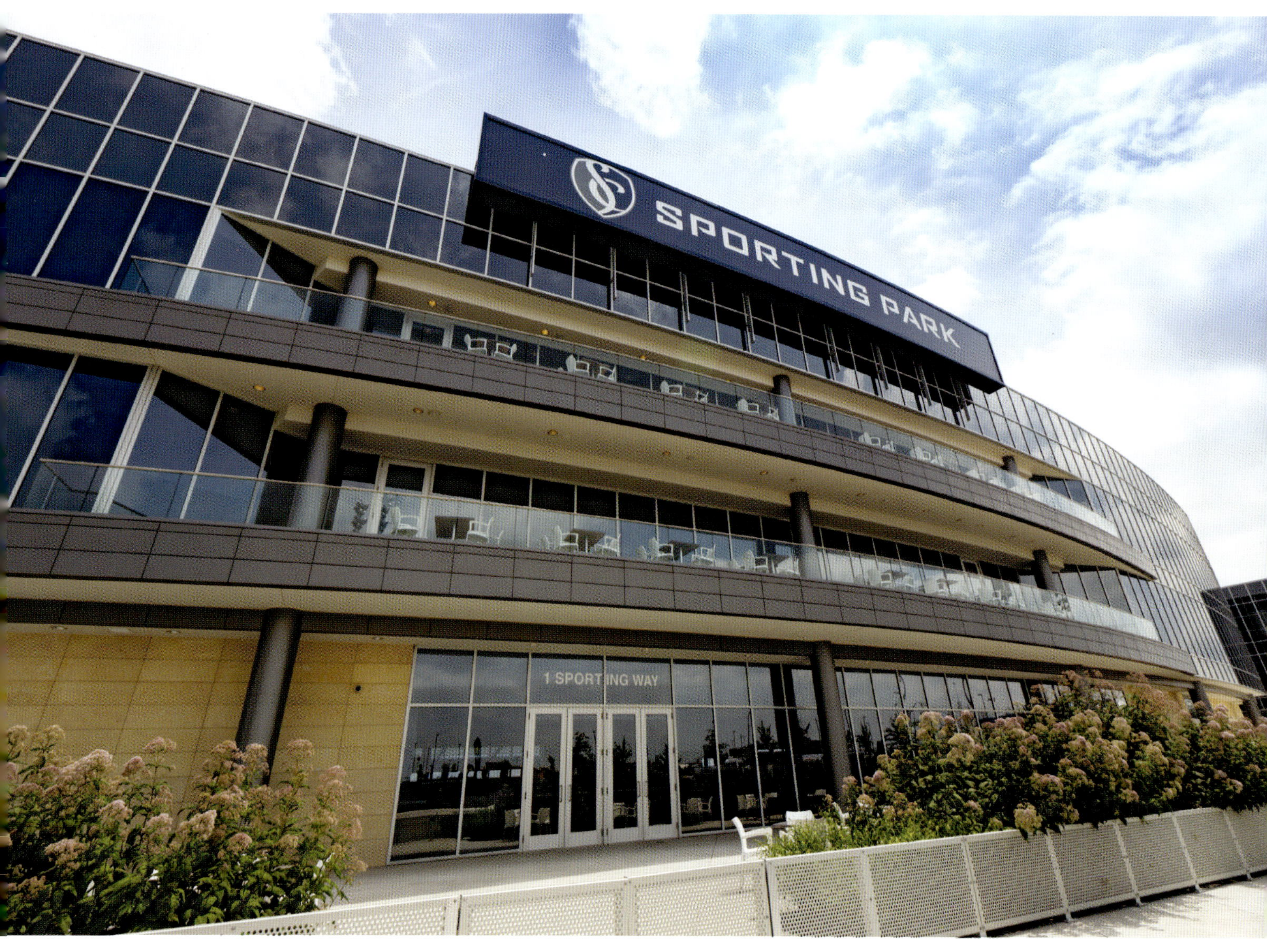

Sporting Park

This state-of-the-art soccer stadium is the anchor to the upcoming US Soccer National Training Center. The soccer village will be home to eight full-sized professional fields, eight youth fields, and a 100,000-square-foot indoor facility. The facility will also house a coaching development center.

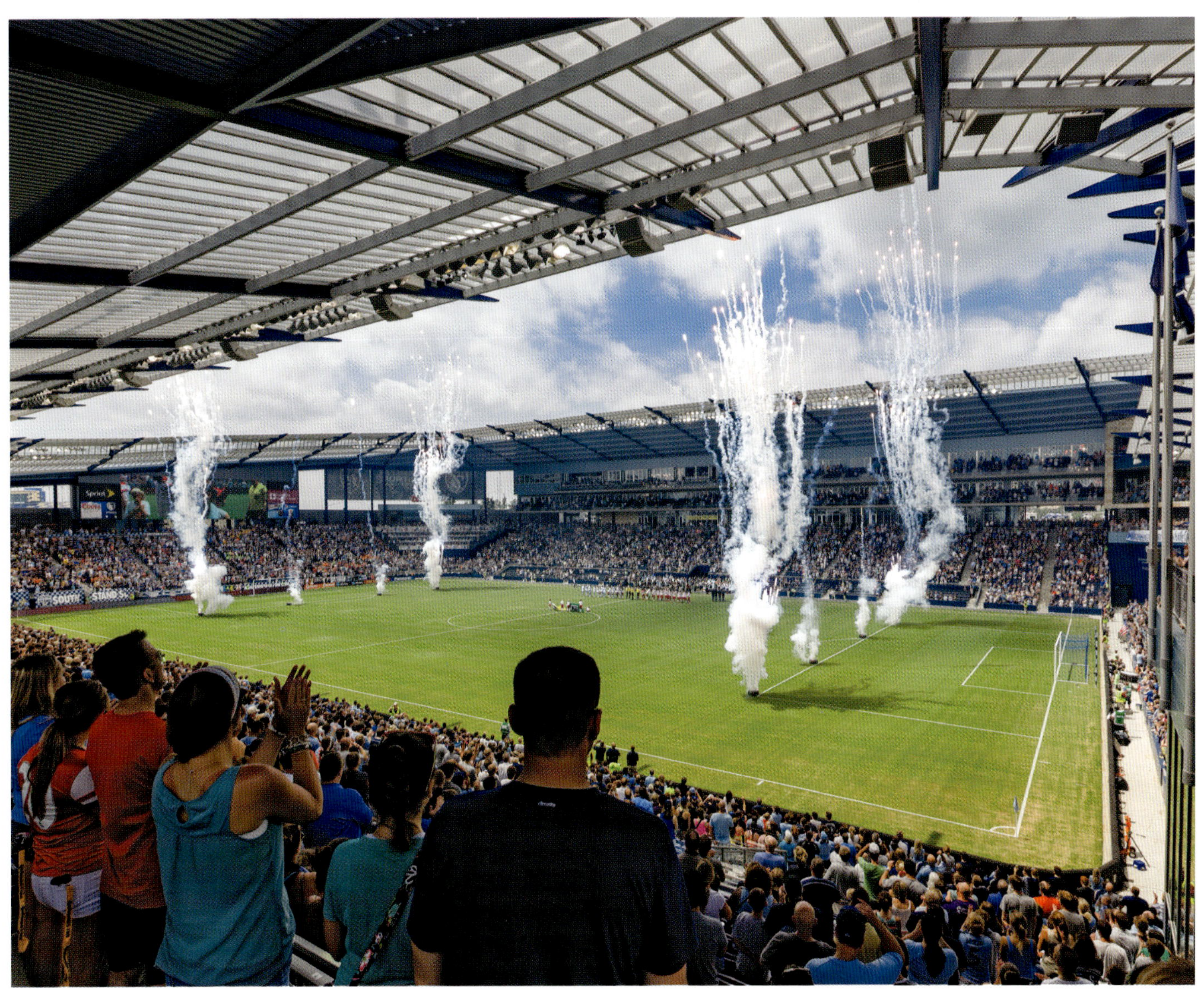

Sporting Park

The city's soccer-specific stadium is home to Sporting Kansas City, but the pitch has also seen World Cup qualifying matches from both the men's and women's national teams. Some of Europe's finest soccer teams have played at Sporting Park, as well, trying their best to conquer the "Blue Hell."

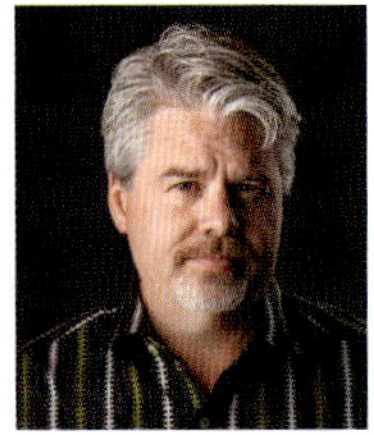

Roger Ridpath is a creative professional with a passion and love for art and photography who welcomed the opportunity to take a fresh look at Kansas City's iconic landmarks through his lens. Using his creative eye and 25 years of experience, Roger enjoyed capturing his hometown's fountains, parks, museums, and other sights. He is a capable travel, portrait, and corporate photographer and has triggered his shutter across the United States and abroad, capturing stunning landscapes, architectural marvels, and the emotions of candid snapshots.

Additionally, Roger is a partner and creative director for an award-winning advertising group where he has worked on major international accounts and helped small local businesses, as well. He has lived his life in the Midwest; he was born in Wichita, Kansas and later earned a degree in fine arts from Wichita State University. Since the early 1990s, he has called Kansas City home, where he lives with his wife and two sons. To learn more about Roger, visit www.ridpathcreative.com.

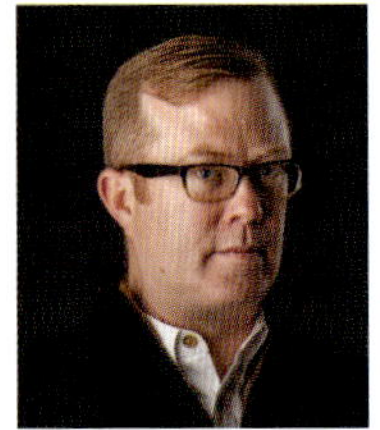

David Banks is often found tapping away at his keyboard. A versatile and experienced writer, he has written or contributed to nearly a dozen books. His professional writing experience has its roots in advertising copy. David has written for major advertising campaigns and crafted more direct marketing than he can remember. Additionally, he was a longtime contributing author for Wired.com, the online edition of the nation's leading source for technology news. He currently writes for a number of online publications.

David has a degree in advertising from the University of Kansas and an MBA from Baker University. He has lived on both coasts, but calls Kansas City home, where he lives with his wife, two daughters, and a son. He runs a small advertising agency on the Country Club Plaza and specializes in client services, user interfaces, and content development. To learn more about David, visit www.davidsbanks.com.